装修
renovación
renovation
تجديد
обновление
rénovation

Nancy Davenport

装修

Cabinet Books
New York

1. George Dudley, *A Workshop for Peace: Designing the United Nations Headquarters* (Cambridge, MA: MIT Press, 1994), p. 213.

2. Lewis Mumford, "The Sky Line: Magic with Mirrors," in Lewis Mumford, *From the Ground Up: Observations on Contemporary Architecture, Housing, Highway Building, and Civic Design* (New York: Harcourt Brace, 1959), p. 41. The essay was originally published in the *New Yorker* in 1951.

3. George Dudley, *A Workshop for Peace*, p. 314. The full quotation runs: "'The world hopes for a symbol of peace,' Harrison said in his final report to Secretary General Trygve Lie. 'We have given them a workshop for peace.'"

Preface
by Reinaldo Laddaga

In the middle of the last century, a series of buildings were erected on the banks of the East River of Manhattan on a site that had been donated by the Rockefeller family and had once been a slaughterhouse and meatpacking facility, earning it the nickname "blood alley." The core of the design was drafted by Oscar Niemeyer and completed by a large group of architects led by Le Corbusier, who solemnly declared that they were "laying down the plans of a world architecture, *world*, not *international*, for therein we shall respect the human, natural and cosmic laws."[1] Not everybody agreed; when the complex was finally opened for operation in 1951, Lewis Mumford wrote that it was "a blend of the grandiose and the obvious," but soon he corrected himself and said that "no one had ever conceived of building a mirror on this scale before and perhaps no one guessed what an endless series of pictures that mirror would reveal."[2]

From the start, the United Nations Headquarters was seen as a grand symbol. This, despite the fact that the founders of the UN conceived of an organization that would be ever changing, continually exceeding its original framework, and that the architects, in tandem with the diplomats, declared that they had built "not a symbol of peace but a workshop of peace."[3] But from the outset, a certain lack of definition affected the organization that the buildings housed—an organization founded at a time of general upheaval in the wake of a bloody conflagration that had engulfed many nations. Universalist ideals ("world cooperation," "world peace") were supposed to be advanced here, but the process of embodying them in documents and plans, offices and calendars, resulted in a long, complex improvisation at the end of which emerged an entity that was to be seen alternatively as necessary (however dysfunctional) or completely crippled by bureaucracy and organizational incoherence. It was not only the mirror walls of the exterior that revealed an endless series of pictures. Inside, a play featuring thousands and thousands of the most diverse characters took place. Sometimes the scenes were dramatic: Patrice Lumumba pleading unsuccessfully, not long before his assassination, with the UN to intervene and use military force to stop the Congolese secessionist leader Tshombe's armies in the region of Katanga; Yasser Arafat delivering a blistering attack on Zionism and obtaining the recognition of Palestinians' right to self-determination. Sometimes they were rather strange: Krishna Menon, Indian envoy, who after giving a seven-hour speech, the longest ever delivered at the Security Council, collapsed from exhaustion and was brought to a hospital, only to rush back to the building as soon as he had recovered so that he could finish his speech, now with a doctor at his side; Nikita Khrushchev banging

his table with a shoe during a meeting of the General Assembly; Fidel Castro complaining of having been evicted from his hotel for keeping live chickens in his room.

Over the course of the decades, the entities and subentities that deliberated and worked in these buildings multiplied, as did, after decolonization, the number of nations that were represented. The mission of the organization expanded exponentially. Its structures became increasingly rhizomatic, and all its various components became increasingly difficult to keep together. Given the lofty ideals that presided over its foundation, it's not surprising that dissolution and cynicism didn't take long to sink in. Perry Anderson was speaking for many others when he wrote the following: "The UN is a political entity without any independent will. If we set aside its specialized agencies, most of which perform useful practical services of one sort or another, the core of the institution—the General Assembly and the Security Council—is a legitimating, not a policy-making, apparatus. Decisions reached by the organisation are in essence embellishments of the relationships of power operative at any given time."[4] Some especially glaring failures (Rwanda 1994, Srebrenica 1995, the Iraq oil-for-food program…) didn't help. But the headquarters remained in more or less its original form: a place for touristic sightseeing for some, a memento of a certain moment of political history for others, a puzzle for most.

But the buildings themselves needed to change, and, at some point around the turn of the millennium, a massive renovation was planned. The work started in 2008, and it took seven years to be completed. Outdated and decayed electrical, heating, and ventilation systems were replaced. The by now iconic interiors were completely gutted, upgraded, and then reconstructed, their character-defining elements restored and returned as closely as possible to their origins. The multinational officers, bureaucrats, and dignitaries that usually occupied the place were moved out; construction workers and maintenance crews took their place. And photographer Nancy Davenport entered the premises with them. For six years, she followed the workers as they broke walls, smashed windows, removed asbestos, and carried bricks and panels, stripping the Security Council Chamber down to its skeleton, with the base of its circular table strangely exposed but still recognizable. We all have seen photographs of the place populated by world leaders sitting in their ample chairs uttering grave sentences; now the voices were those of workers trying to communicate over the noise of machines, the banal sounds of modern construction. An odd phrase appeared here and there, written on the Sheetrock walls, all mentioning a name: "Jimmy Buckles." Who was Jimmy Buckles? And who was the audience for these cryptic messages? Did the workers write such things on all their job sites, or were they unconsciously adopting some of the habits of the place?

4. Perry Anderson, "Our Man," *The London Review of Books*, vol. 29, no. 9 (10 May 2007), p. 9.

What was the relationship between what had happened before—in the days when the buildings weren't as dirty and destroyed—and these transitional times? It was possible to see in the passing present of the renovation traces of the prehistory of the site, the time when instead of the clean, glass buildings that we all know, there were the brick-and-wood edifices of the slaughterhouse and blood spilled on floors that were not made of marble. A haunting quality suffused the half-destroyed, half-built edifice, and it almost seemed that it wouldn't be a bad place for Castro's chickens to roam around. The sound of the hammers breaking walls echoed the sound of Khrushchev's shoe banging on a table, and some of the machines probably didn't look that different from the one that Krishna Menon's doctor must have used to monitor his blood pressure while the diplomat completed his speech. For a time, it was possible to imagine the process taking place as the execution of a plan by some unknown functionary to construct miniaturized representations of the bombed cities, wastelands, and places of devastation that so many people had discussed, for good or bad, on this site over the years.

This is the temporal and spatial disorientation that Davenport sought to document. She took photographs, interviewed the workers, the maintenance crews, and interpreters, and recorded their conversations. She noted their ethical codes and work-site etiquette. She was intrigued by the way their discussions resonated, as if a commentary by turns hilarious and tragic, with the intense debate that was simultaneously raging in the Security Council over its procedures and the need to expand its membership—the need, in other words, to chart a new future for an institution that was being physically torn apart only to be returned to its original state. Lewis Mumford, at the time when he despised the design, critiqued the UN Headquarters as architecture in which "the future is frozen solidly in the form of the present,"[5] but now one could see the ice melting. This book collects mementos of this deliquescence (recent photographs, transcripts, archival images, and items from the artist's own immense collection of vintage UN paraphernalia) and remixes graphic forms and visual citations to convey the curious life of this unstable extraterritorial space, half-abandoned but still allowing, to borrow the words of Perry Anderson, "a glimpse of the history of possibility."[6]

5. Lewis Mumford, "United Nations Assembly," in *From the Ground Up*, p. 59. The essay was originally published in the *New Yorker* in 1953.

6. Perry Anderson, *Spectrum: From Right to Left in the World of Ideas* (London: Verso, 1995), p. 76.

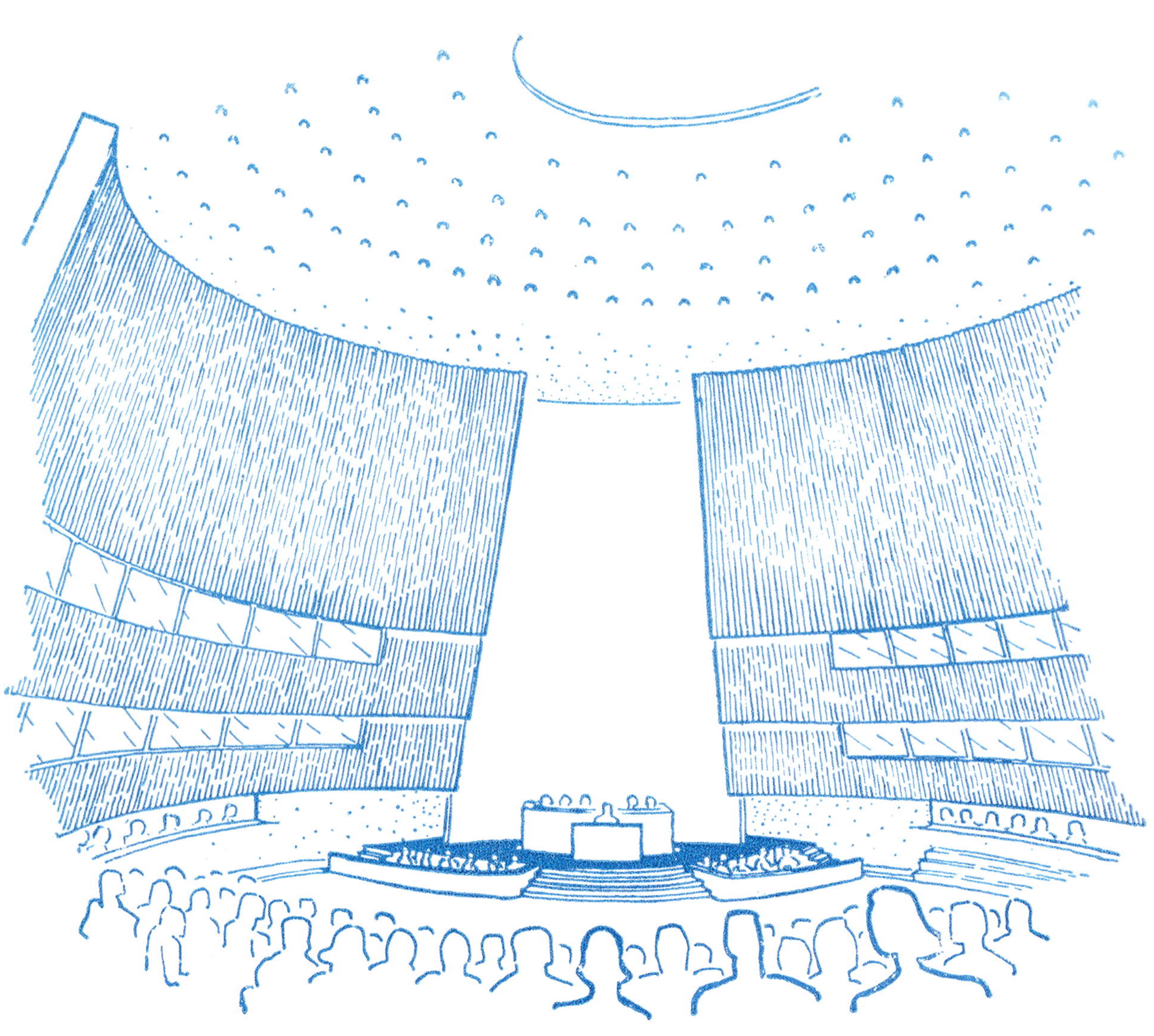

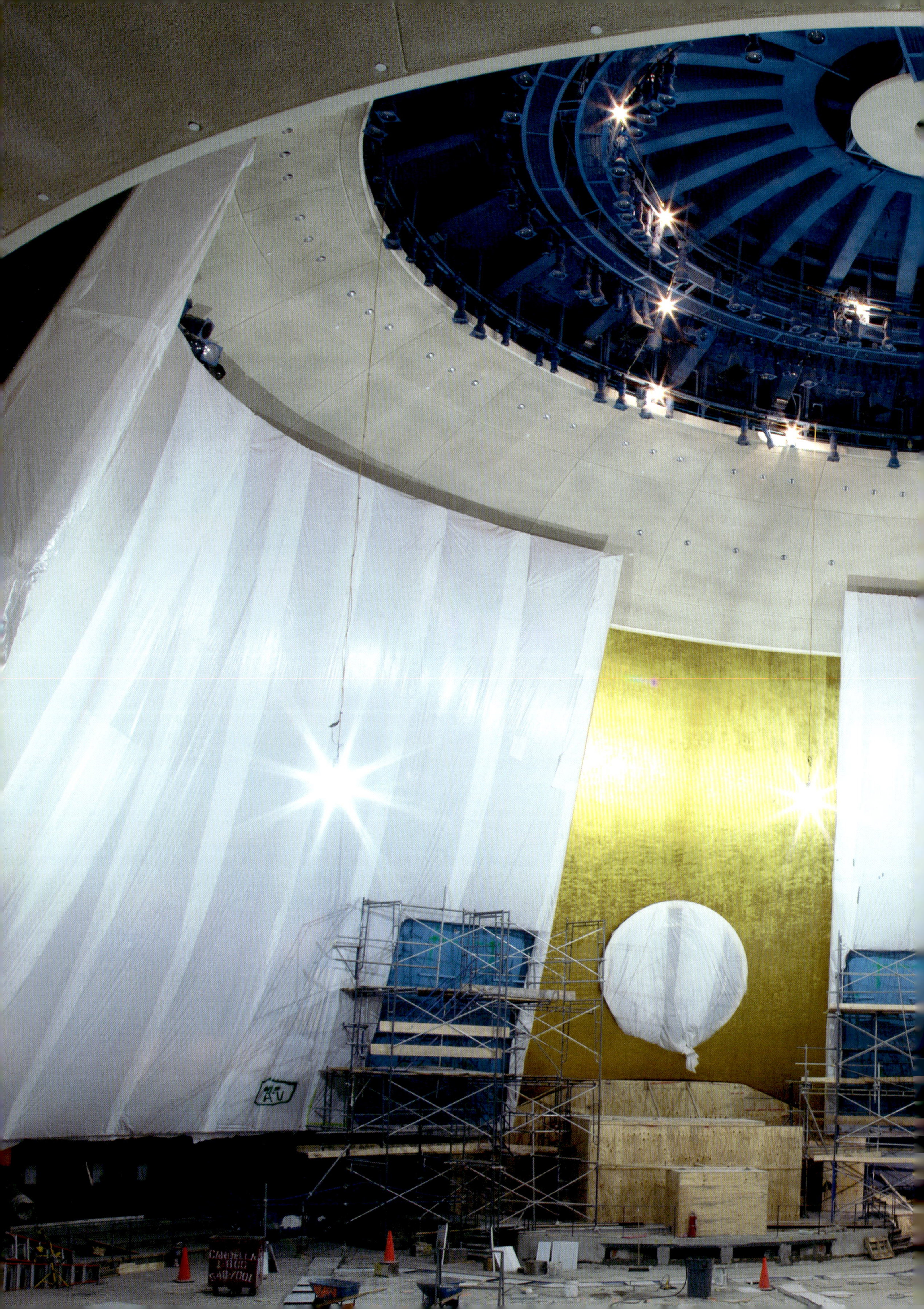

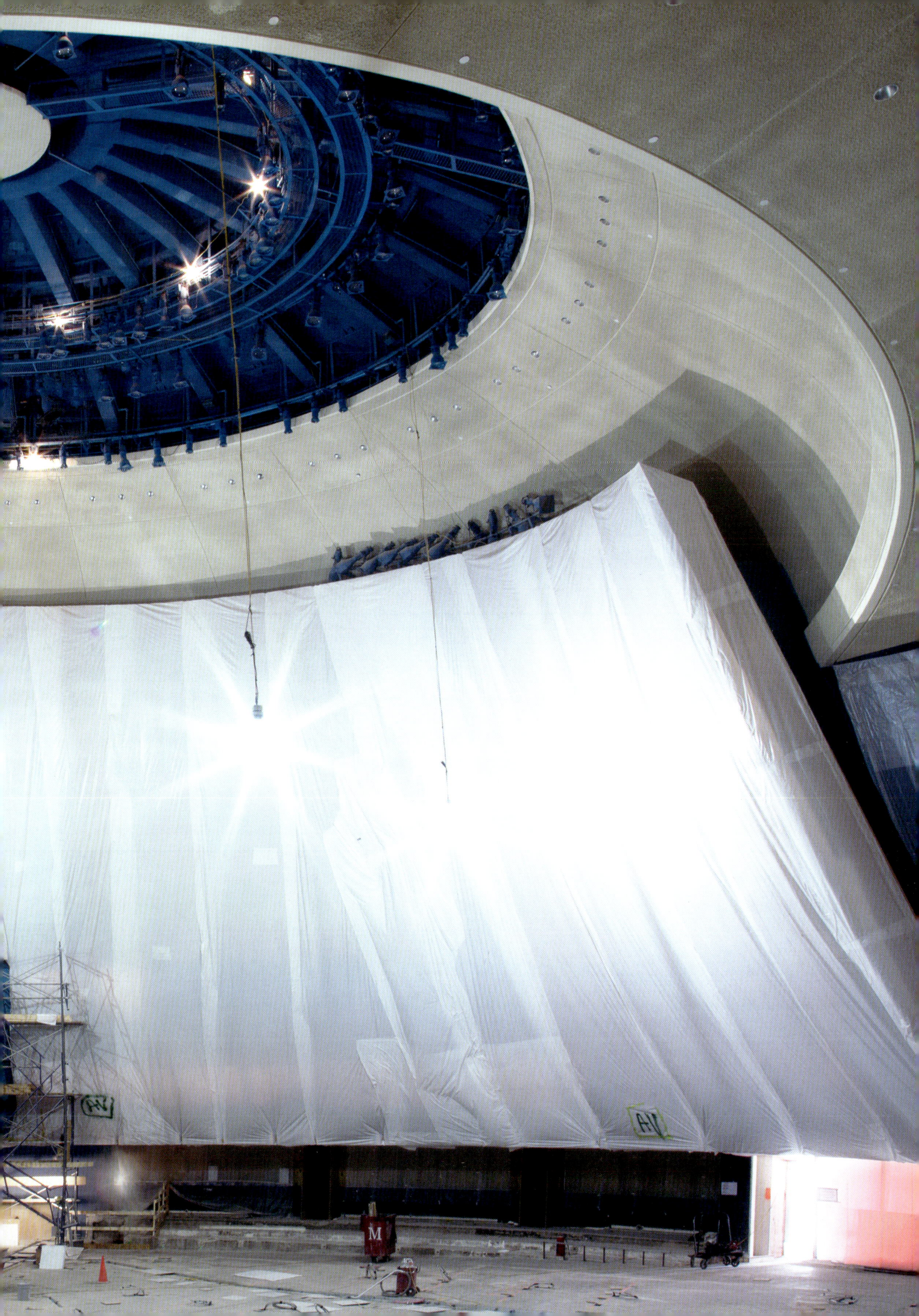

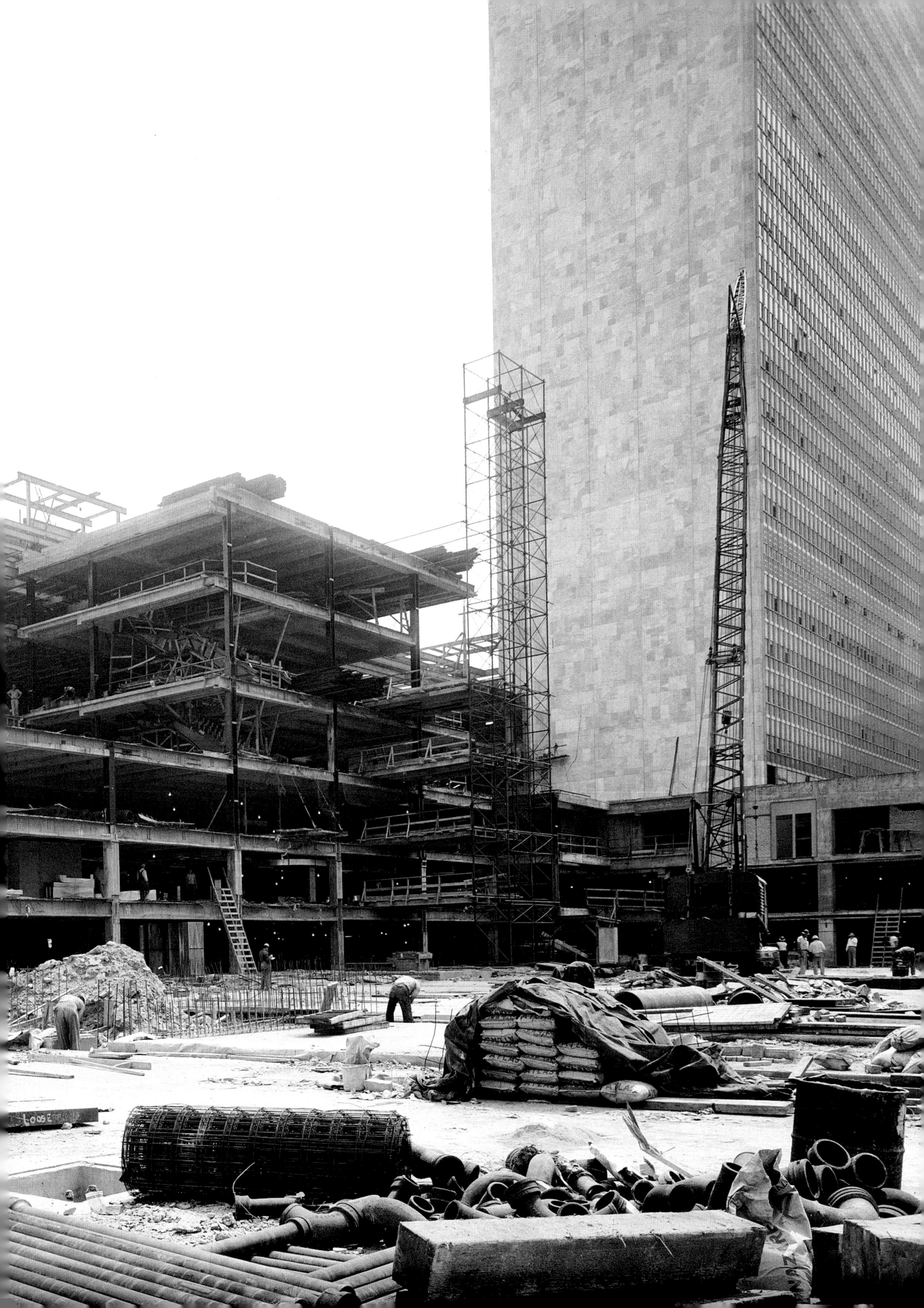

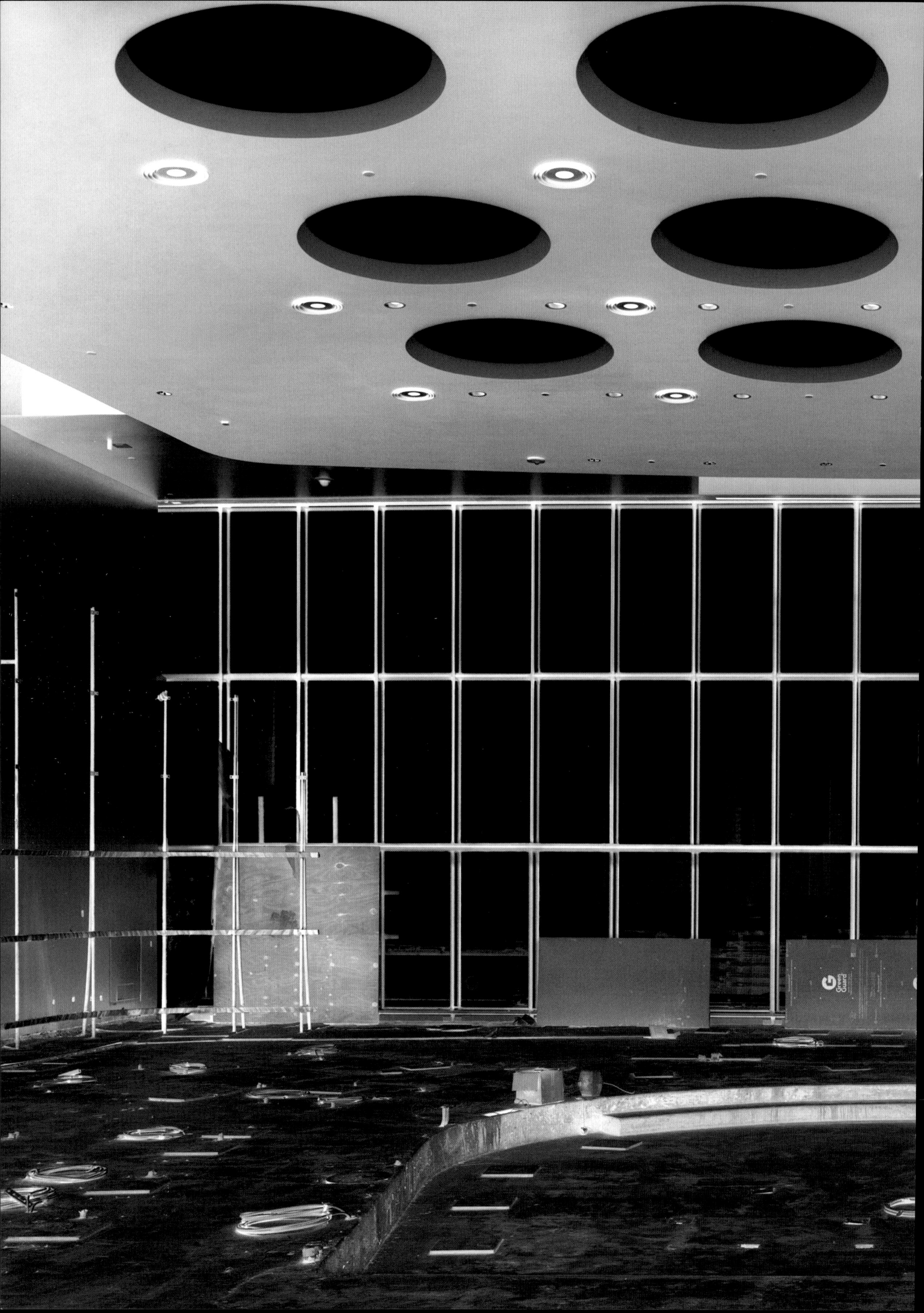

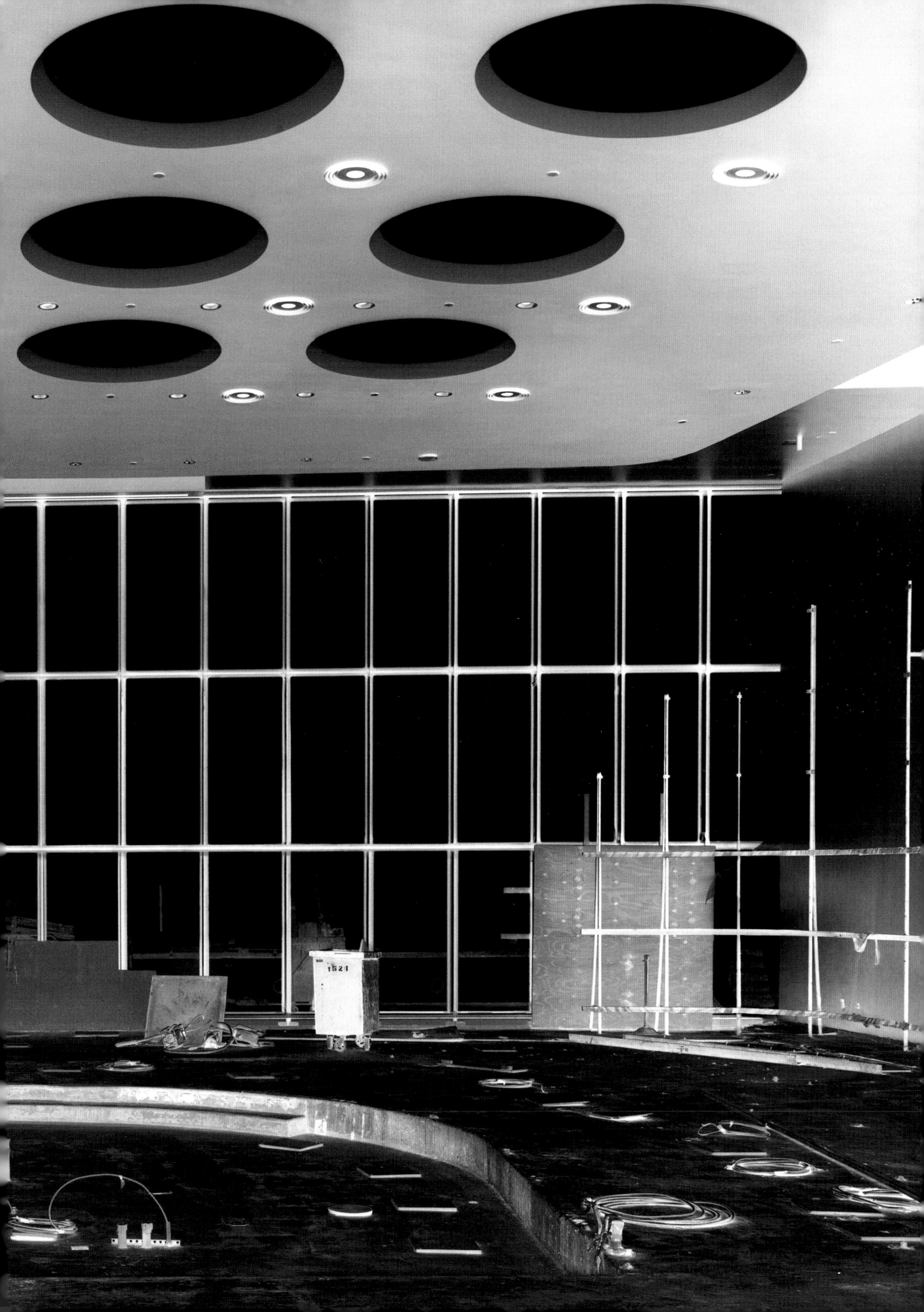

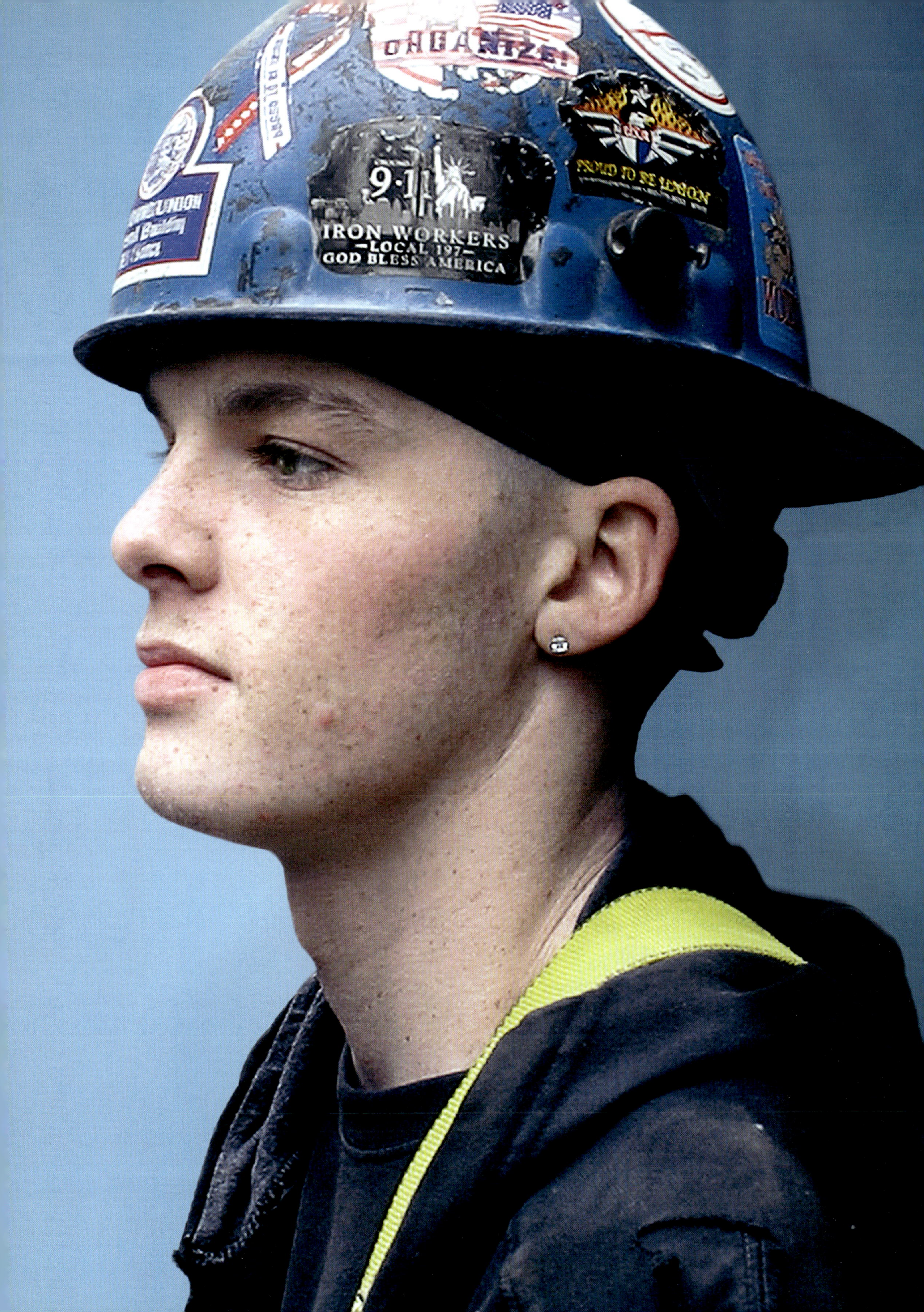

ORGANIZE
9-1
IRON WORKERS
—LOCAL 197—
GOD BLESS AMERICA
PROUD TO BE UNION
UNION

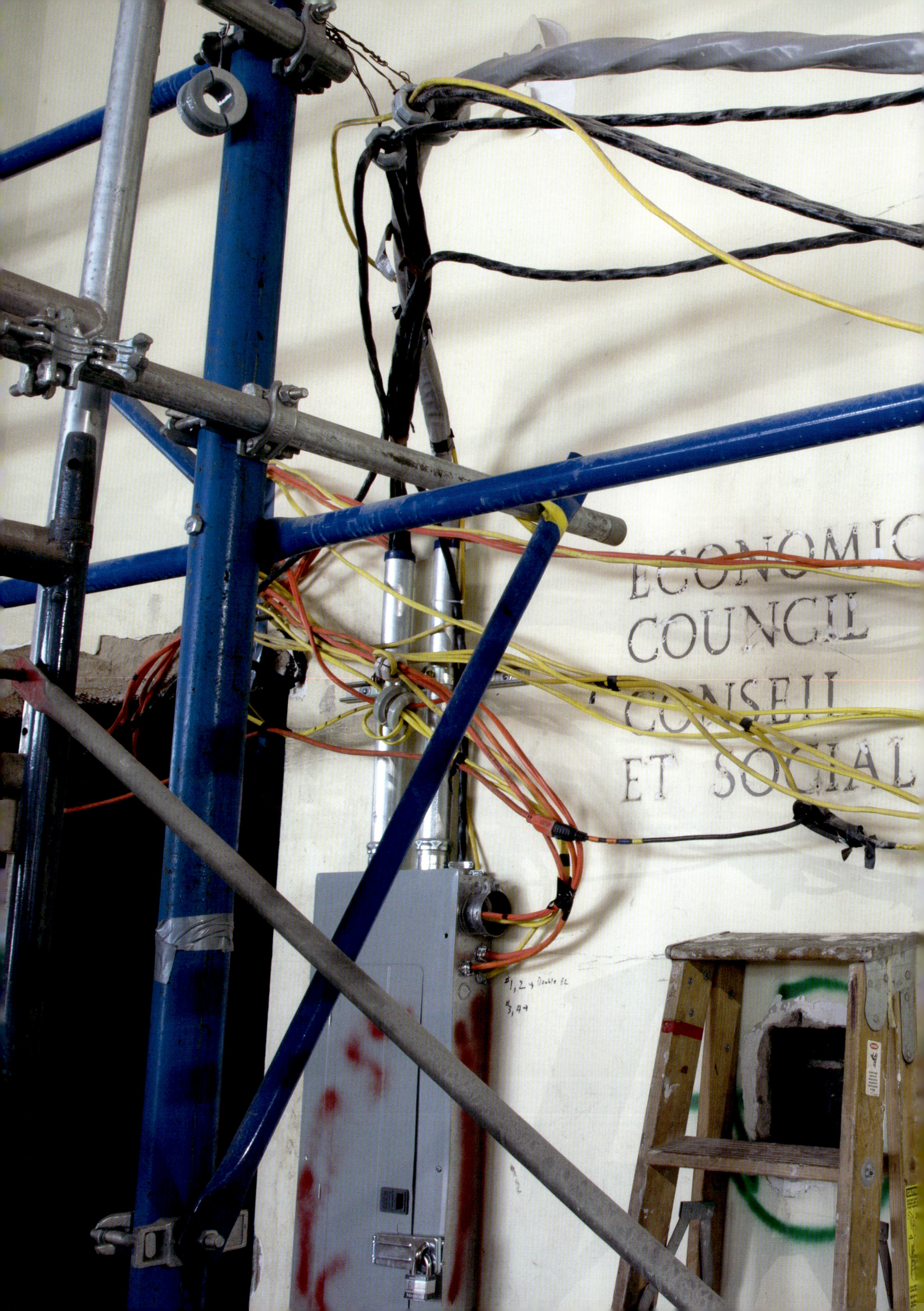

ECONOMIC
COUNCIL
CONSEIL
ET SOCIAL

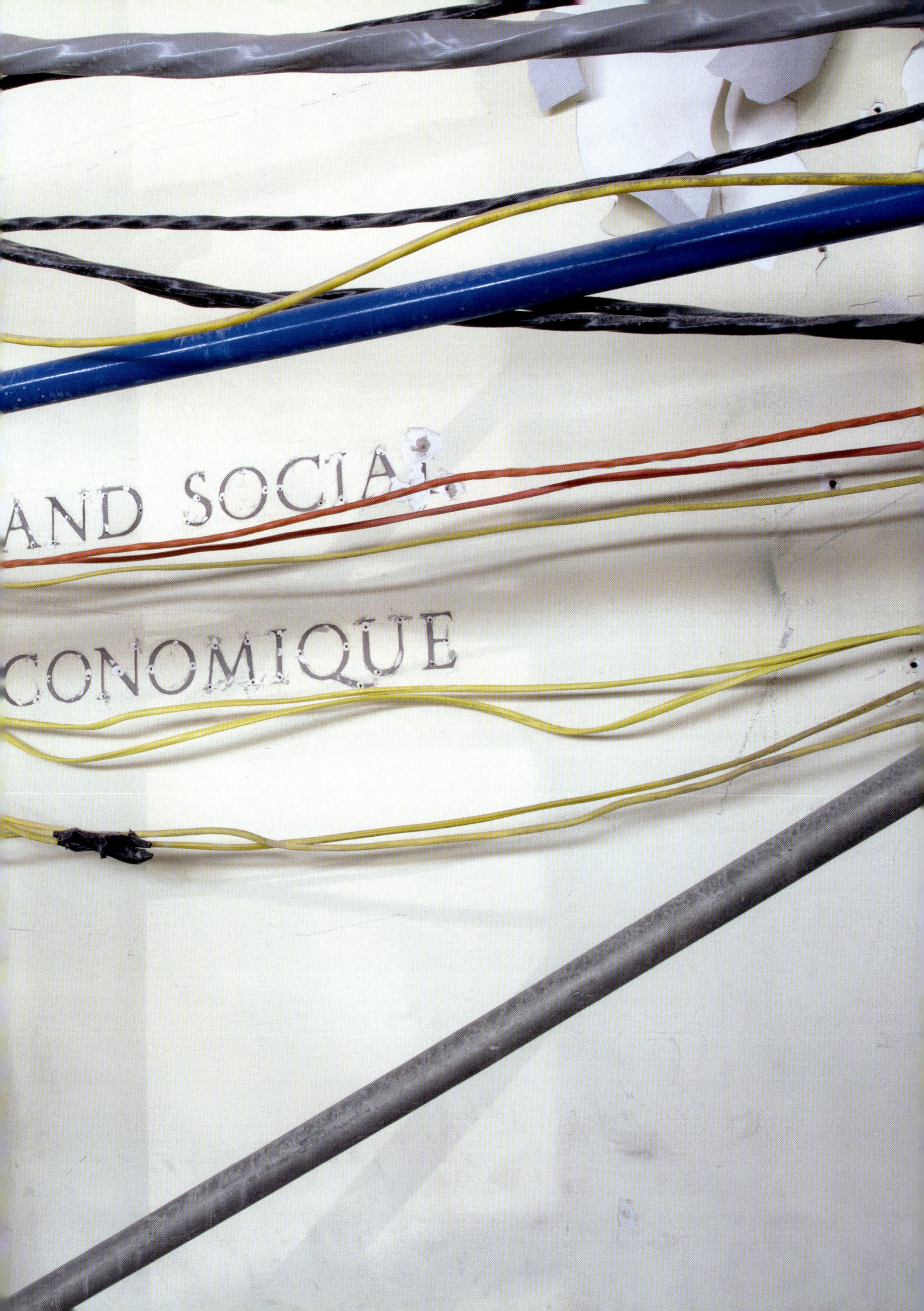
AND SOCIAL
CONOMIQUE

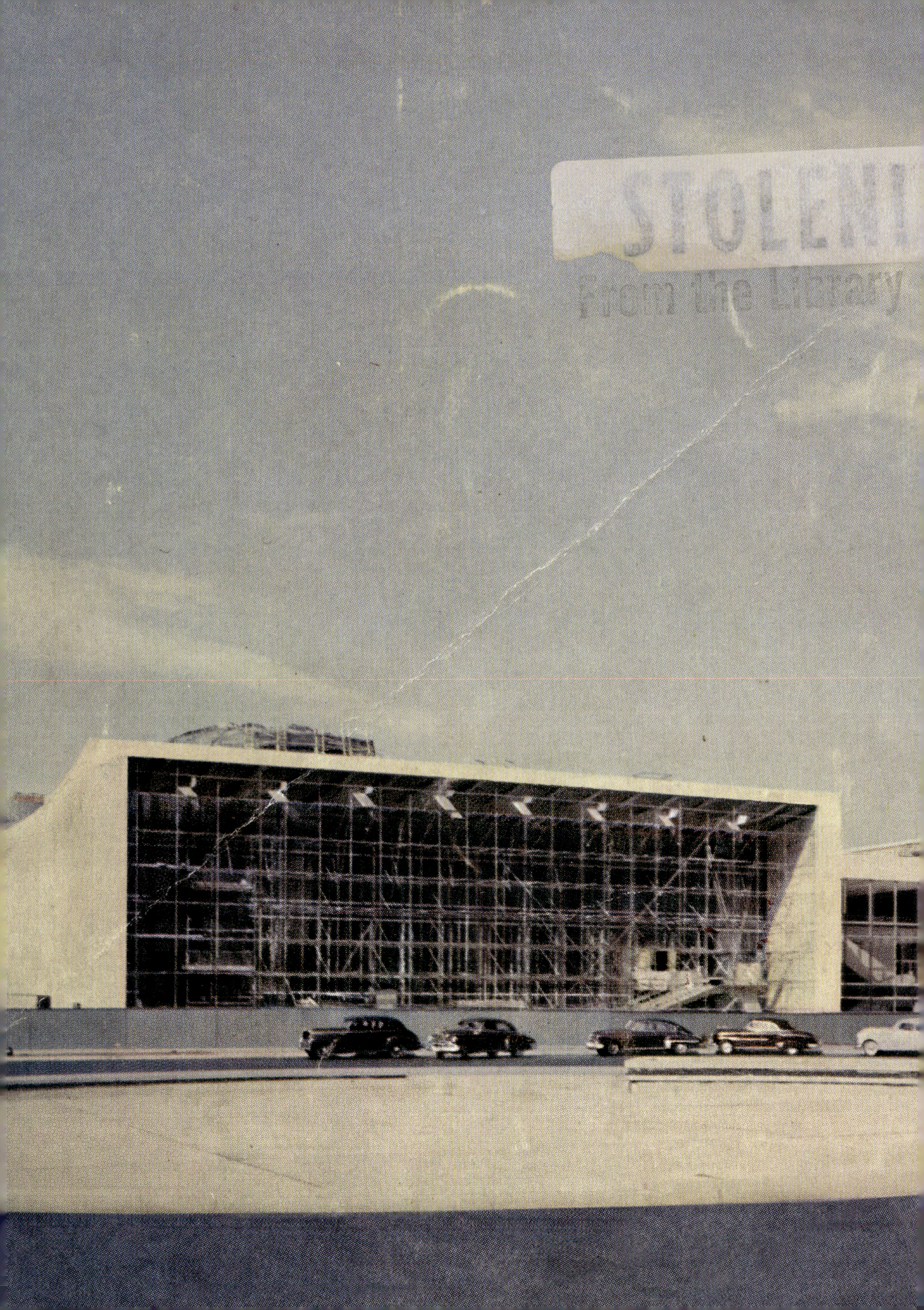

STOLEN
From the Library

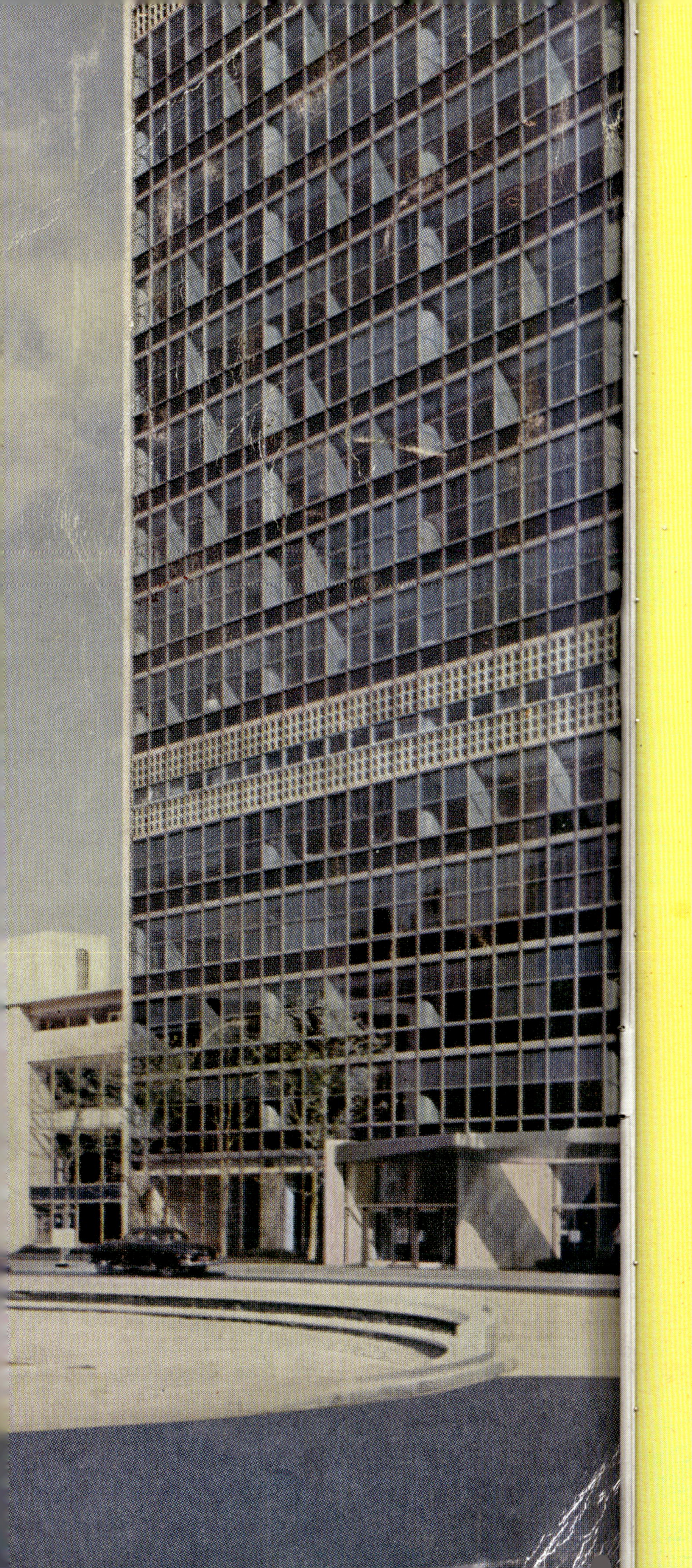

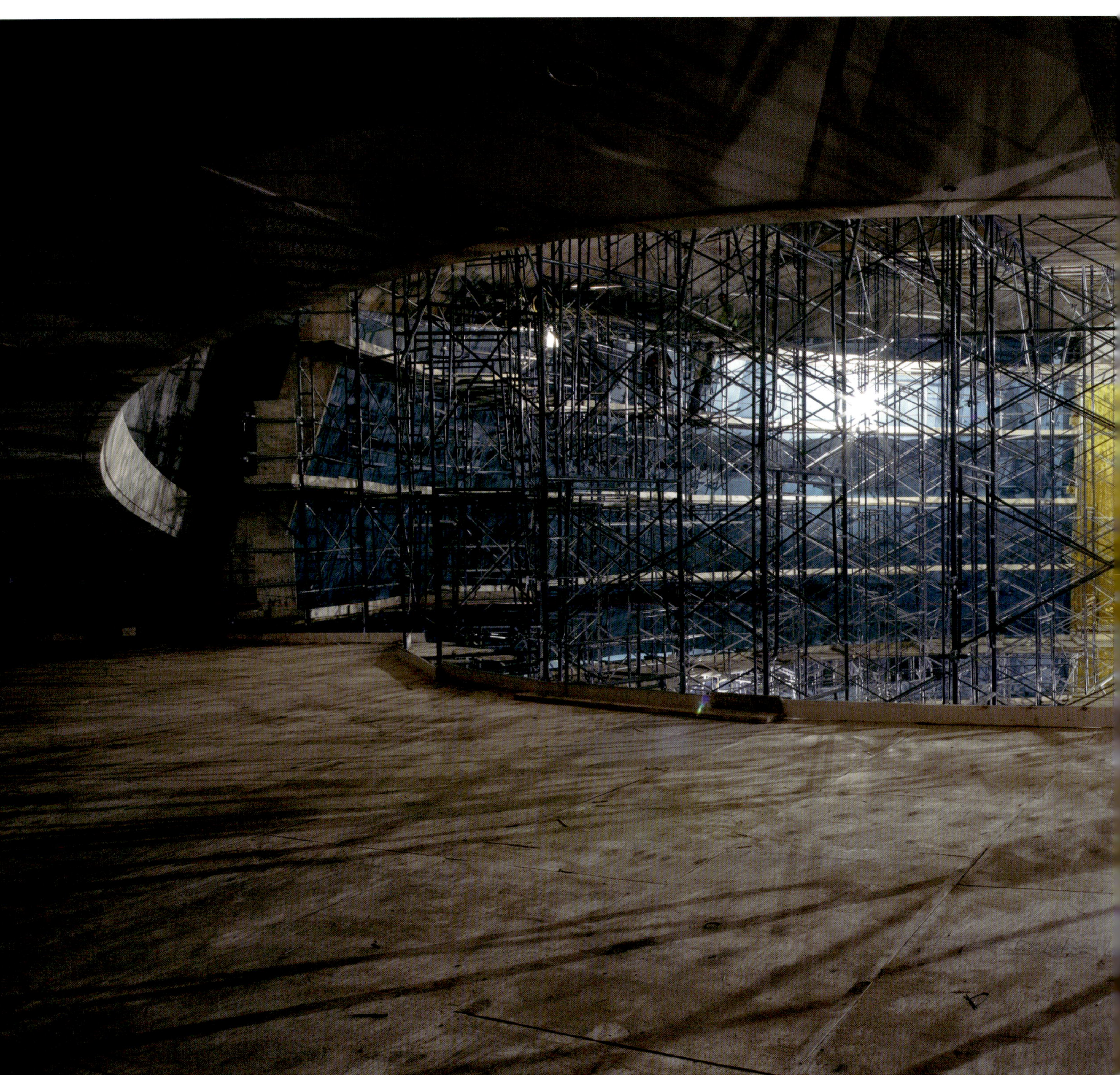

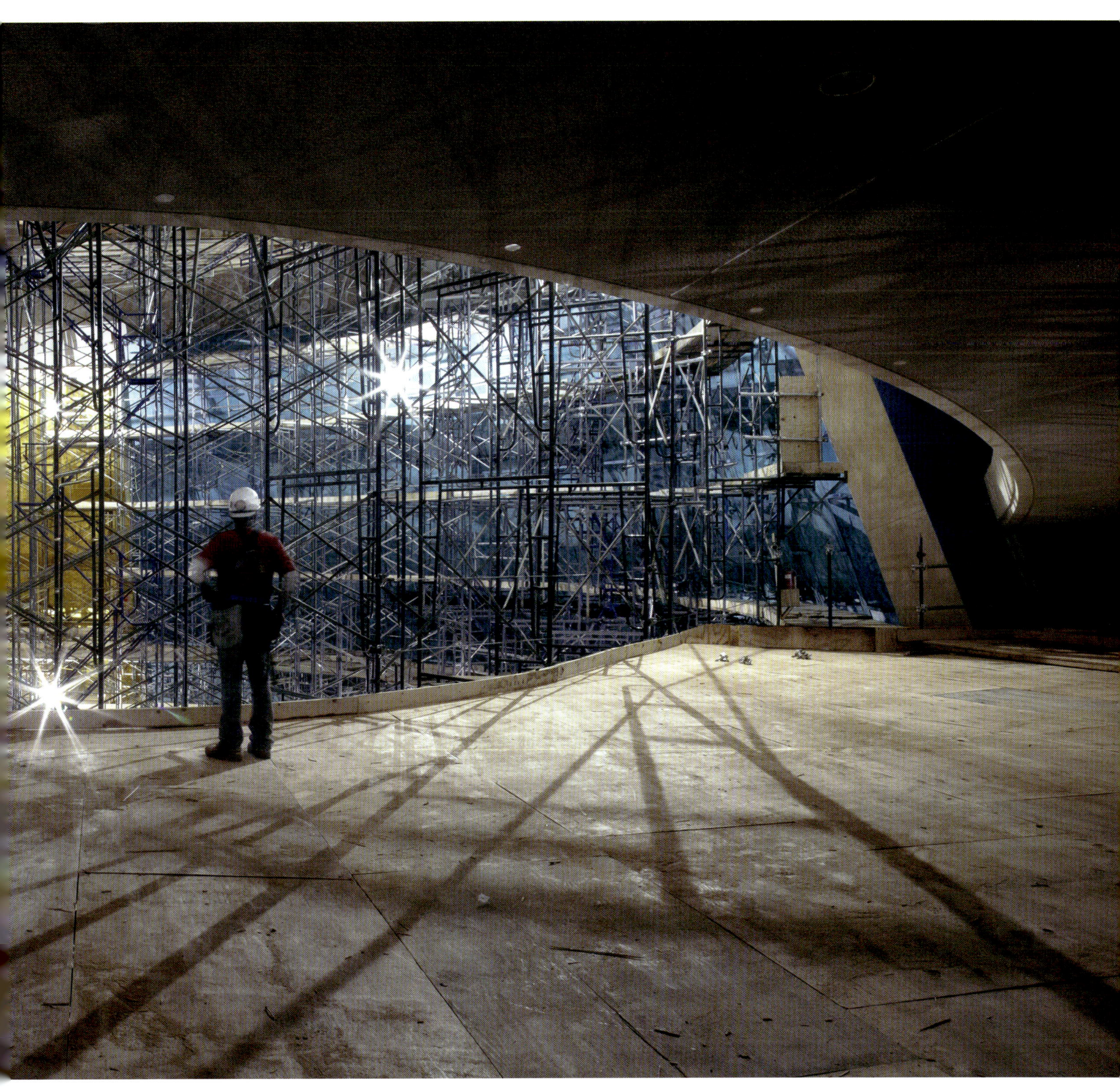

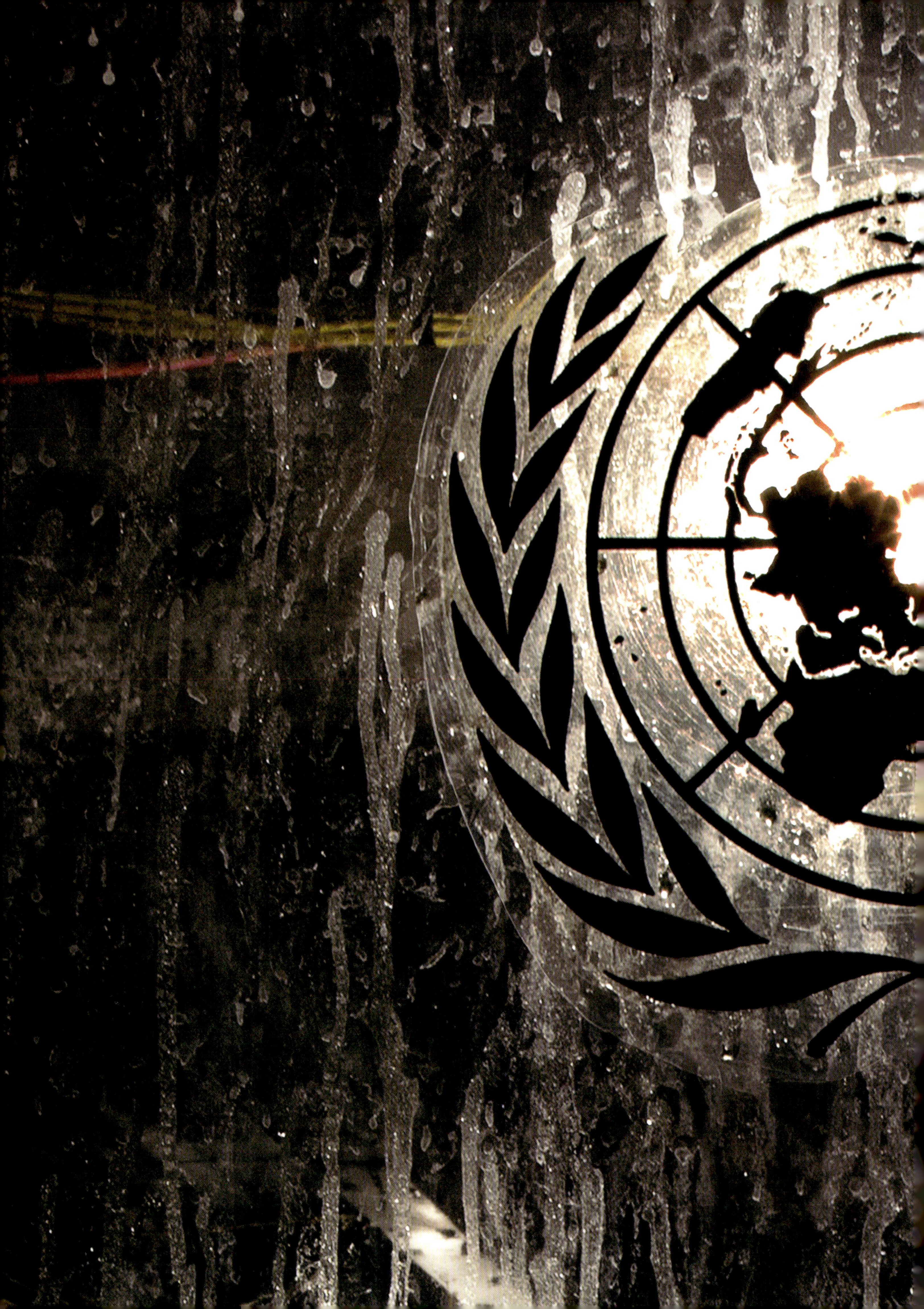

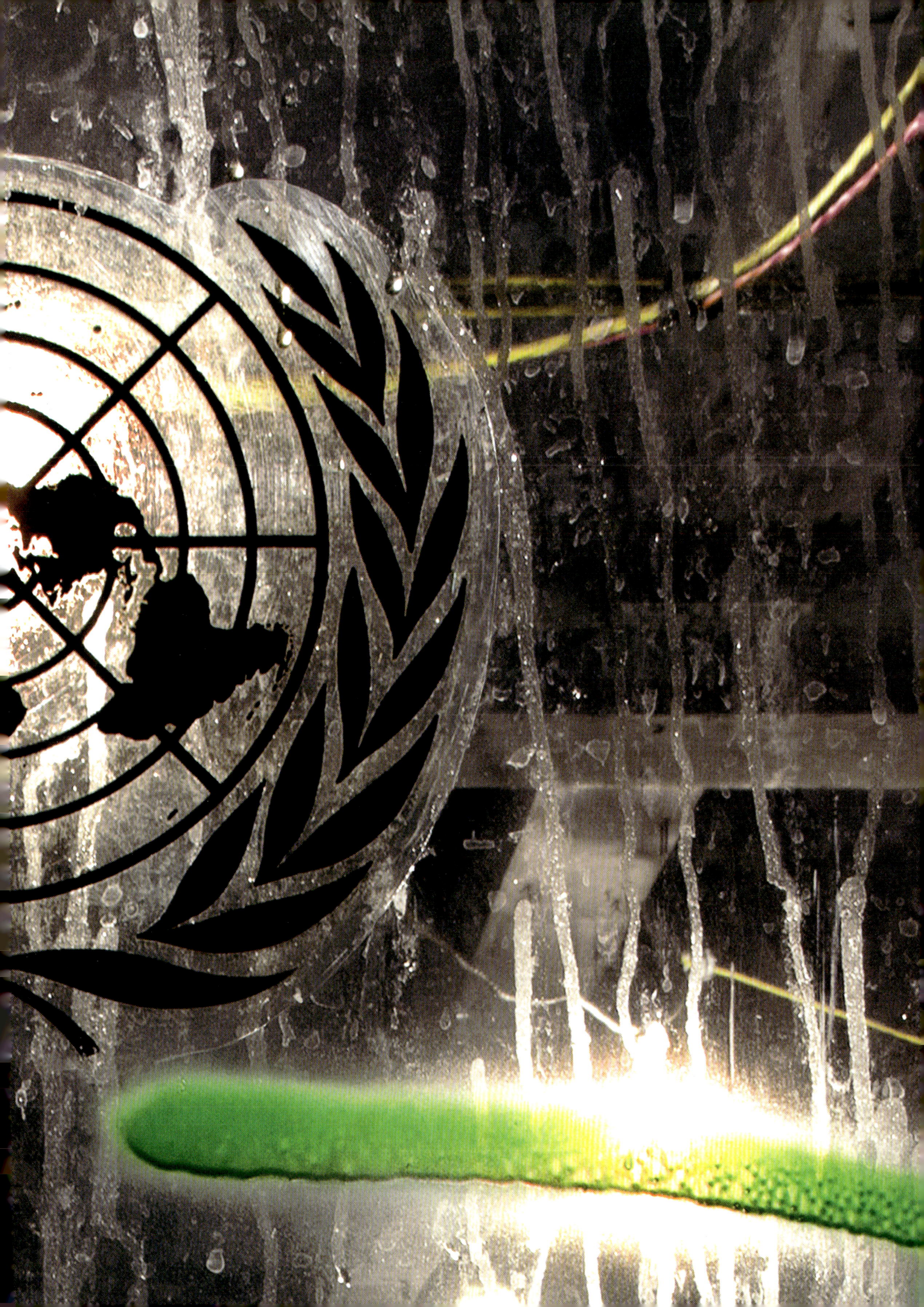

HEADQUARTERS
A DESCRIPTION AND APPRAISAL

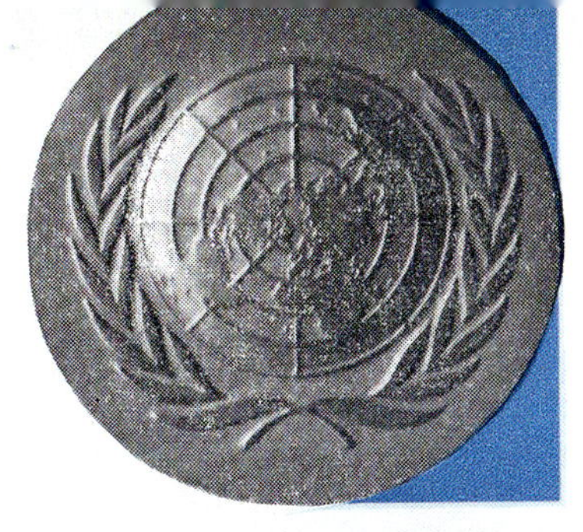

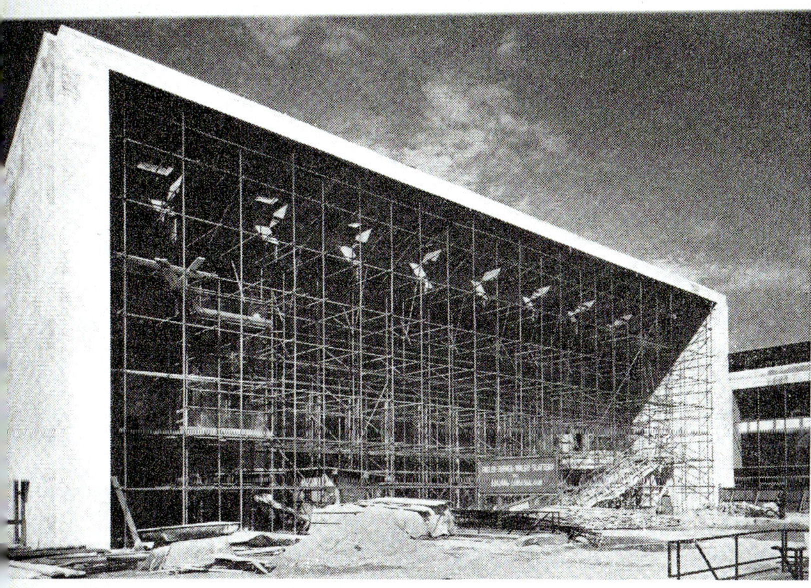

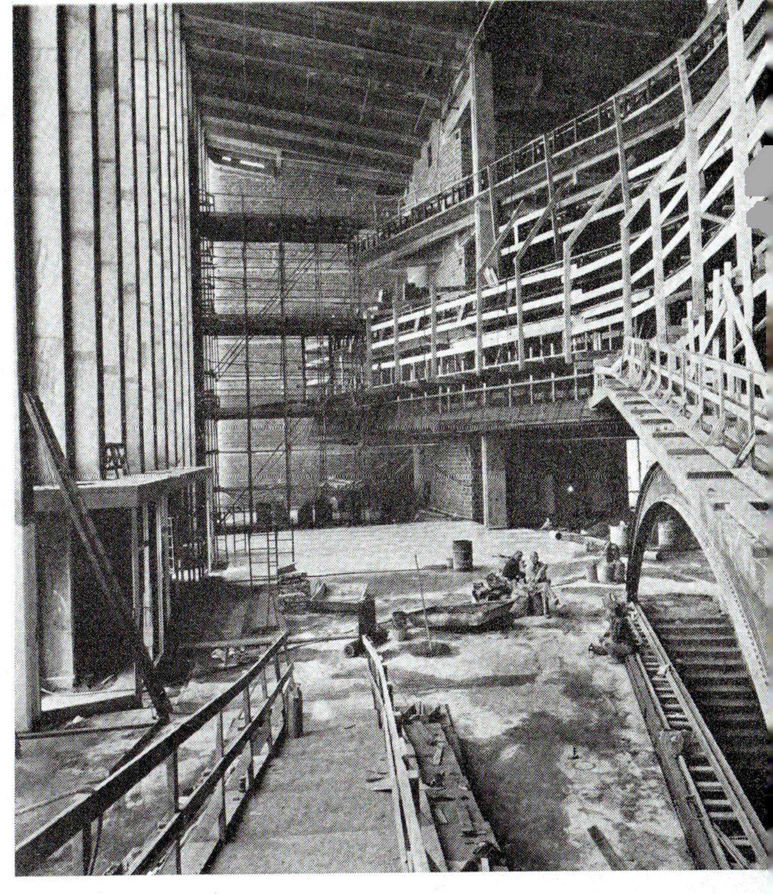

Joseph W. Molitor

acteristic form of American architecture, and it is in the technique of office buildings that our greatest advances have been made. It is somehow fitting that the Secretariat should become the symbol of the U.N. — an up-ended filing case for human beings, their hopes, their fears and their aspirations for a steady job. That is the new American Dream, a steady job, that is what we hope a United World will bring us, in the terms of peace and security; and of that the Secretariat is a just, if unconscious, expression.

The planning of the U.N. group is a triumph of clarity and ingenuity, a putting together and sorting out of an almost incredible variety of elements and functions. It is also a triumph of technical skill, of structural ability, of mechanical engineering. Almost every possible device of a mechanical nature has been used to further the comfort of the users of the buildings, to speed up communication, to disseminate information quickly and accurately. It is, in other words, a very fine example of American architectural skill.

It is not, however, much more than that; and perhaps it could not be. Our architectural genius today, and in the United States particularly, lies in the design of buildings for the use of business. Our most successful

structures, esthetically as well as technically, are office buildings and factories. We are accomplished in the design of residences, too; but none of these classes of architecture speaks to the deep symbolic needs of our being, they have little emotional impact. The Secretariat is the U.N. to the world. By its simplicity of form and dominating mass it has become the symbol for U.N. The General Assembly building does not dominate either by its physical presence or its spiritual content. It is not that the effort to have the General Assembly provide the symbol was not made: it was. The failure is not the fault of the architects, but of a time in which no emotional symbols are possible because there is no deep belief, no emotional content in our lives. Symbols are not "created": they exist or they do not exist. The non-existent symbolism that was consciously striven for in the General Assembly got transferred subconsciously and necessarily to the real and existing symbol, the building which houses what we most believe in — paper-work, files, reports, pay-rolls, publicity. Symbols, great art, are not created *ad hoc;* they are inherent in the cultural and emotional heritage, and appear as such, whether we like them or not.

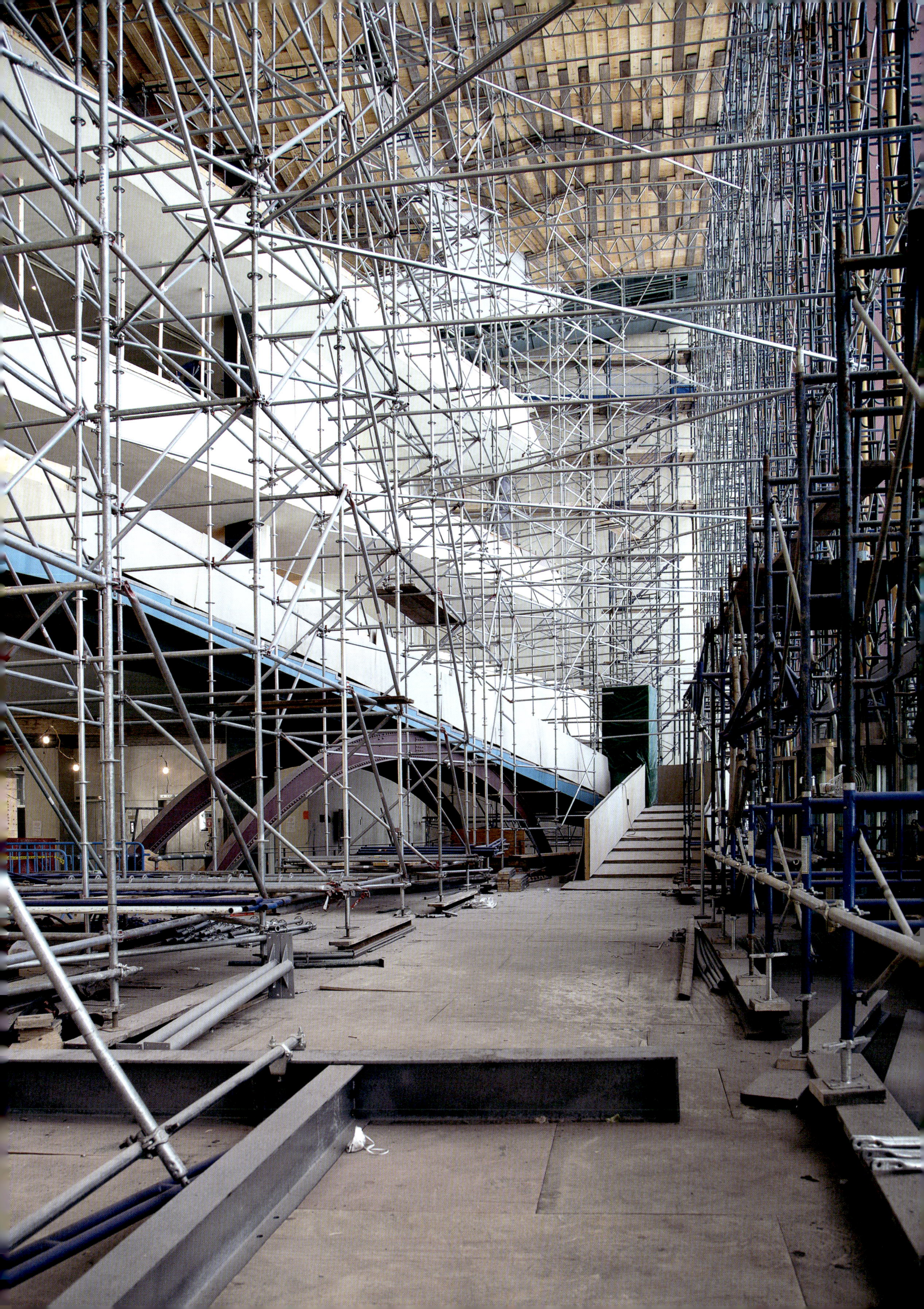

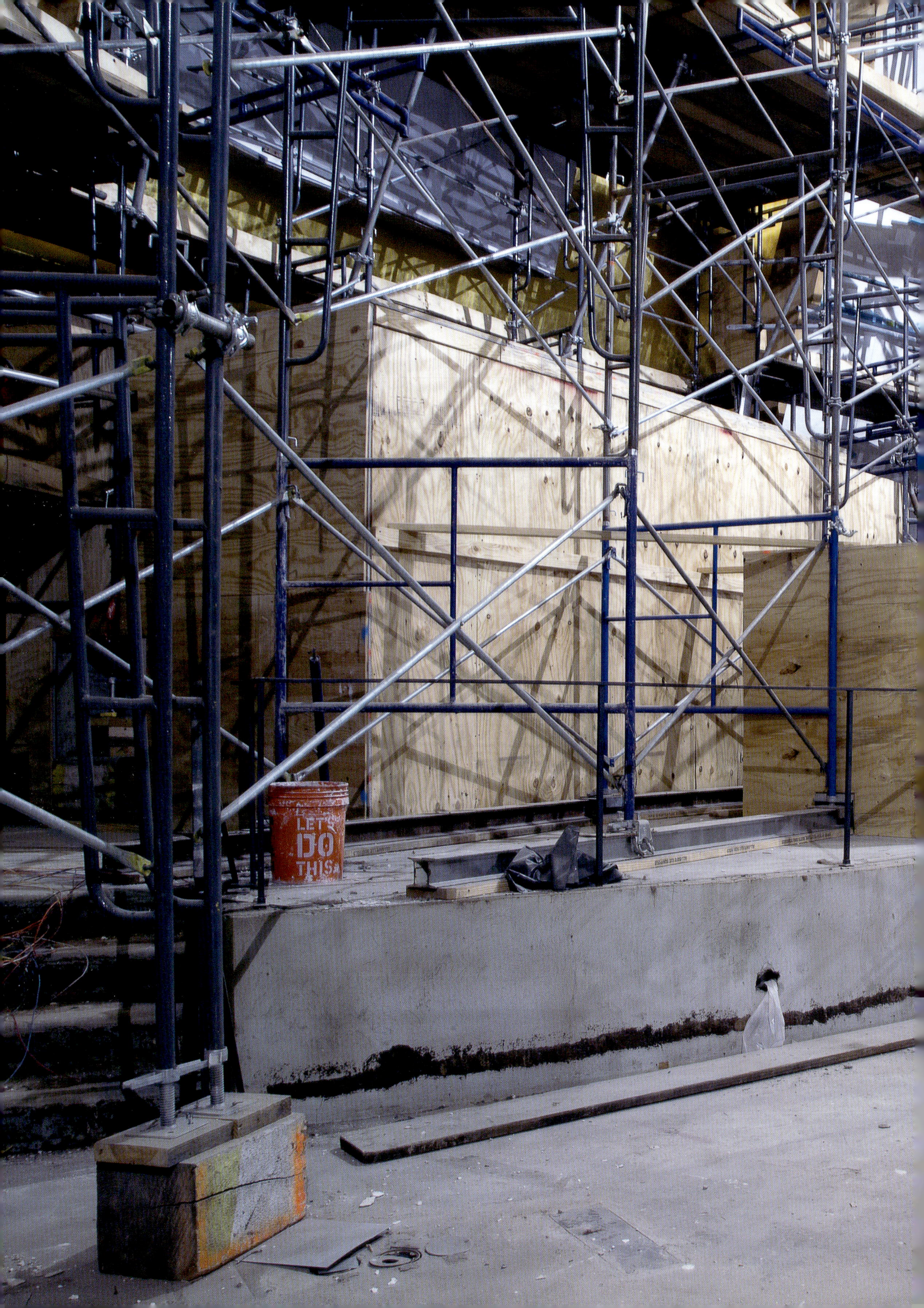

LET'S
DO
THIS

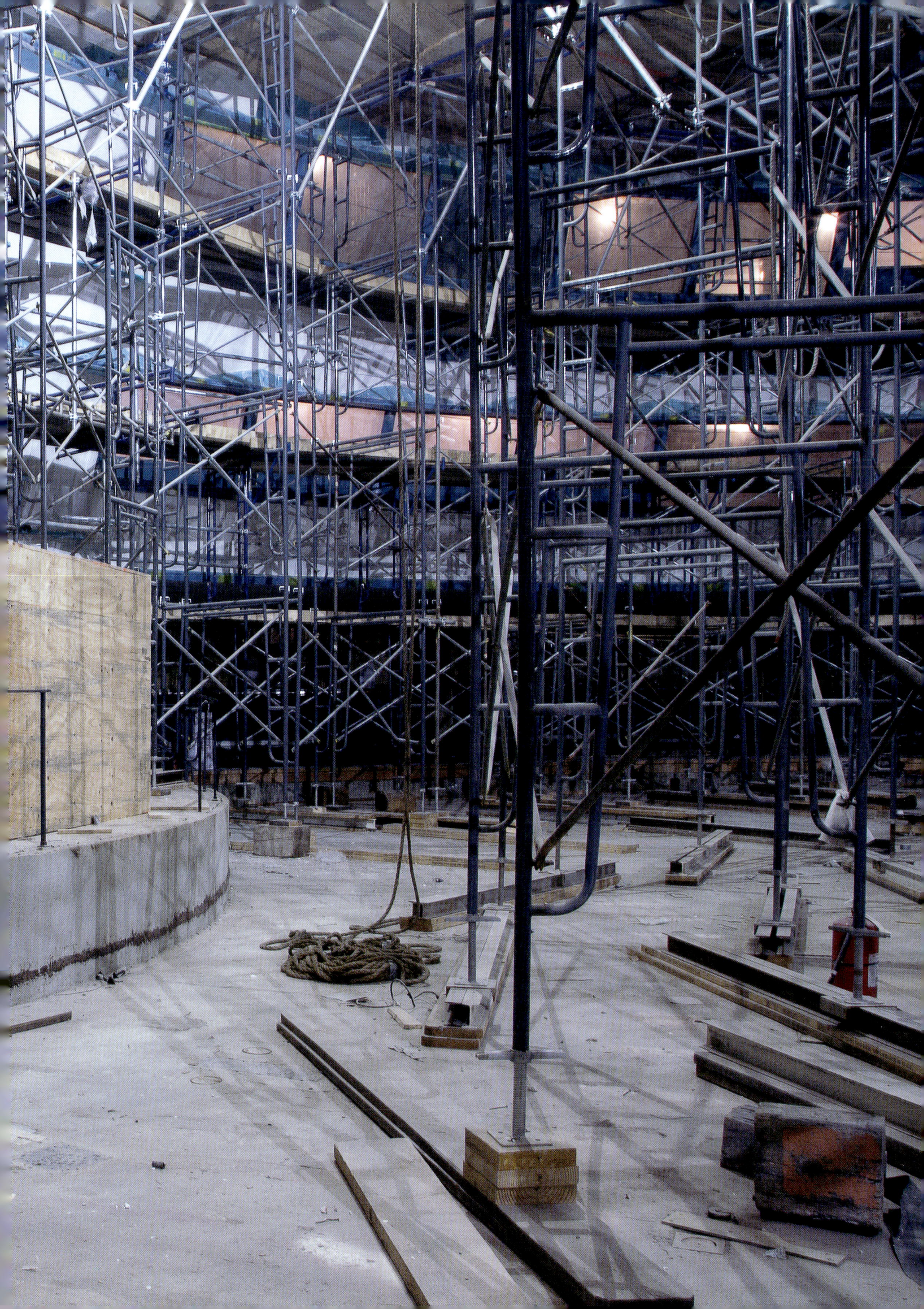

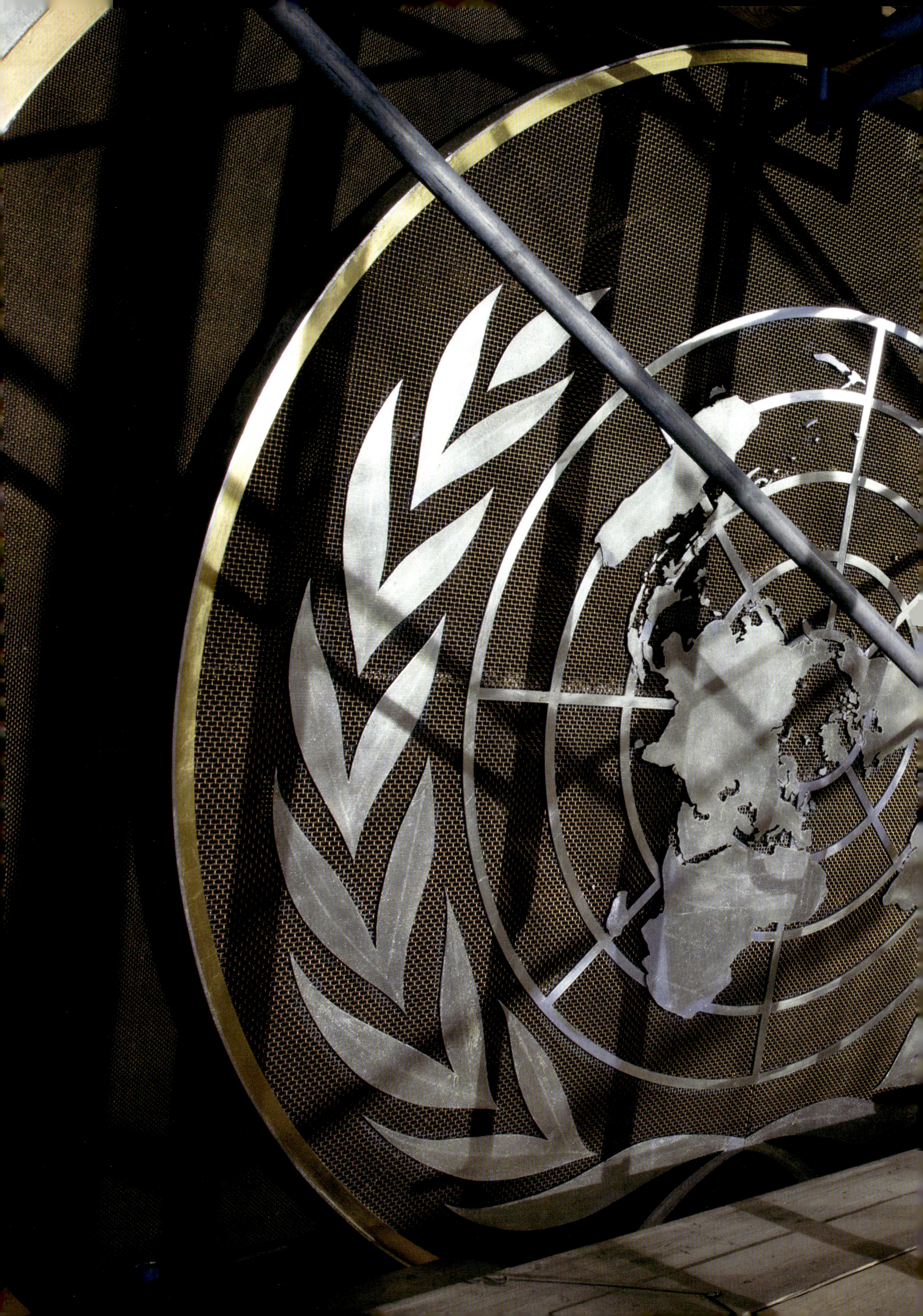

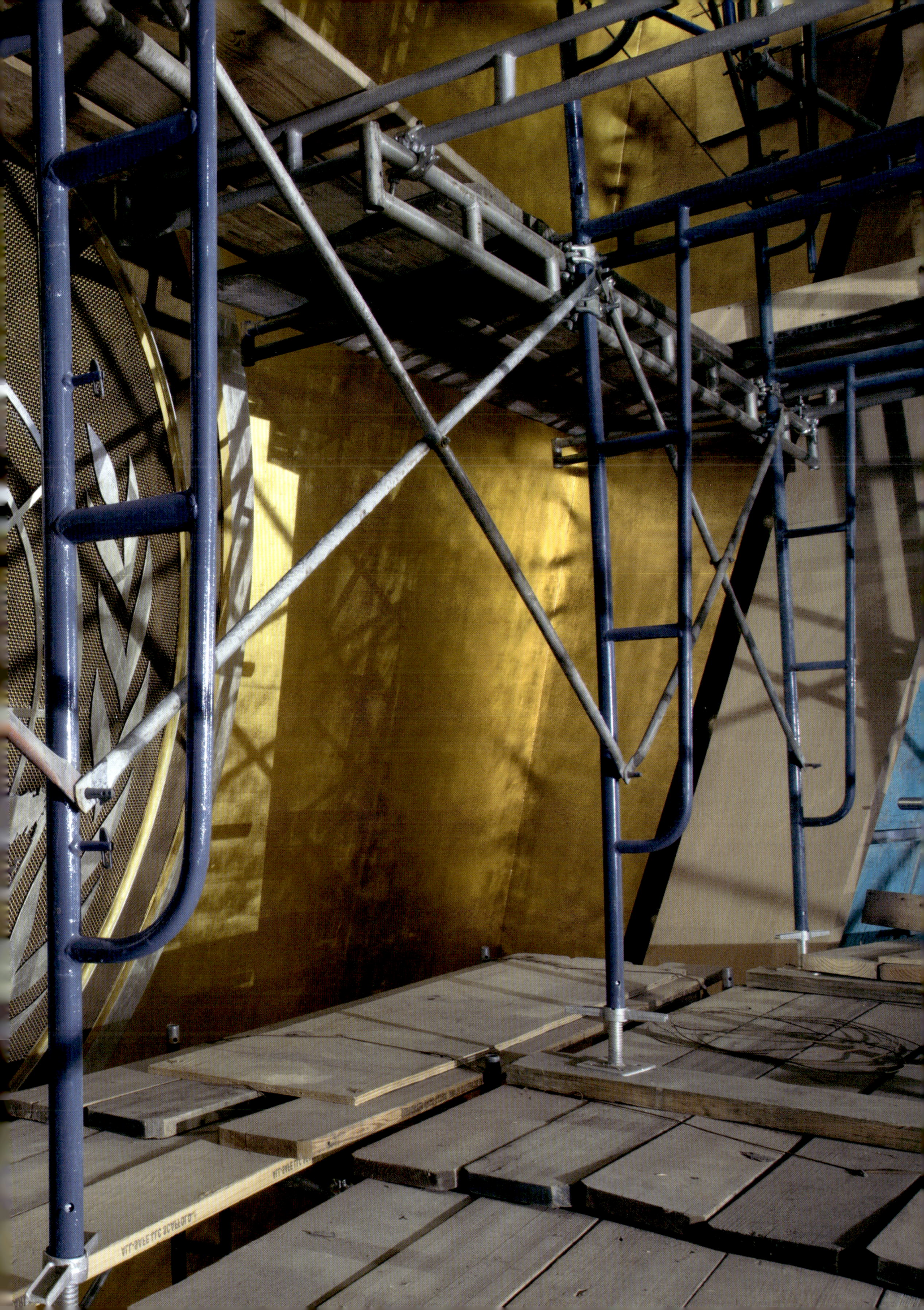

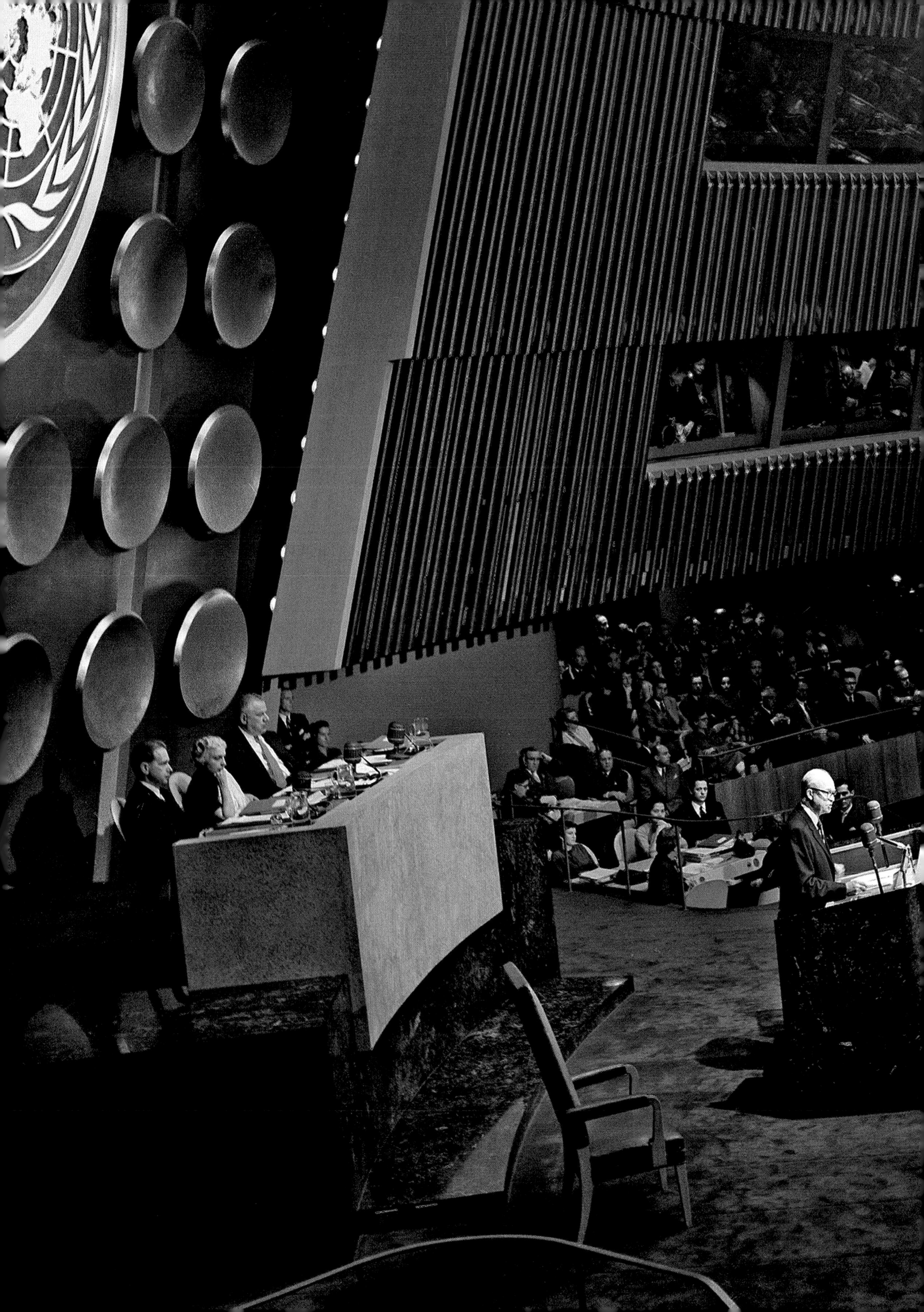

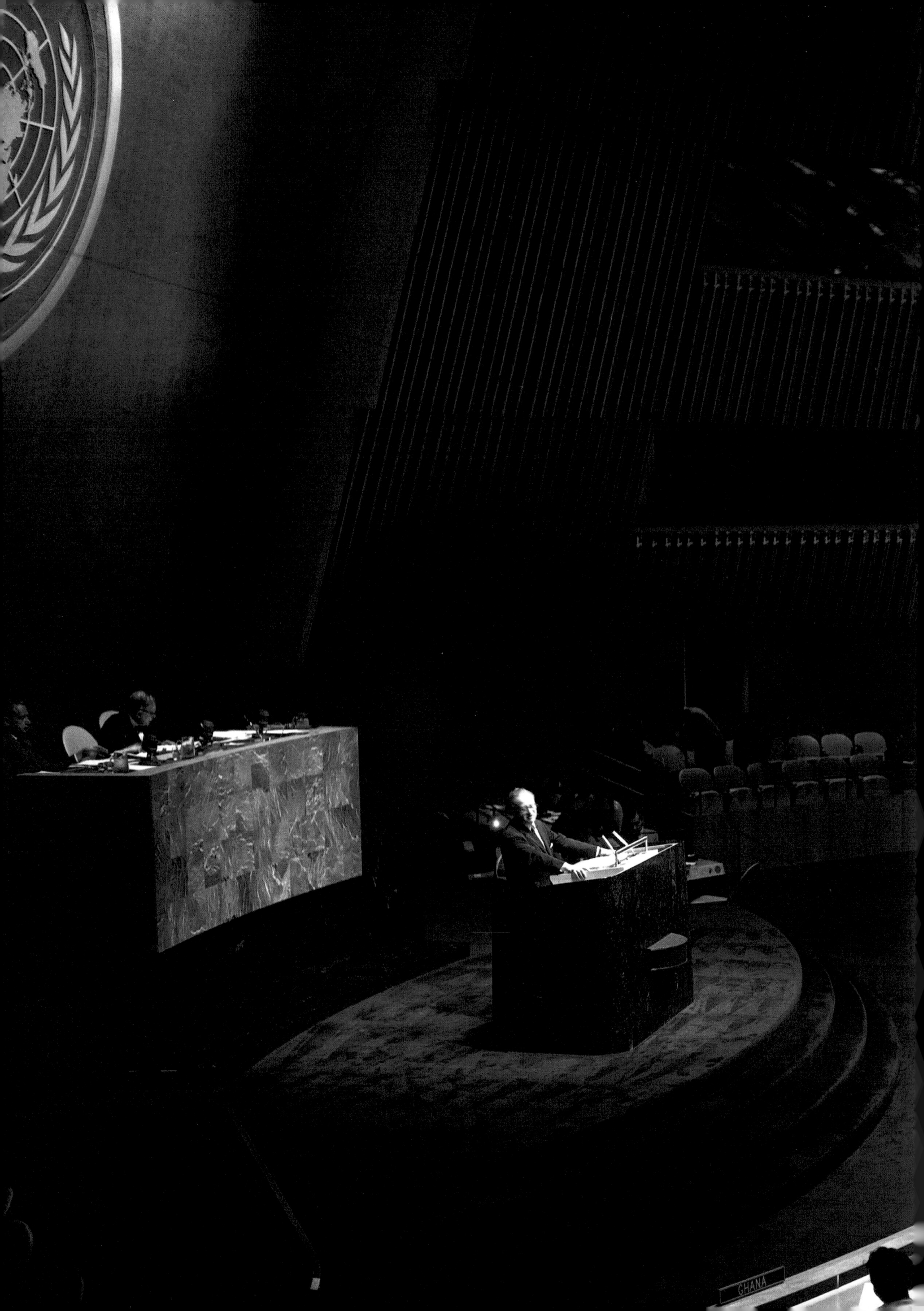

GHANA

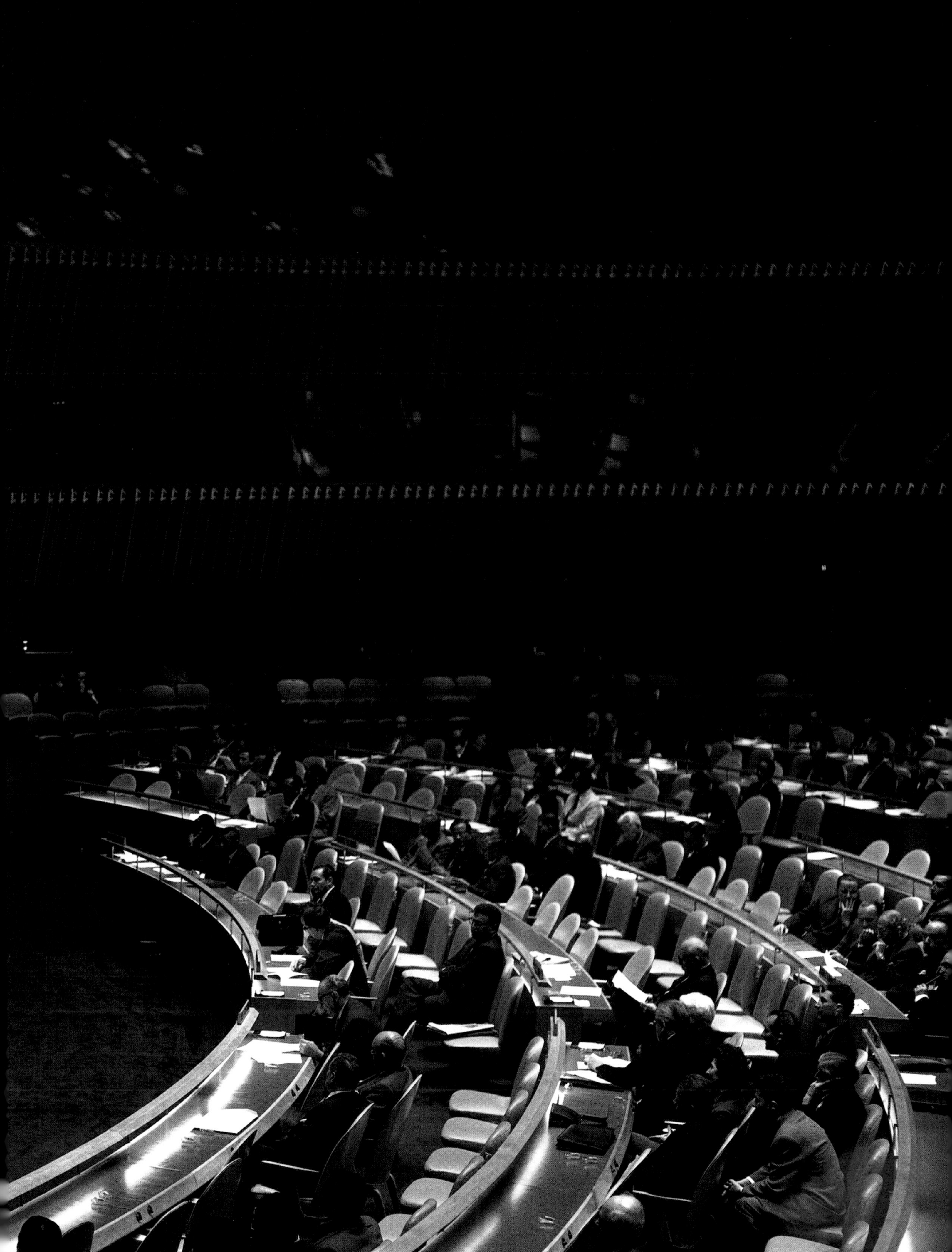

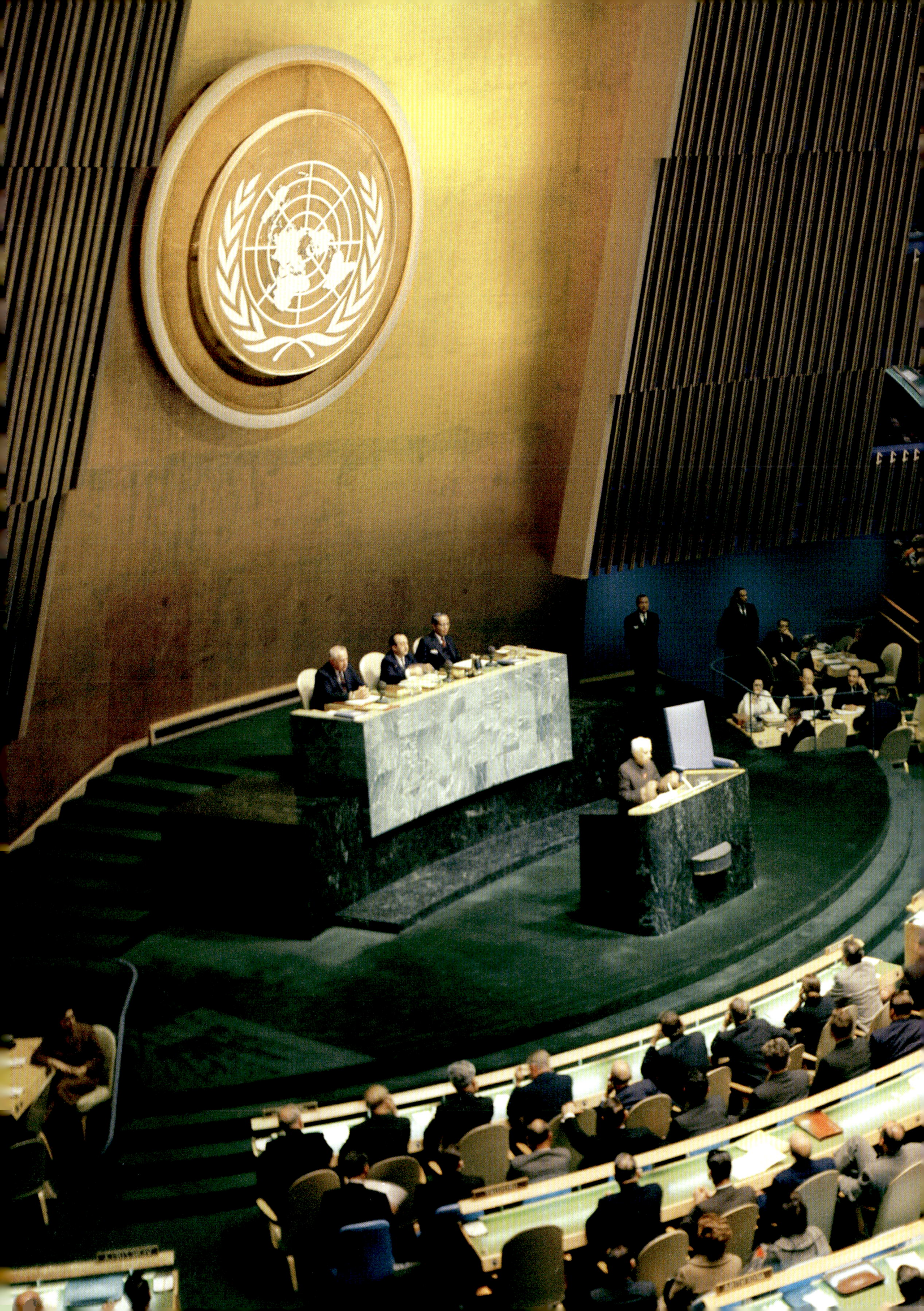

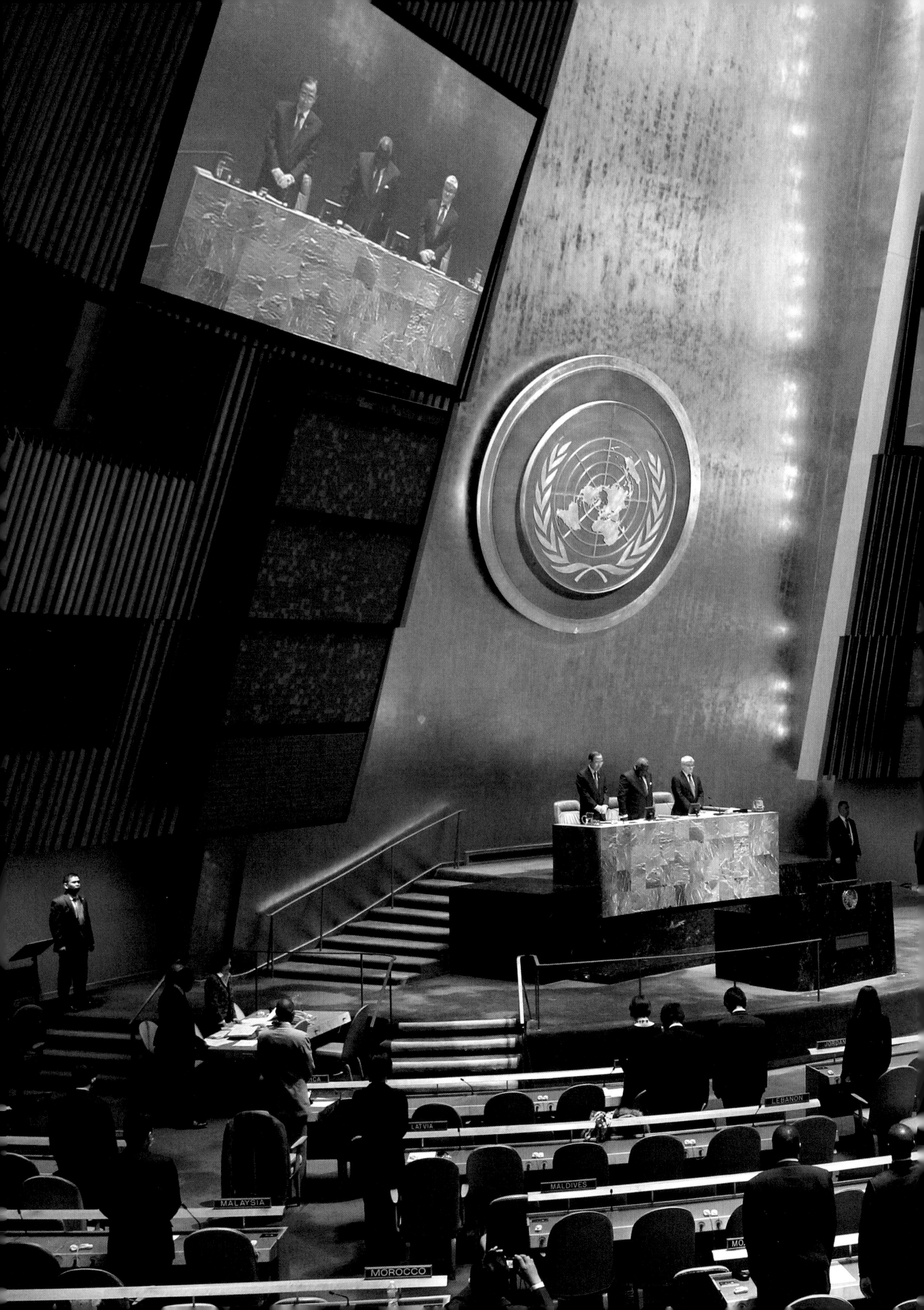

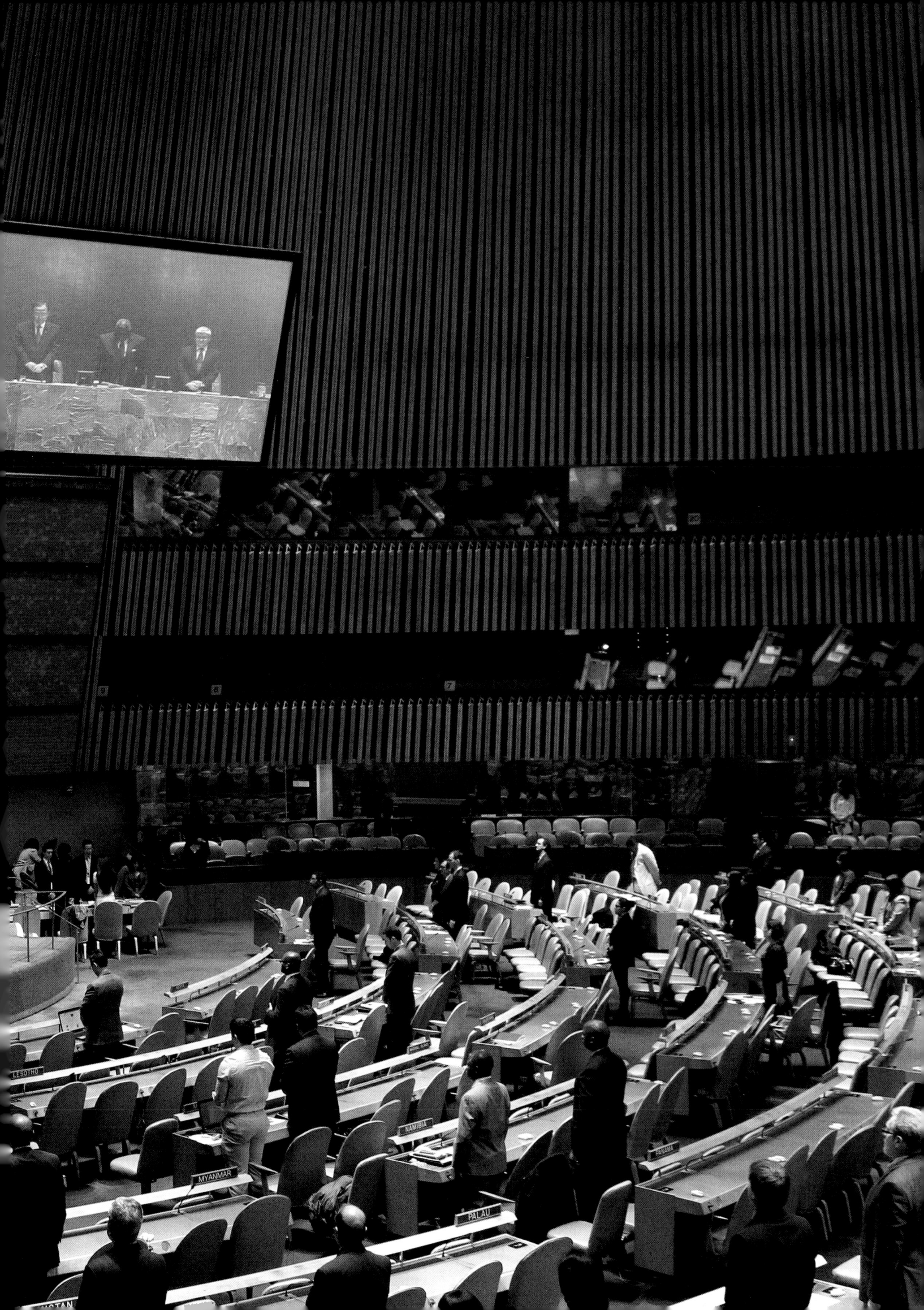

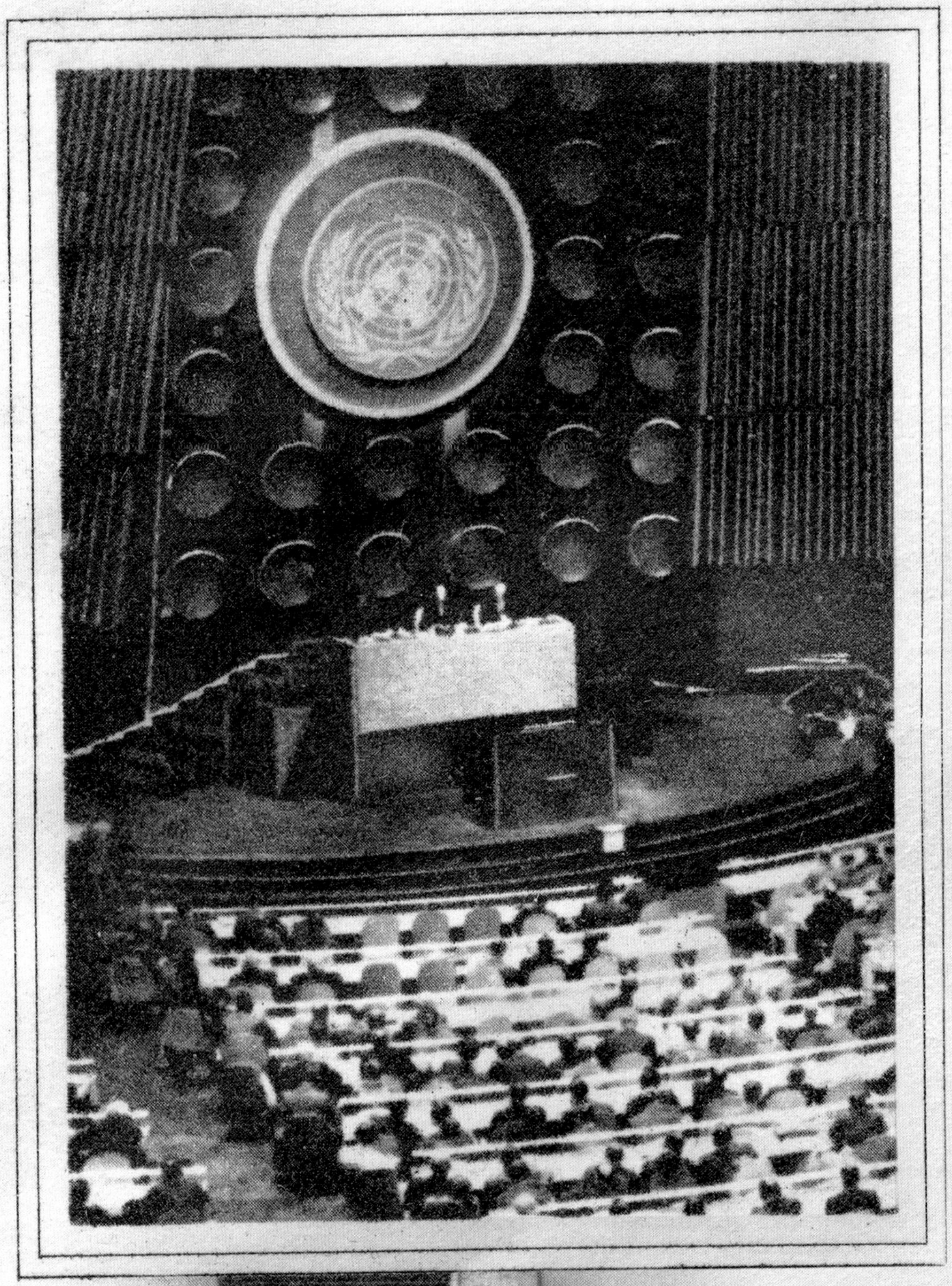

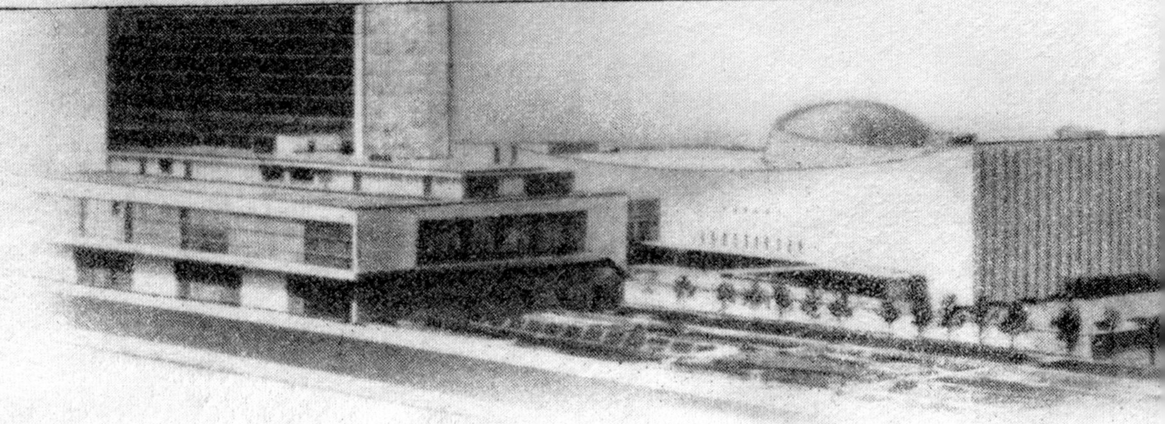

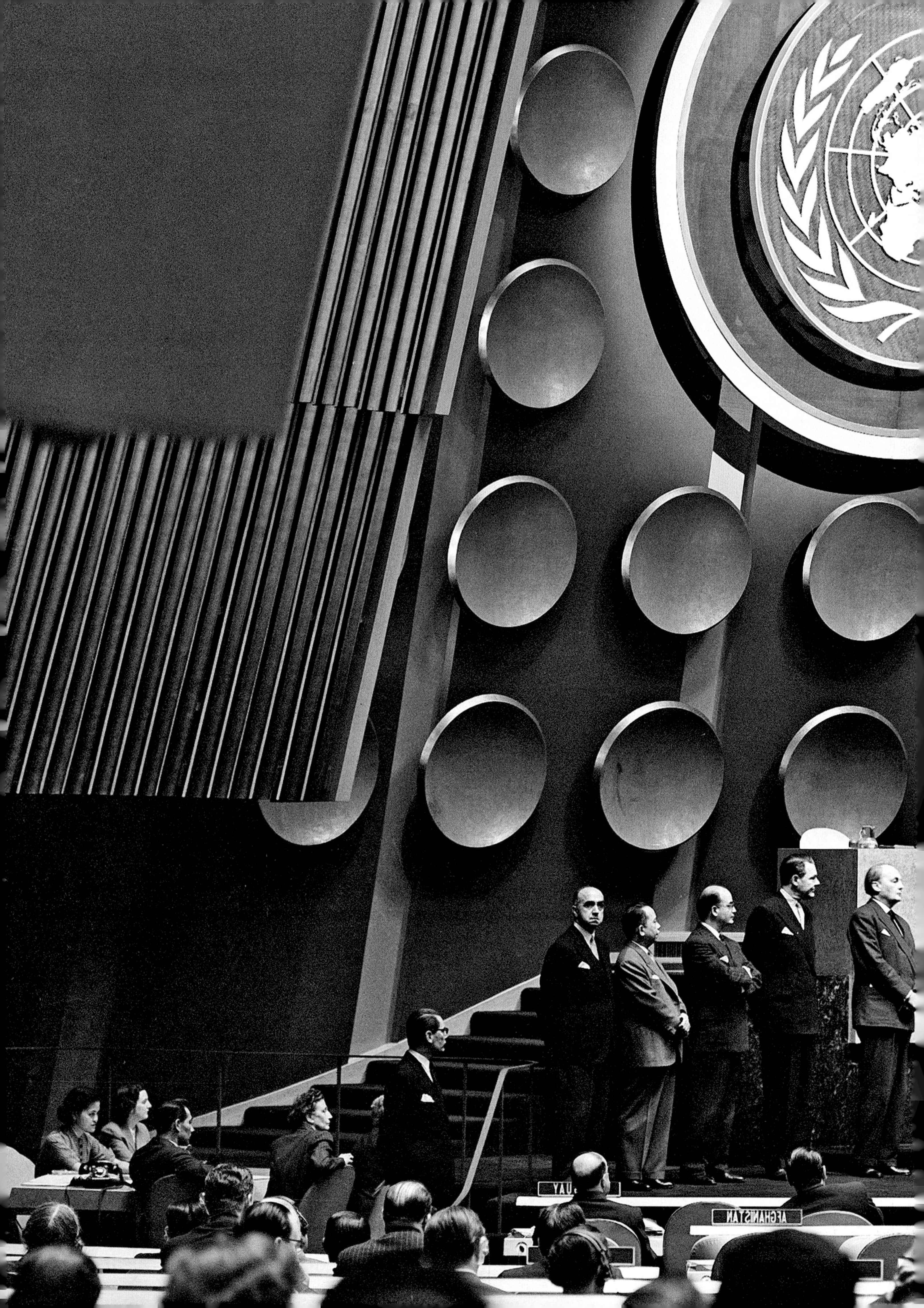
URUGUAY
AFGHANISTAN

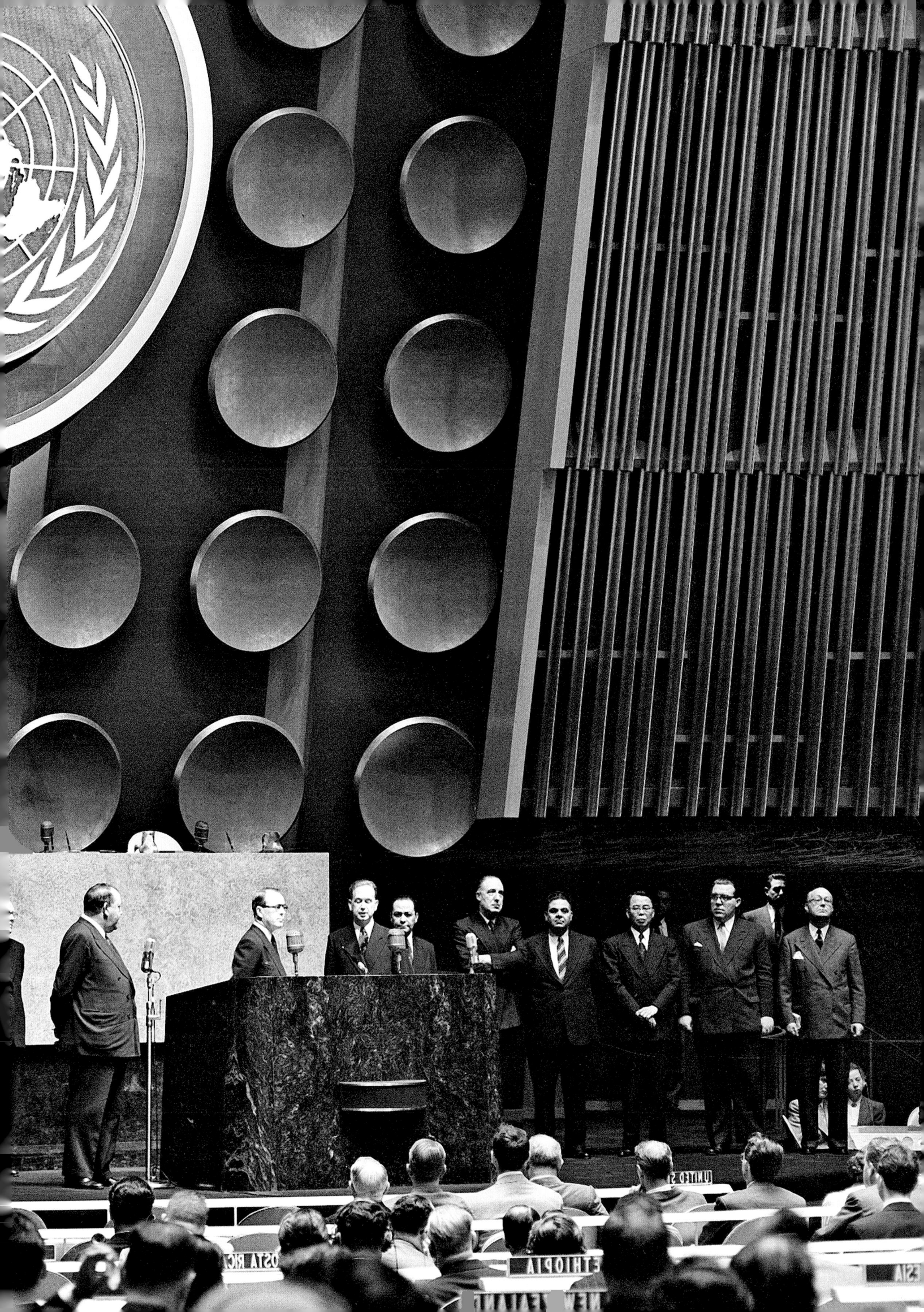

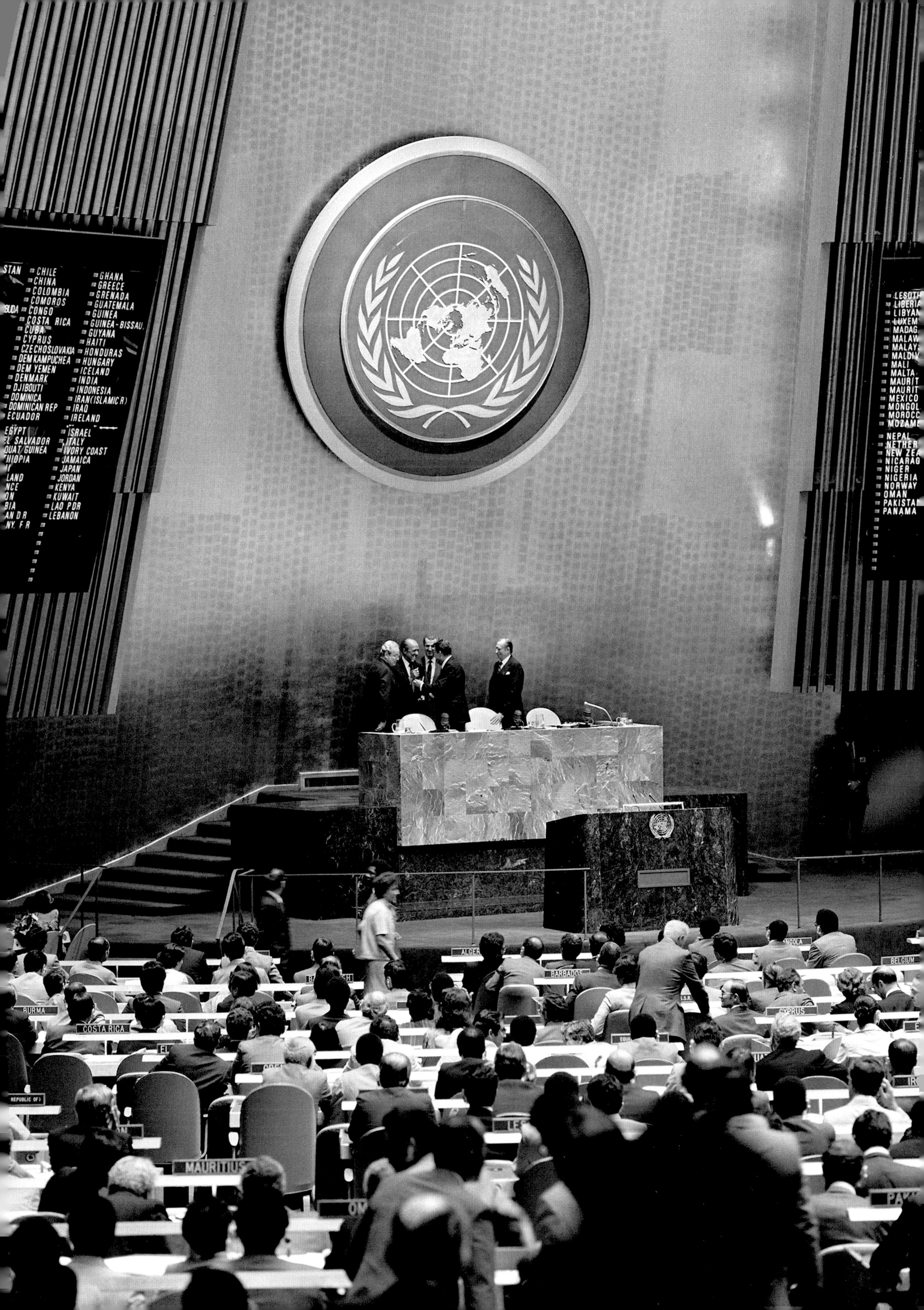

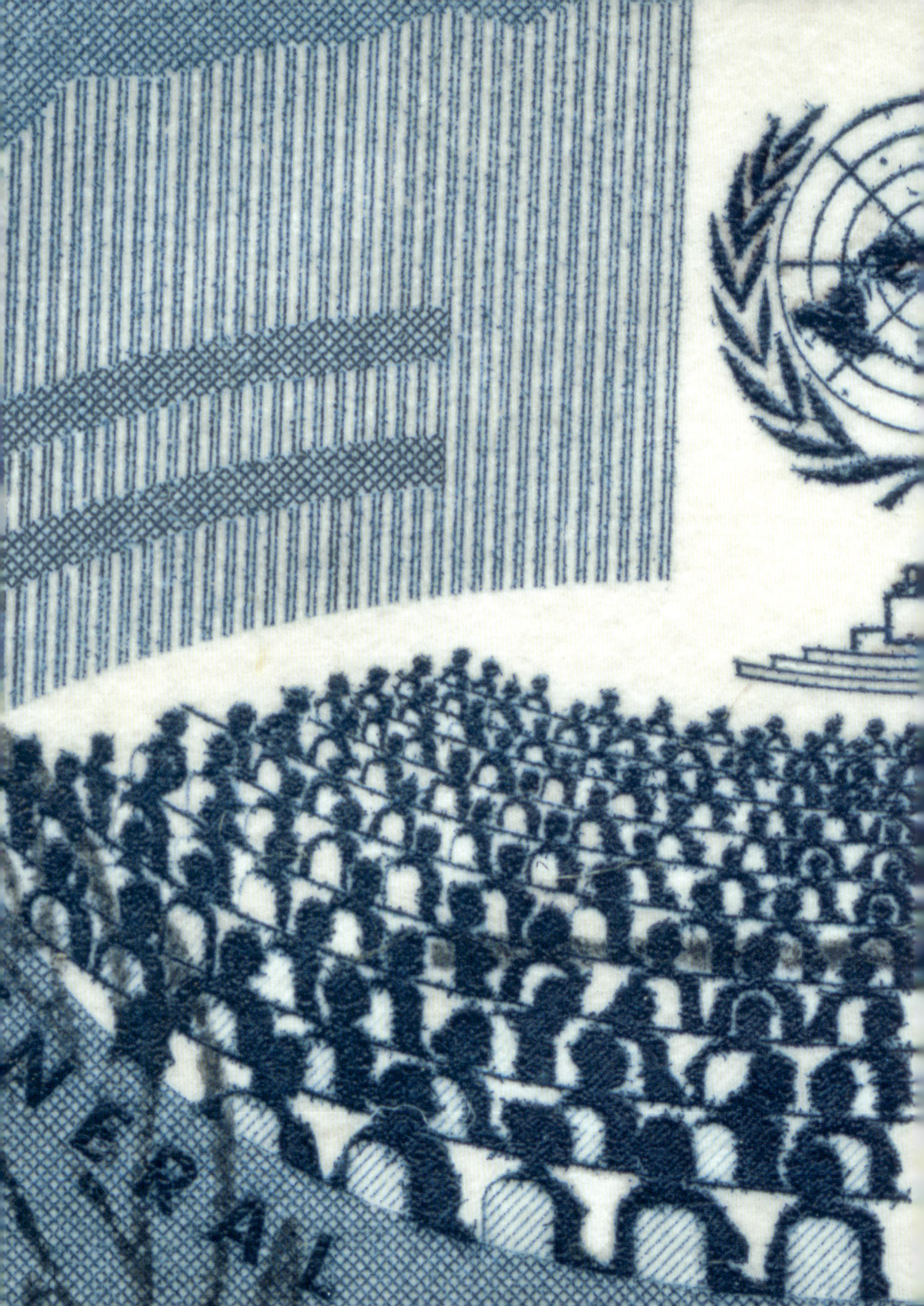

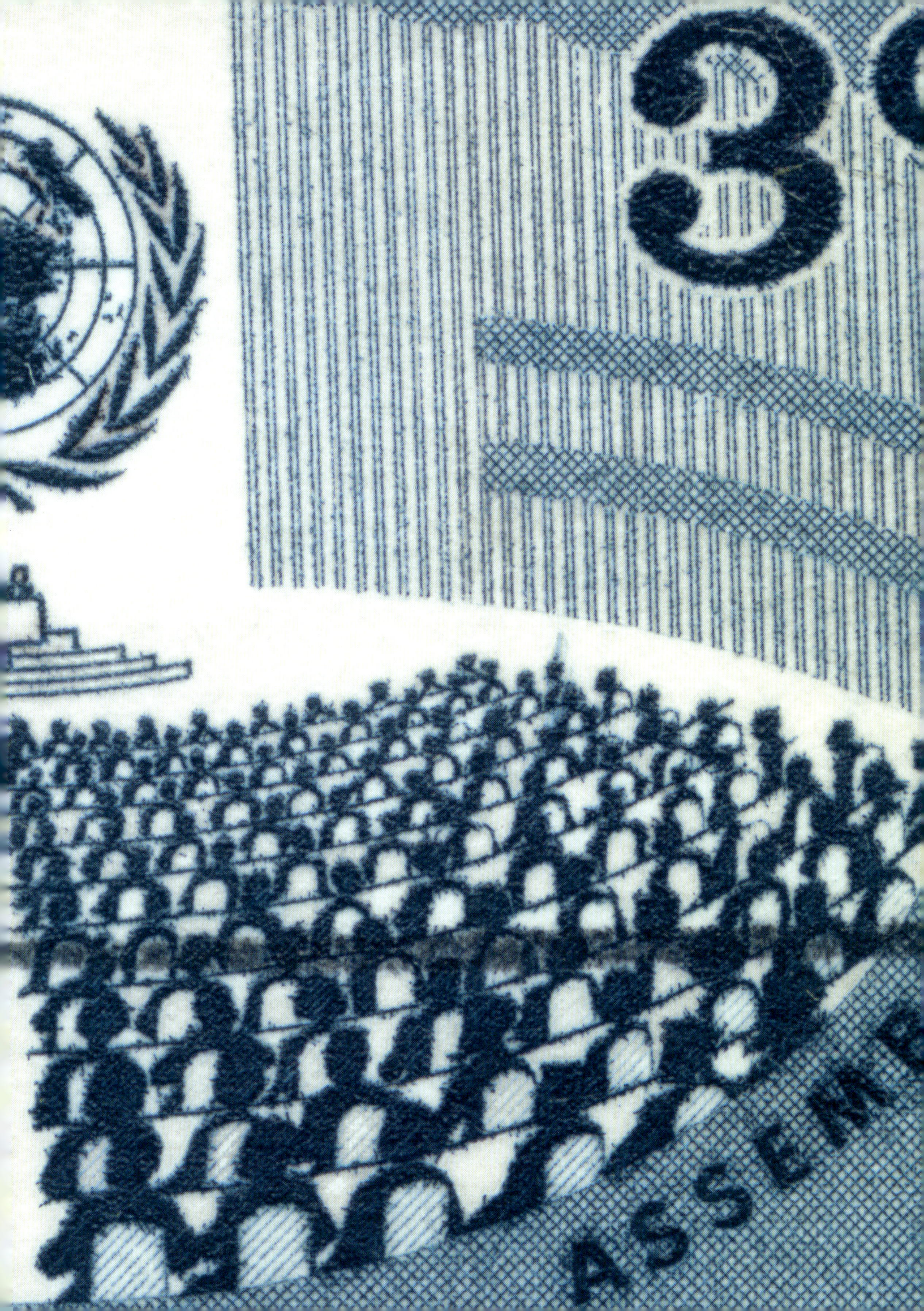

3
ASSEMB

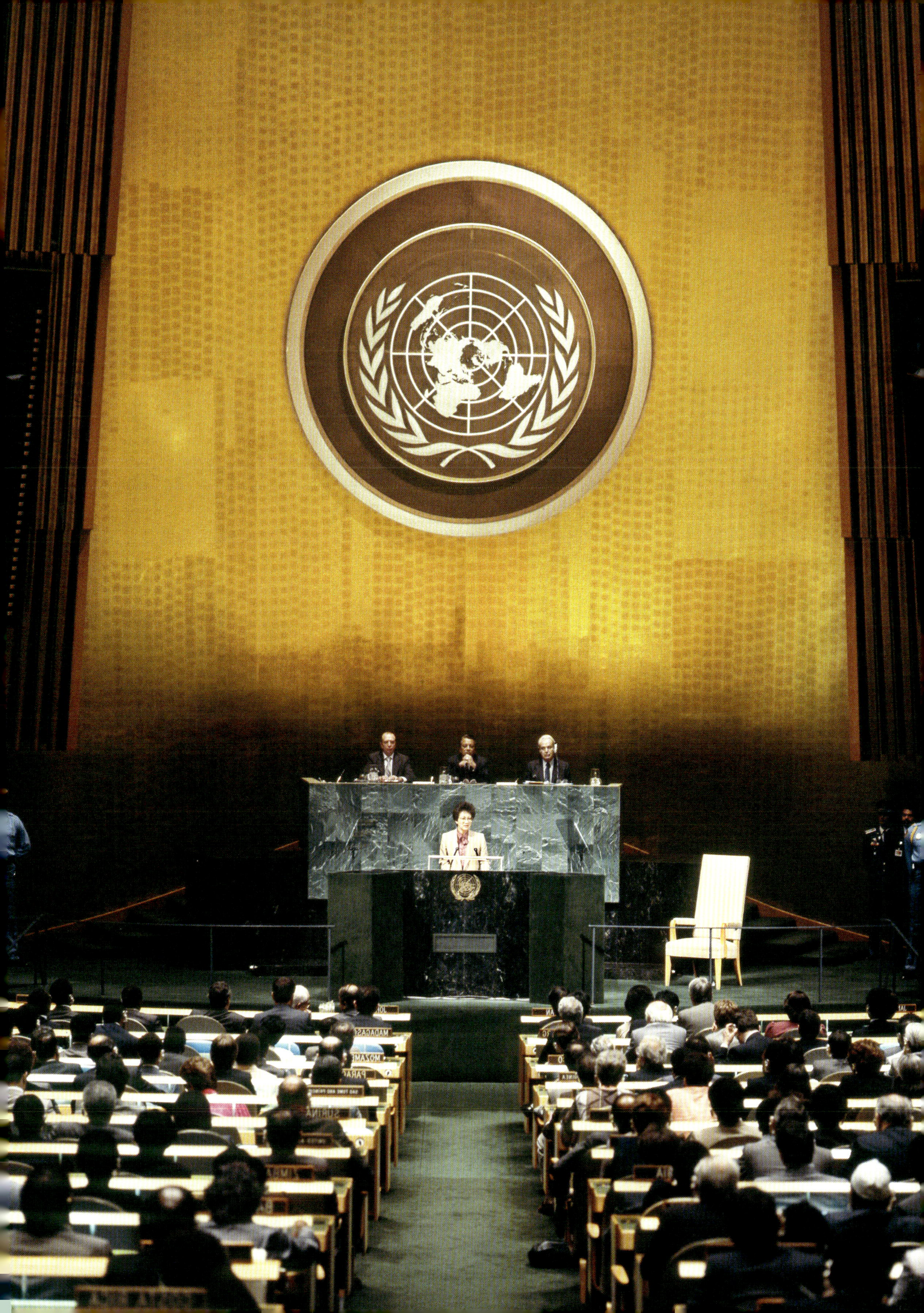

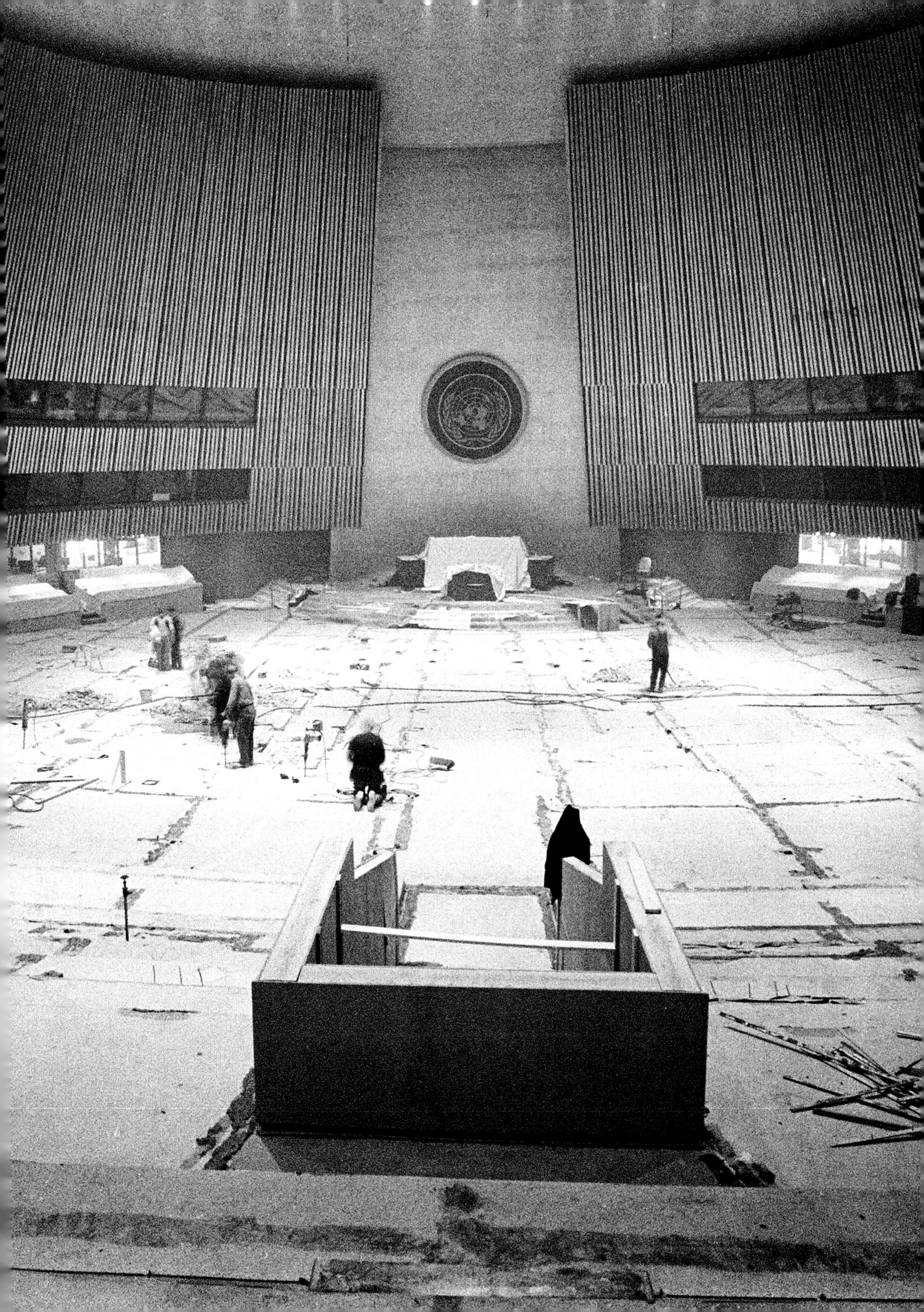

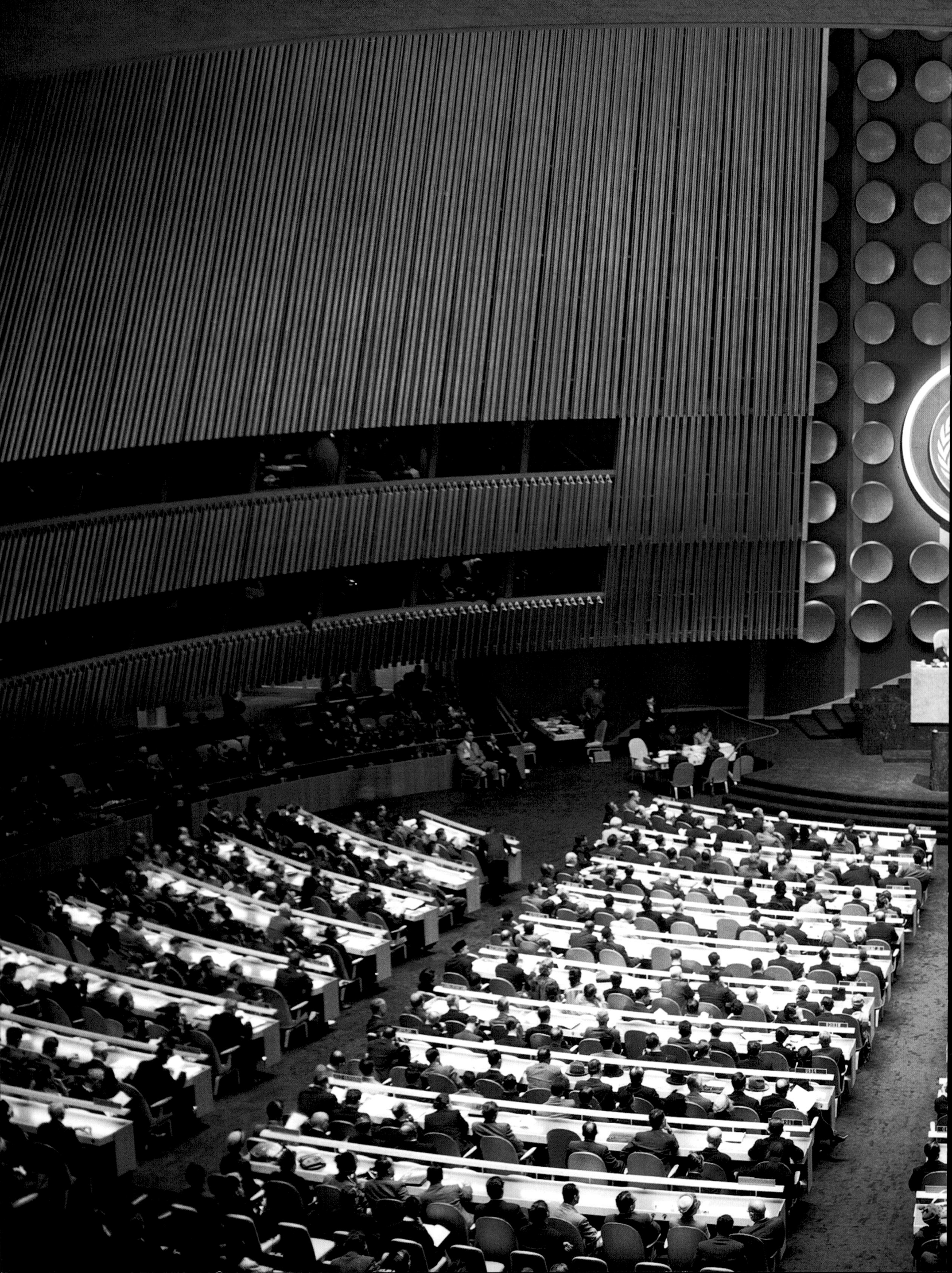

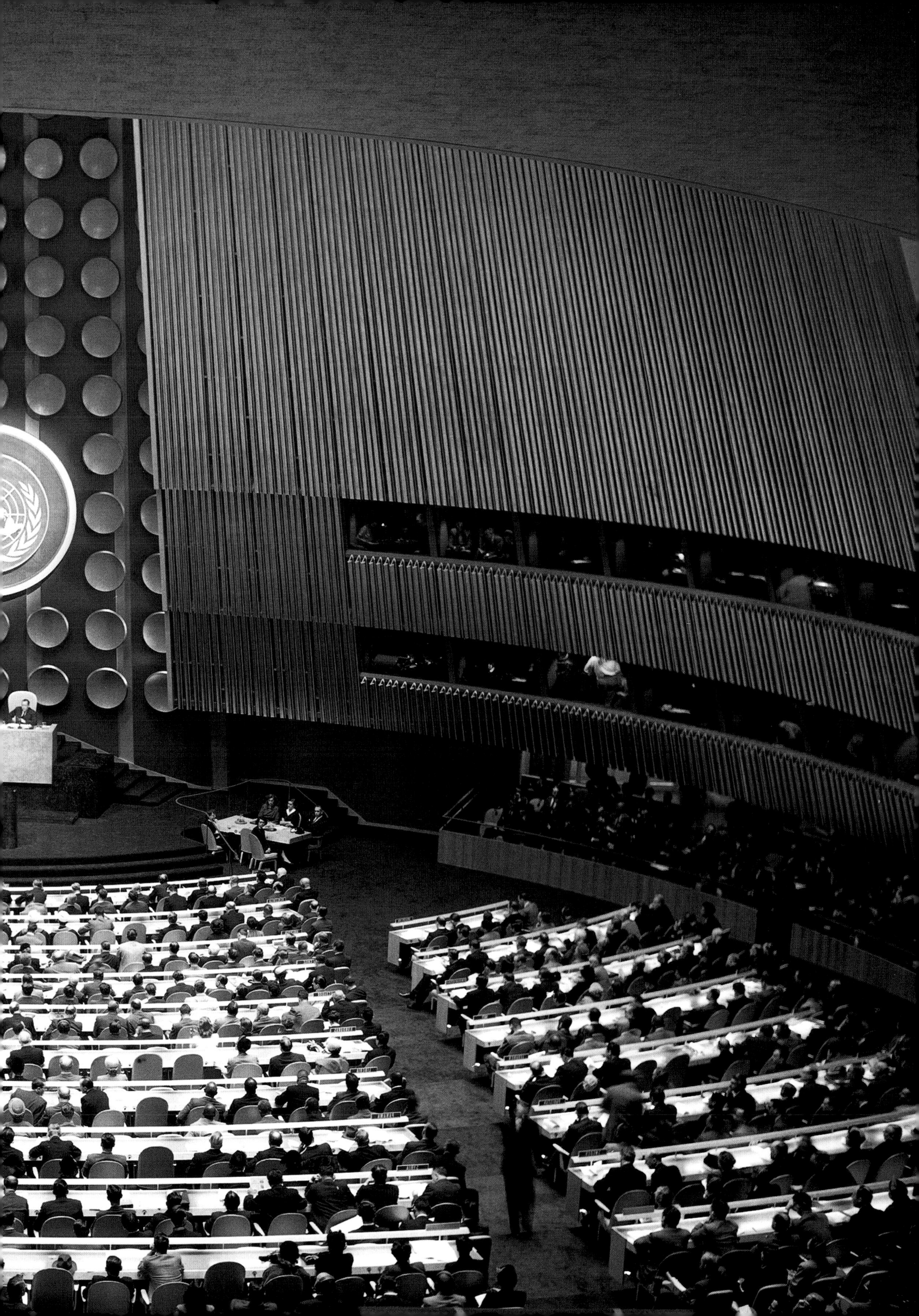

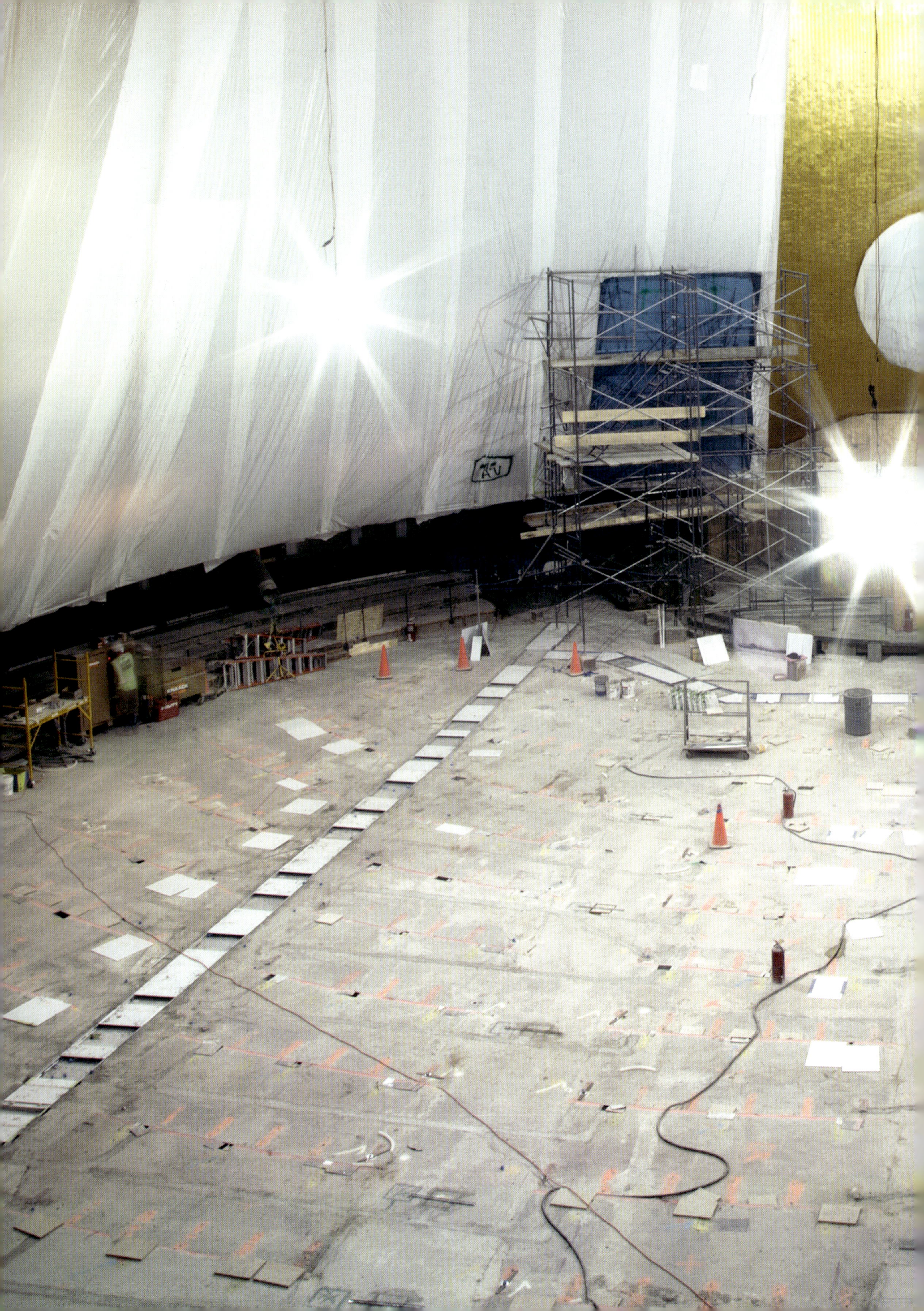

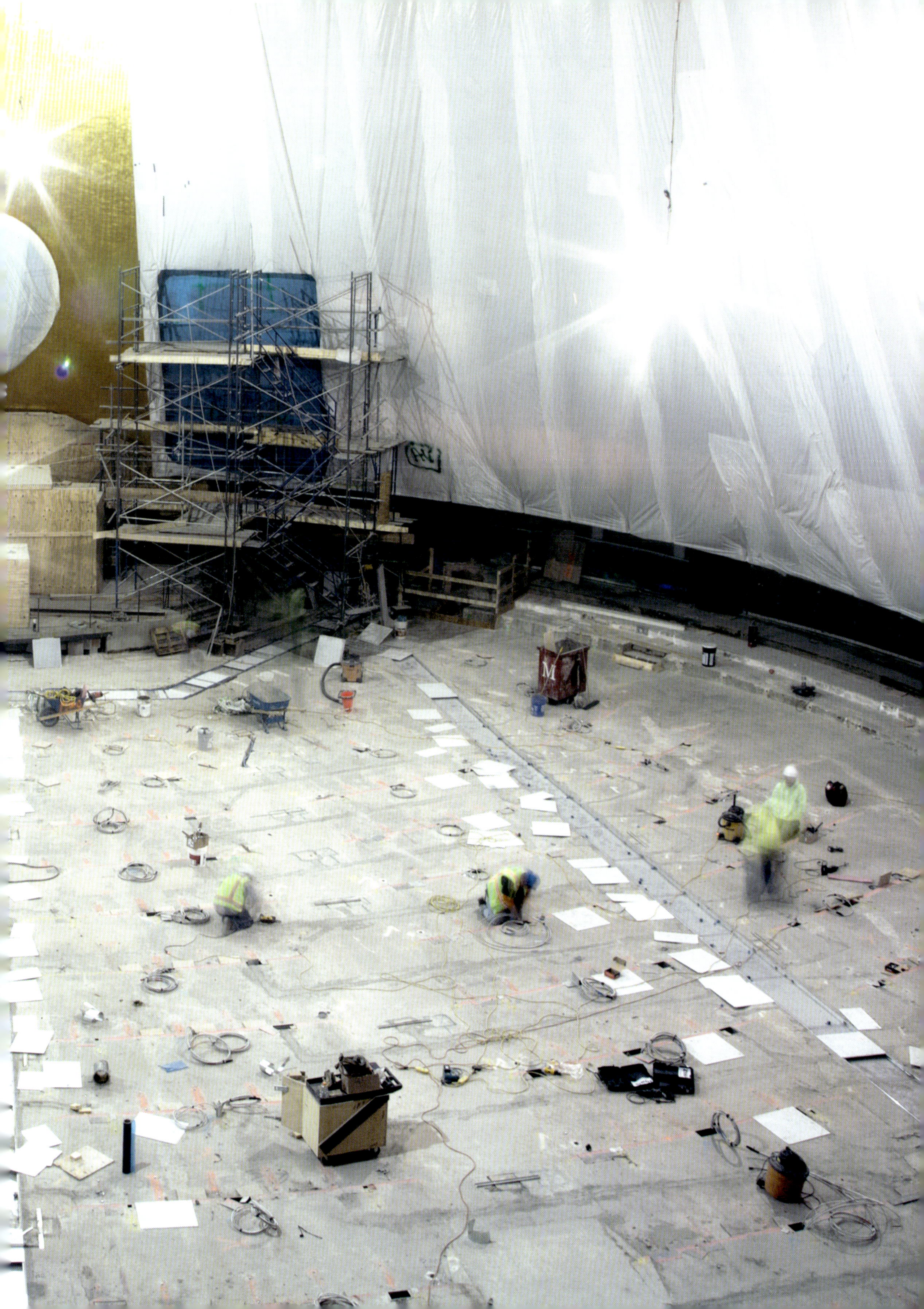

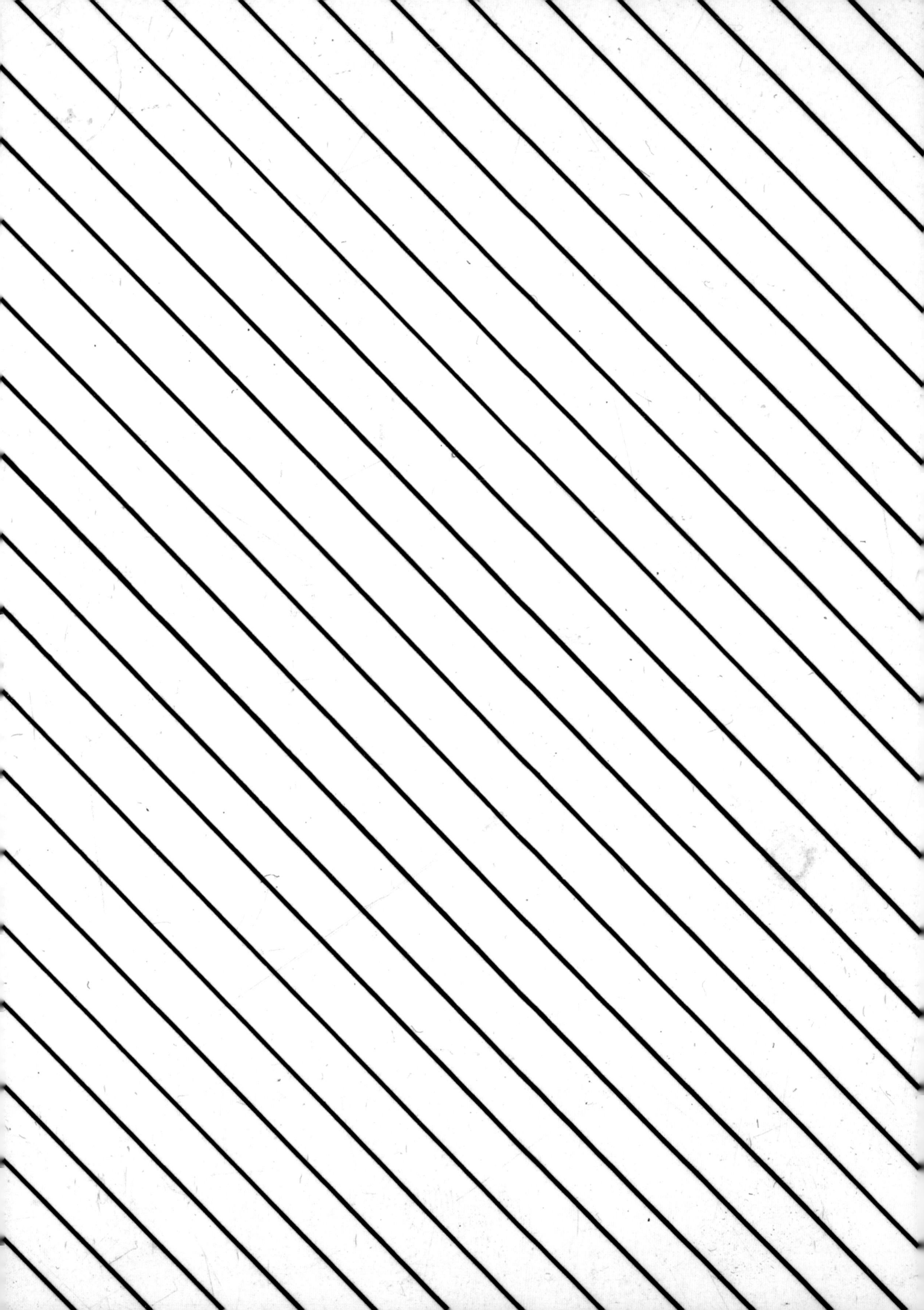

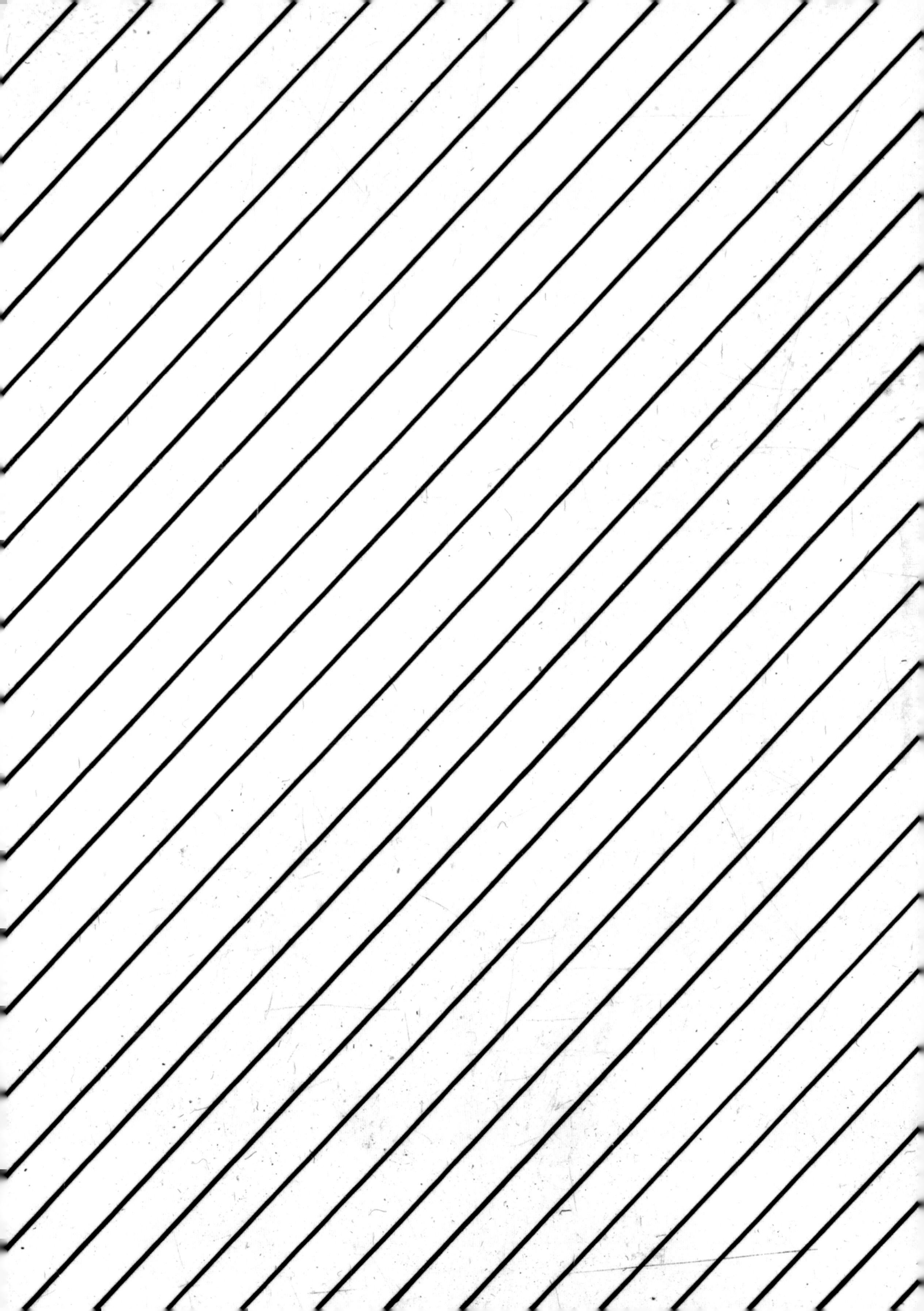

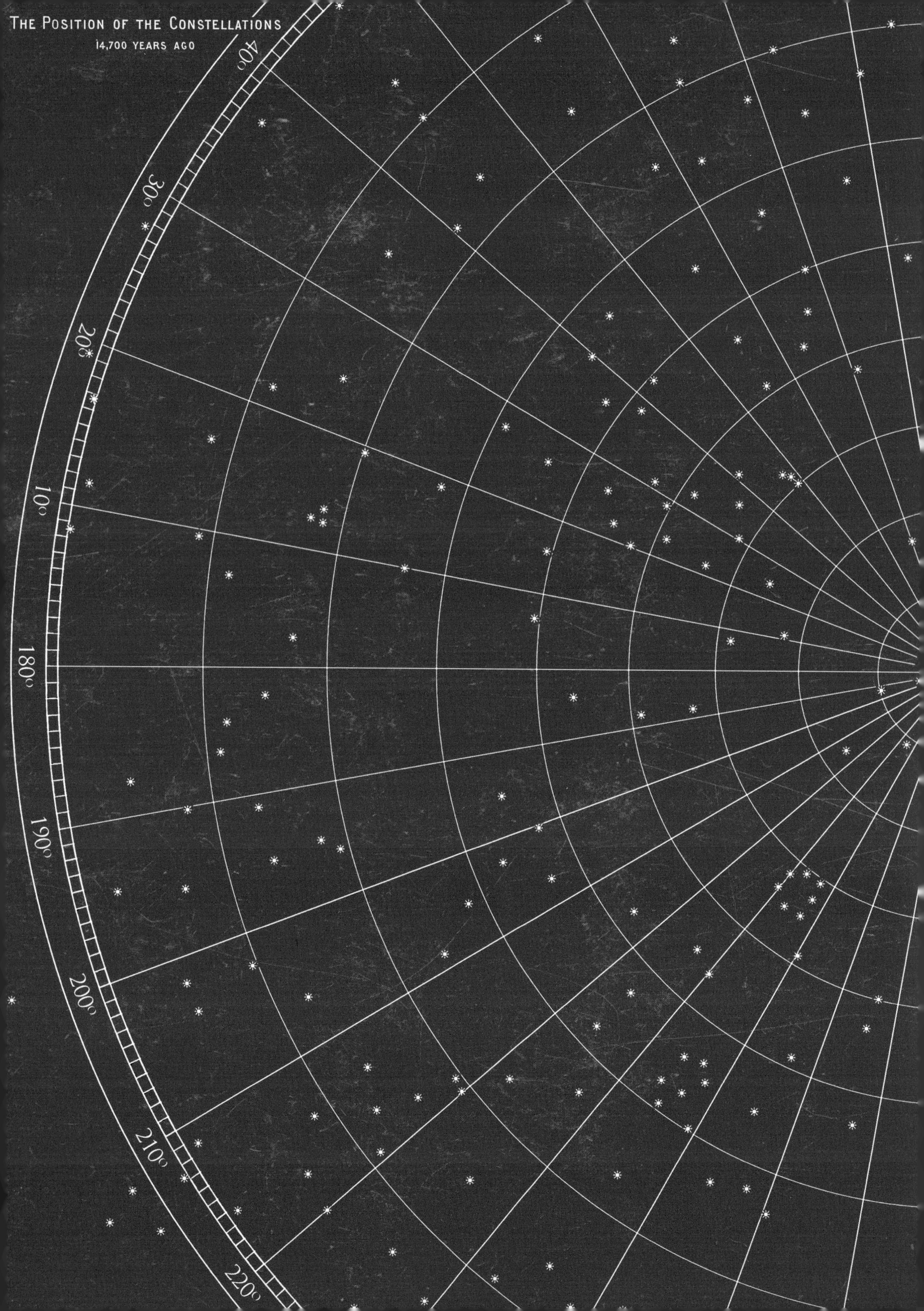

THE POSITION OF THE CONSTELLATIONS
14,700 YEARS AGO
40°
30°
20°
10°
180°
190°
200°
210°
220°

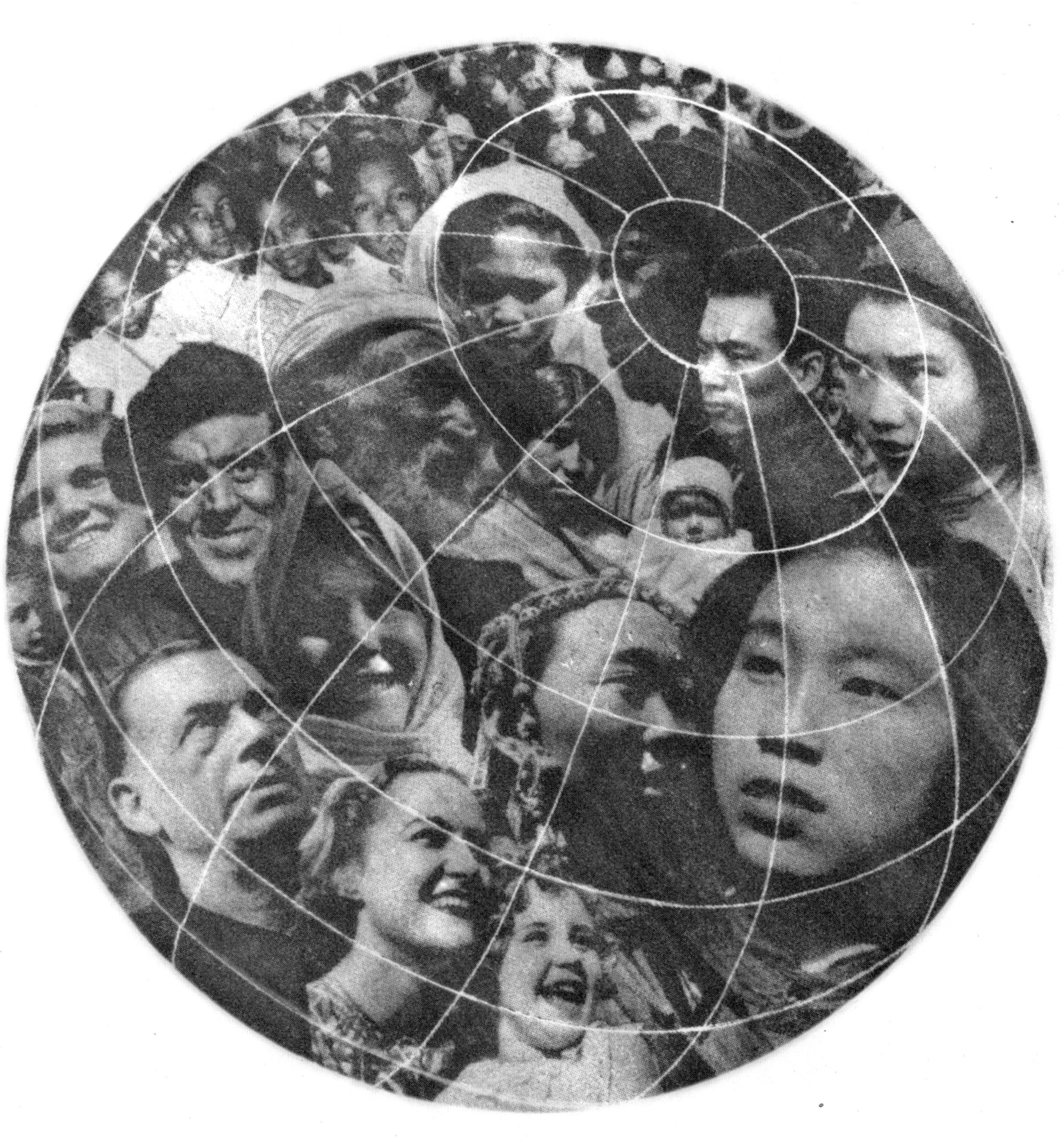

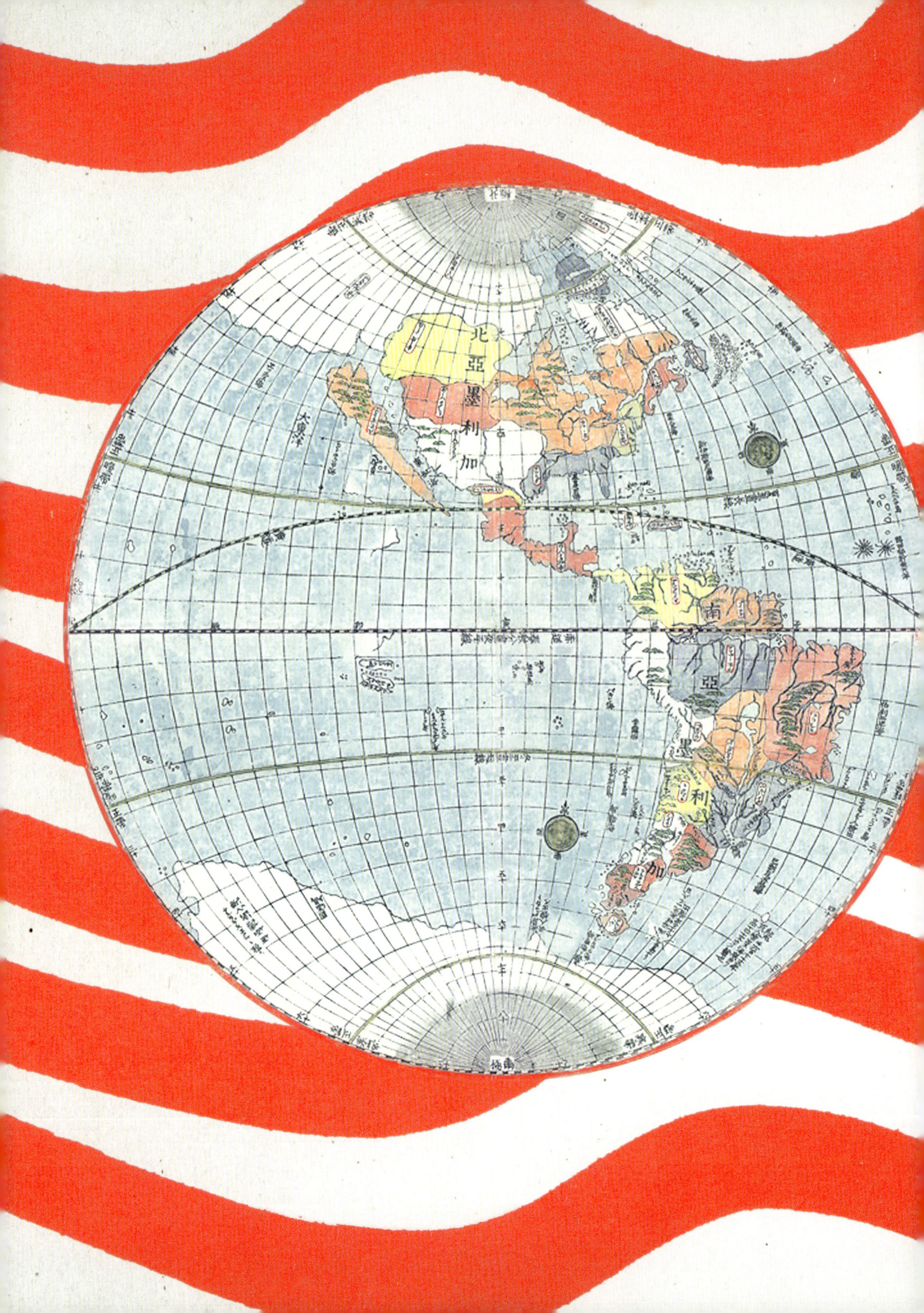

北亞墨利加
南亞墨利加
大東洋

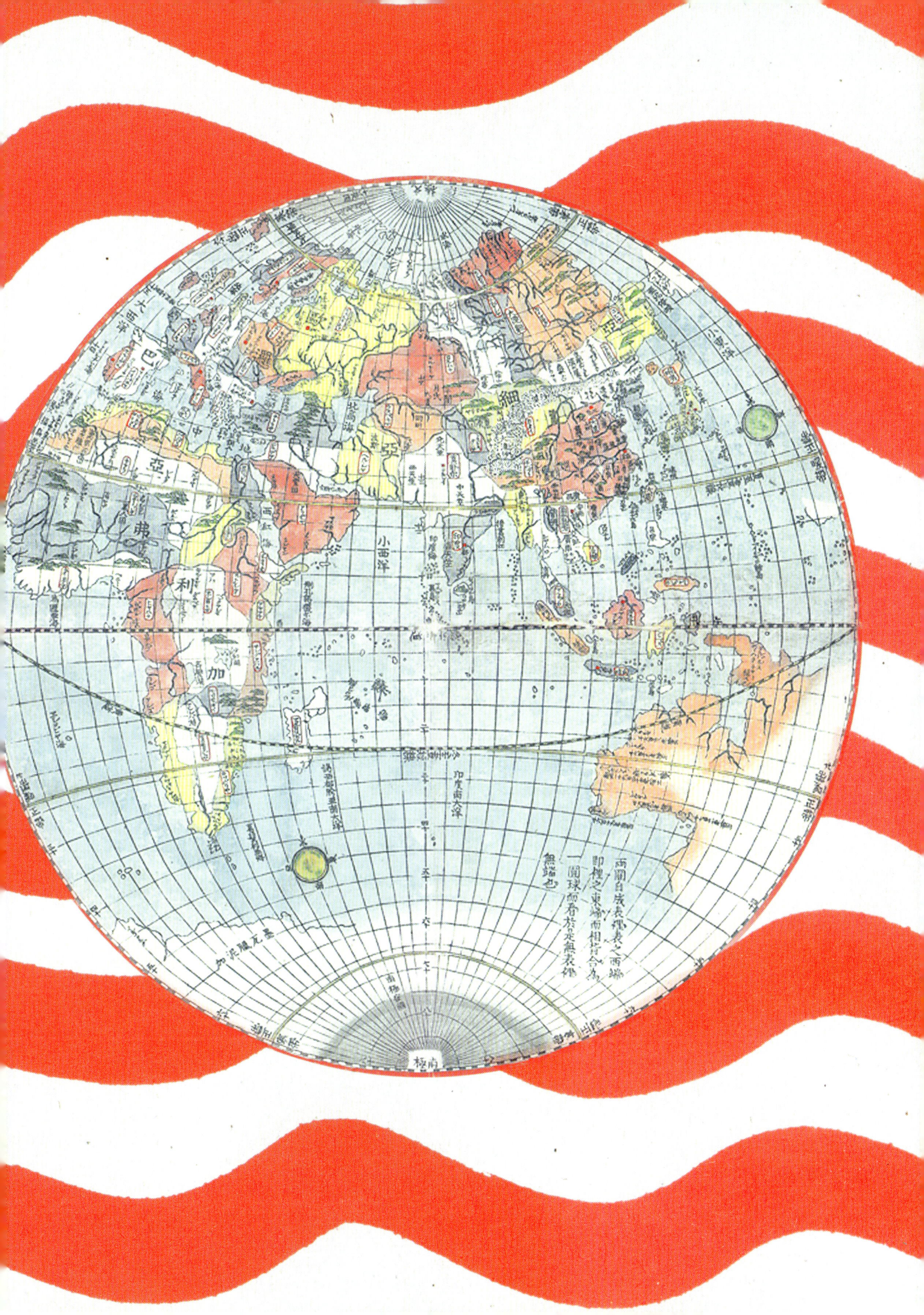

北極
南極
細亞
亞弗利加
亞墨利加
弗
中亞
小西洋
印度大洋
兩間自戌表裏義之兩端
即裡之東端衛相對合為
一圓球而看於定無表裡
無端也

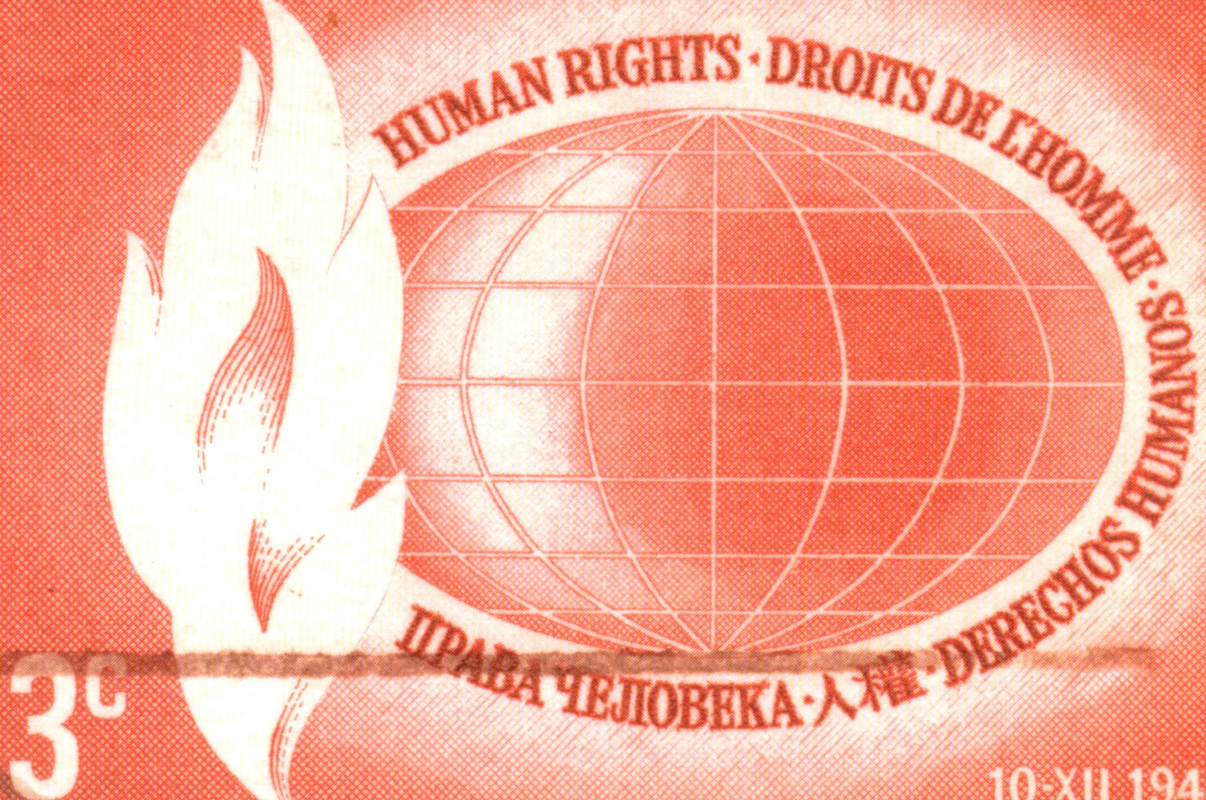
UNITED NATIONS 聯合國
NACIONES UNIDAS
NATIONS UNIES
HUMAN RIGHTS · DROITS DE L'HOMME · DERECHOS HUMANOS
ПРАВА ЧЕЛОВЕКА · 人權
3
10·XII 1948-56
ОБЪЕДИНЕННЫЕ НАЦИИ

UNITED NATIONS 聯合國
NACIONES UNIDAS
NATIONS UNIES
HUMAN RIGHTS · DROITS DE L'HOMME · DERECHOS HUMANOS
ПРАВА ЧЕЛОВЕКА · 人權
3c
10·XII 1948-56
ОБЪЕДИНЕННЫЕ НАЦИИ

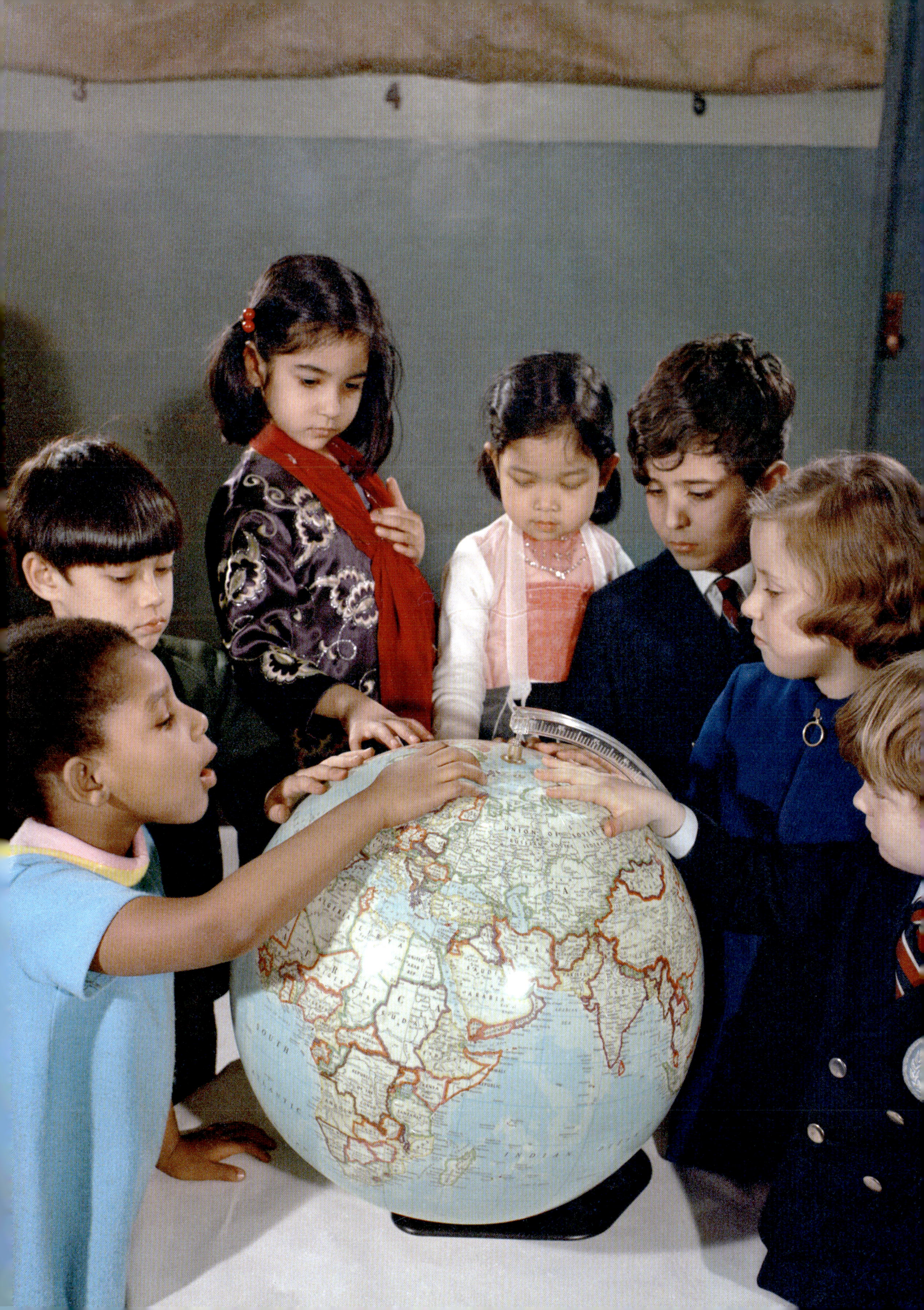

UNION OF SOVIET
SOUTH
ARABIA
SOUTH
ATLANTIC
INDIAN OCEAN

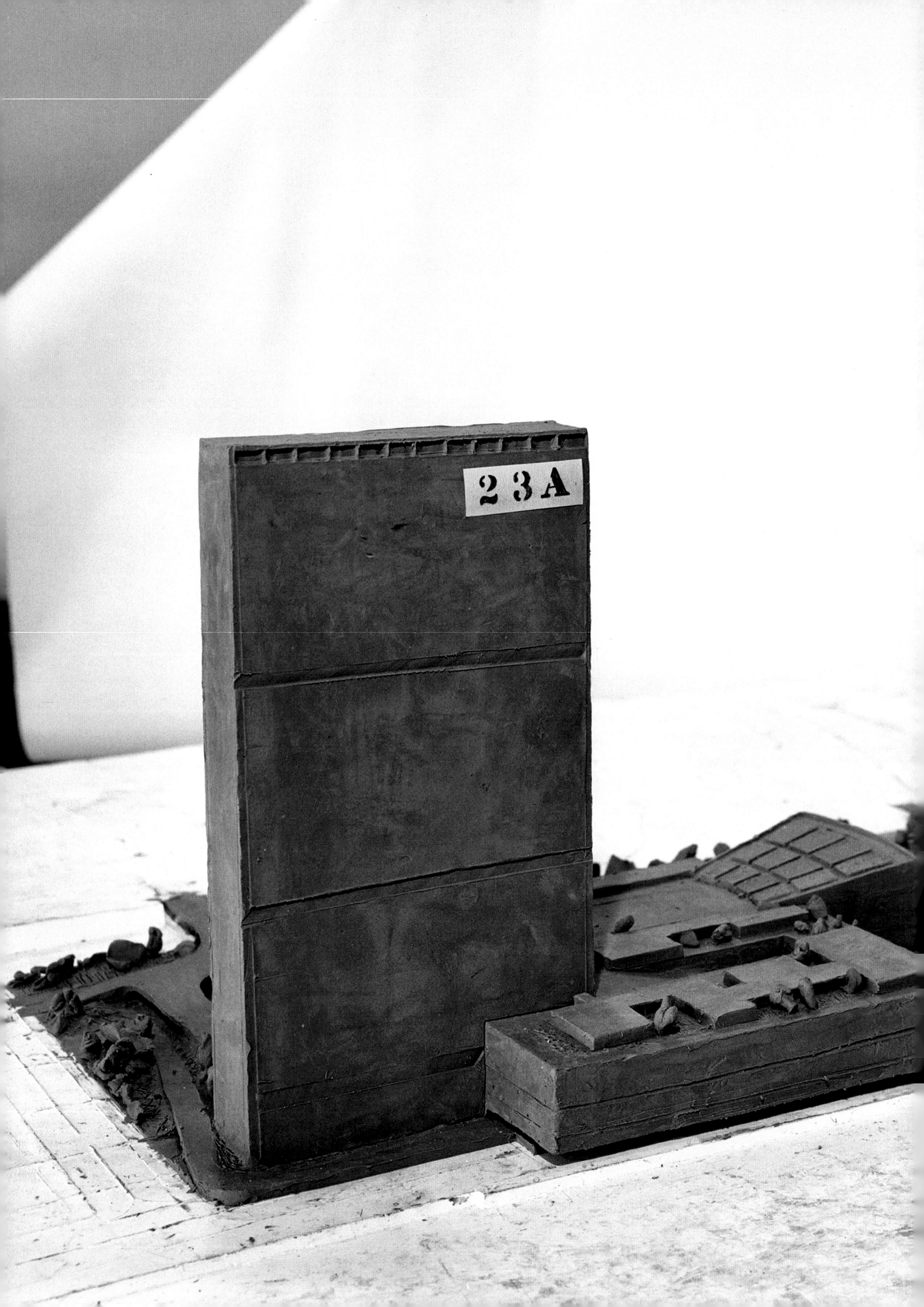

23A

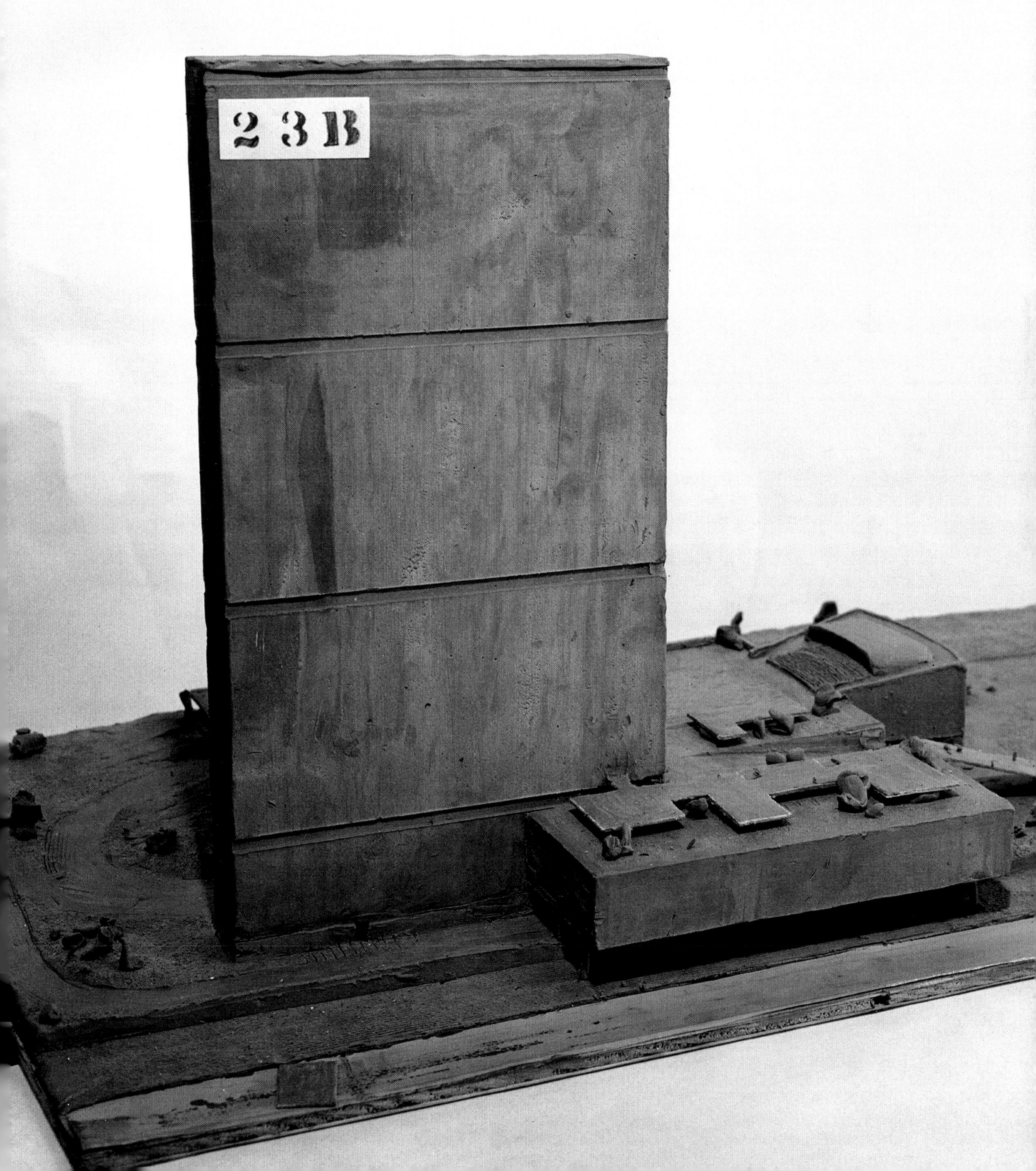

2 3 B

ON THE EDGE OF GREATNESS

The Diaries of John Humphrey,
First Director of the United Nations
Division of Human Rights

Volume 1, 1948-1949

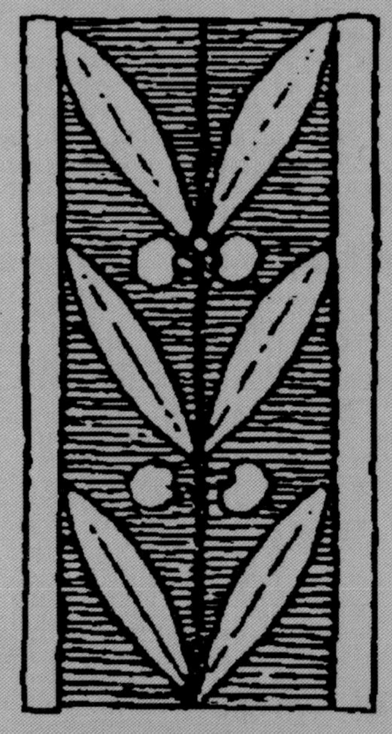

ON THE EDGE OF GREATNESS

The Diaries of John Humphrey,
First Director of the United Nations
Division of Human Rights

•

Volume 2, 1950-1951

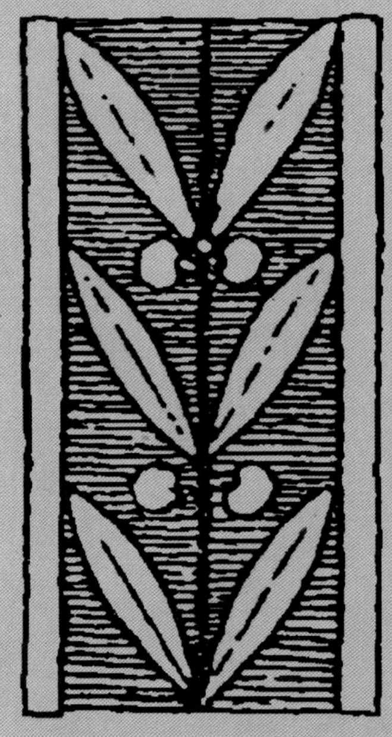

XXX — Every one is entitled to adequate
food and housing.

XVI — Every one has the right to social
security. ~~To this end the State
must promote the public
public health and safety~~
This right includes the right to
health in so far as

XXXI — Every one has the right to
leisure.

XXXII — Every one has the right to culture & to the
enjoyment of the arts.

XXXIII — Every one has the right to share in
the benefits of science.

XXXIV — ~~Every one has the right~~
The State should promote public
health and safety

within the limits
of the economic capacity
+ development

XXXIV — Every one has the right to social
security. To this end each the State shall promote
public health and safety +

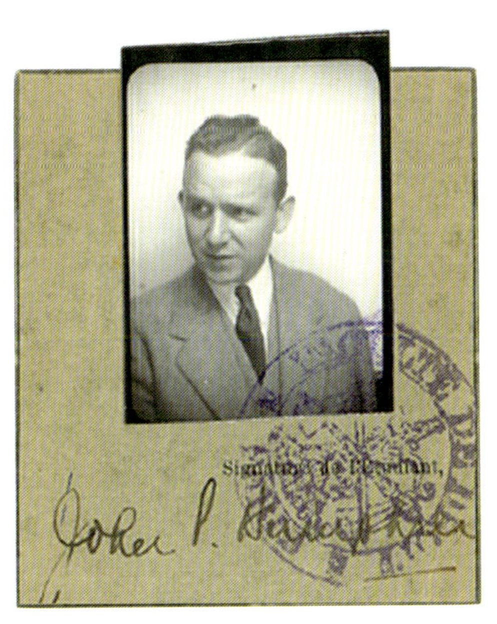

Signature de l'étudiant,

1. That their... be respect for human ... rights
   and freedoms of the world is to know peace
2. That man does not have rights only: he owes
   duties to the society (both national and

The provisions of this International Bill of Rights
shall be deemed fundamental principles of
international law and of the national law of
each of the member States of the United Nations.
Its observance is therefore a matter of international
concern and it shall be within the jurisdiction
of the United Nations to discuss any violation
thereof.

a) It is the duty of the State to respect and maintain the
   rights enunciated in the Bill of Rights.

2. In the exercise of his rights every one is limited
   by the rights of others and by the just
   requirements of the democratic State.

3. Every one has the right to life.

4. Every one has the right to personal liberty

1b Every one owes a duty of loyalty to his State
   and to the international community of

我聯合國人民

同茲決心

欲免後世再遭今代人類兩度身歷慘不堪言之戰禍，重伸基本人權，人格尊嚴與價值，以及男女與大小各國平等權利之信念。

創造適當環境，俾克維持正義，尊重由條約與國際法其他淵源而起之義務，久而弗懈。

促成大自由中之社會進步及較善之民生。

並為達此目的

力行容恕，彼此以善鄰之道，和睦相處。

集中力量，以維持國際和平及安全。

接受原則，確立方法，以保證非為公共利益，不得使用武力。

運用國際機構，以促成全球人民經濟及社會之進展。

用是發奮立志，務當同心協力，以竟厥功‧

爰由我各本國政府，經齊集金山市之代表各將所奉全權證書，互相校閱，均屬妥善，議定本聯合國憲章，並設立國際組織，定名聯合國。

聯合國憲章序言

Мы, народы
ОБЪЕДИНЕННЫХ НАЦИЙ

преисполненные решимости избавить грядущие поколения от бедствий войны, дважды в нашей жизни принесшей человечеству невыразимое горе,

и вновь утвердить веру в основные права человека, в достоинство и ценность человеческой личности, в равноправие мужчин и женщин и в равенство прав больших и малых наций, и

создать условия, при которых могут соблюдаться справедливость и уважение к обязательствам, вытекающим из договоров и других источников международного права, и

содействовать социальному прогрессу и улучшению условий жизни при большей свободе,

и в этих целях проявлять терпимость и жить вместе, в мире друг с другом, как добрые соседи, и

объединить наши силы для поддержания международного мира и безопасности, и

обеспечить принятием принципов и установлением методов, чтобы вооруженные силы применялись не иначе, как в общих интересах, и

использовать международный аппарат для содействия экономическому и социальному прогрессу всех народов,

**решили объединить наши усилия
для достижения этих целей.**

Согласно этому наши соответственные правительства через представителей, собравшихся в городе Сан-Франциско, предъявивших свои полномочия, найденные в надлежащей форме, согласились принять настоящий Устав Организации Объединенных Наций и настоящим учреждают международную организацию под названием "Объединенные Нации".

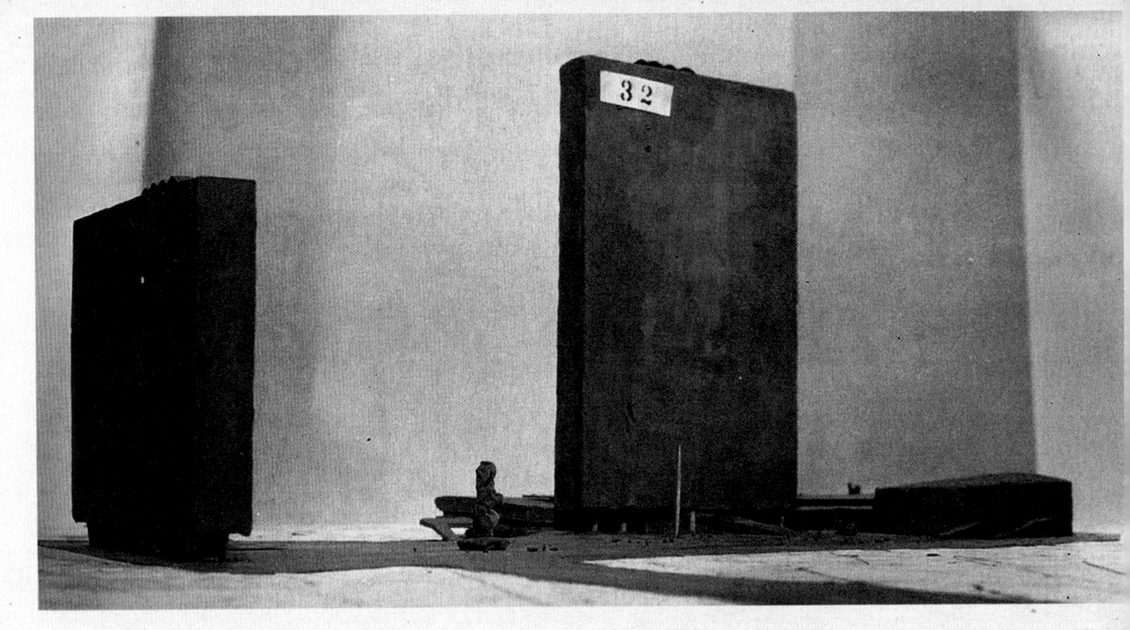

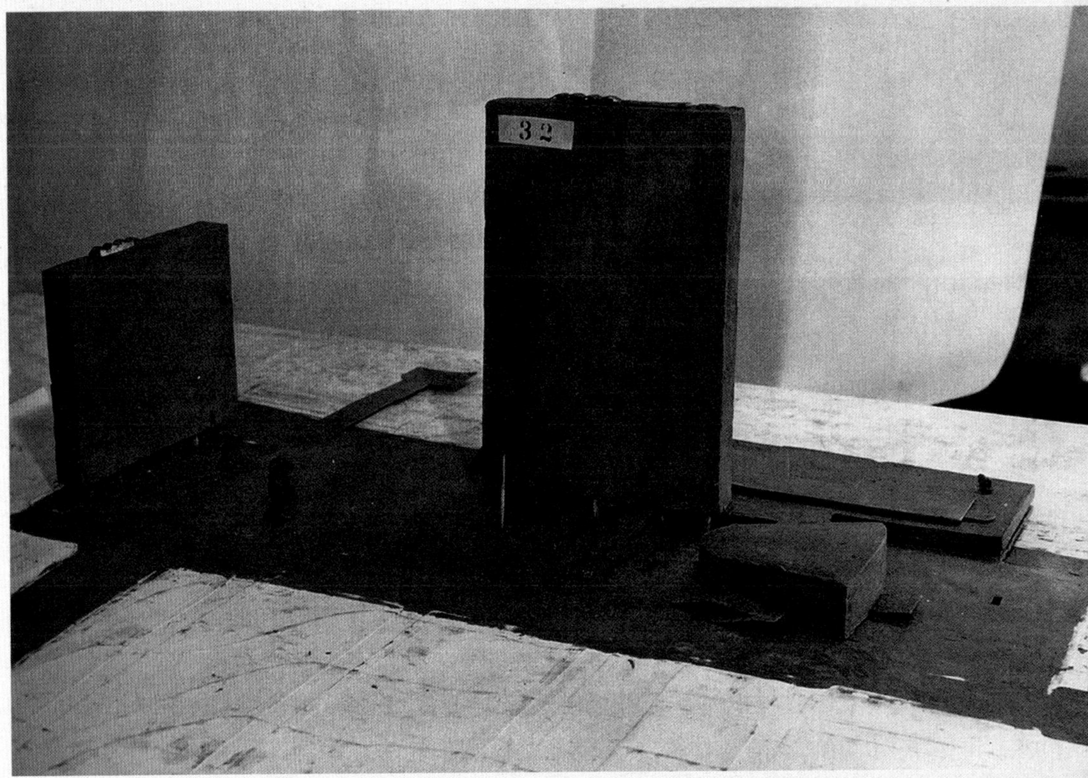

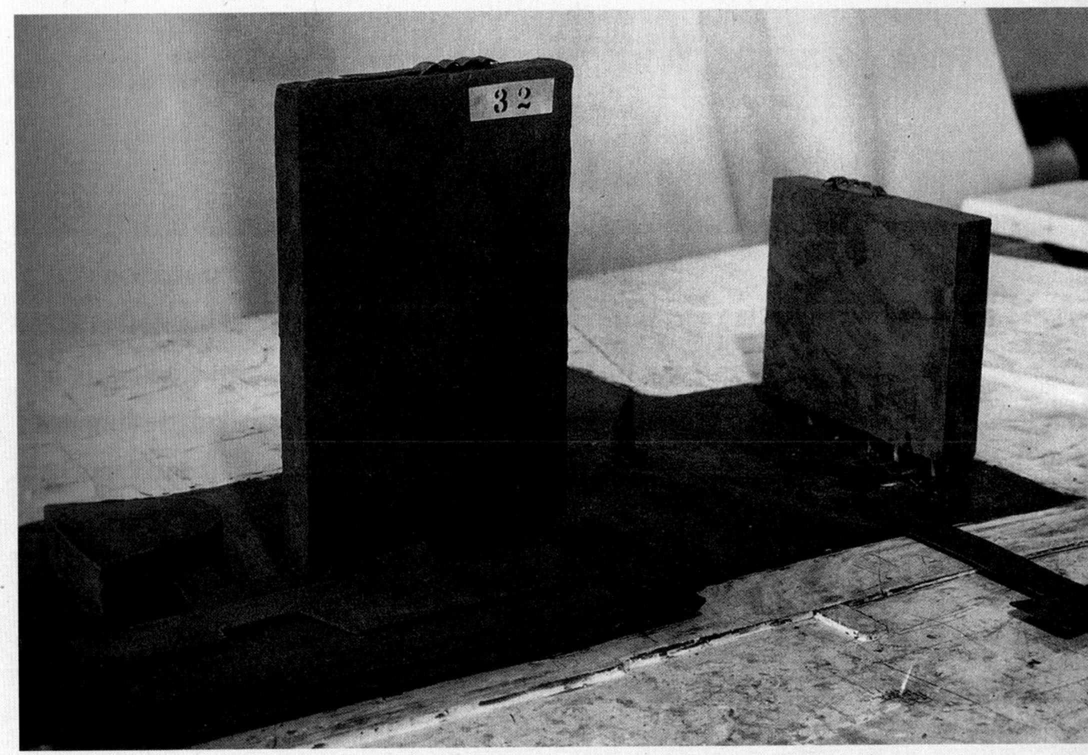

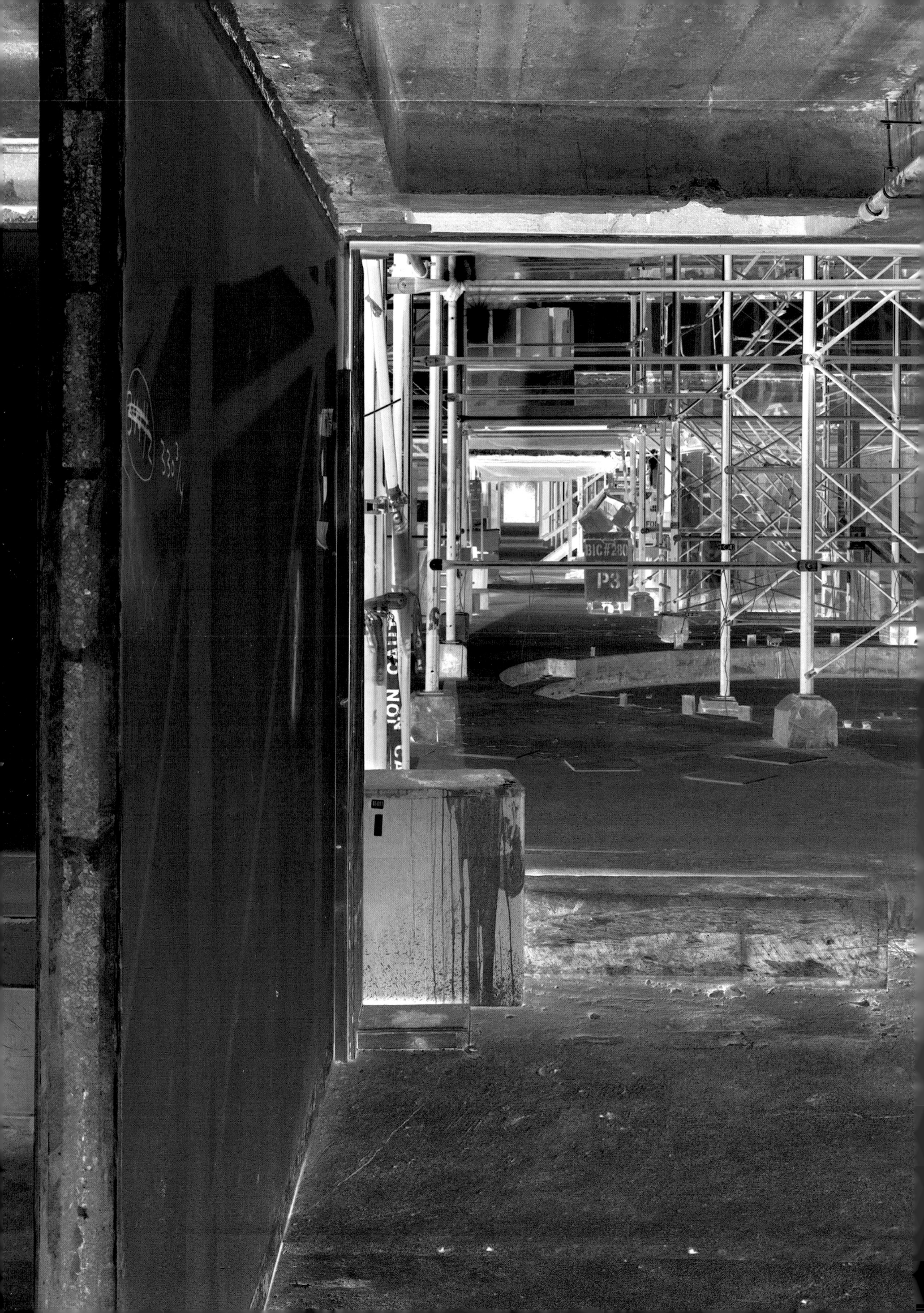

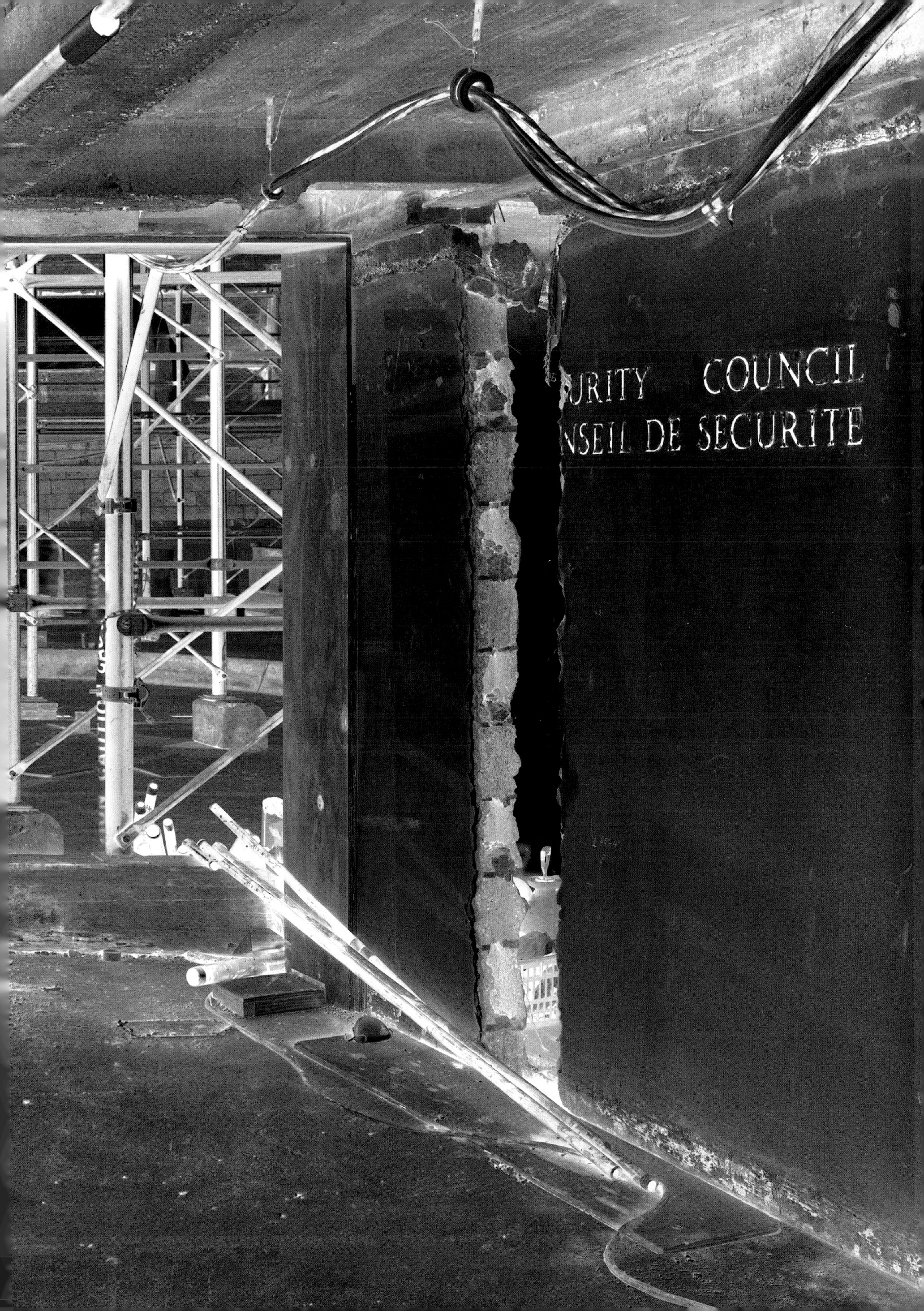

URITY   COUNCIL
NSEIL DE SECURITE

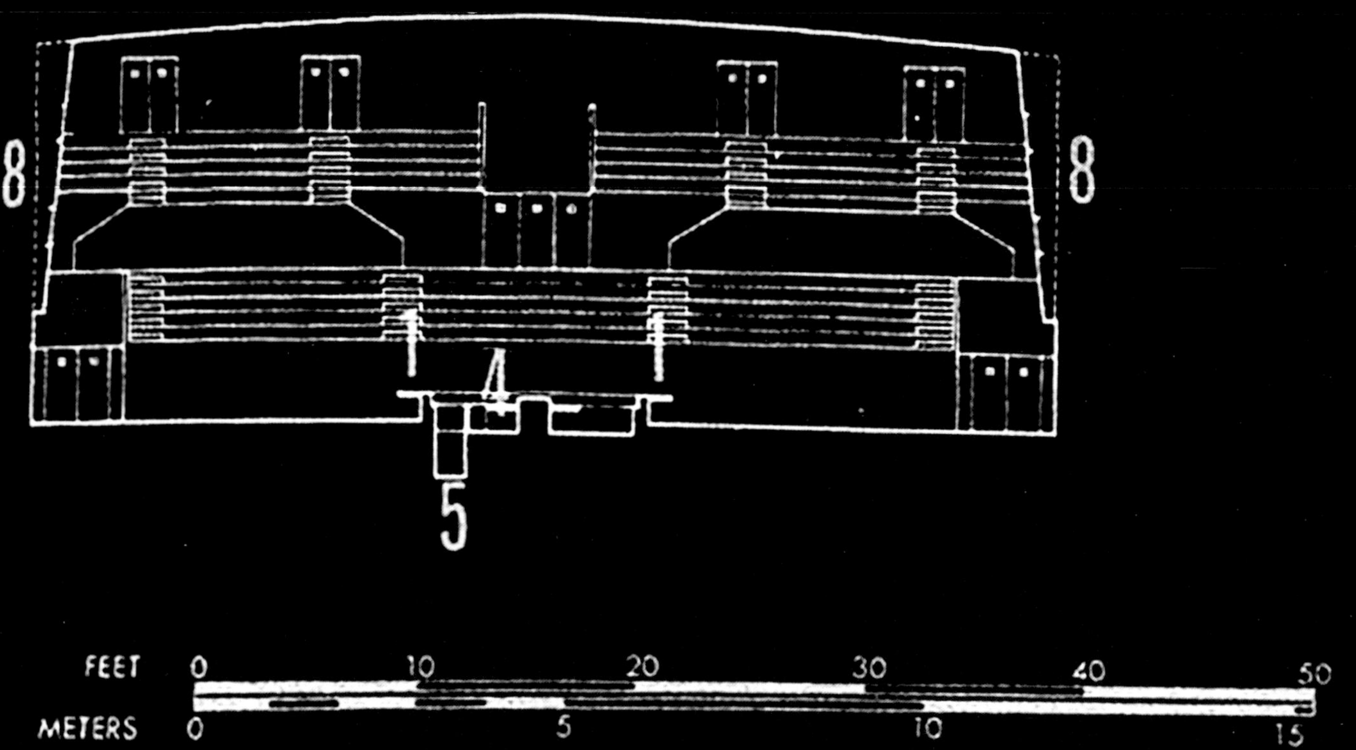
8
8
4
5
FEET
0   10   20   30   40   50
METERS
0   5   10   15

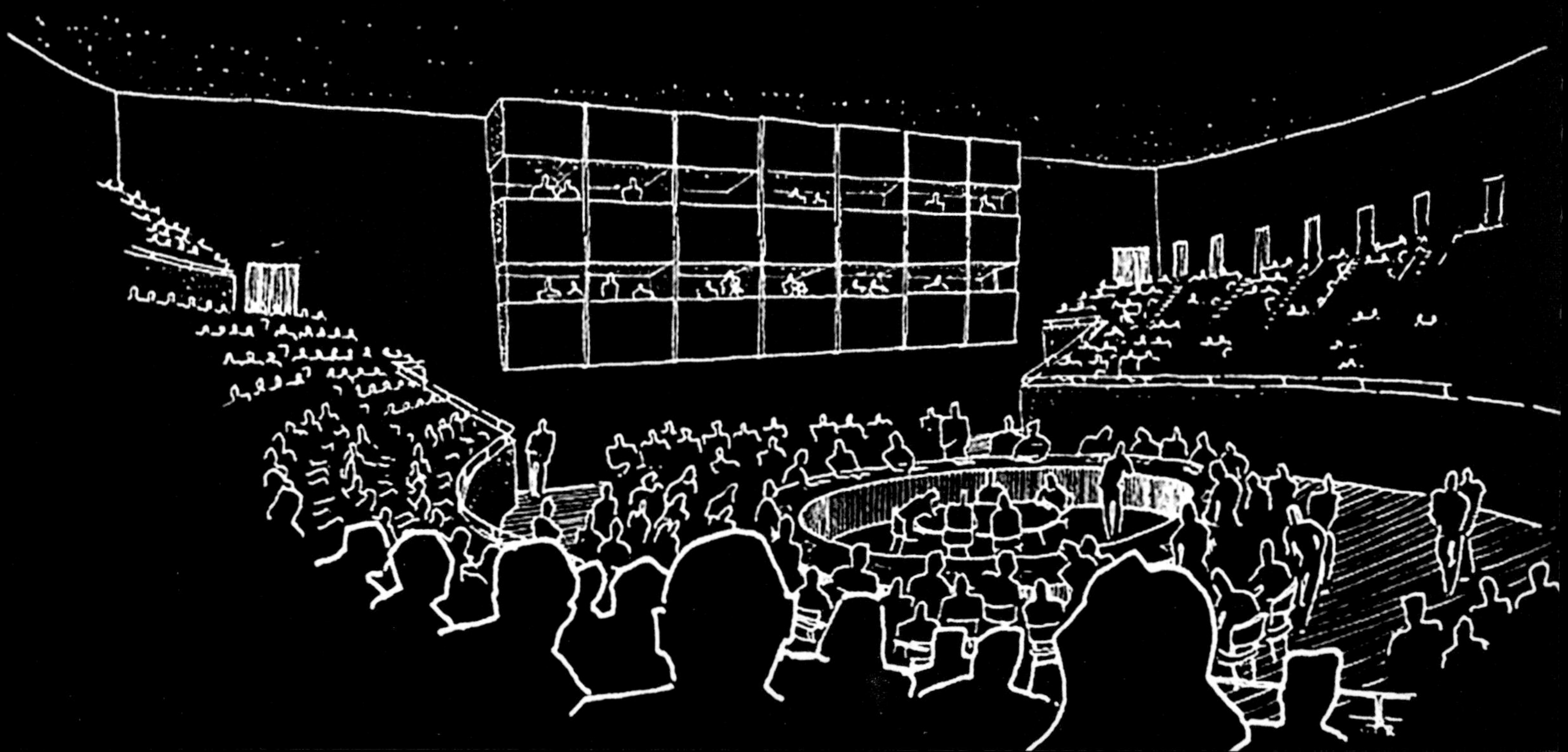

get started, Mrs. Roosevelt invited Chang, Malik, an

her Washington Square apartment on the weekend

ssion's adjournment.

hrey's recollection of the meeting was similar, down

's polite and indirect admonition to avoid an excessiv

on.[40] "Before the tea party was over," he wrote, "they

uld prepare a preliminary draft." He began working

ary 21, 1947, he permitted himself to preen a bit in a

er, Ruth: "I am now playing the role of a Jefferson,

e responsibility for drawing up the first draft of the I

ights. I have been working on it for three days now."

r years the scrupulous Humphrey took pains to ackno

ration "had no father in the sense that Thomas Jeffer

the Declaration of Independence," because "literally

. contributed to its drafting."[43] What a pity that Hu

o learn that the Declaration of Independence had n

The Preamble shall refer to the four freedoms and to the provisions of

the Charter relating to human rights and shall enunciate the following

principles:

1. that there can be no peace unless human rights and

   freedoms are respected;

2. that man does not have rights only; he owes duties to

   the society of which he forms part;

3. that man is a citizen both of his State and of the world.

4. that there can be no human freedom or dignity unless war is abolished.

Mrs. R. suggested that the preamble also say that there can be no human rights without peace.

1. Every one owes a duty of loyalty to his State and to the ~~inter-national society of which he forms part.~~ United Nations He must accept his just

    share of responsibility for the performance of social duties and

    also his share of any sacrifices ~~made necessary by the exigencies of life in common.~~ common

Preliminary dispositions

2. In the exercise of his rights every one is limited by the rights

    of others and by the just requirements ~~of the democratic~~ his State and of the United Nations.

3. Every one has the right to life. This right can be denied only

    to persons who have been convicted under general law of some

    crime against society to which the death penalty is attached.

Right to life, etc.

4. No one shall be subjected to torture, or to any unusual punishment

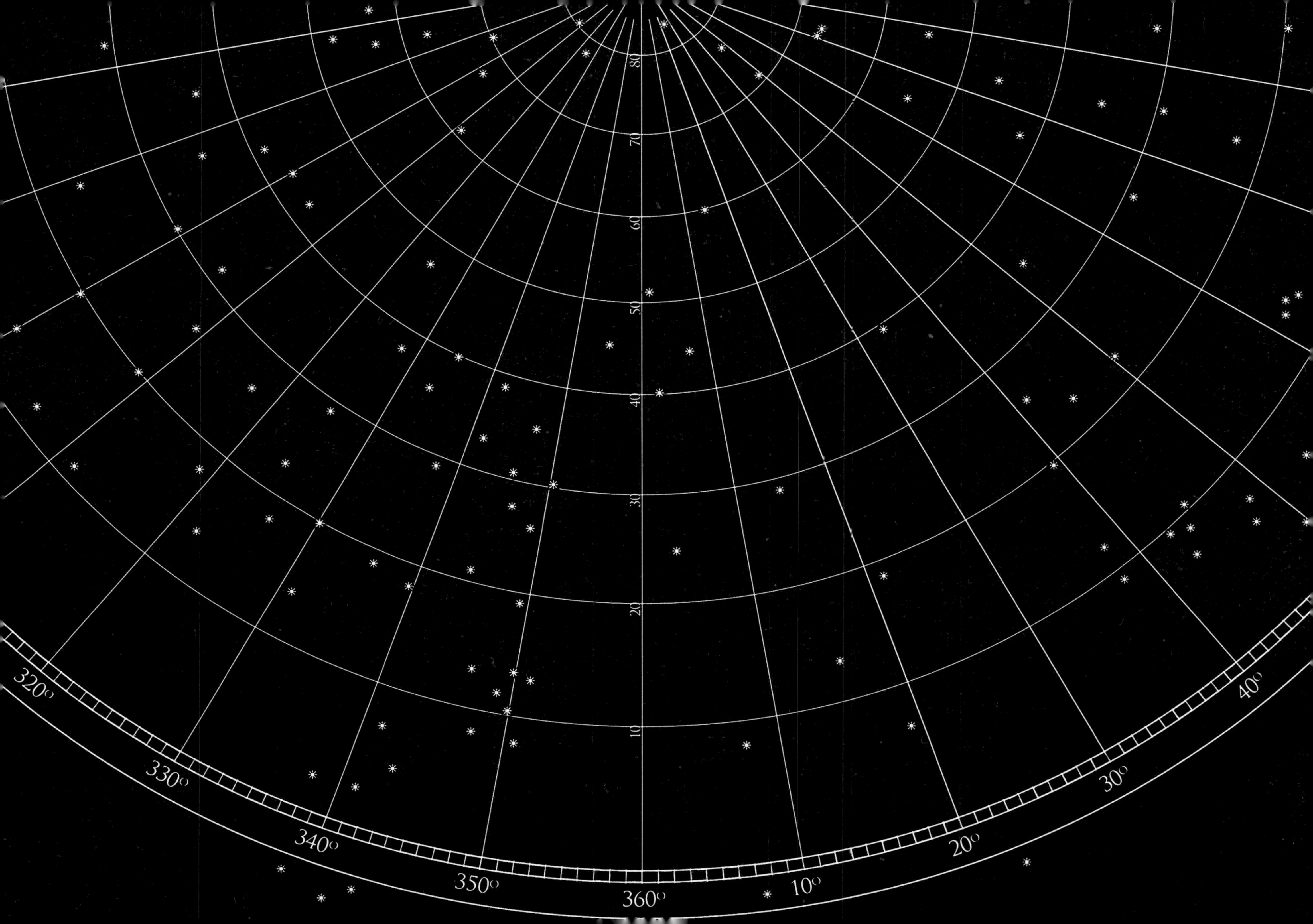

80
70
60
50
40
30
20
10
320°
330°
340°
350°
360°
10°
20°
30°
40°

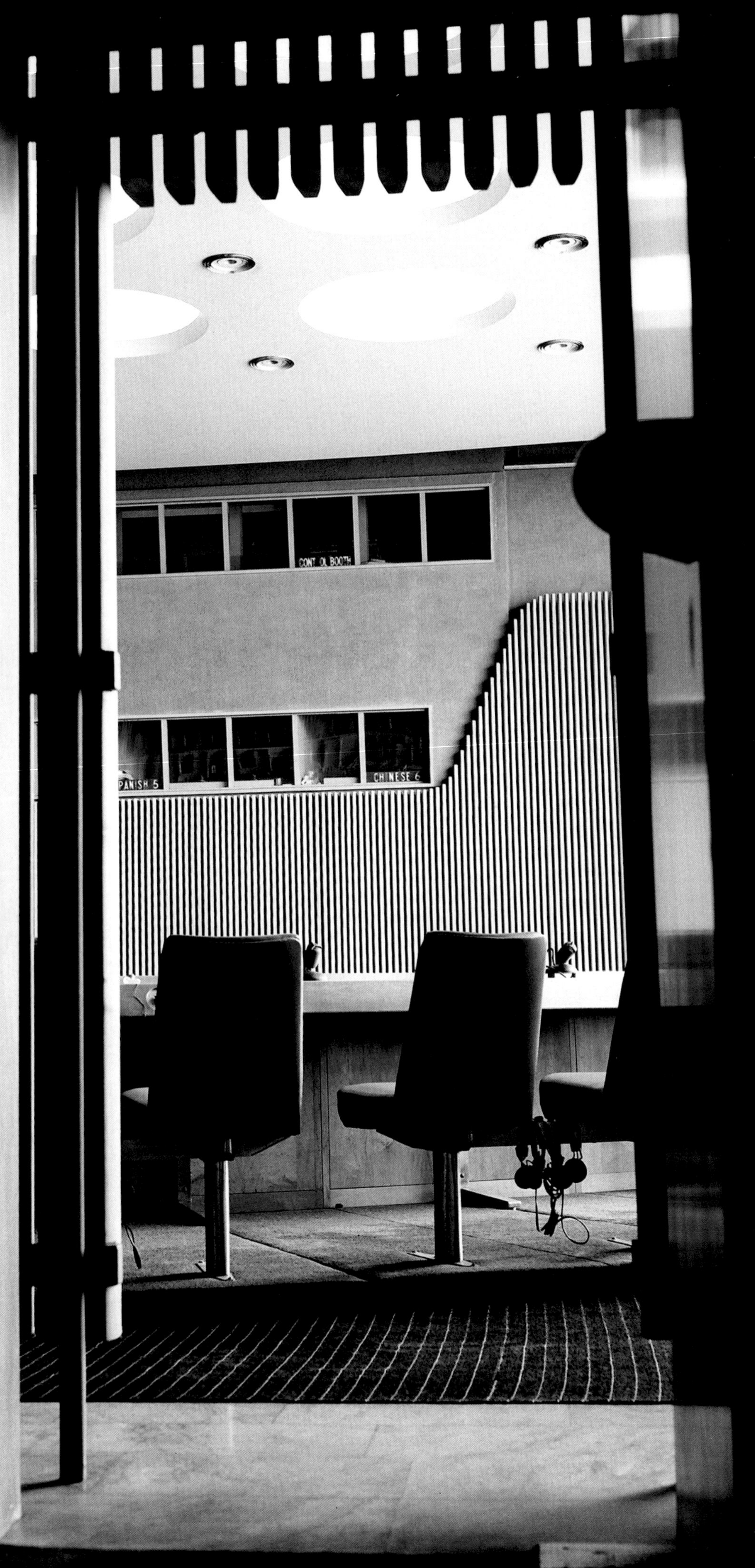

CONTROL BOOTH
SPANISH 5
CHINESE 6

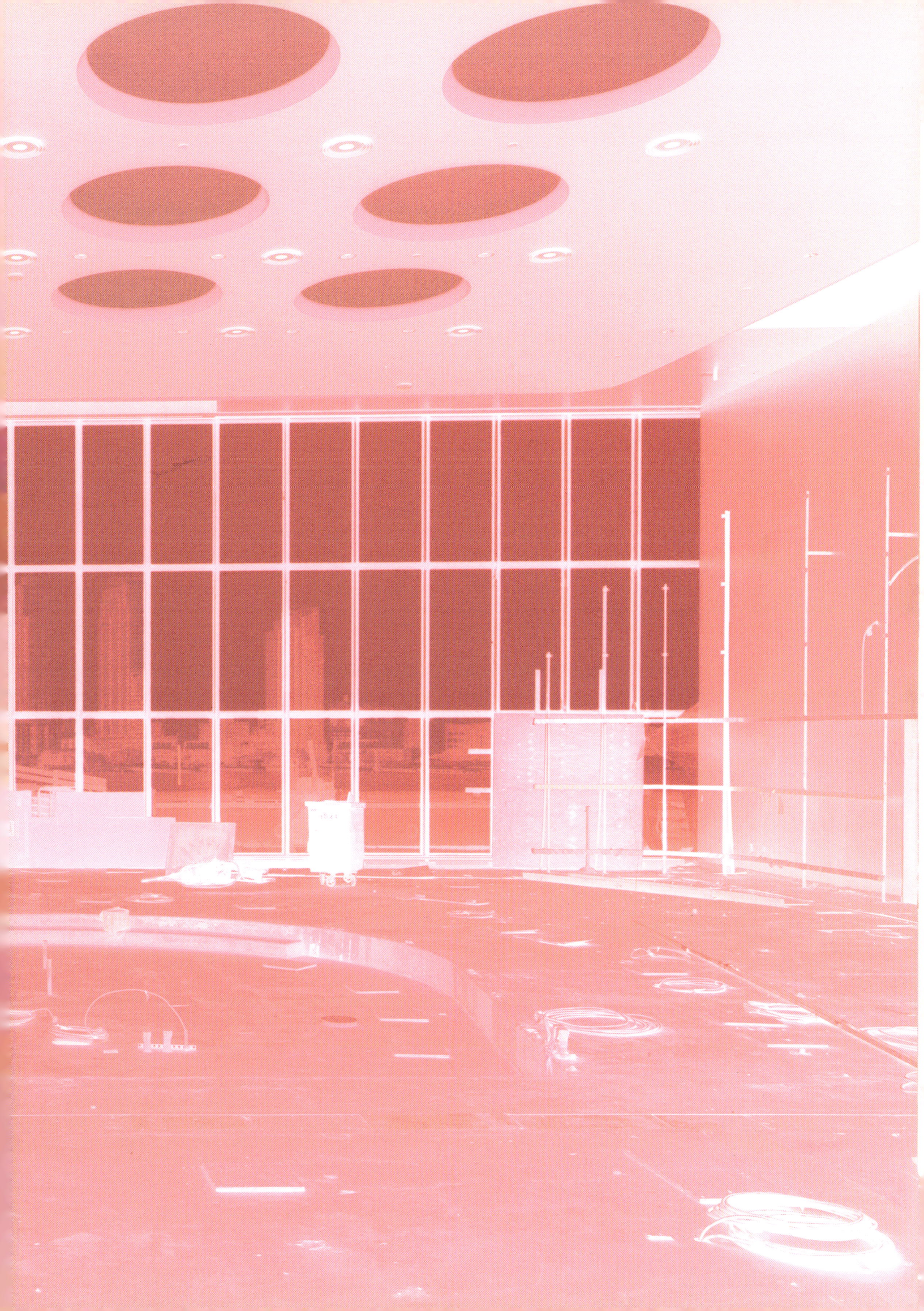

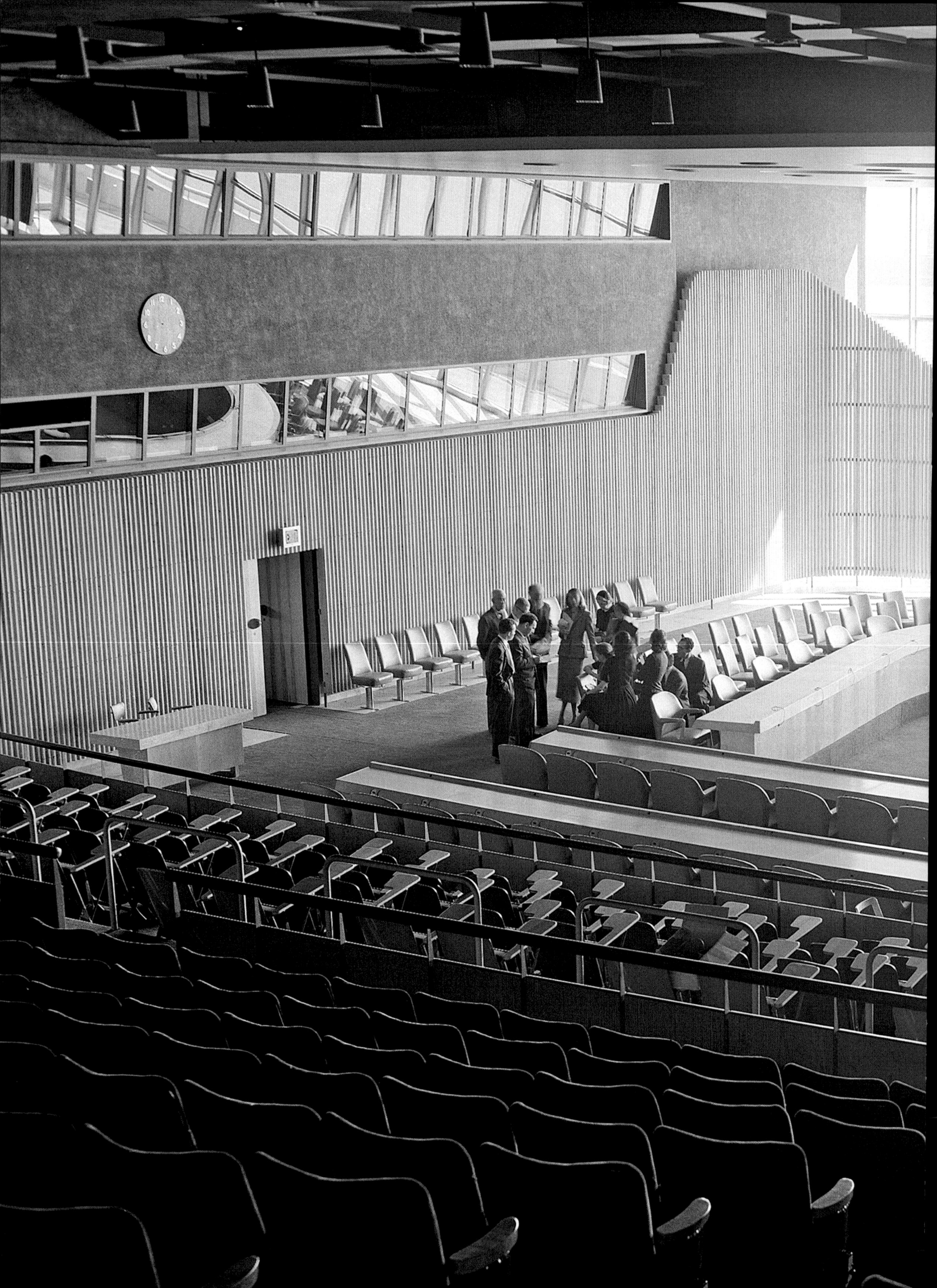

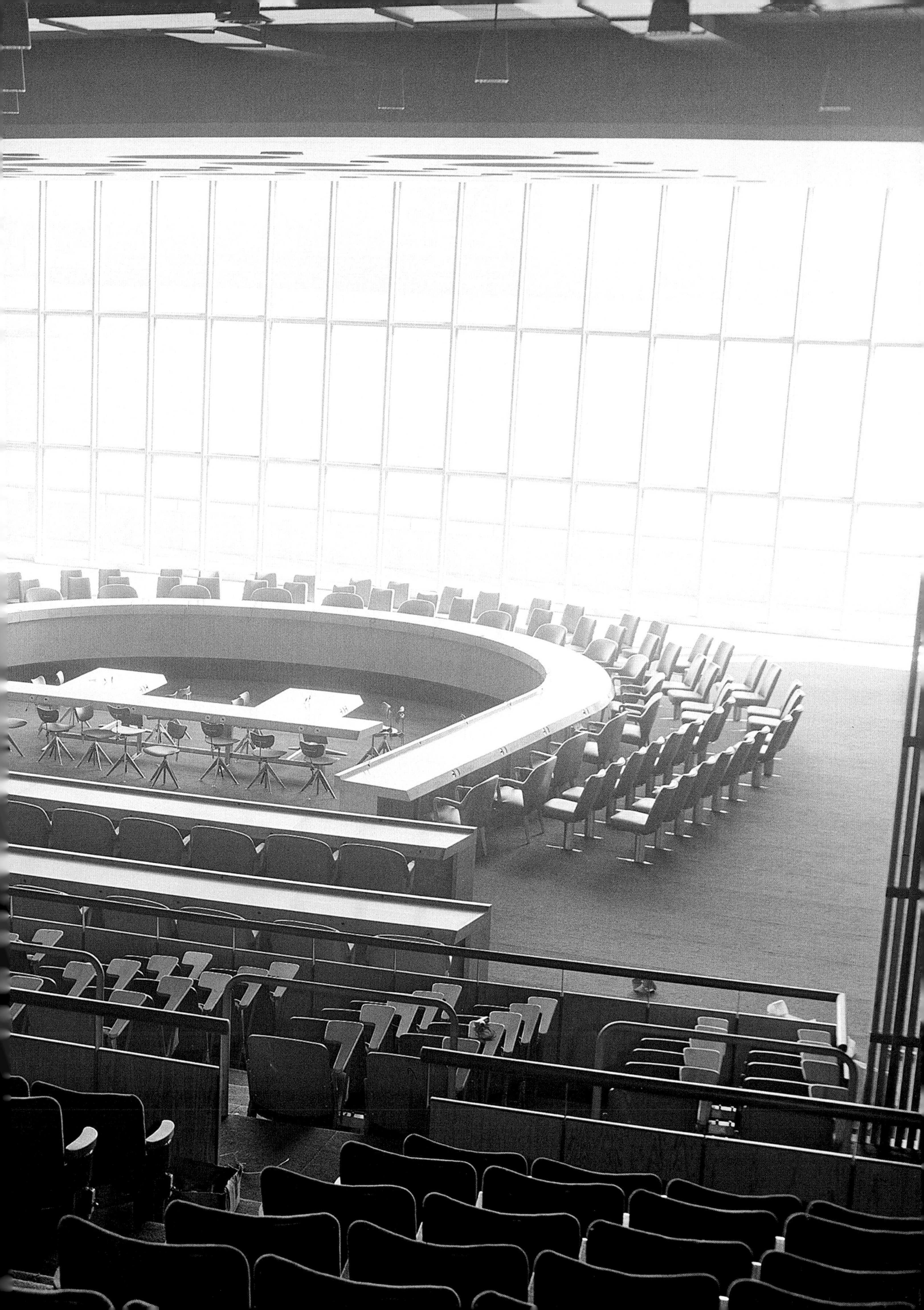

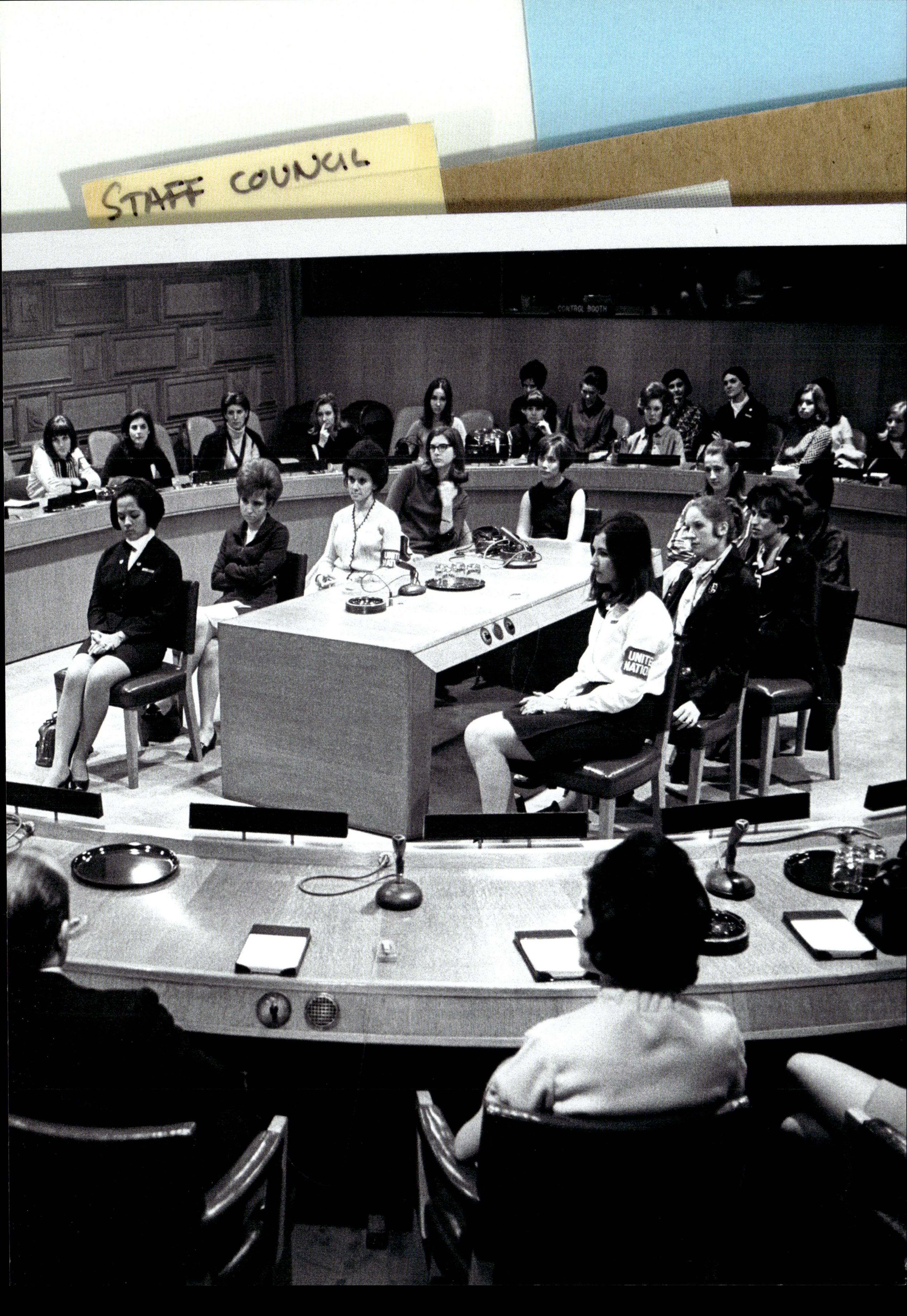

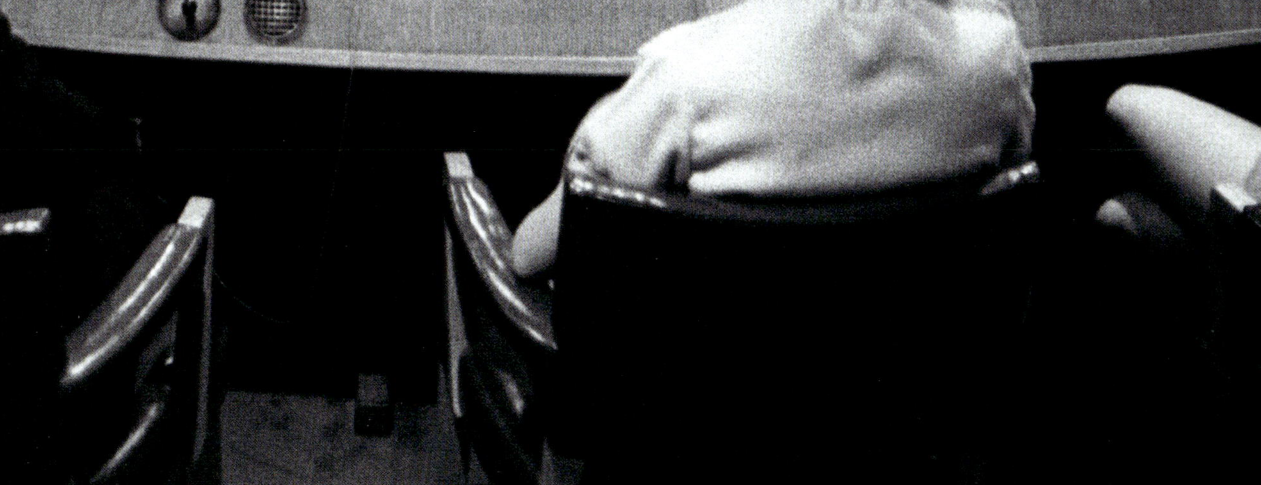
STAFF COUNCIL

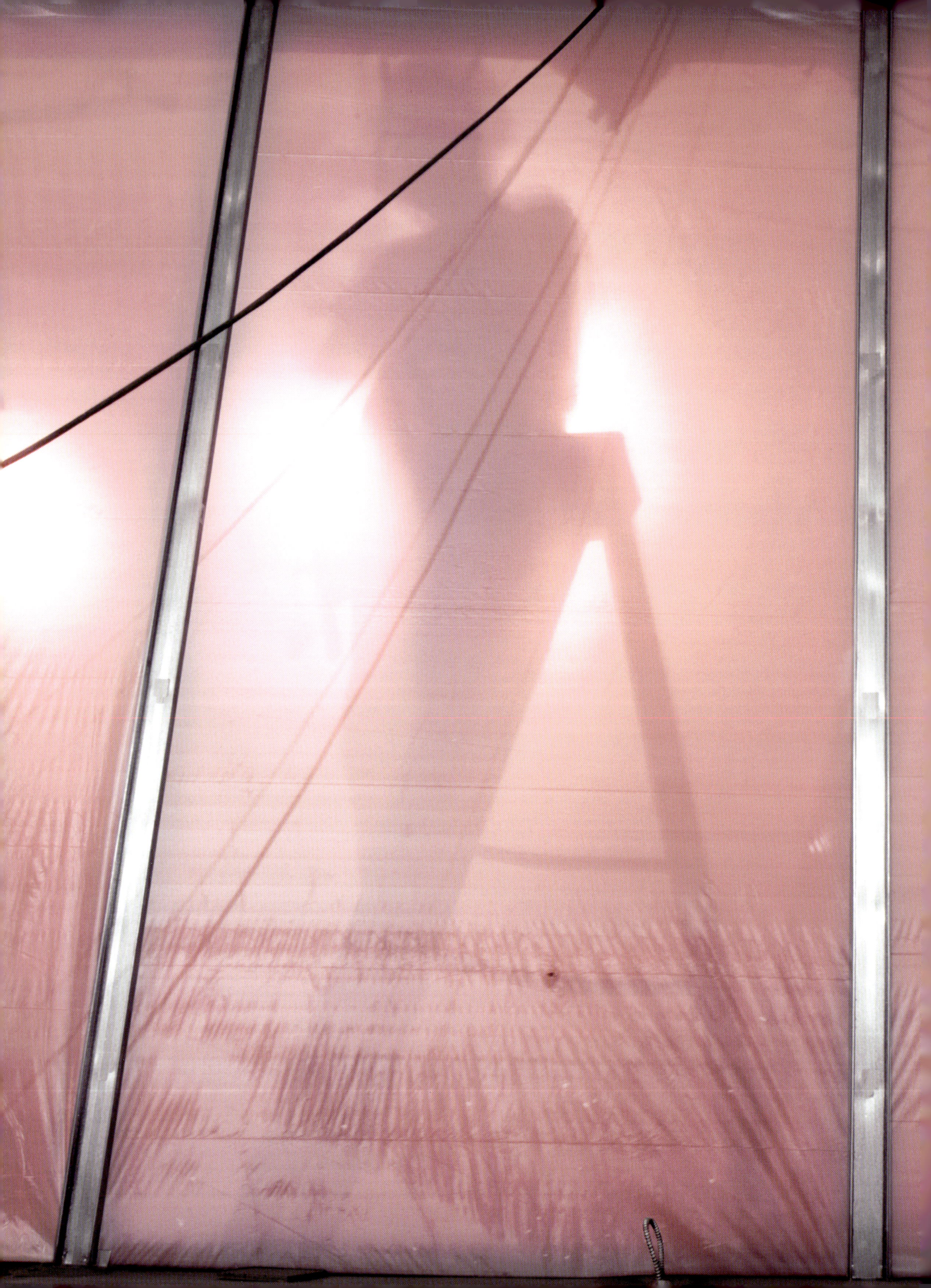

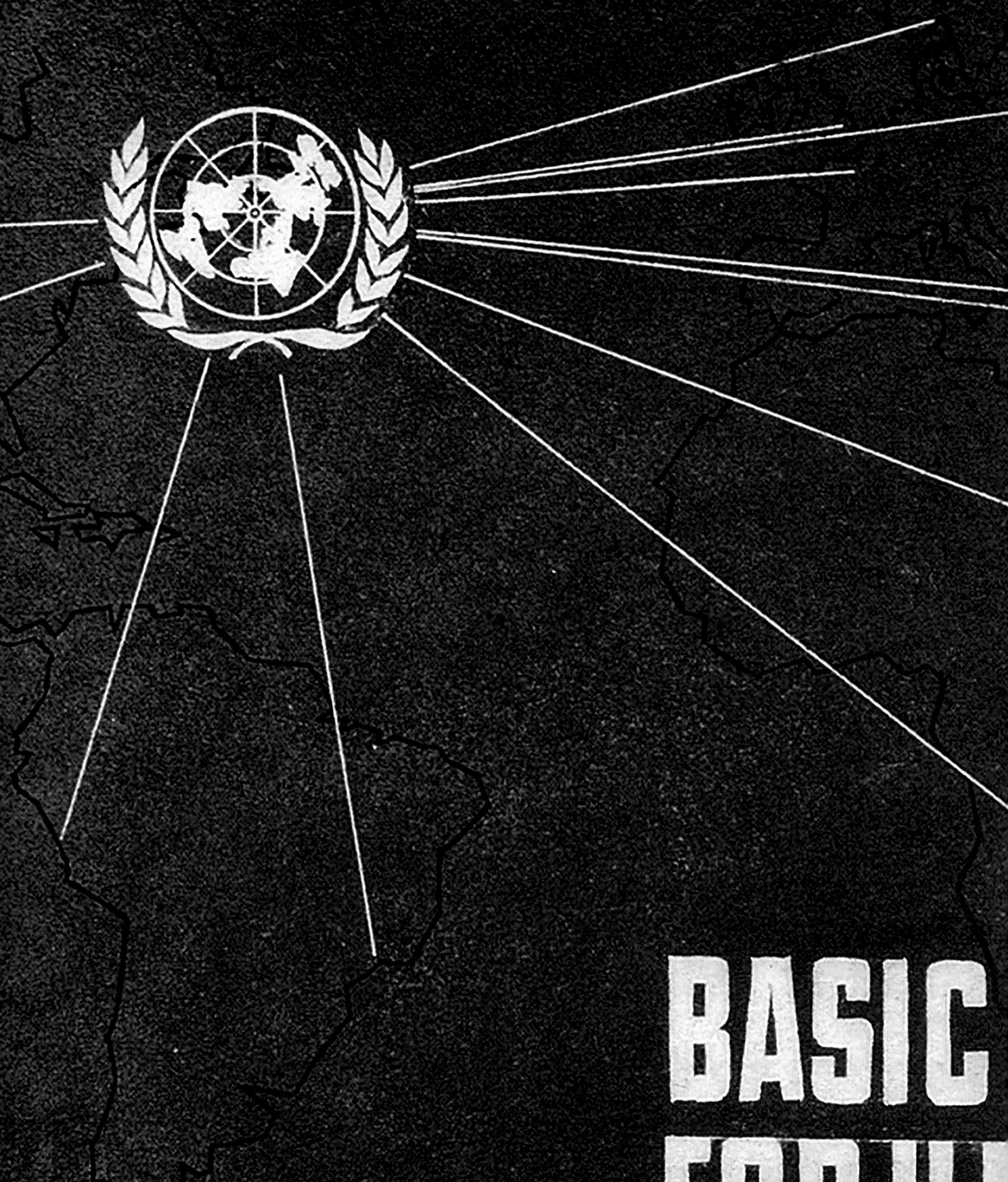

BASIC
FOR U.N

REQUIREMENTS
HEADQUARTERS

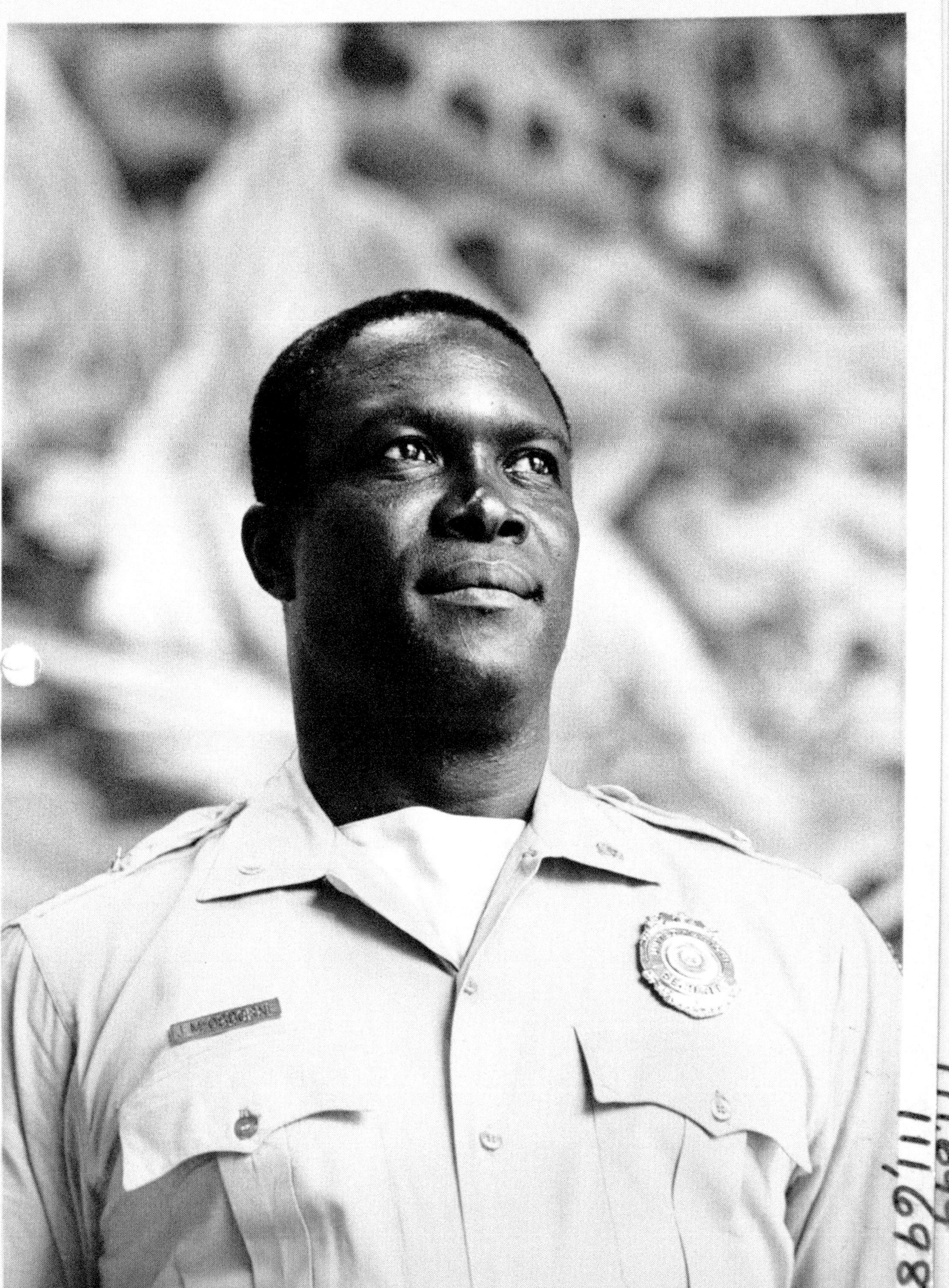

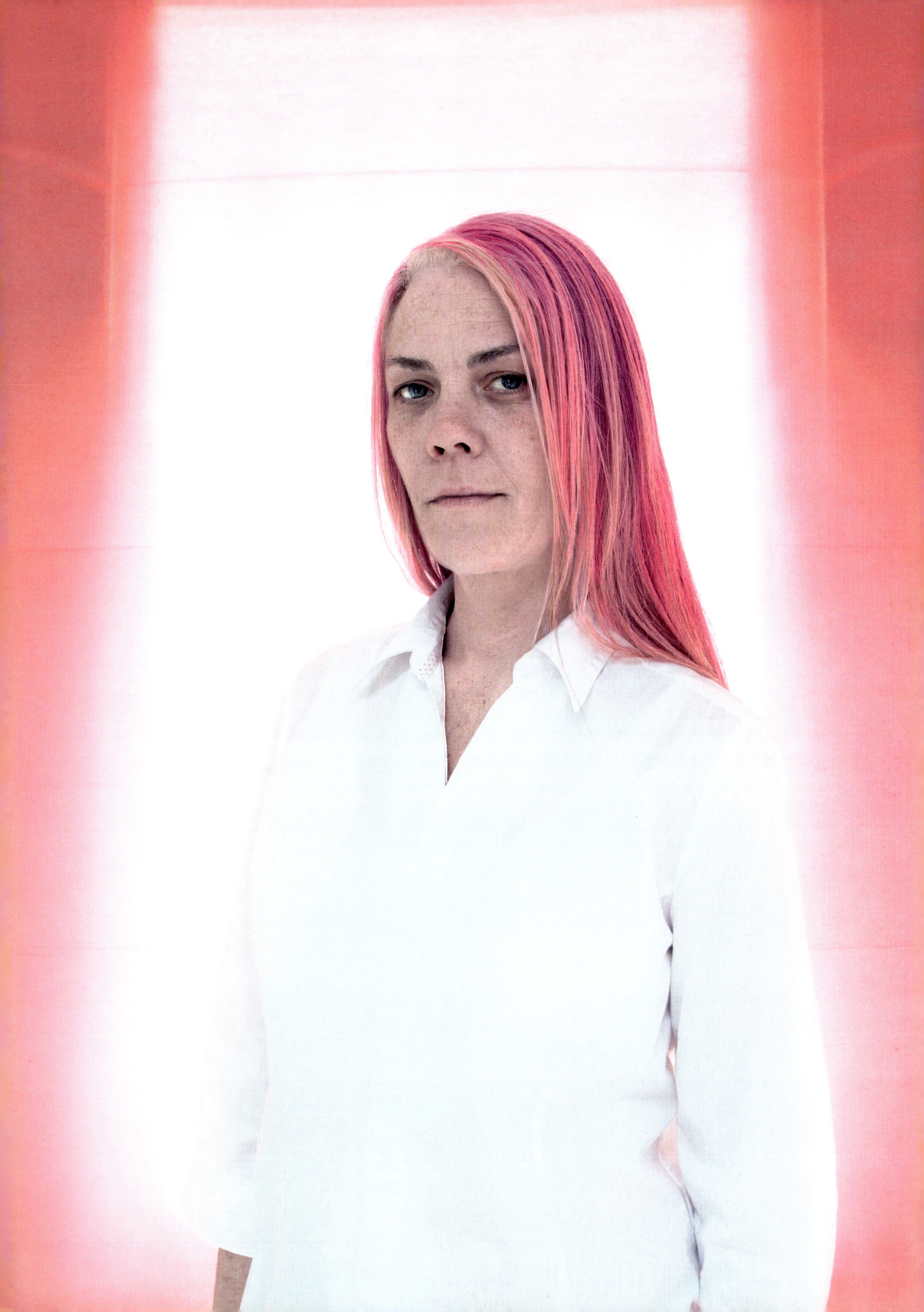

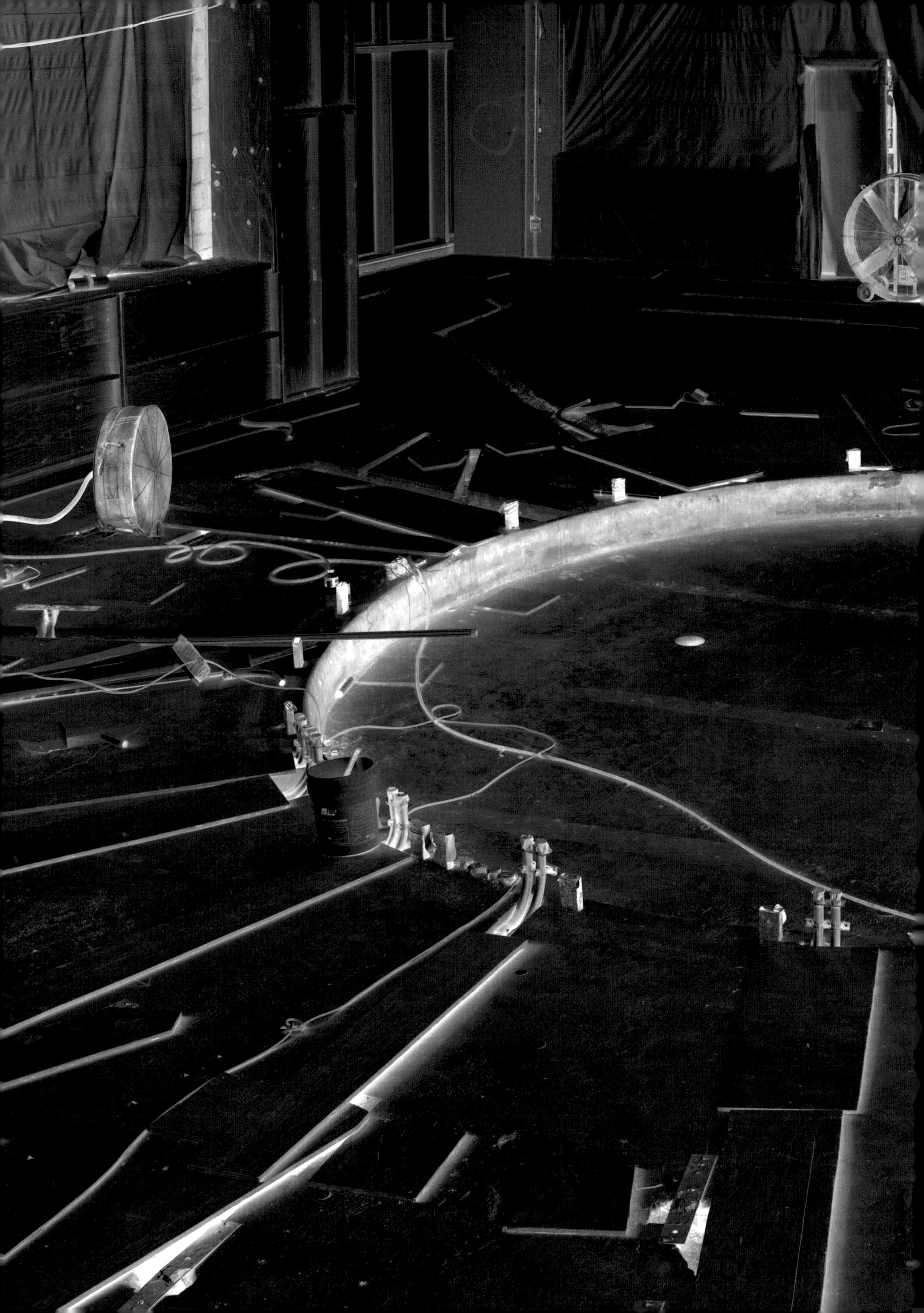

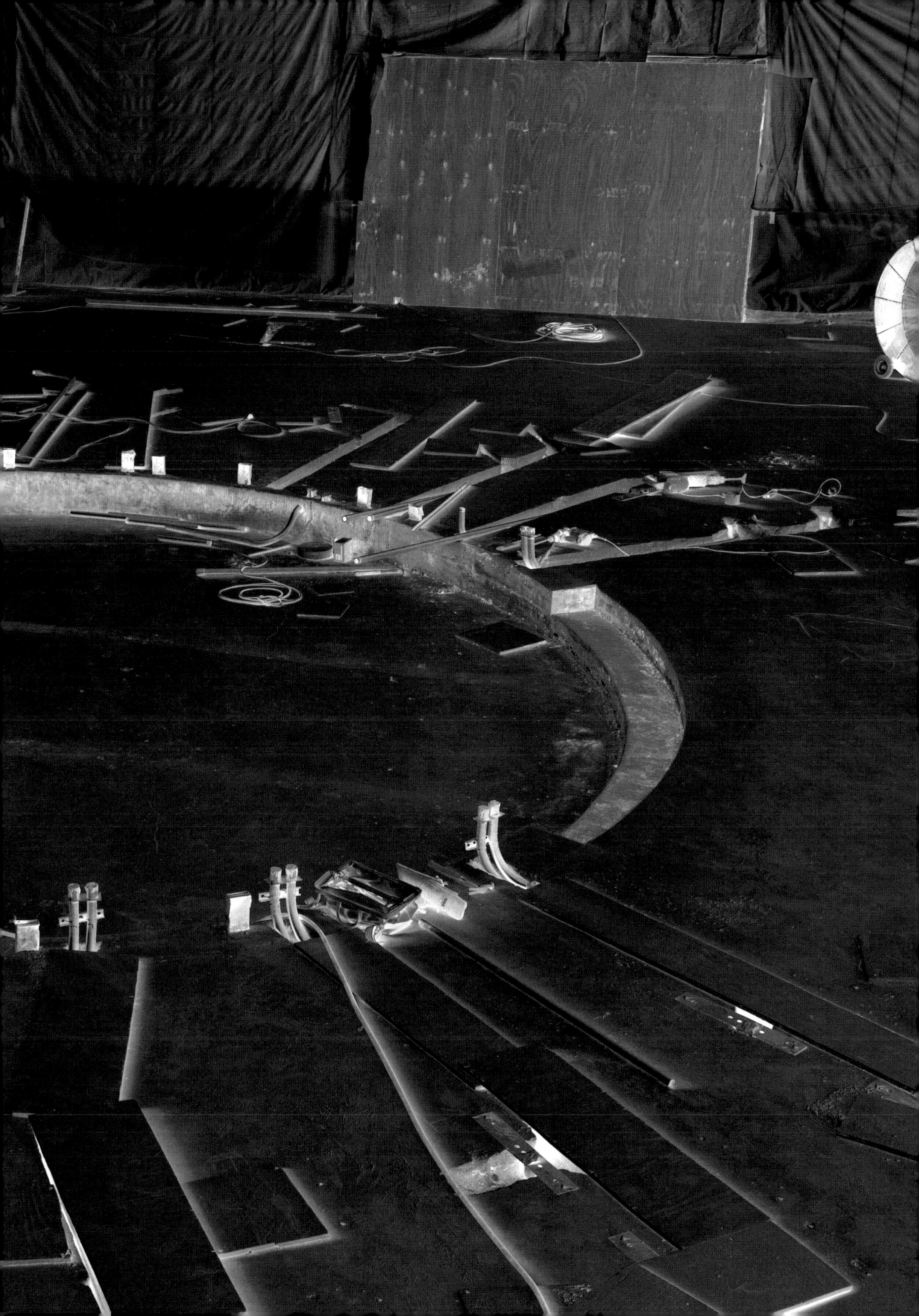

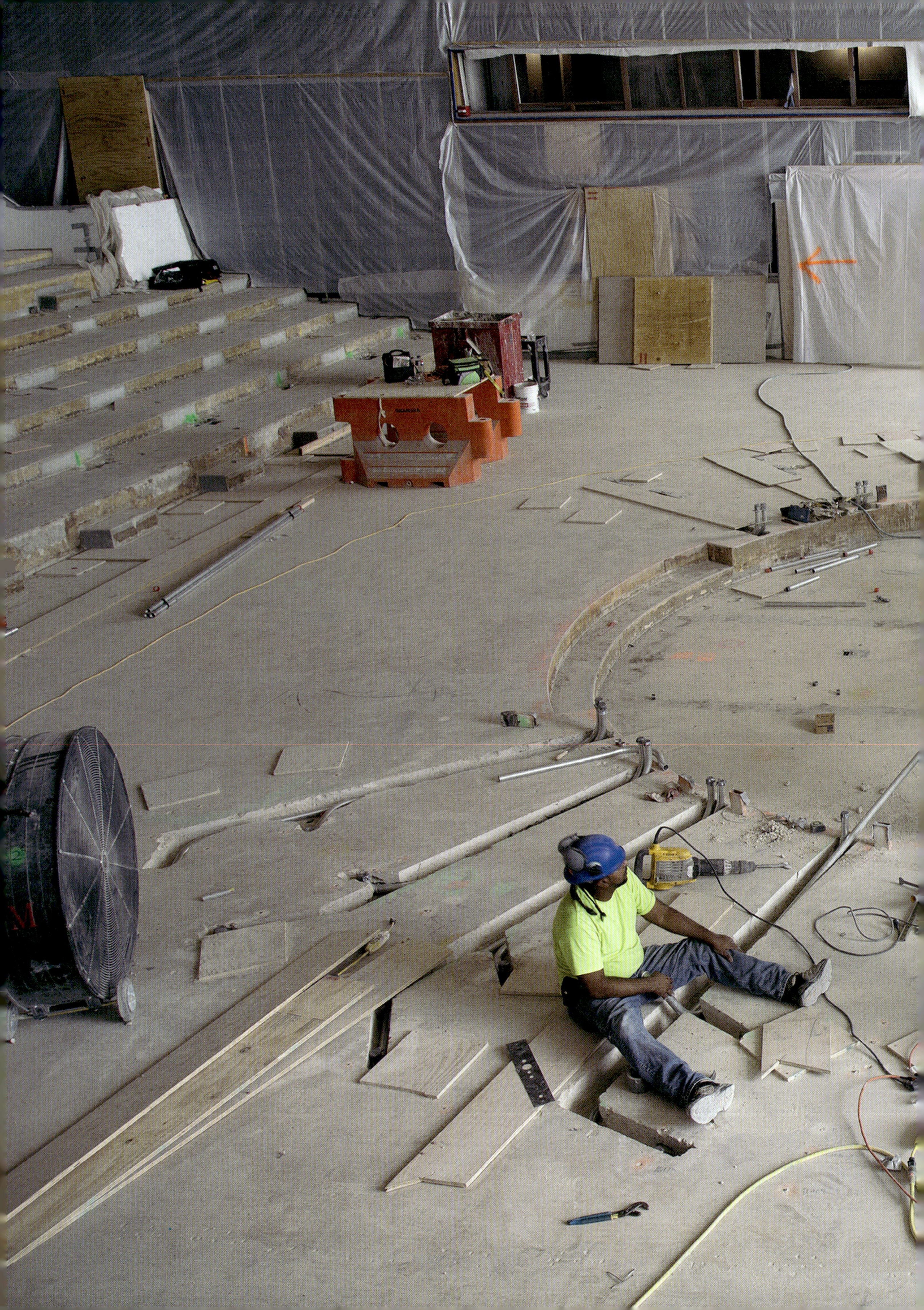

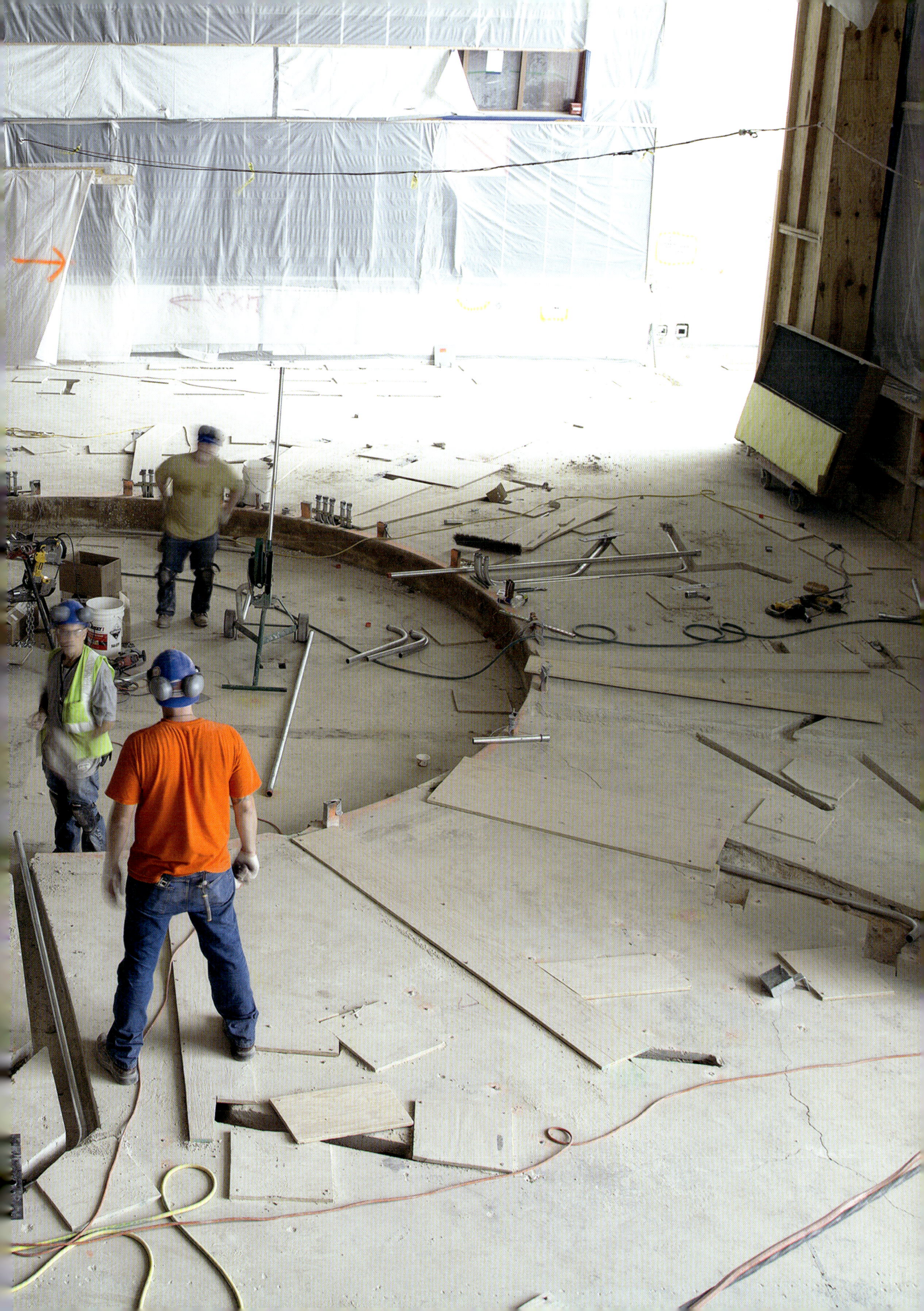

                              ND
Could you tell me why "Buckles" or "Jimmy Buckles" is
written everywhere around the Security Council Chamber?
Who is Jimmy Buckles?

                              DG
I don't actually know the guy, but I did hear the story.
They used to take little side bets on the football games
every Sunday and there was a certain fellow who put money
on the same boxes every week, he always took the same
three boxes. So one day, he wrote his name in the grid as
usual, placed his bet. Then the foreman comes up and wants
to place the same bet...

                              RS
Buckles was running the football pool.

                              DG
Right. Buckles was doing the boxes and says that he didn't
get the first guy's money in time... so he says.

                              RS
So he says.

                              DG
Buckles crossed the first name out, put the foreman's name
in, and this is the box that hits. The box hits $2,000.
Quite a stir ensues. Now there's two guys claiming the
winning box. Big uproar for $2,000. So the word goes
around he gave away this fellow's box to the foreman --
who just happens to be giving out the overtime.

                              RS
Everyone says the foreman pressured him...

                              DG
He buckled under pressure.

He used to be called "Pesci" because he looks like Joe
Pesci. Now they start calling him Jimmy Buckles. They
start writing on the walls about "Buckles" and "Buckling"
and all this other stuff. It got blown up out of
proportion, every lift has a "Buckles" haiku, every gang
box has some "Buckle-ism"...

                              RS
There are "Buckles" everywhere.

                              DG
It got so bad that the UN actually sent round a memo
saying: "Who is Jimmy Buckles?" and "No more Mr.
Buckles"...

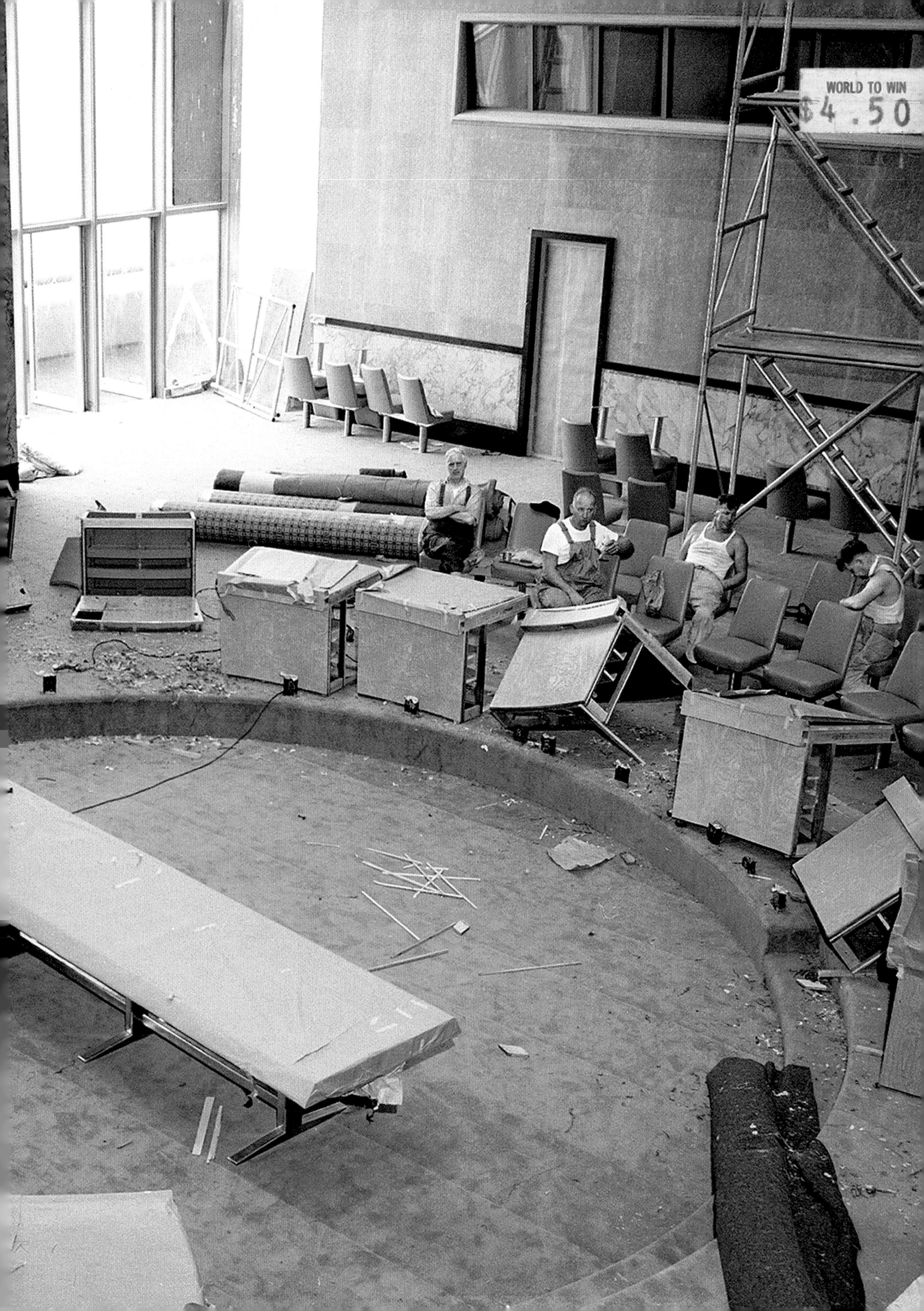

WORLD TO WIN
$4.50

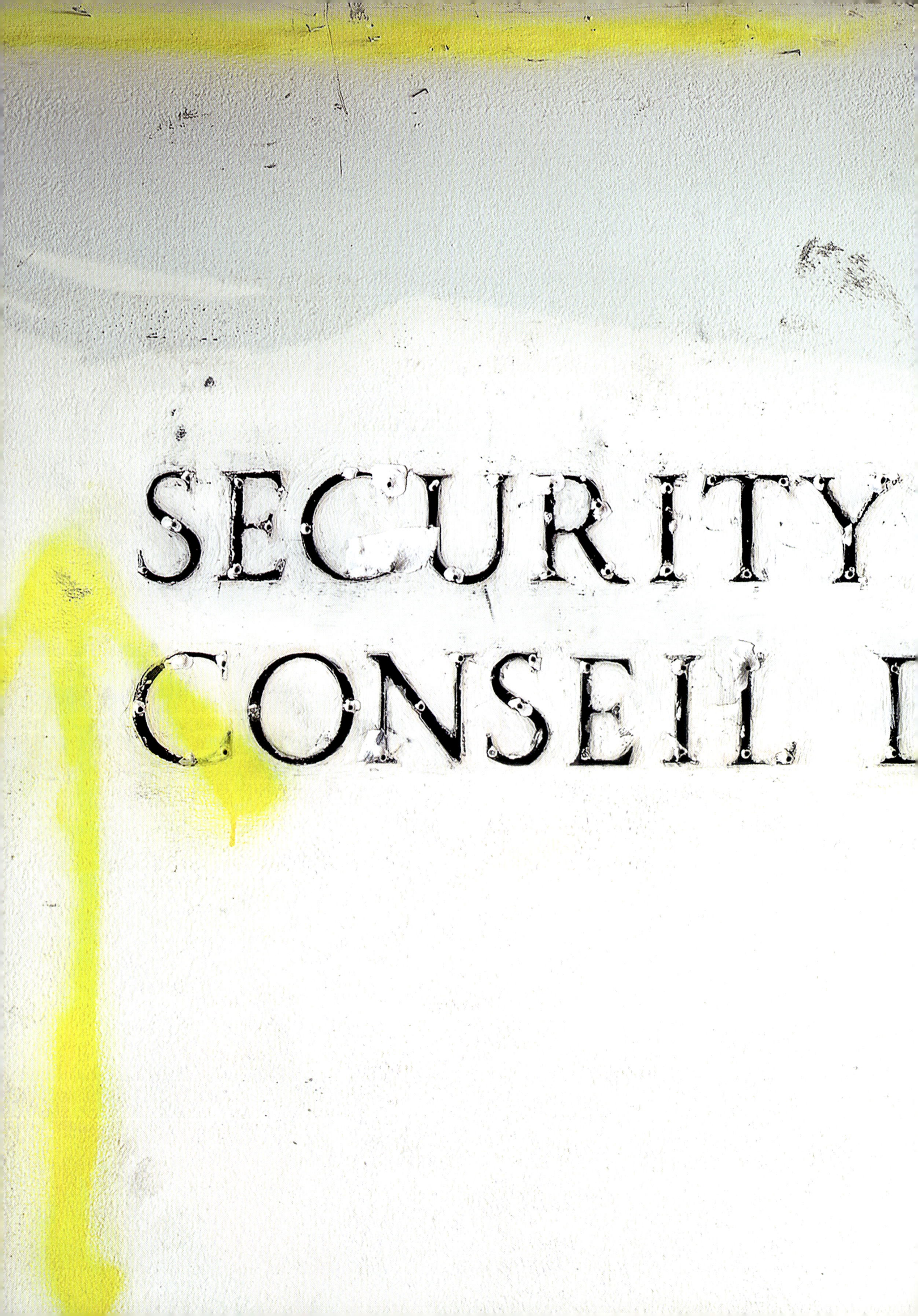

SECURITY
CONSEIL

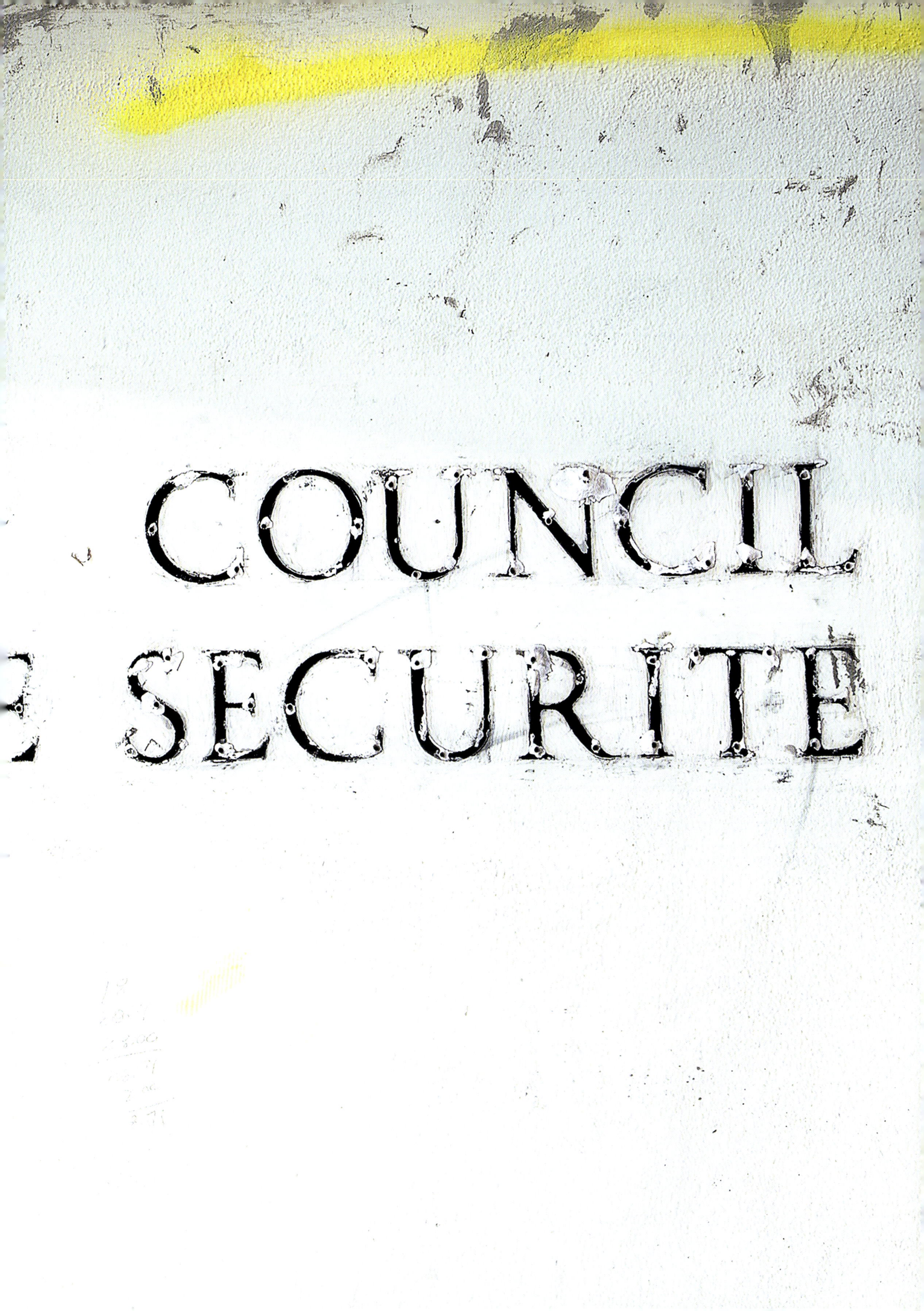

COUNCIL

SECURITE

                    ND
How did Jimmy Buckles react?

                    DG
He didn't mind, actually. He liked being notorious.

                    ND
Was this the only time that Jimmy Buckles -- buckled?

                    DG
That we know of.

                    RS
When the memo came around, here's the UN asking,
"Who is Jimmy Buckles?" Everyone was talking. Now,
I think he's proud of being Buckles.

                    ND
And his first name is really Jimmy?

                    RS
No, actually his real name is Dave.

                    ND
Is he still working at the United Nations? Maybe I could
find him.

                    DG
Yeah, he might be around.

                    RS
I heard a rumor he got laid off.

                    ND
Why would Jimmy Buckles get laid off? Do you think he got
fired... for buckling?

        (pause)

                    RS
Nah.

                    DG
I don't know. If he buckled in one case, maybe he'd buckle
somewhere else. You can't trust him anymore.

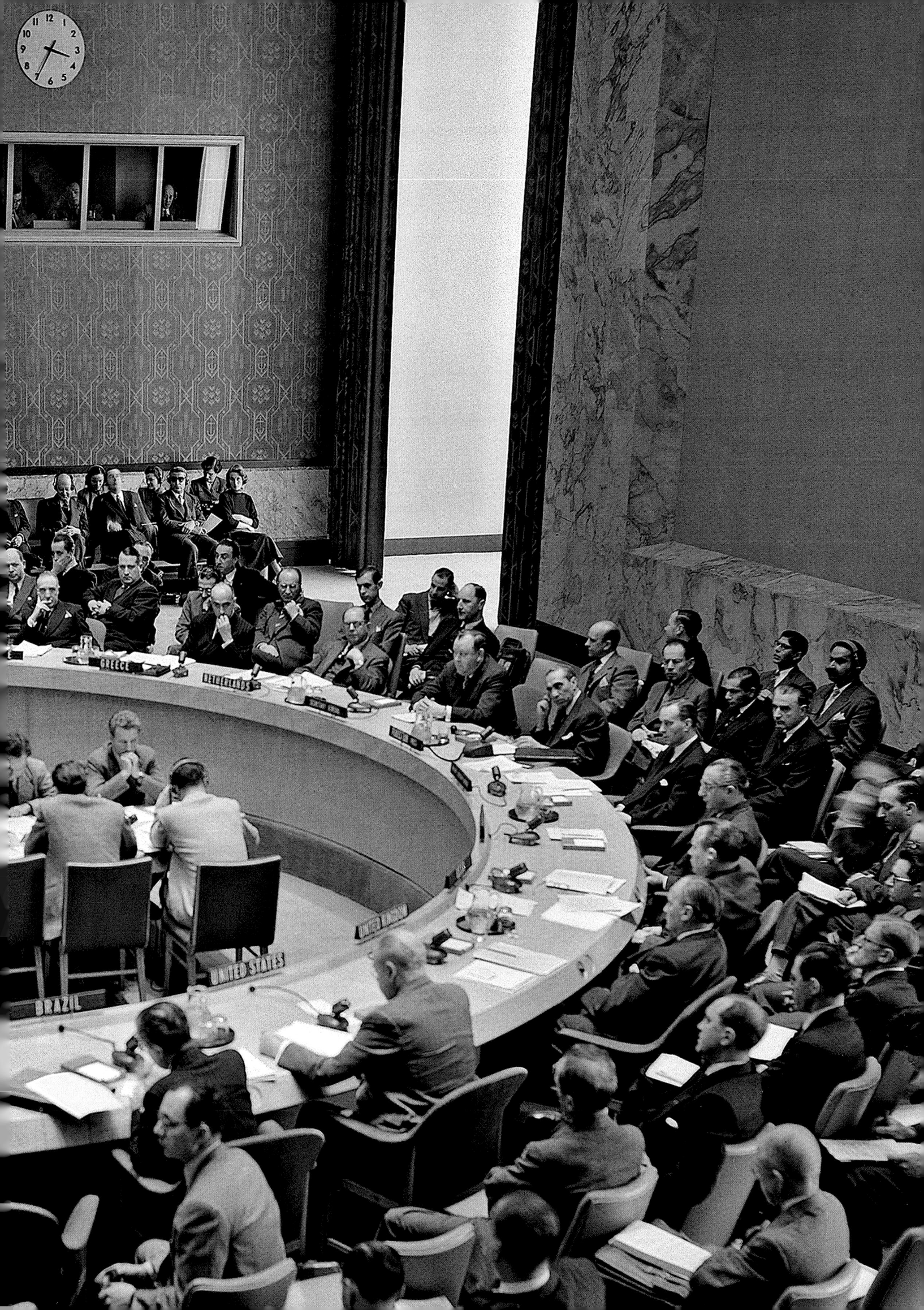

GREECE
NETHERLANDS
UNITED STATES
UNITED KINGDOM
BRAZIL

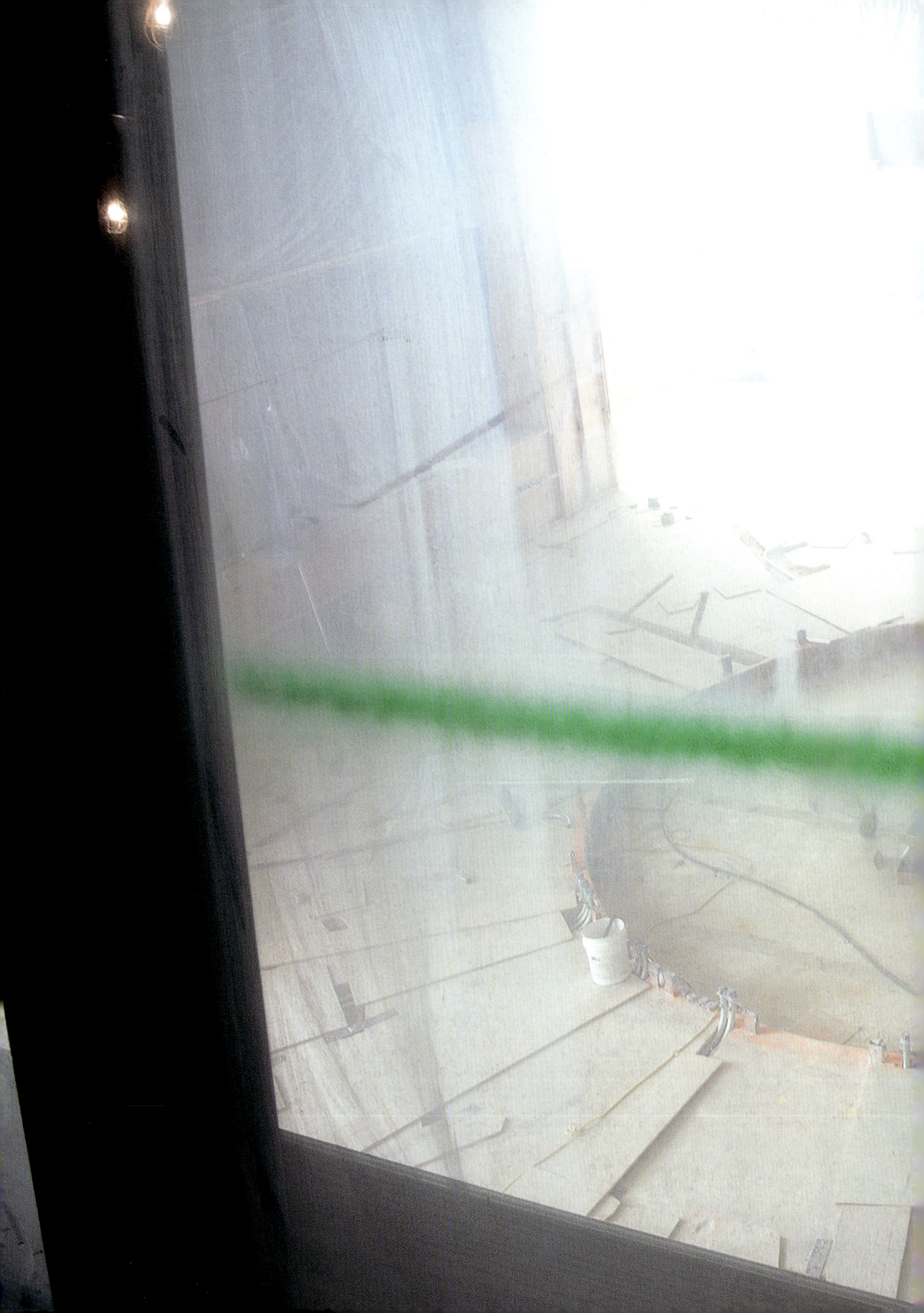

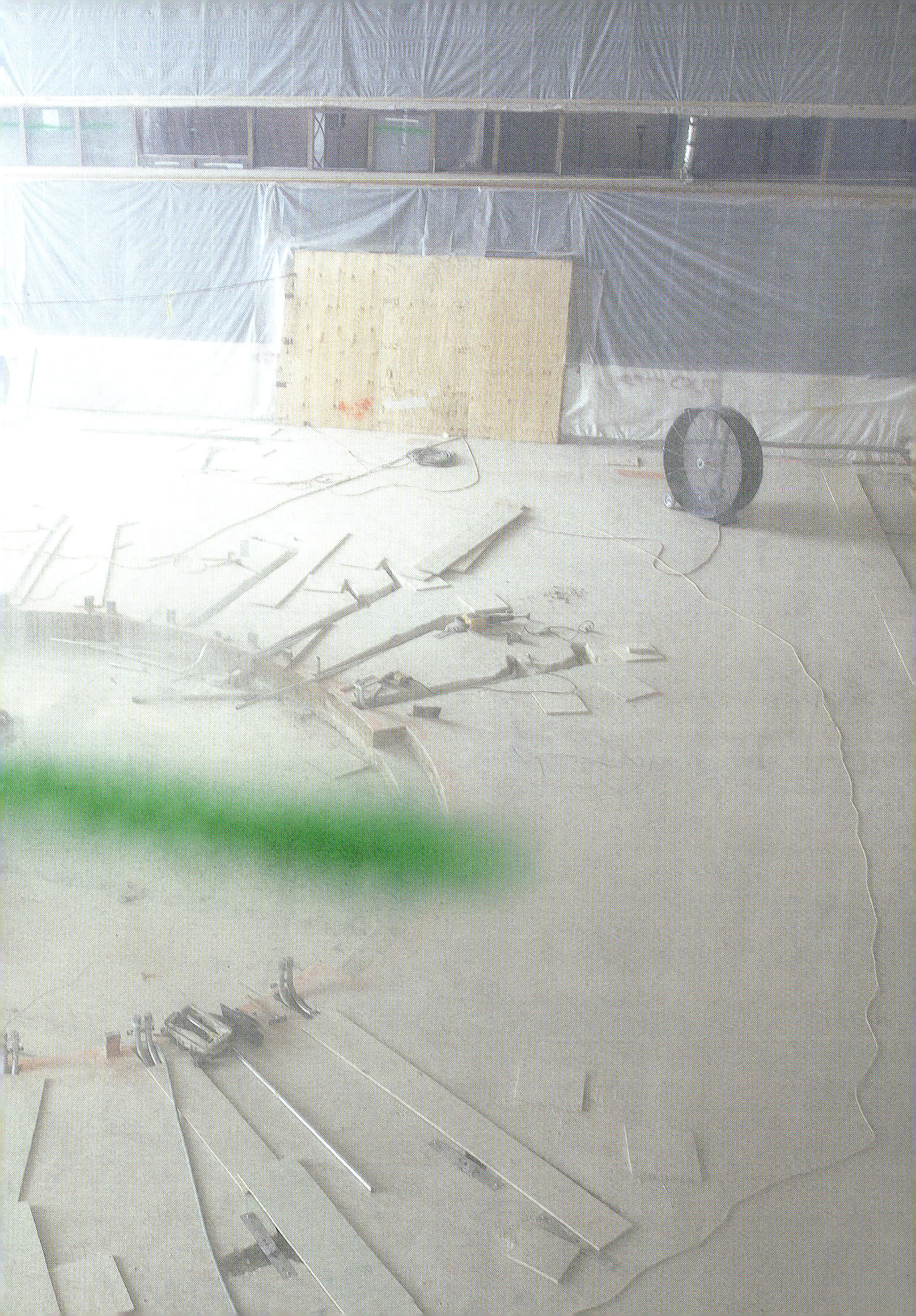

                              ND
Do you know Jimmy Buckles?

                              GM
Well, we know the story.

                              BL
There was a football pool, you know, with boxes that you
buy. People always want the best odds; the best numbers
get taken pretty fast. Jimmy promised one guy certain
numbers and then weaseled out. He sold the same boxes to
another guy... that's why he's called "Buckles."

                              GM
Actually, he sold them to the foreman -- that's how he
really buckled.

                              AP
He gave them to the foreman. He got his overtime. Now
"Buckles" is written everywhere, the floors, the walls,
every piece of equipment...

                              BL
I've seen a "Buckles" going down the highway on the side
of a truck.

                              GM
"Buckles Condo" is written on all the garbage bins.

                              AP
     (laughs)

"Buckles Condo."

                              GM
On low beams downstairs, it says: "Mind your head...
everyone except Buckles."

     (all laugh)

                              BL
Yeah, Buckles is a little guy, something like four feet
tall.

                              GM
So, that's pretty much the story. Jimmy sold out.
Somebody said, "You buckled. I can't believe you," and it
just took off.

                              ND
          I heard his name is not Jimmy.

                              BL
          No. Actually, he likes to be called "Pesci."

                              AP
          He thinks he's Joe Pesci. He's got the Italian mug and
          looks angry all the time.

                              ND
          So, he does look like Joe Pesci?

                              GM
          Nah, he doesn't look like him at all. But he thinks so.

                              AP & BL
              (together)

          He thinks he does...

                              BL
          He likes to play the tough guy.

                              AP
          He's a nervous wreck.

                              GM
          I think the Buckle-isms are poetry. All the trades started
          writing. I'm sure most of them don't know who Buckles is;
          they just rode with it.

                              ND
          Do you know him?

                              GM
          Oh yeah, I worked with Buckles last year.

                              ND
          I guess you saw the memo sent around by the UN: "Who is
          Jimmy Buckles?" After the memo, did people stop writing?

                              AP
          Nah, it's never going to end.

                              BL
          He buckled.

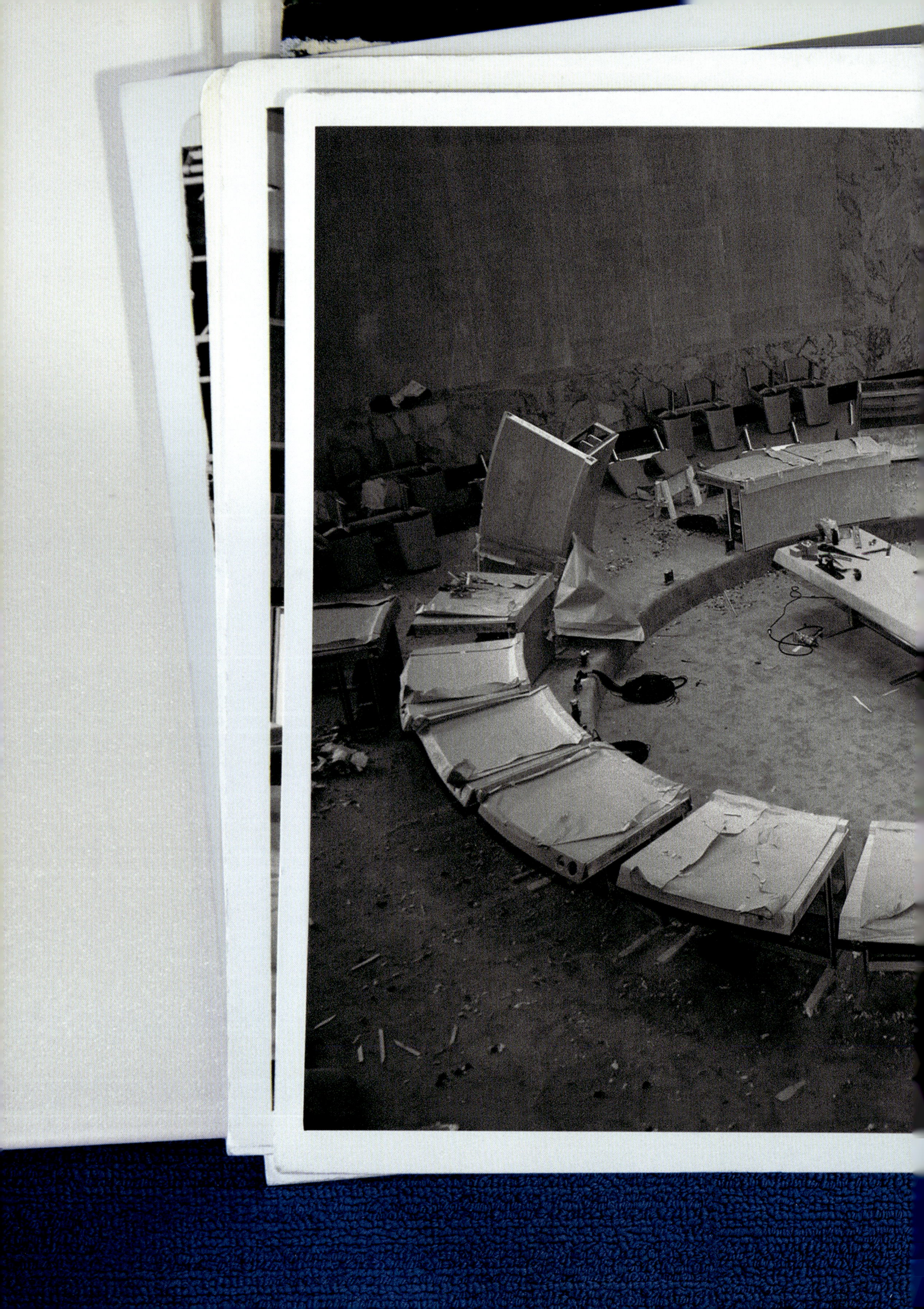

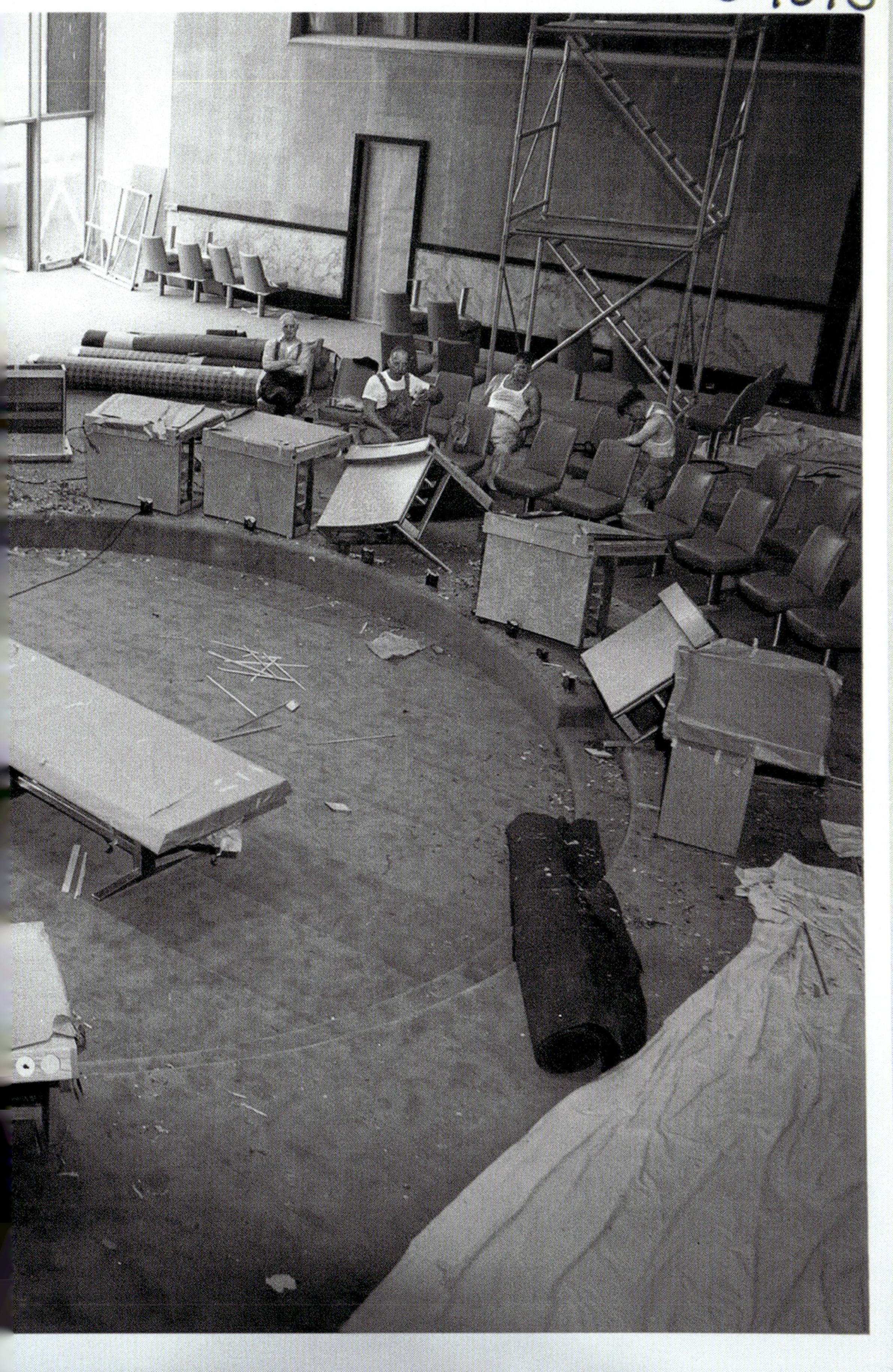

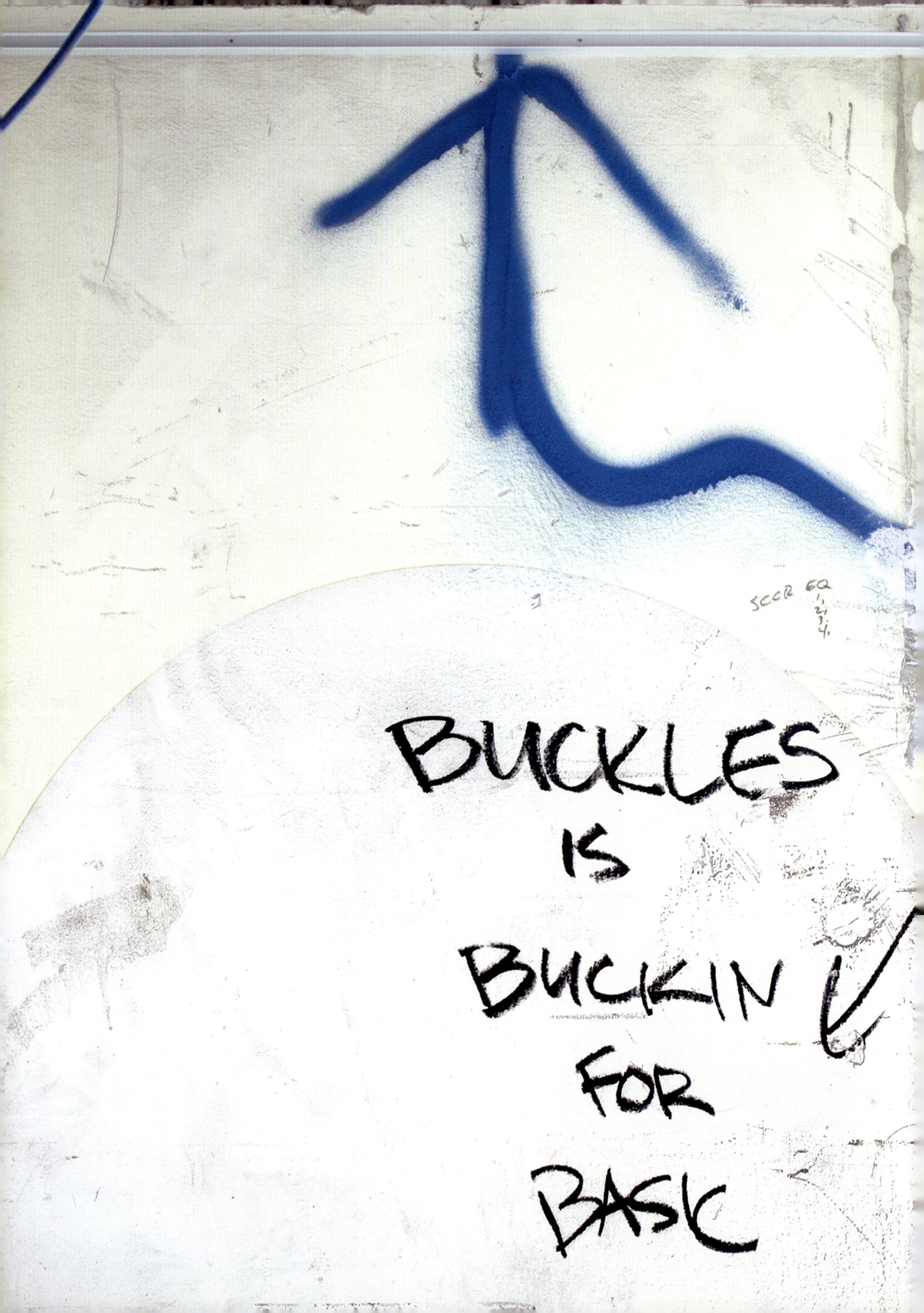

BUCKLES
IS
BUCKIN
FOR
BASC

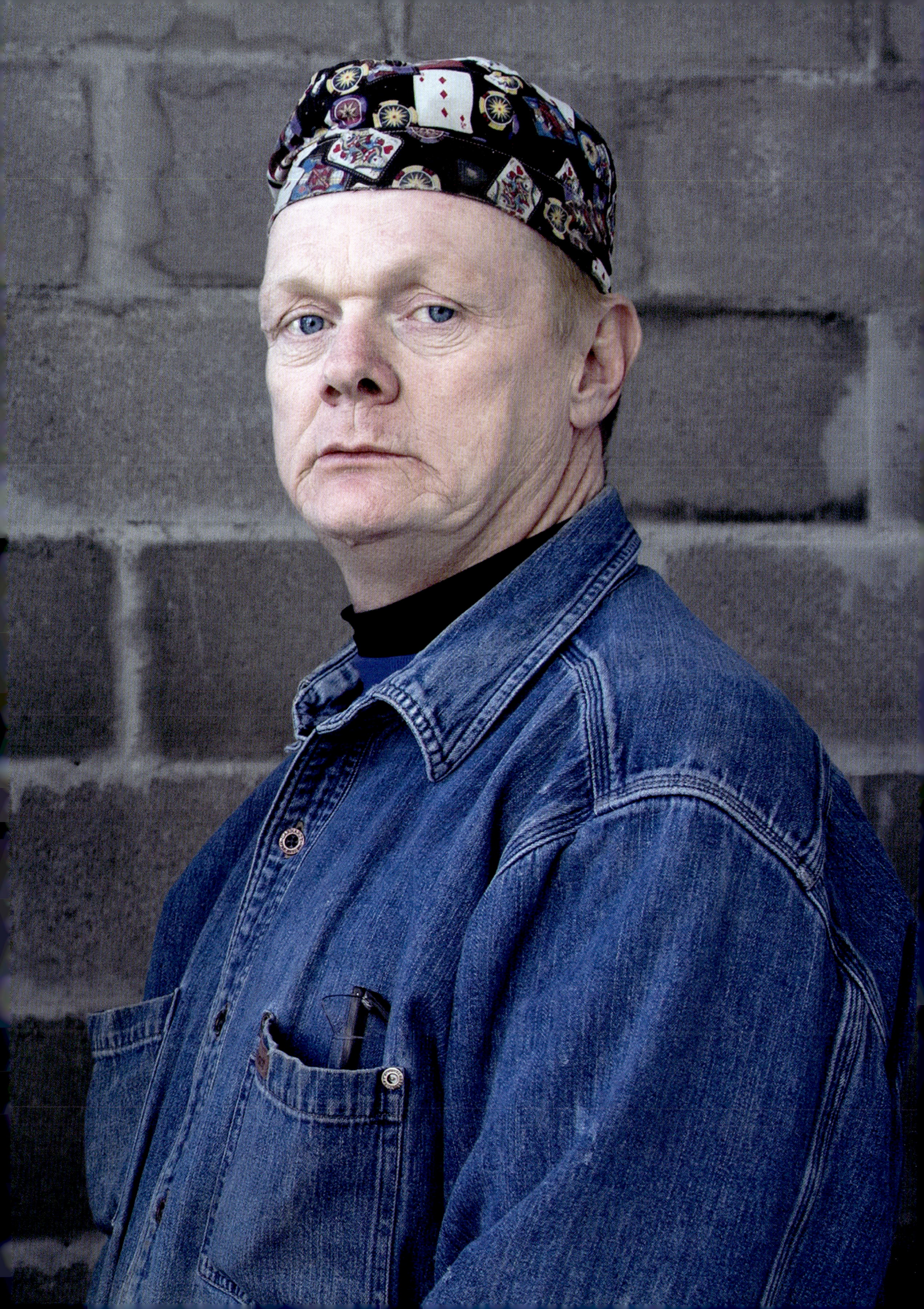

                          ND
Who is Jimmy Buckles?

                          MB
Buckles is notorious. He's the guy who got into trouble
with the electricians.

                          ND
So they are writing "Jimmy Buckles" on everything; how do
you get into trouble with electricians?

                          MB
They are ribbing him... he doesn't respect the trade. If
your name is written all over the walls, it's not good.

                          JF
It has nothing to do with the electricians. He walks
around with an attitude, like he can't get laid off. So
everyone comes down on him.

                          MB
Ok, well, that's only what I heard. I don't know Buckles
personally.

                          JF
He has no skills, he stands around looking at other guys
working.

                          TZ
No, no, it's about a football pool. He tried to beat the
pool.

                          VS
No, that's not right. He buckled.

                          TZ
Meaning?

                          VS
One guy claimed a box and Buckles gave his word. A minute
later, he gave the box away... to the foreman.

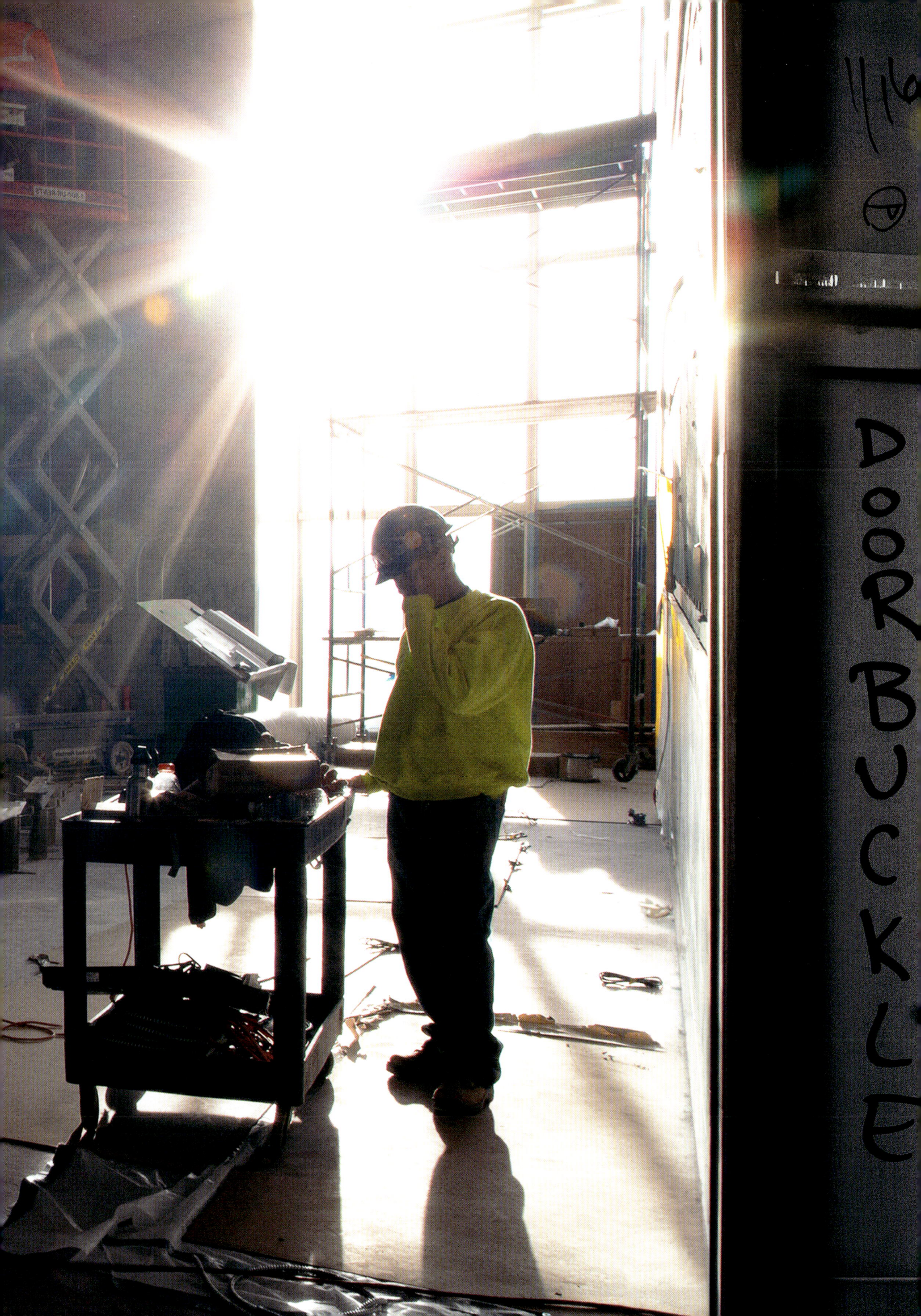
11/16
DOOR
BUCKLE

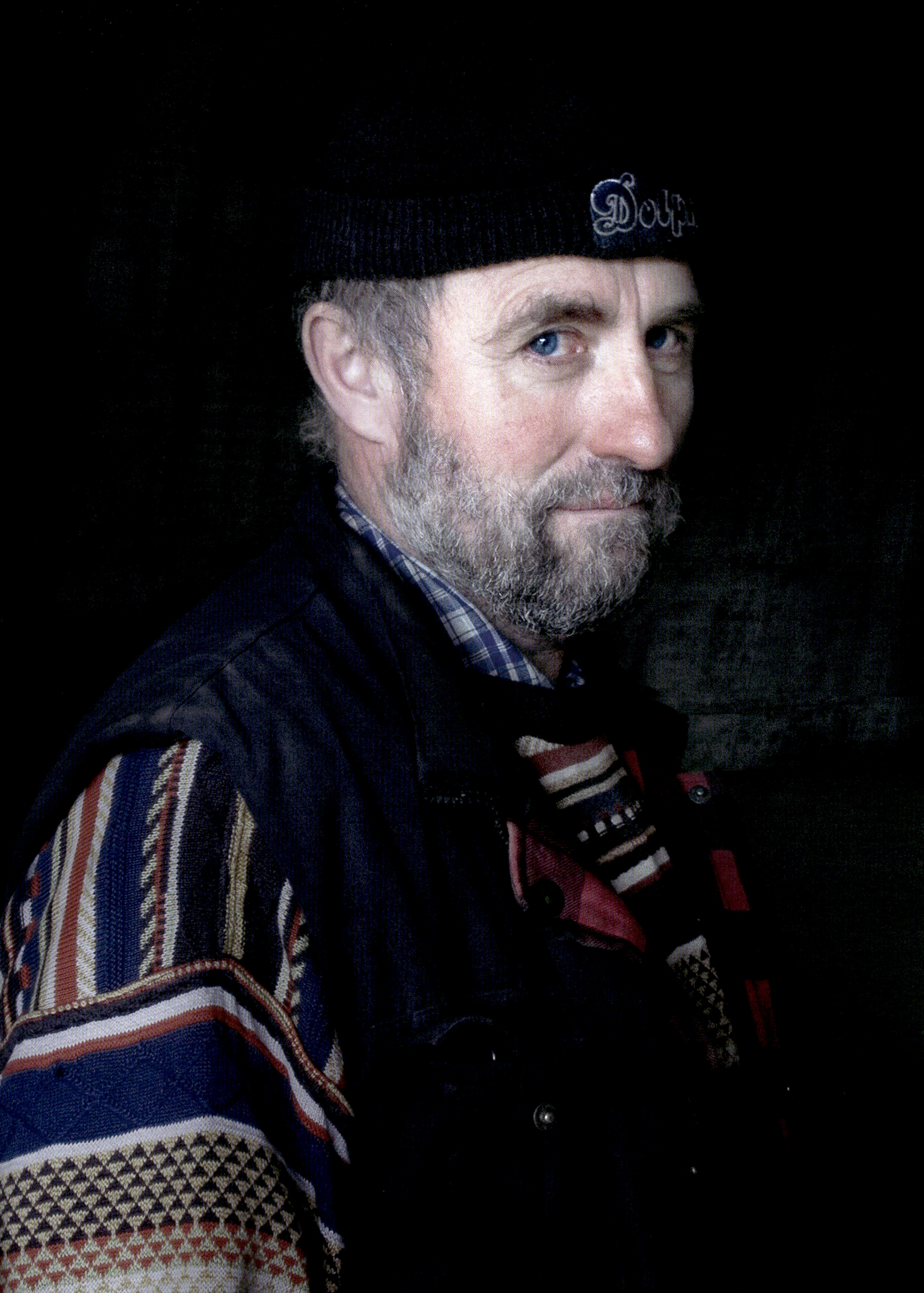

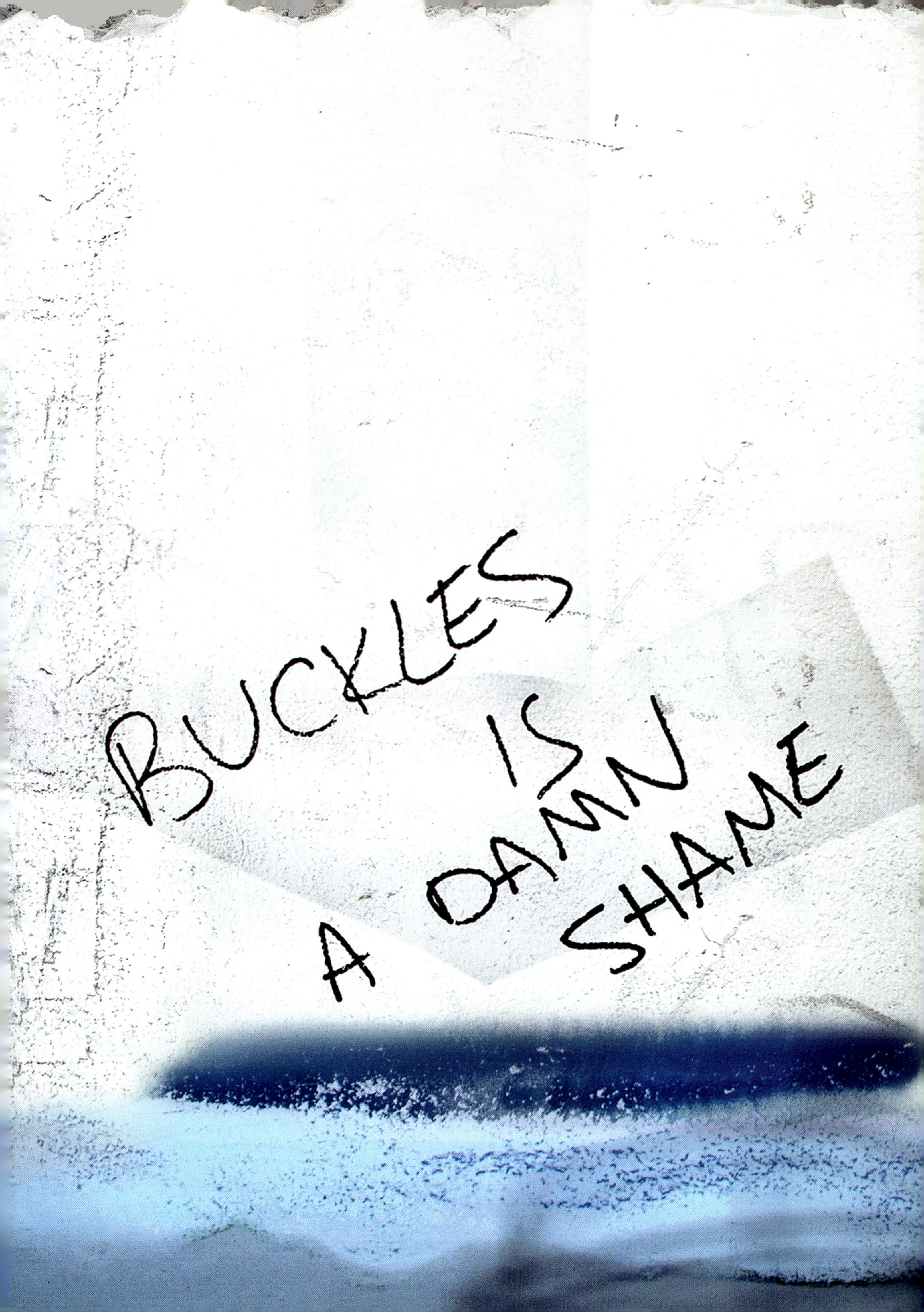

BUCKLES
IS
A DAMN
SHAME

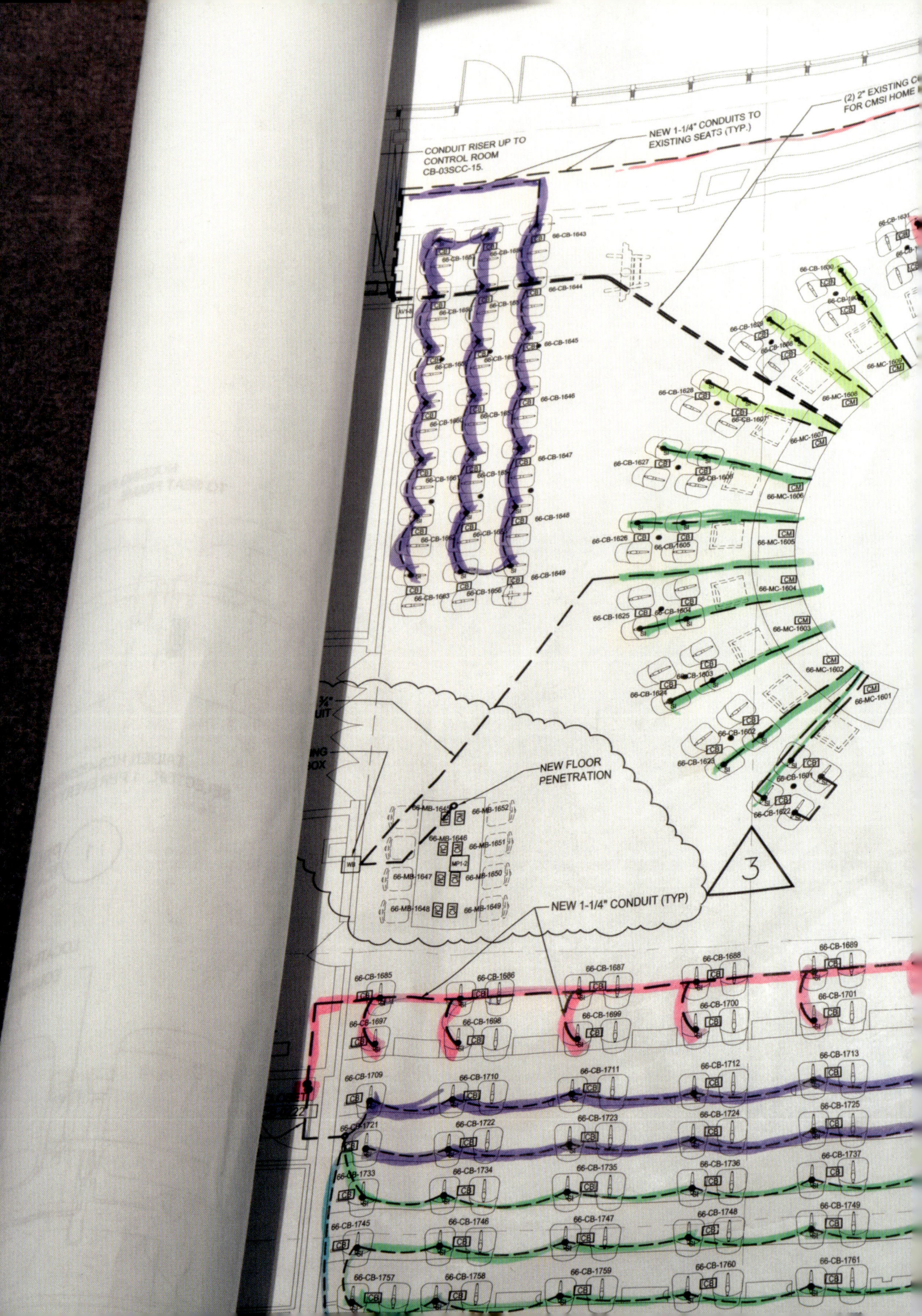

(2) 2" EXISTING C
FOR CMSI HOME
NEW 1-1/4" CONDUITS TO
EXISTING SEATS (TYP.)
CONDUIT RISER UP TO
CONTROL ROOM
CB-03SCC-15.
66-CB-1651
66-CB-1643
66-CB-1644
66-CB-1645
66-CB-1646
66-CB-1647
66-CB-1648
66-CB-1649
66-CB-1683
66-CB-1656
66-CB-1631
66-CB-1630
66-CB-1629
66-CB-1628
66-CB-1627
66-CB-1626
66-CB-1625
66-CB-1624
66-CB-1623
66-CB-1622
66-CB-1621
66-CB-1609
66-CB-1608
66-CB-1607
66-CB-1606
66-CB-1605
66-CB-1604
66-CB-1603
66-CB-1602
66-CB-1601
66-MC-1609
66-MC-1608
66-MC-1607
66-MC-1606
66-MC-1605
66-MC-1604
66-MC-1603
66-MC-1602
66-MC-1601
NEW FLOOR
PENETRATION
66-MB-1645
66-MB-1646
66-MB-1647
66-MB-1648
66-MB-1652
66-MB-1651
66-MB-1650
66-MB-1649
MP1-2
W8
NEW 1-1/4" CONDUIT (TYP)
3
66-CB-1685
66-CB-1686
66-CB-1687
66-CB-1688
66-CB-1689
66-CB-1697
66-CB-1698
66-CB-1699
66-CB-1700
66-CB-1701
66-CB-1709
66-CB-1710
66-CB-1711
66-CB-1712
66-CB-1713
66-CB-1721
66-CB-1722
66-CB-1723
66-CB-1724
66-CB-1725
66-CB-1733
66-CB-1734
66-CB-1735
66-CB-1736
66-CB-1737
66-CB-1745
66-CB-1746
66-CB-1747
66-CB-1748
66-CB-1749
66-CB-1757
66-CB-1758
66-CB-1759
66-CB-1760
66-CB-1761

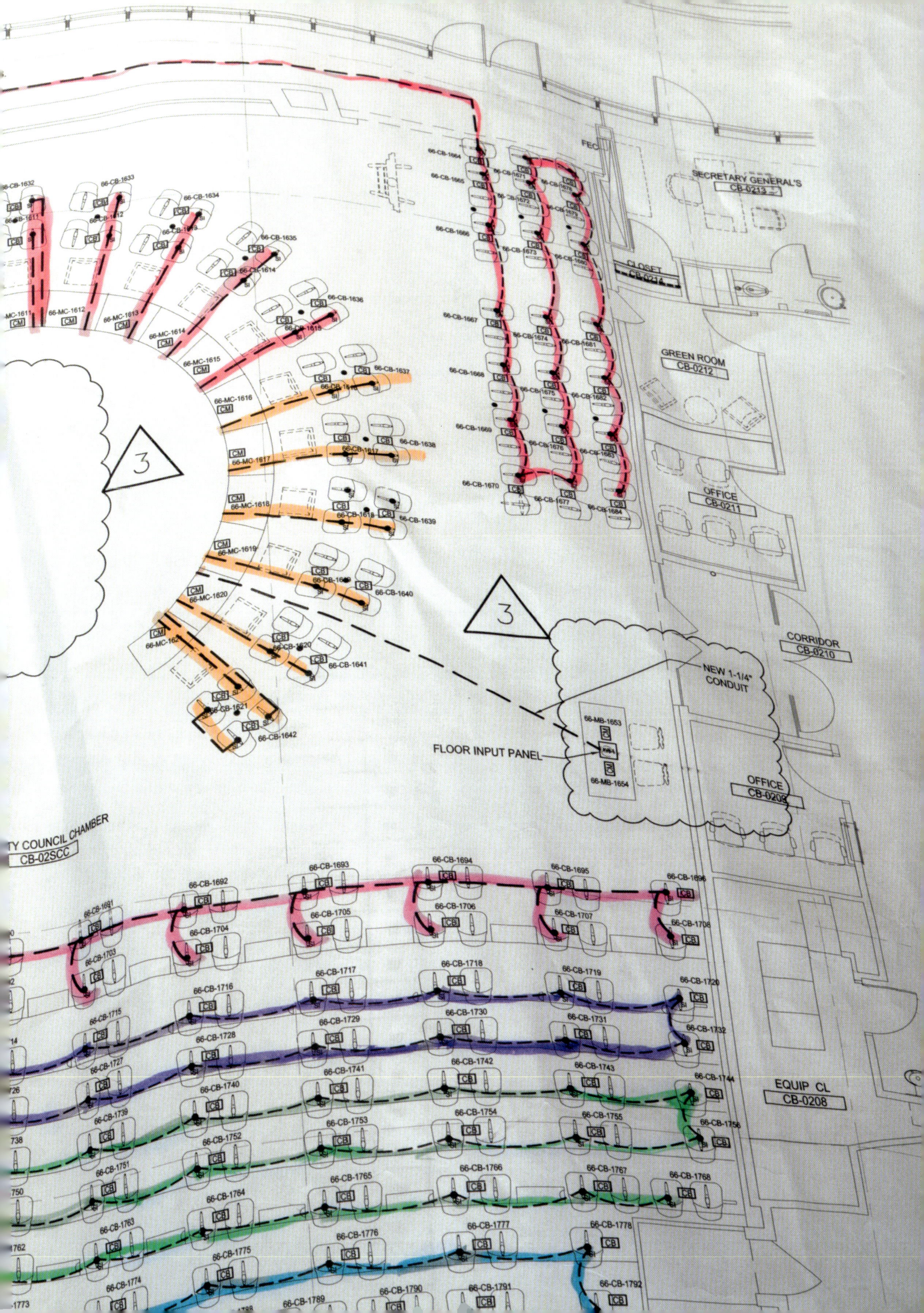

66-CB-1632
66-CB-1633
66-CB-1634
66-CB-1635
66-CB-1636
66-CB-1637
66-CB-1638
66-CB-1639
66-CB-1640
66-CB-1641
66-CB-1642
66-CB-1611
66-CB-1612
66-CB-1613
66-CB-1614
66-CB-1615
66-CB-1616
66-CB-1617
66-CB-1618
66-CB-1619
66-CB-1620
66-CB-1621
66-MC-1611
66-MC-1612
66-MC-1613
66-MC-1614
66-MC-1615
66-MC-1616
66-MC-1617
66-MC-1618
66-MC-1619
66-MC-1620
66-MC-1621
CM
CB
3
66-CB-1664
66-CB-1665
66-CB-1666
66-CB-1667
66-CB-1668
66-CB-1669
66-CB-1670
66-CB-1671
66-CB-1672
66-CB-1673
66-CB-1674
66-CB-1675
66-CB-1676
66-CB-1677
66-CB-1678
66-CB-1679
66-CB-1681
66-CB-1682
66-CB-1683
66-CB-1684
FEC
SECRETARY GENERAL'S
CB-0213
CLOSET
CB-0214
GREEN ROOM
CB-0212
OFFICE
CB-0211
CORRIDOR
CB-0210
NEW 1-1/4"
CONDUIT
66-MB-1653
66-MB-1654
FLOOR INPUT PANEL
OFFICE
CB-0209
CITY COUNCIL CHAMBER
CB-02SCC
66-CB-1691
66-CB-1692
66-CB-1693
66-CB-1694
66-CB-1695
66-CB-1696
66-CB-1703
66-CB-1704
66-CB-1705
66-CB-1706
66-CB-1707
66-CB-1708
66-CB-1715
66-CB-1716
66-CB-1717
66-CB-1718
66-CB-1719
66-CB-1720
66-CB-1727
66-CB-1728
66-CB-1729
66-CB-1730
66-CB-1731
66-CB-1732
66-CB-1739
66-CB-1740
66-CB-1741
66-CB-1742
66-CB-1743
66-CB-1744
EQUIP CL
CB-0208
66-CB-1751
66-CB-1752
66-CB-1753
66-CB-1754
66-CB-1755
66-CB-1756
66-CB-1763
66-CB-1764
66-CB-1765
66-CB-1766
66-CB-1767
66-CB-1768
66-CB-1773
66-CB-1774
66-CB-1775
66-CB-1776
66-CB-1777
66-CB-1778
66-CB-1789
66-CB-1790
66-CB-1791
66-CB-1792
3
CB

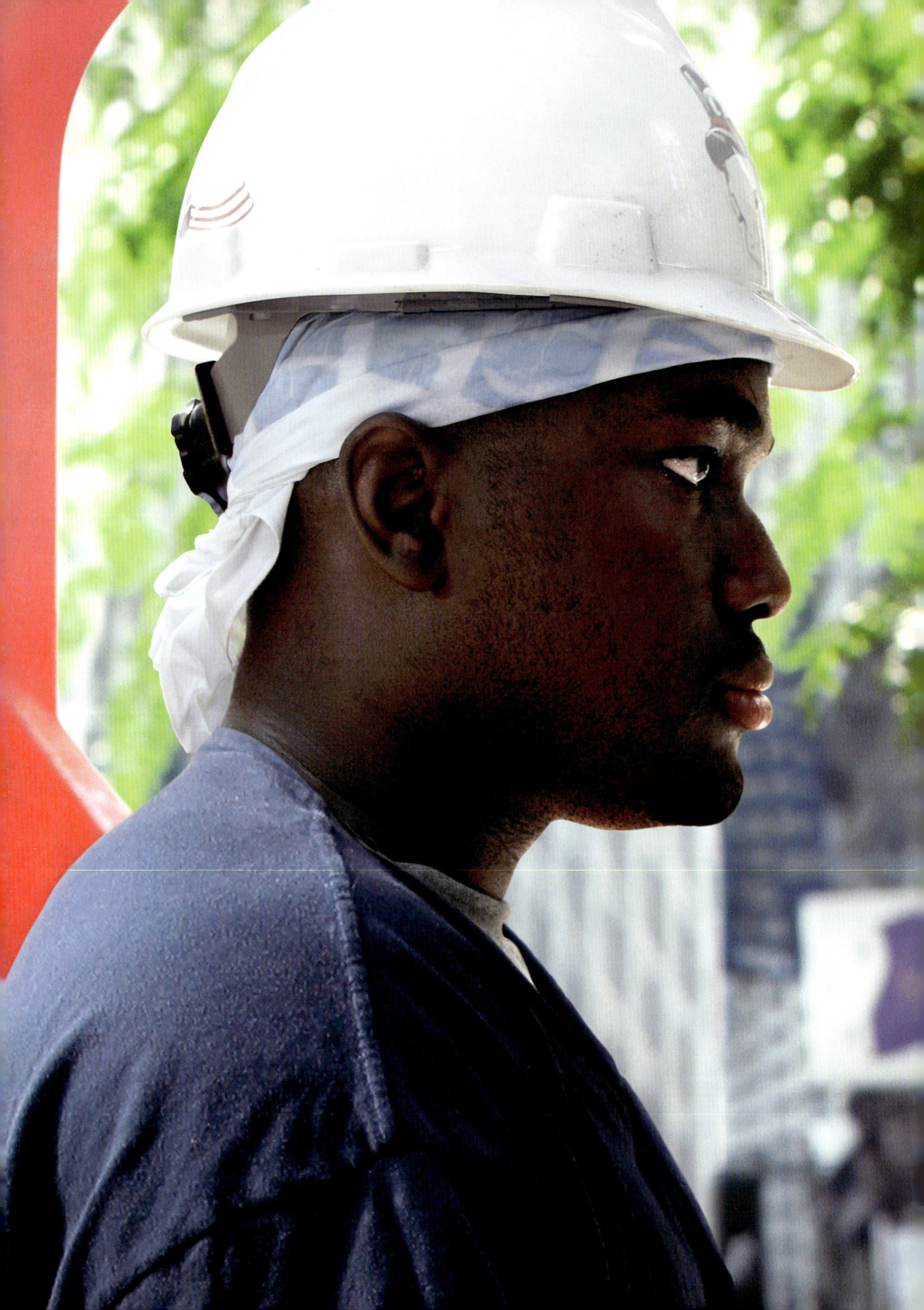

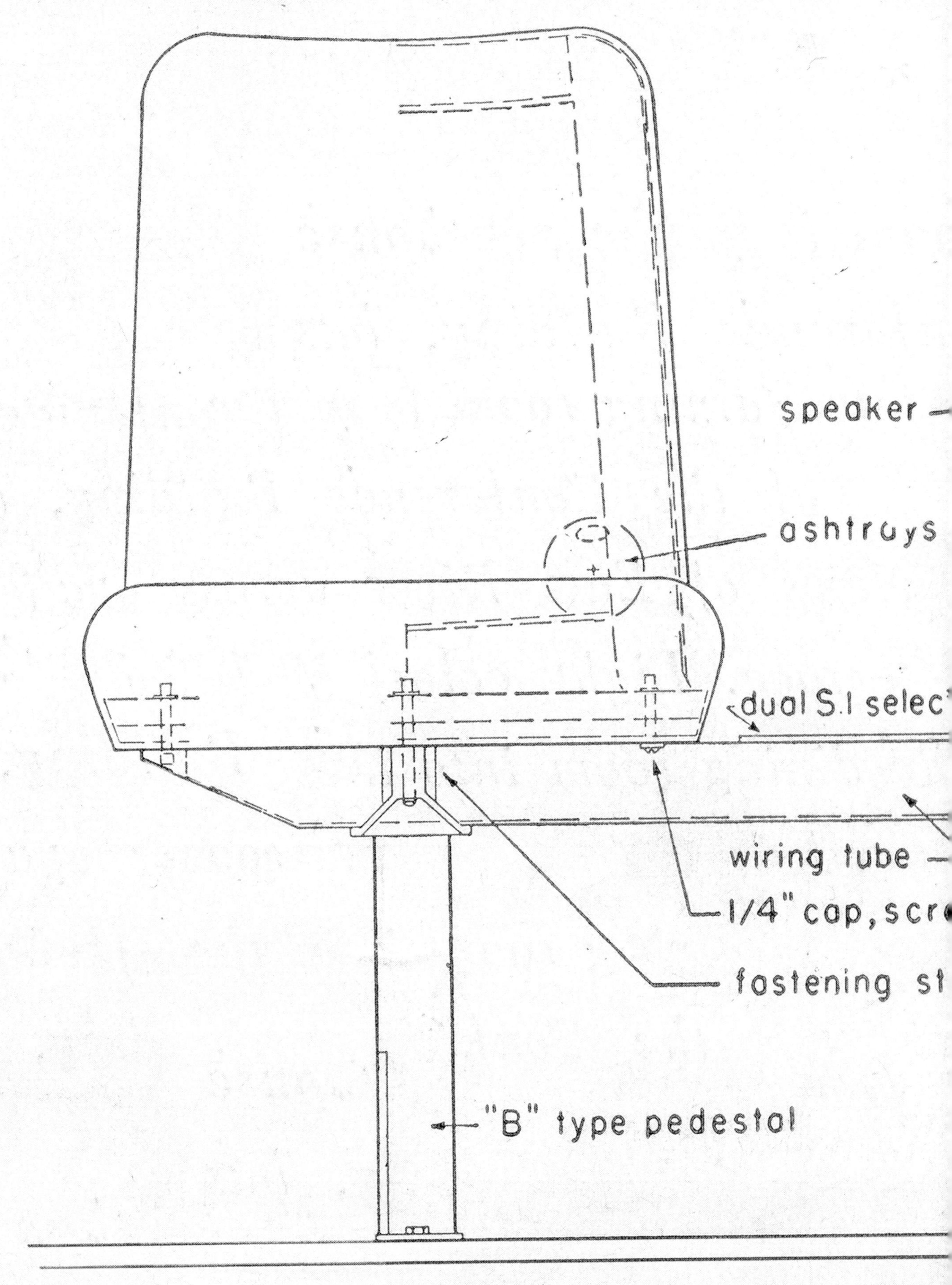

speaker
ashtrays
dual S.I selec
wiring tube
1/4" cap, scre
fastening st
"B" type pedestal

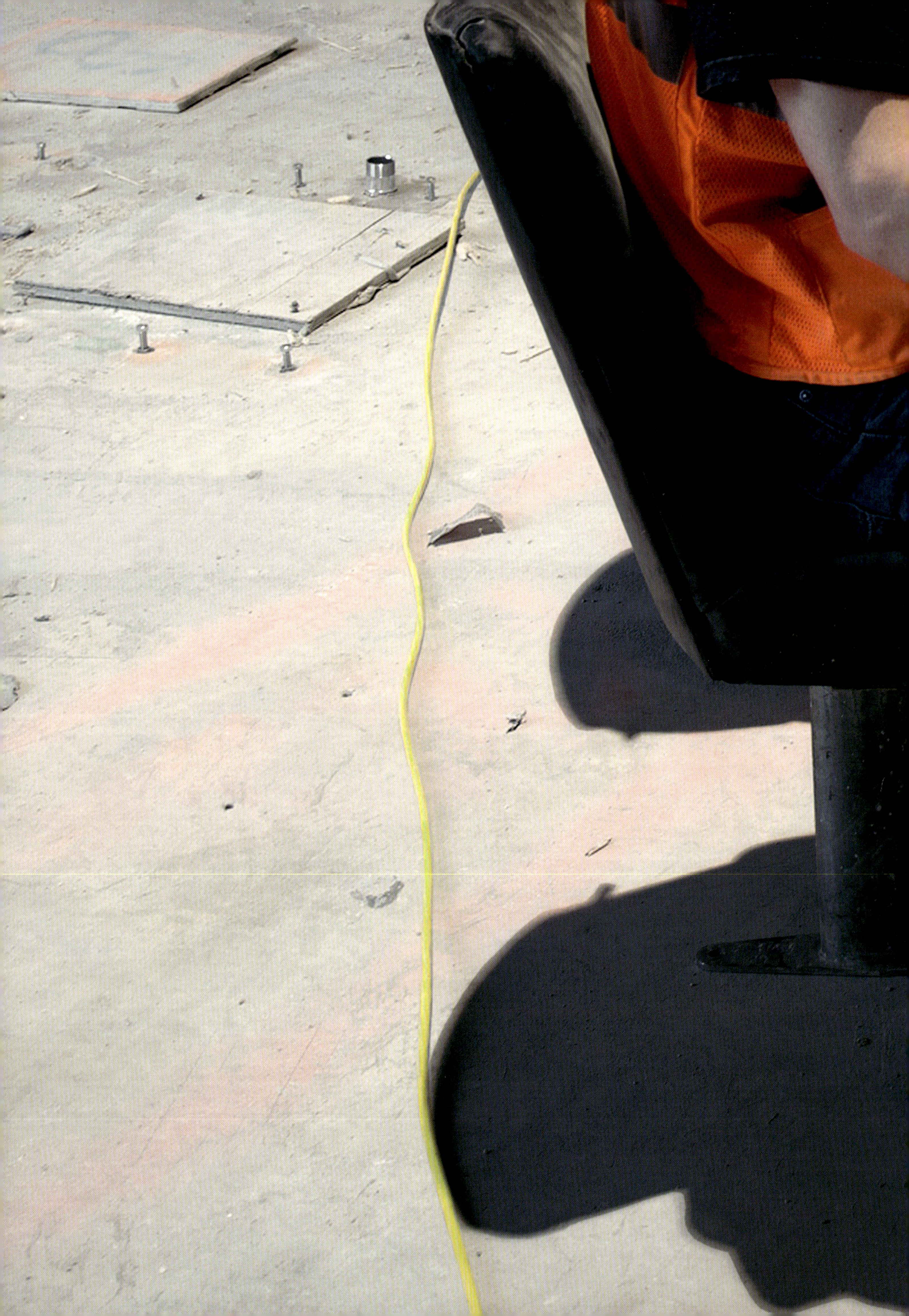

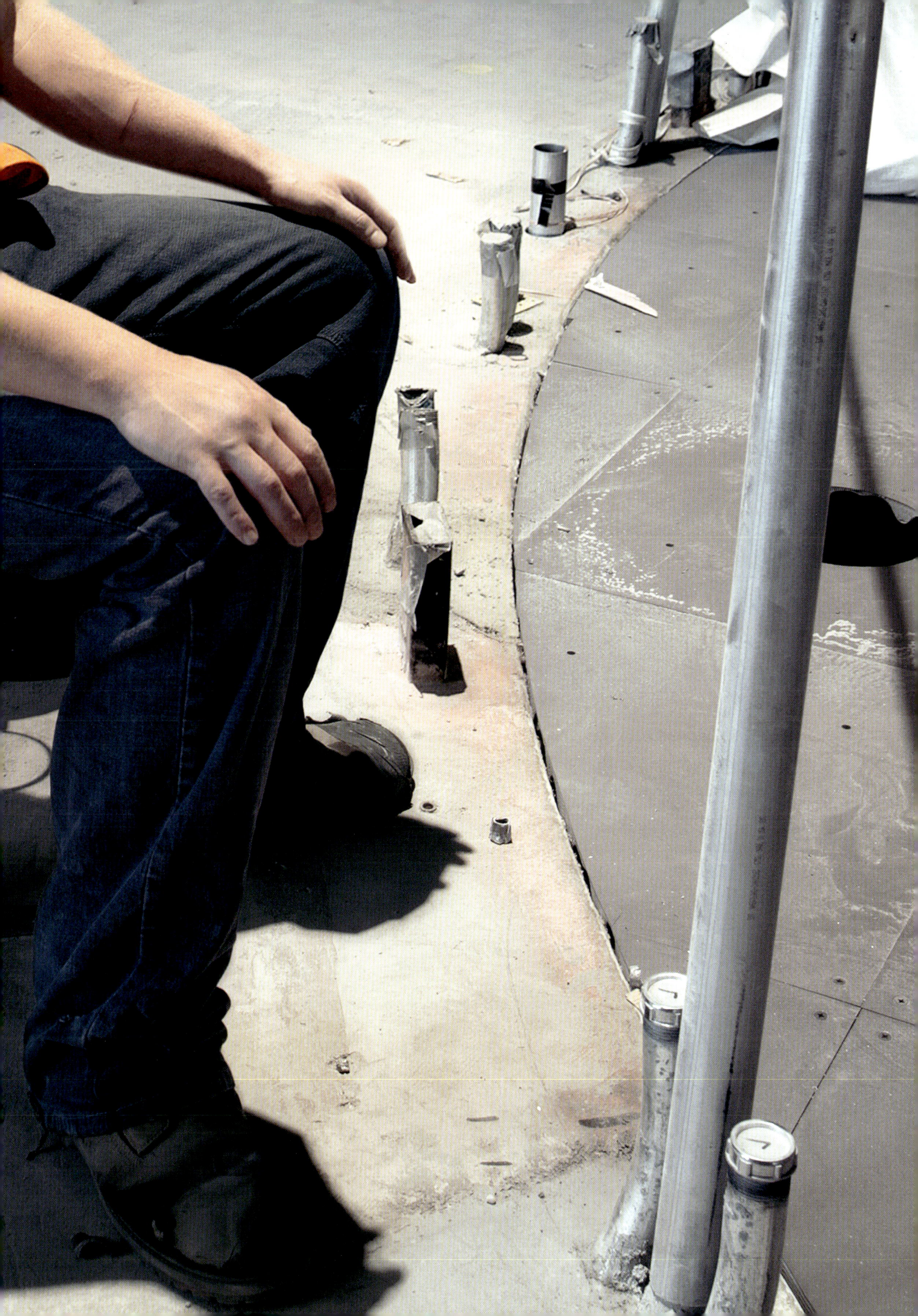

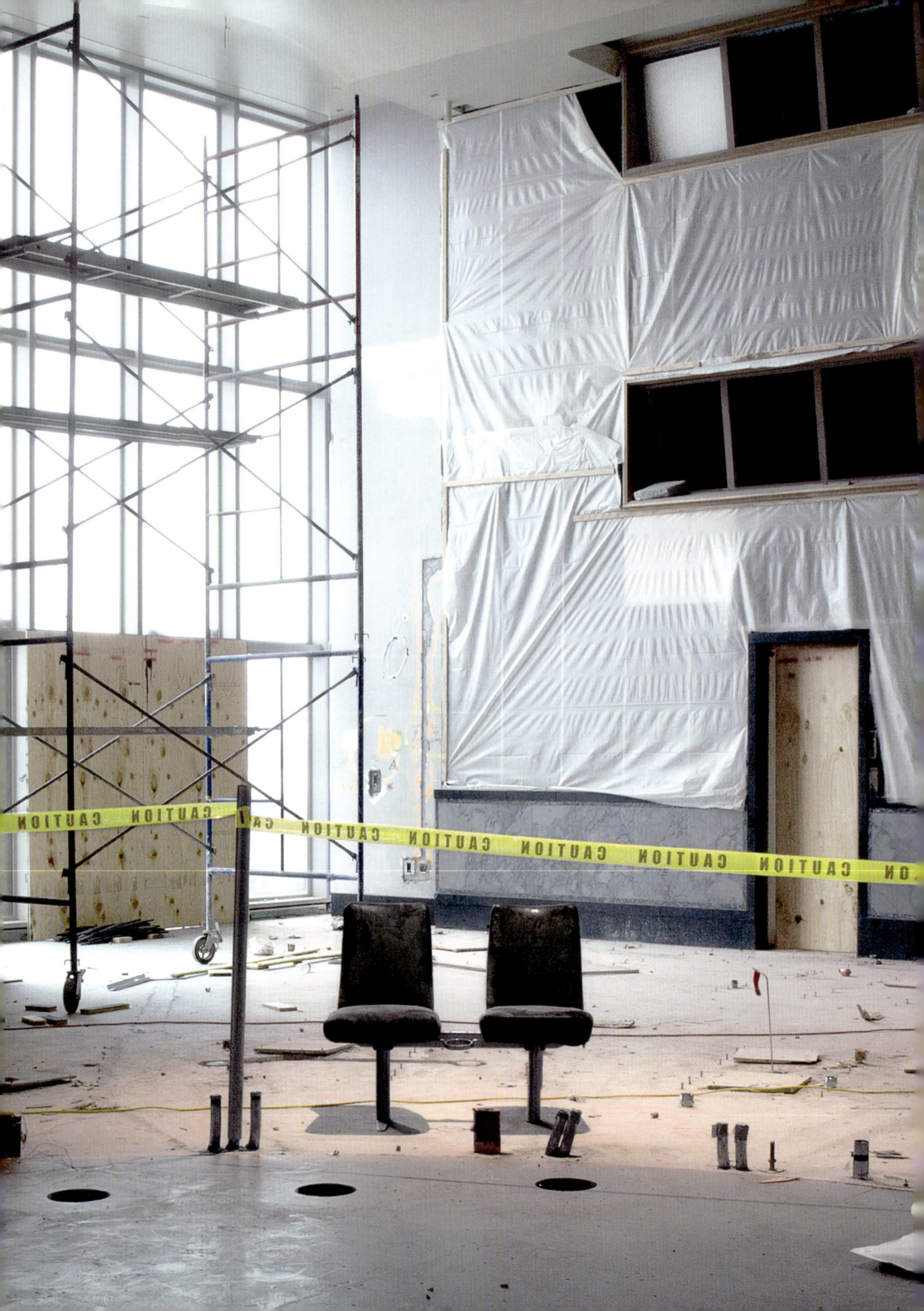
CAUTION CAUTION CAUTION CAUTION CAUTION CAUTION

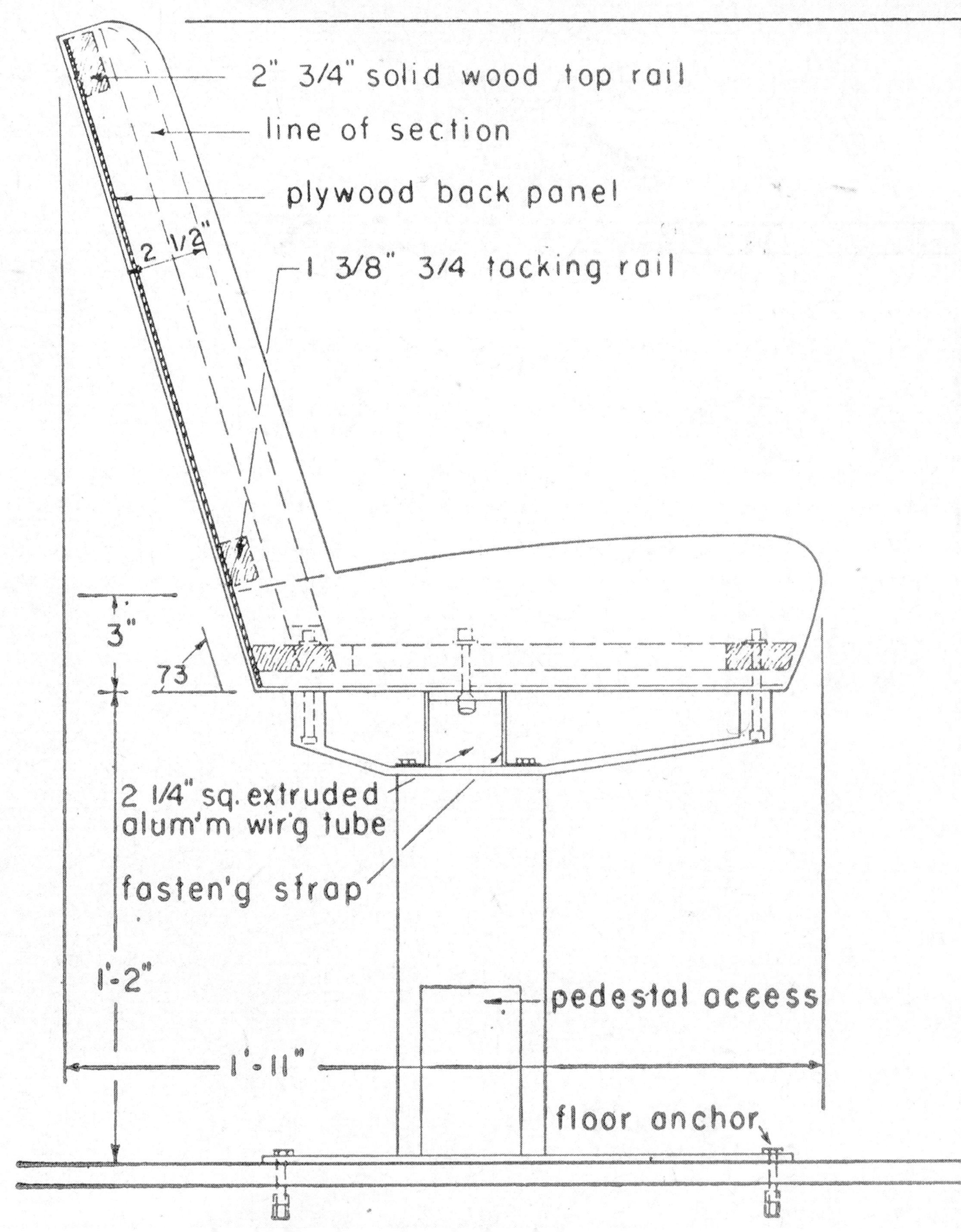

2" 3/4" solid wood top rail
line of section
plywood back panel
1 3/8" 3/4 tacking rail
2 1/2"
3"
73
2 1/4" sq. extruded alum'm wir'g tube
fasten'g strap
1'-2"
1'-11"
pedestal access
floor anchor

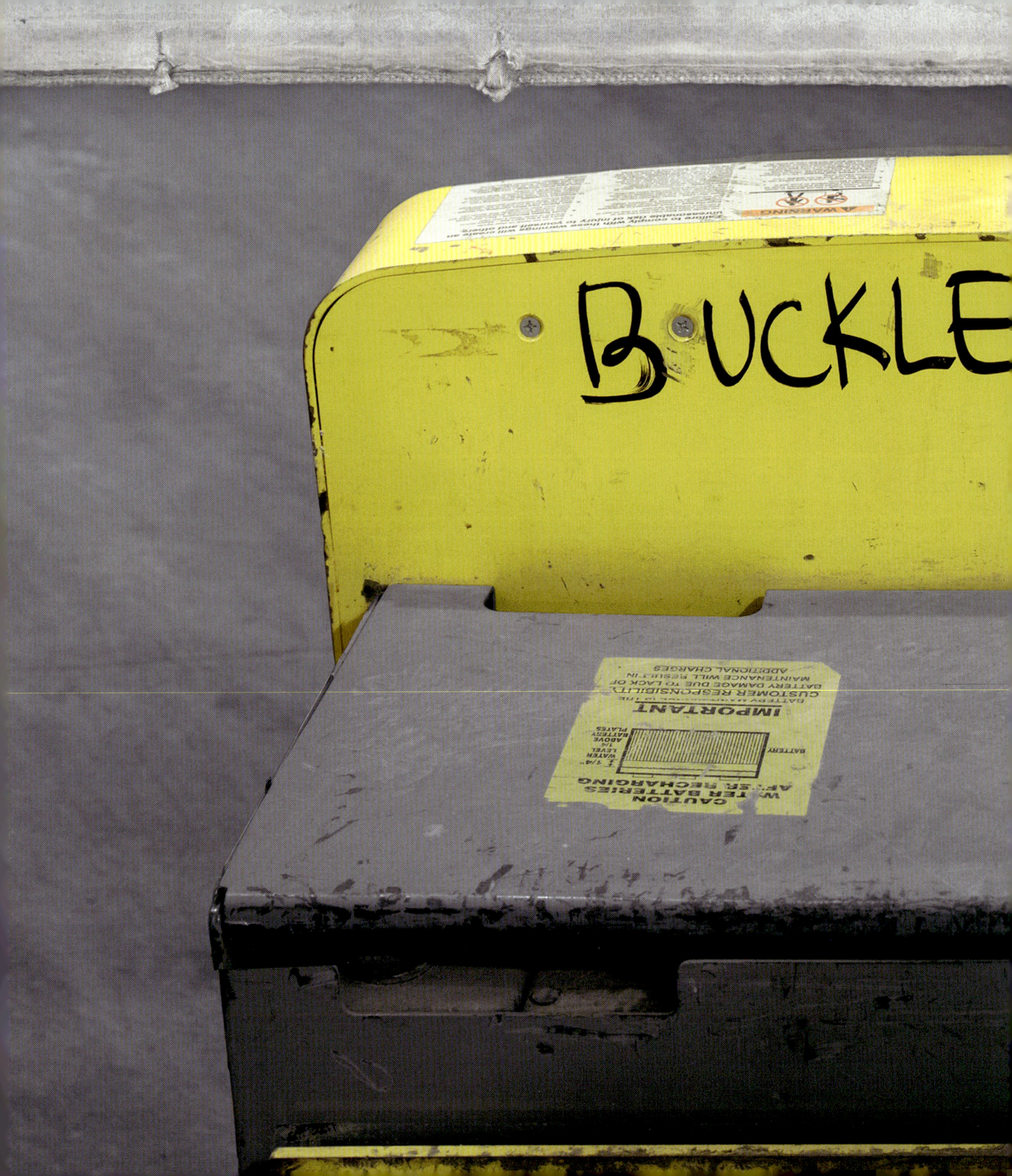

BUCKLE

CAUTION
WATER BATTERIES
AFTER RECHARGING

IMPORTANT
CUSTOMER RESPONSIBILITY.
BATTERY DAMAGE DUE TO LACK OF
MAINTENANCE WILL RESULT IN
ADDITIONAL CHARGES.

WATER
LEVEL
ABOVE
BATTERY
PLATES

MOBILE
Please Read!
1) Battery Must Be Charged A Minimum Of 8 Hour
(1 hour phone/message/etc)
2) Check Battery Water After Every Charge
(water must be above plates & below ...)
3) Plug Charger Into Battery (Not Machine)
4) Be Sure Your Electrical Supply Remains On After
Work Hours !
THANK YOU!

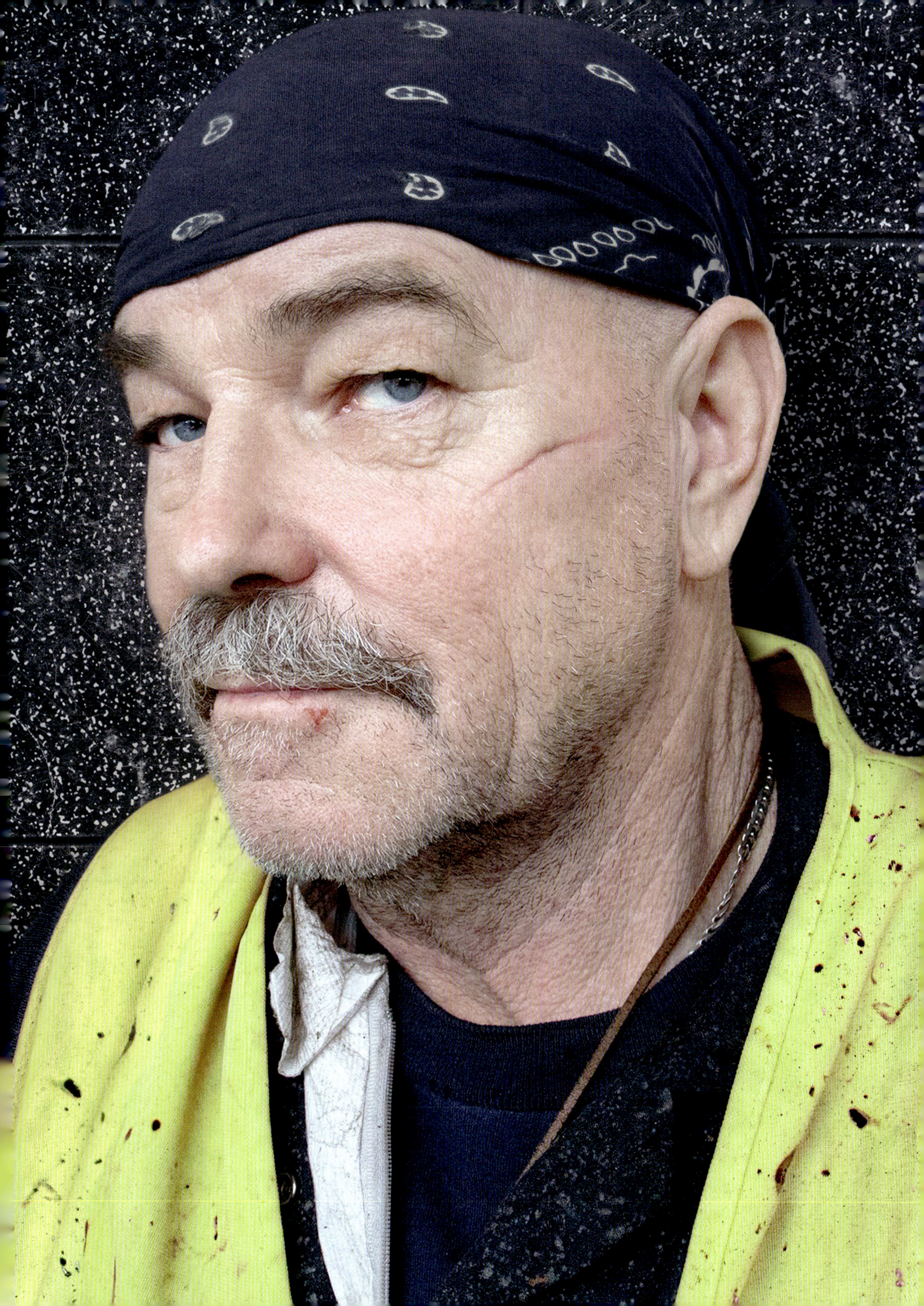

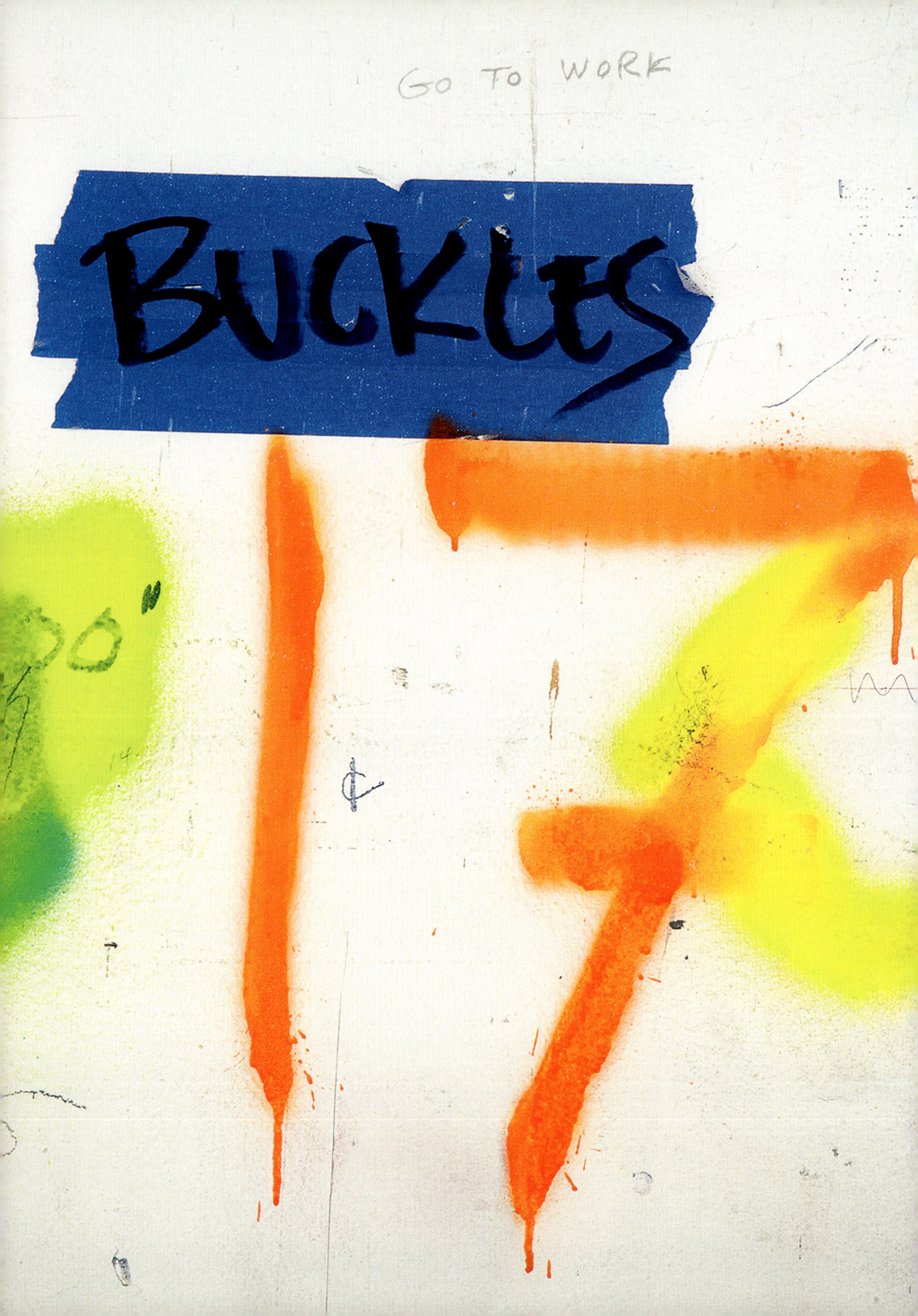

GO TO WORK

BUCKLES

17

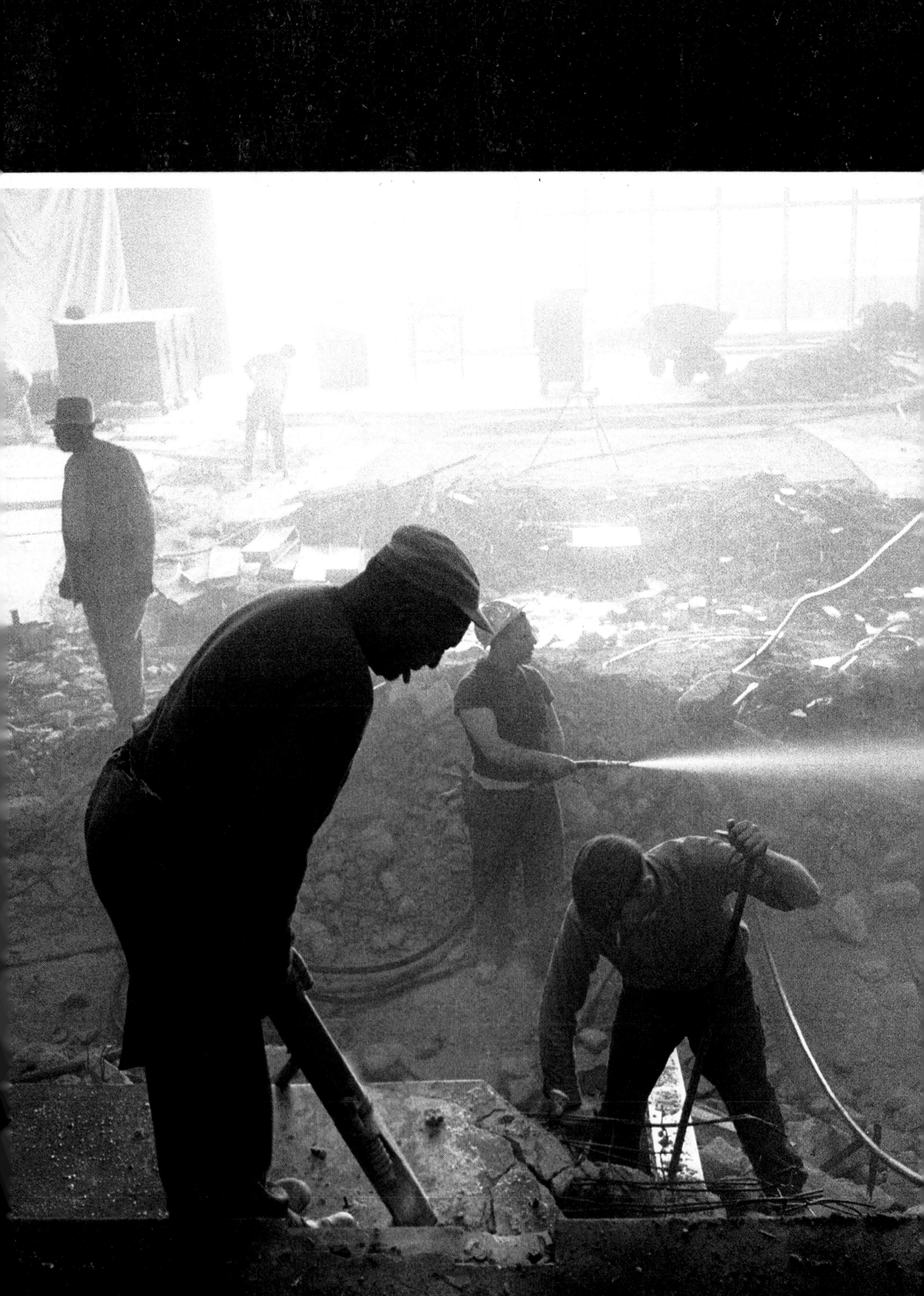

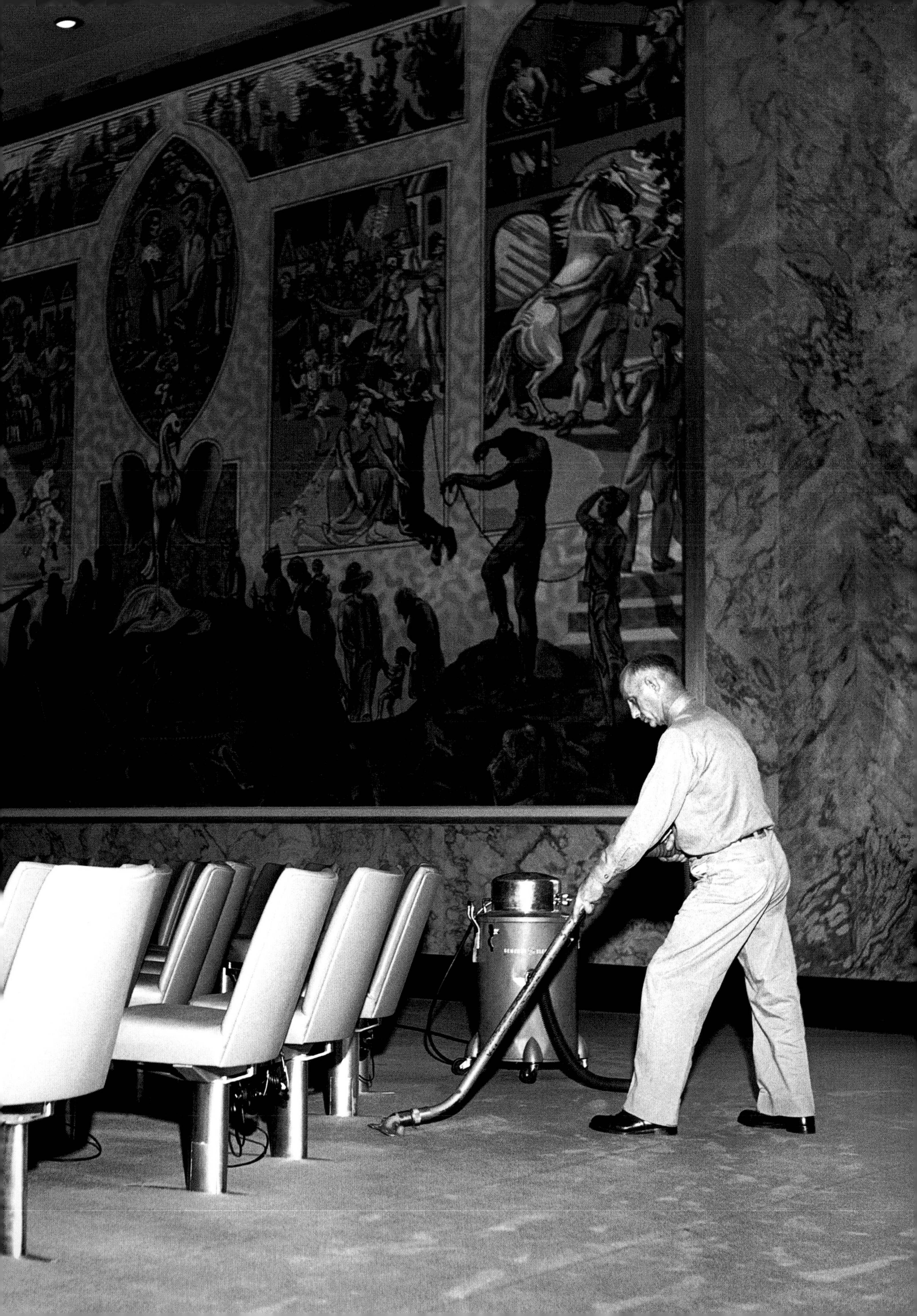

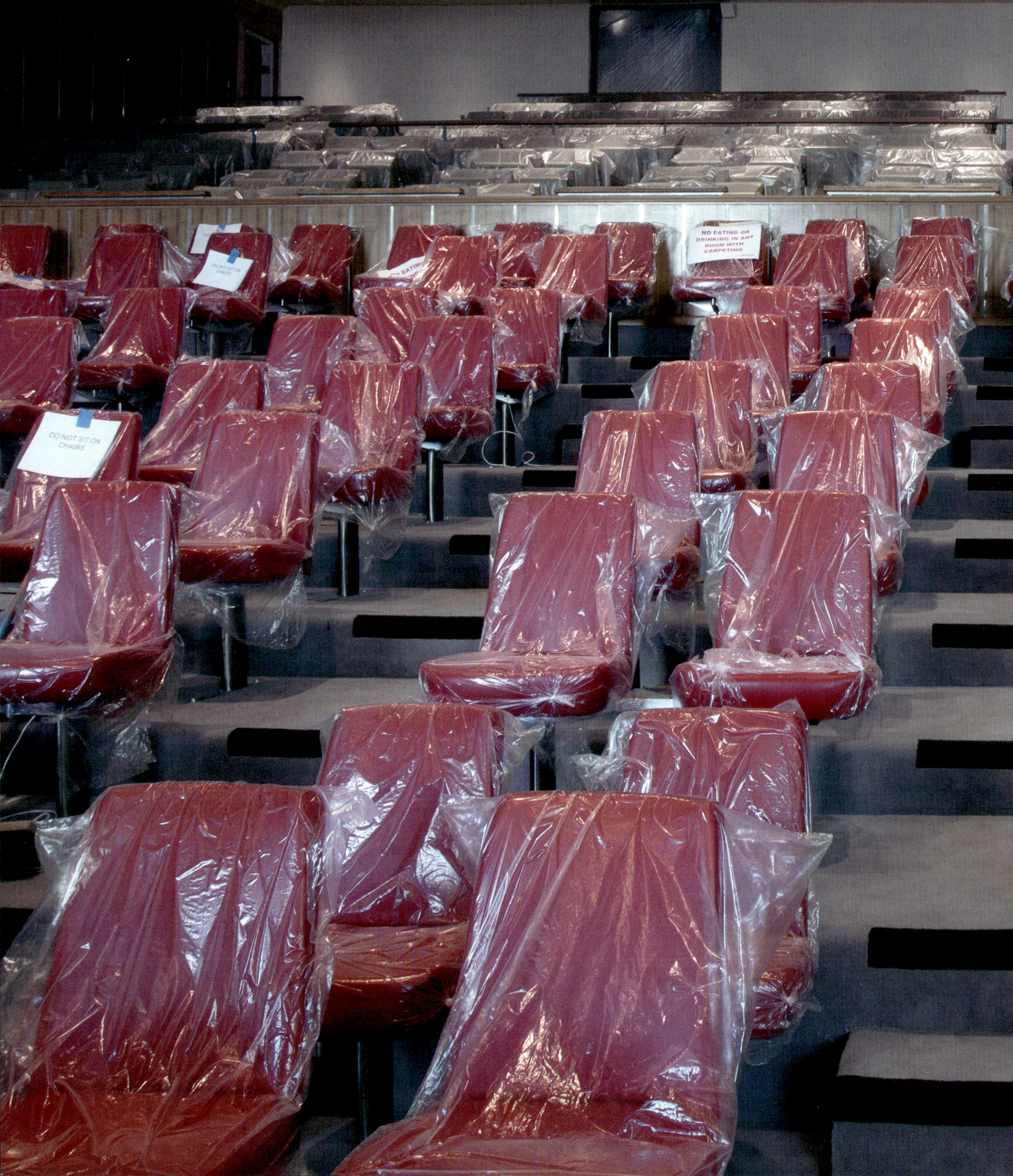

DO NOT SIT ON CHAIRS
NO EATING OR DRINKING IN ANY ROOM WITH CARPETING

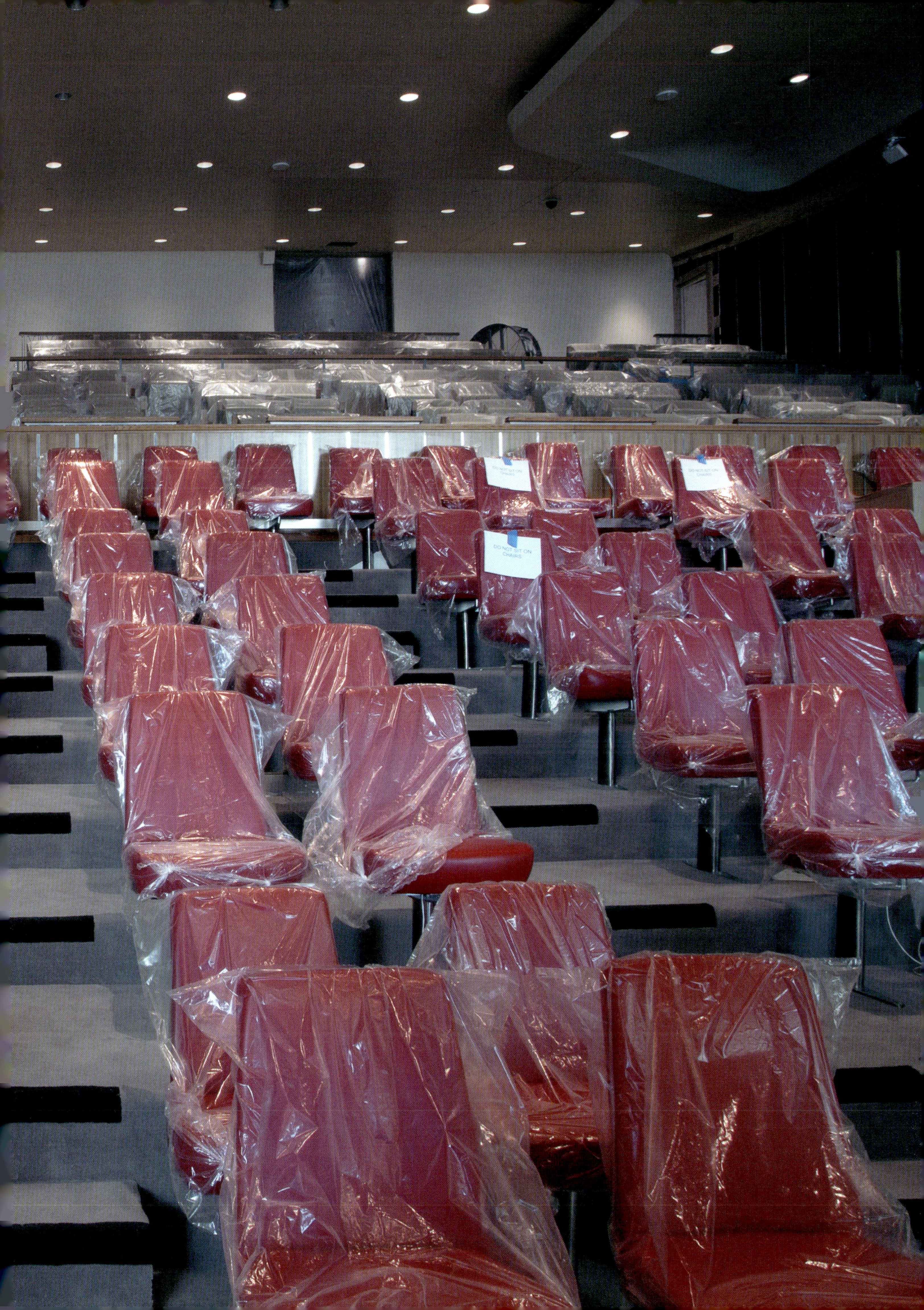
DO NOT SIT ON
CHAIRS
DO NOT SIT ON
CHAIRS
DO NOT SIT ON
CHAIRS

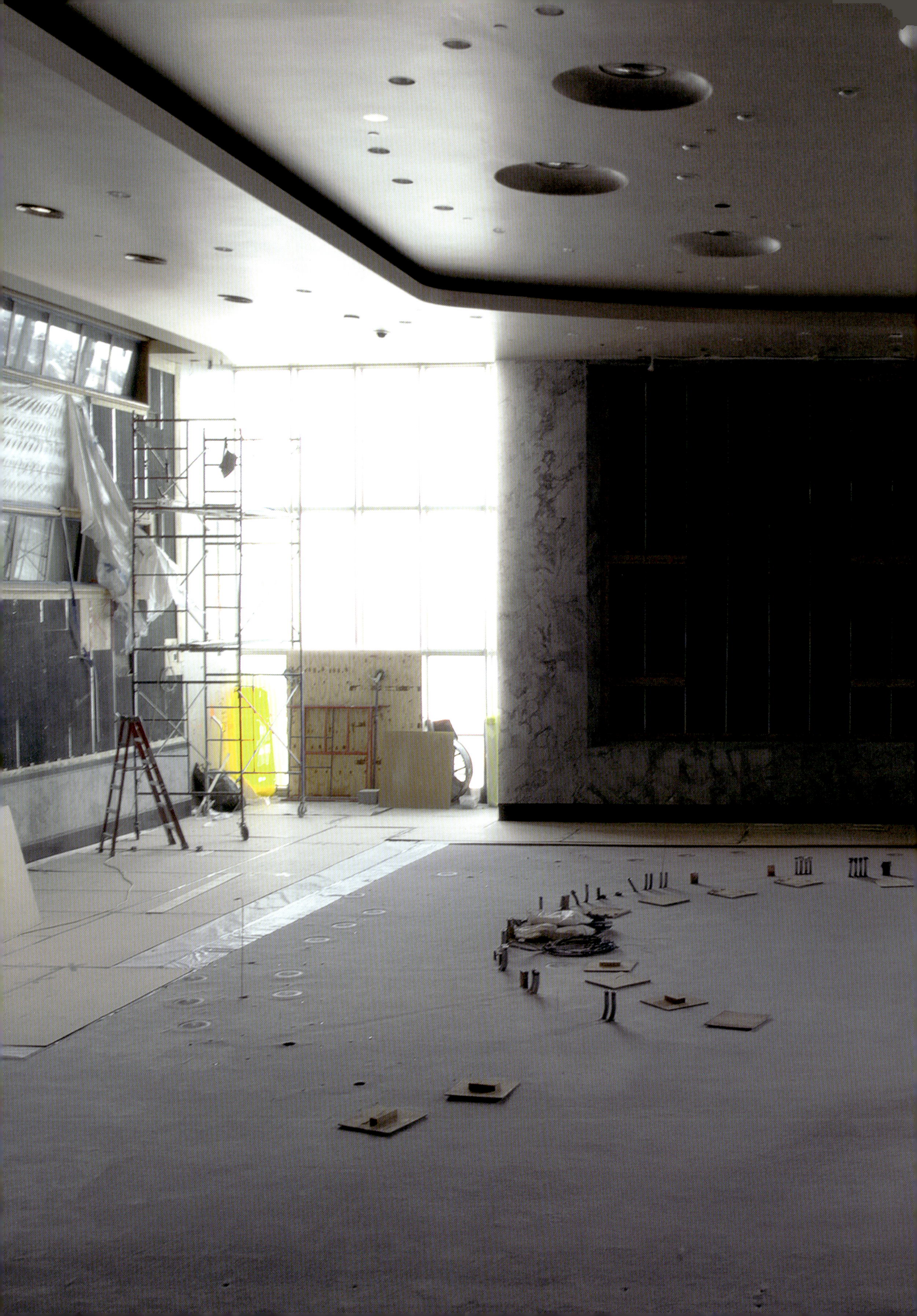

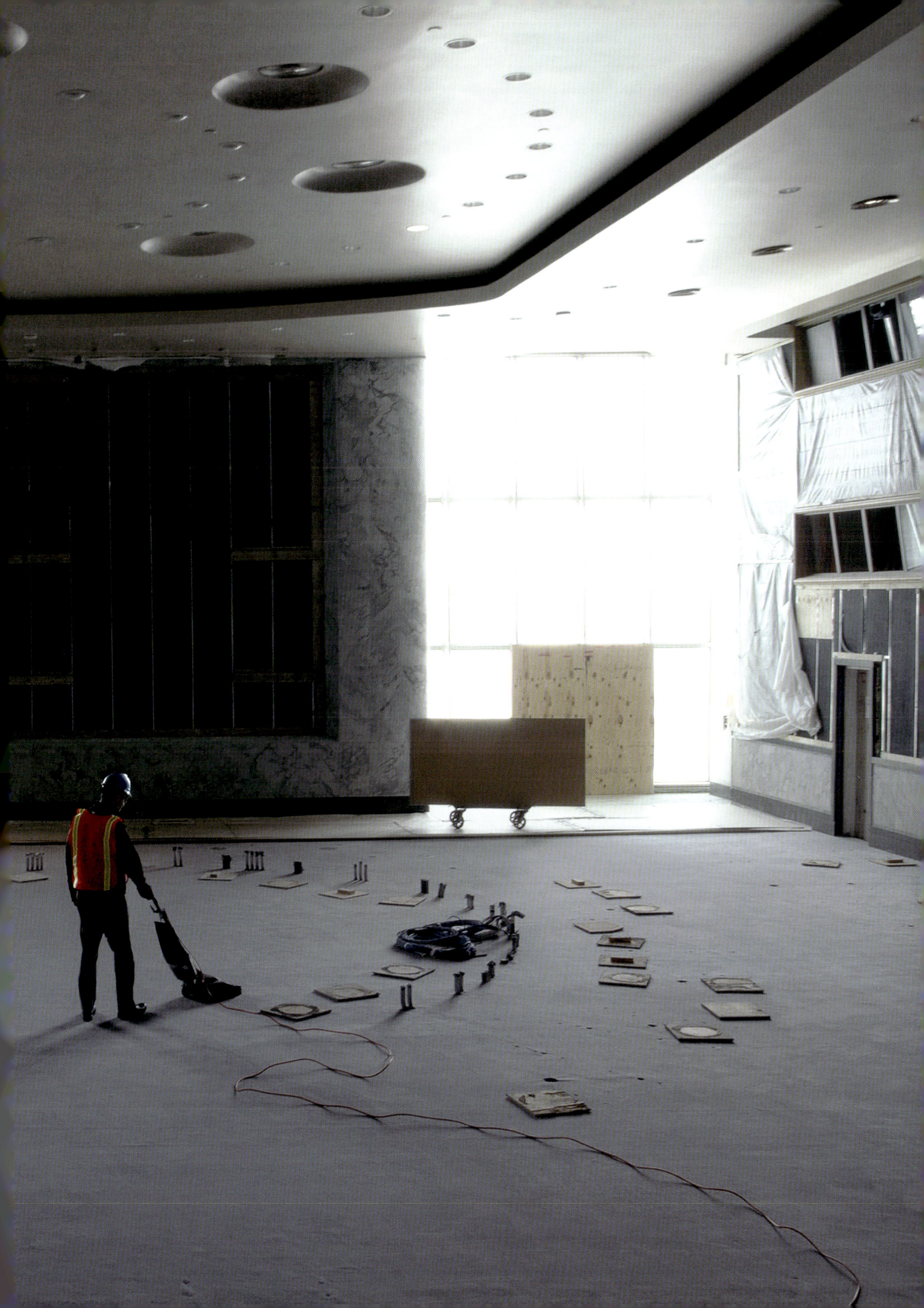

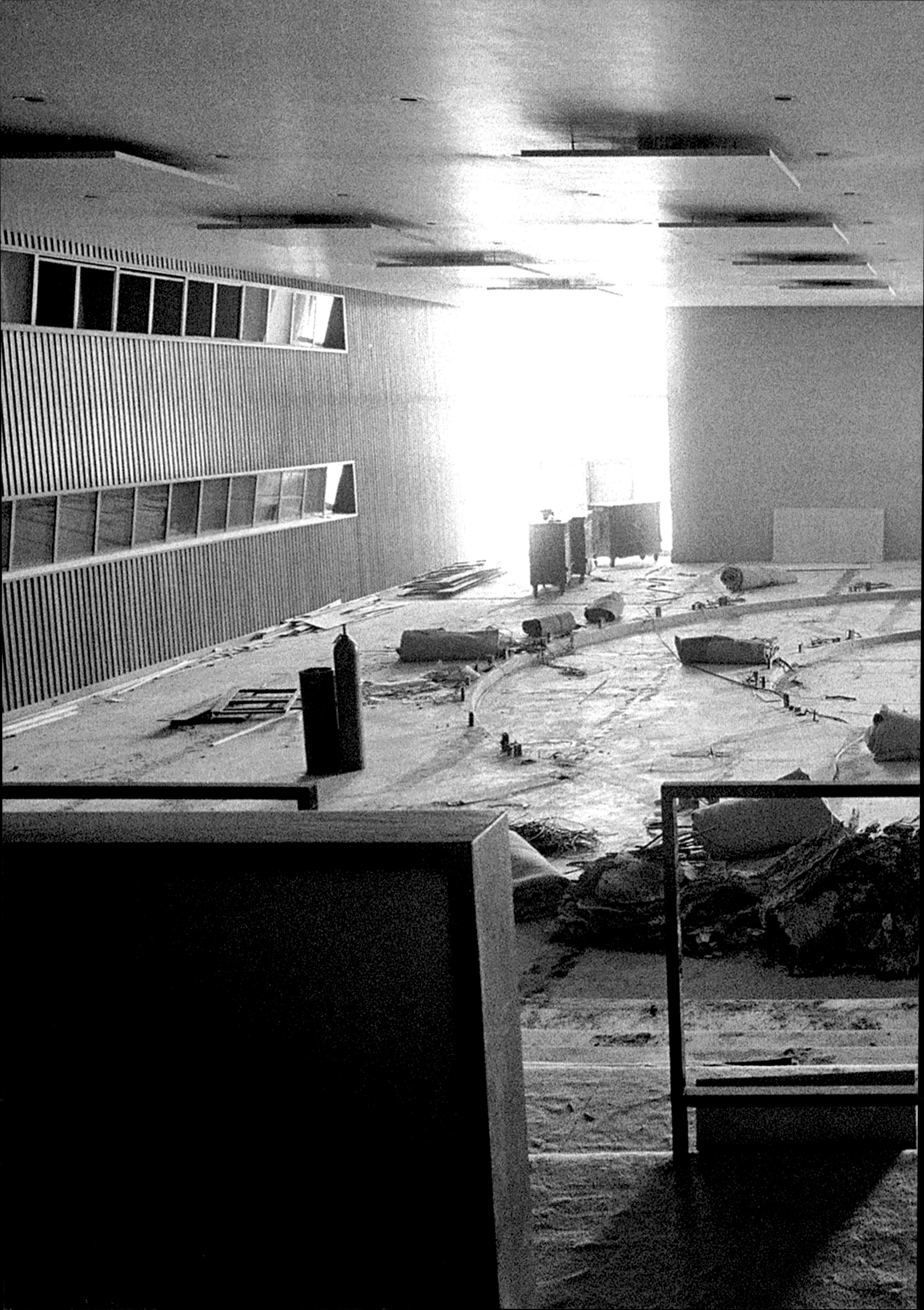

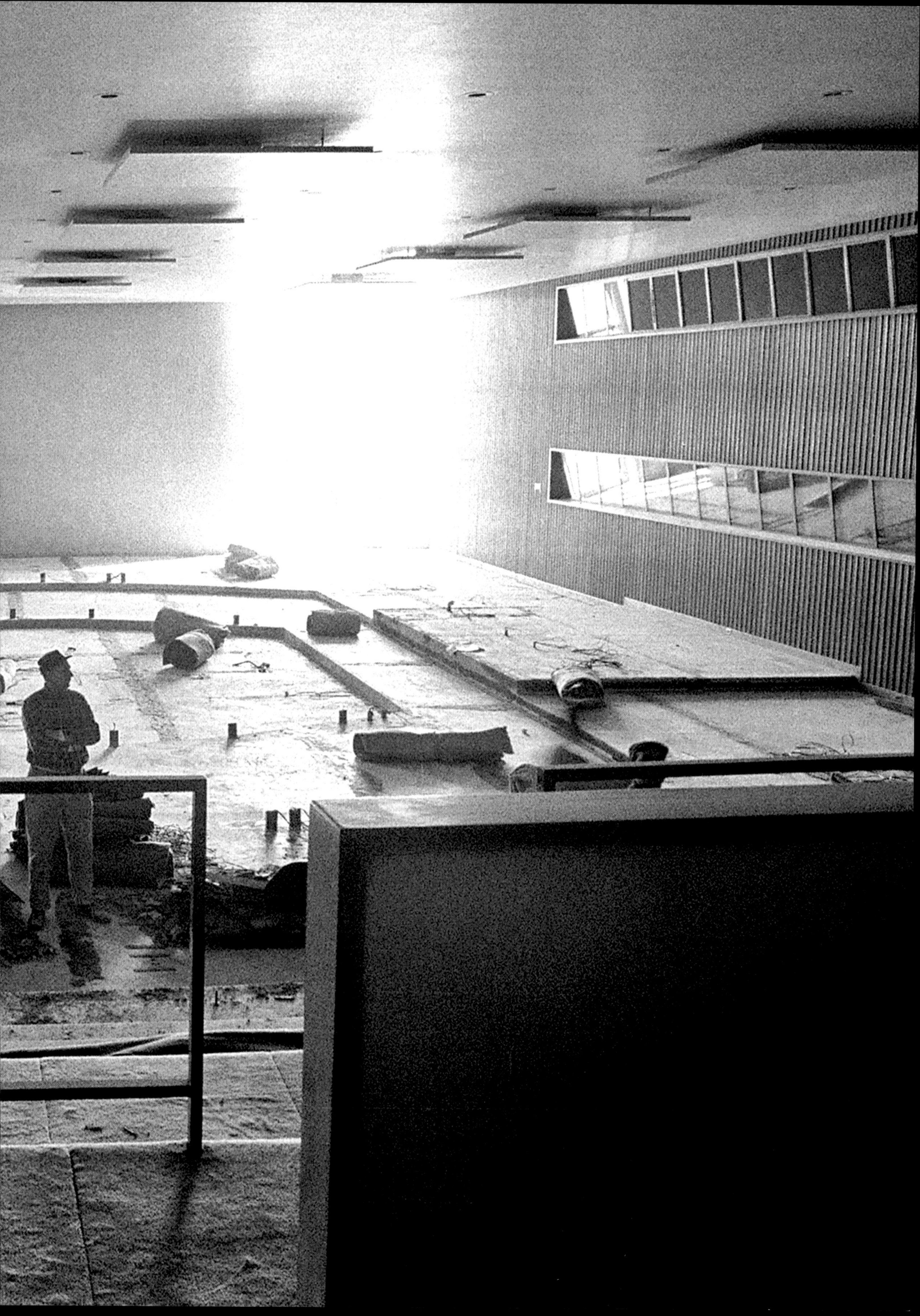

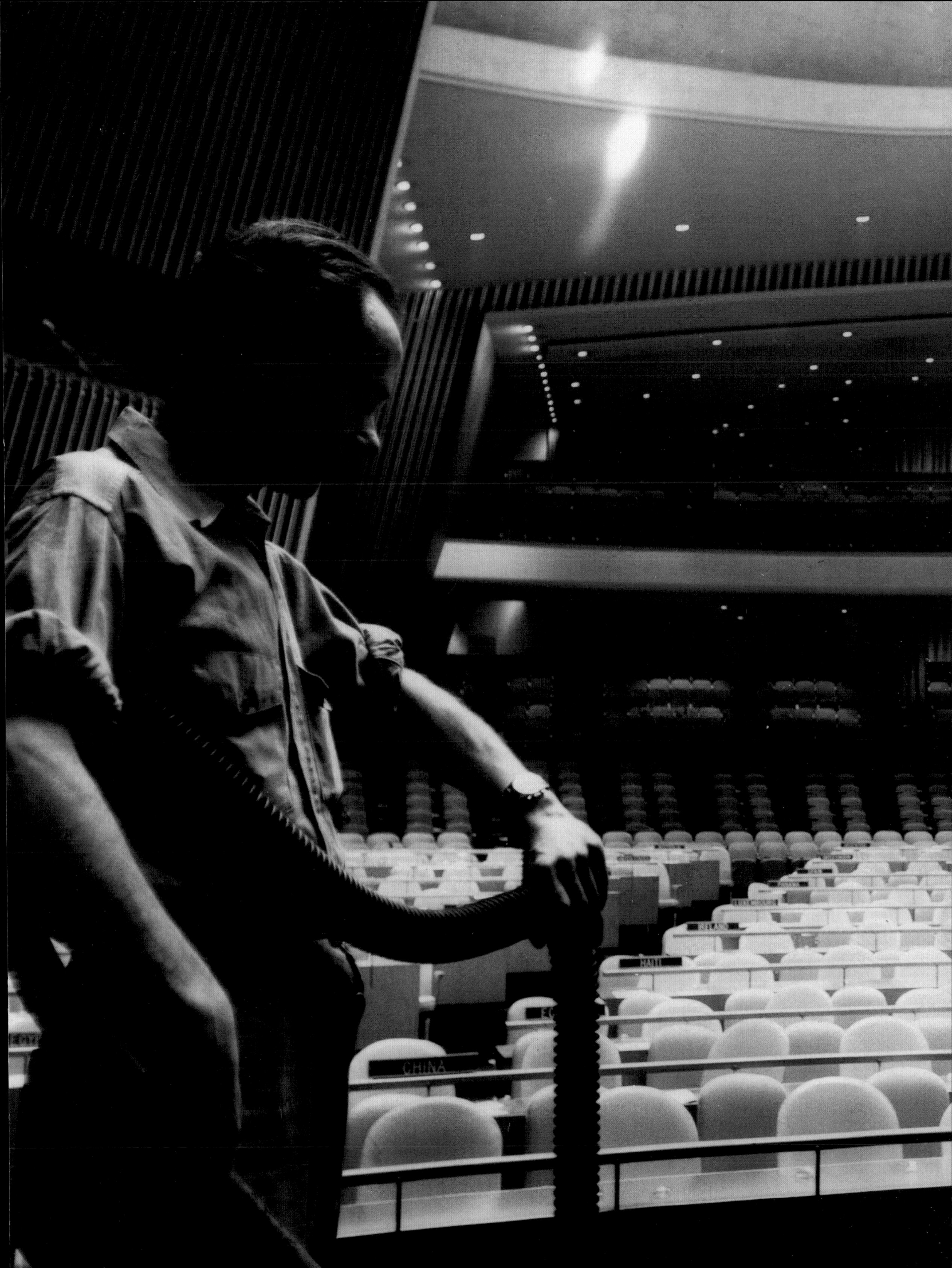
LUXEMBOURG
IRELAND
HAITI
CHINA

NXP 1102119 . . . . NEW YORK BUREAU

CLEANING UP

UNITED NATIONS, N.Y.: -- THE MAKERS OF
HISTORY HAVE PICKED UP THEIR PORTFOLIOS AND
GONE HOME. LOUIS MANCUSO, A CLEANING MAN AT
UNITED NATIONS HEADQUARTERS, LOOKS AT HIS
WATCH AND PREPARES TO CARRY OUT HIS CHORES.
THE NEW HUNGARIAN CRISIS HAS GIVEN THE U.N.
ANOTHER MAJOR PROBLEM TO TACKLE, SO LOU CAN
LOOK TO ANOTHER BIG CLEAN-UP JOB TOMORROW.
WHEN PEOPLE SAY THE WORLD'S IN A MESS, LOU
NODS AND PROCLAIMS: "YOU CAN SAY THAT AGAIN!"
NX-1
CREDIT (UNITED PRESS PHOTO)   11-2-56   (JB)

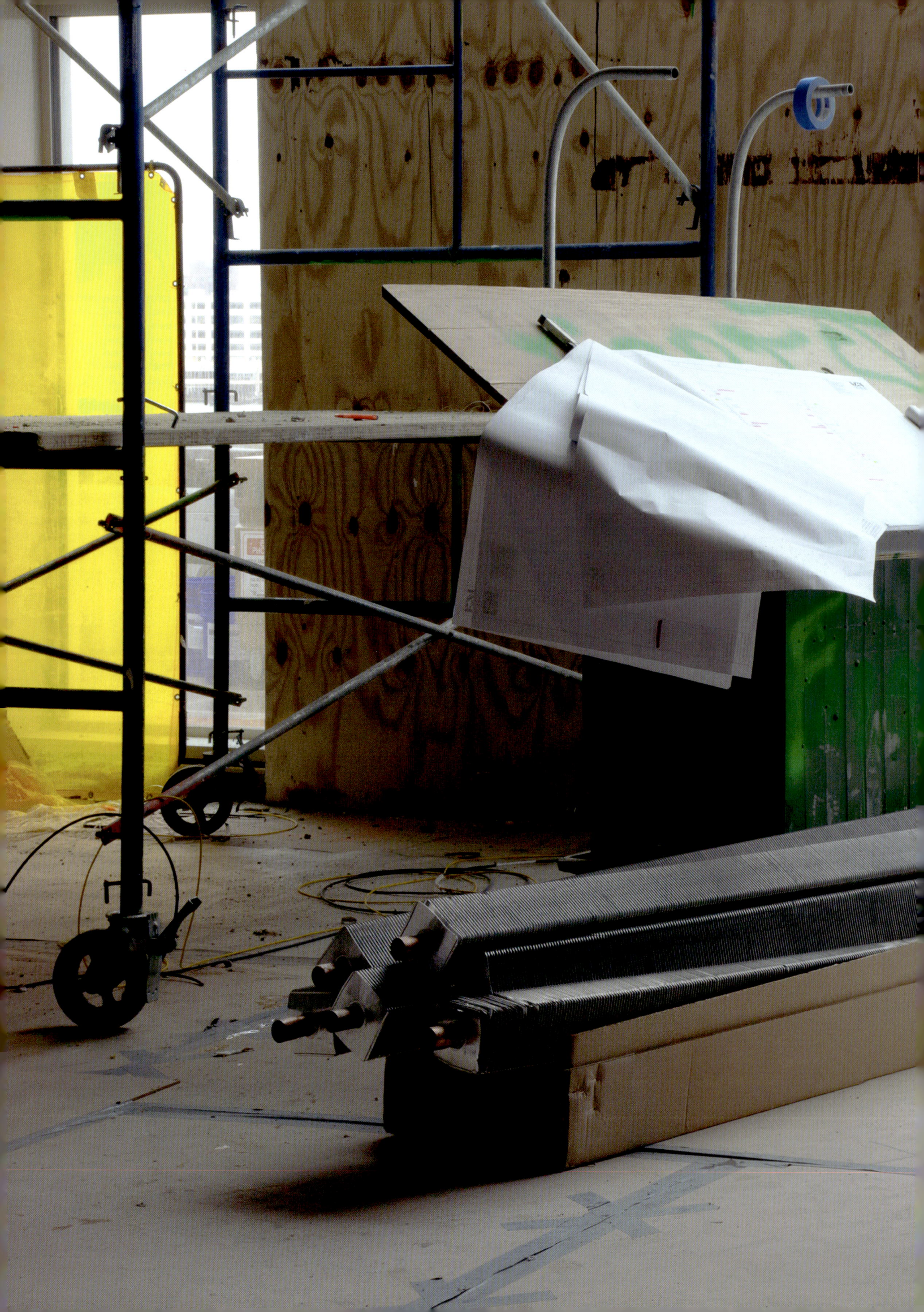

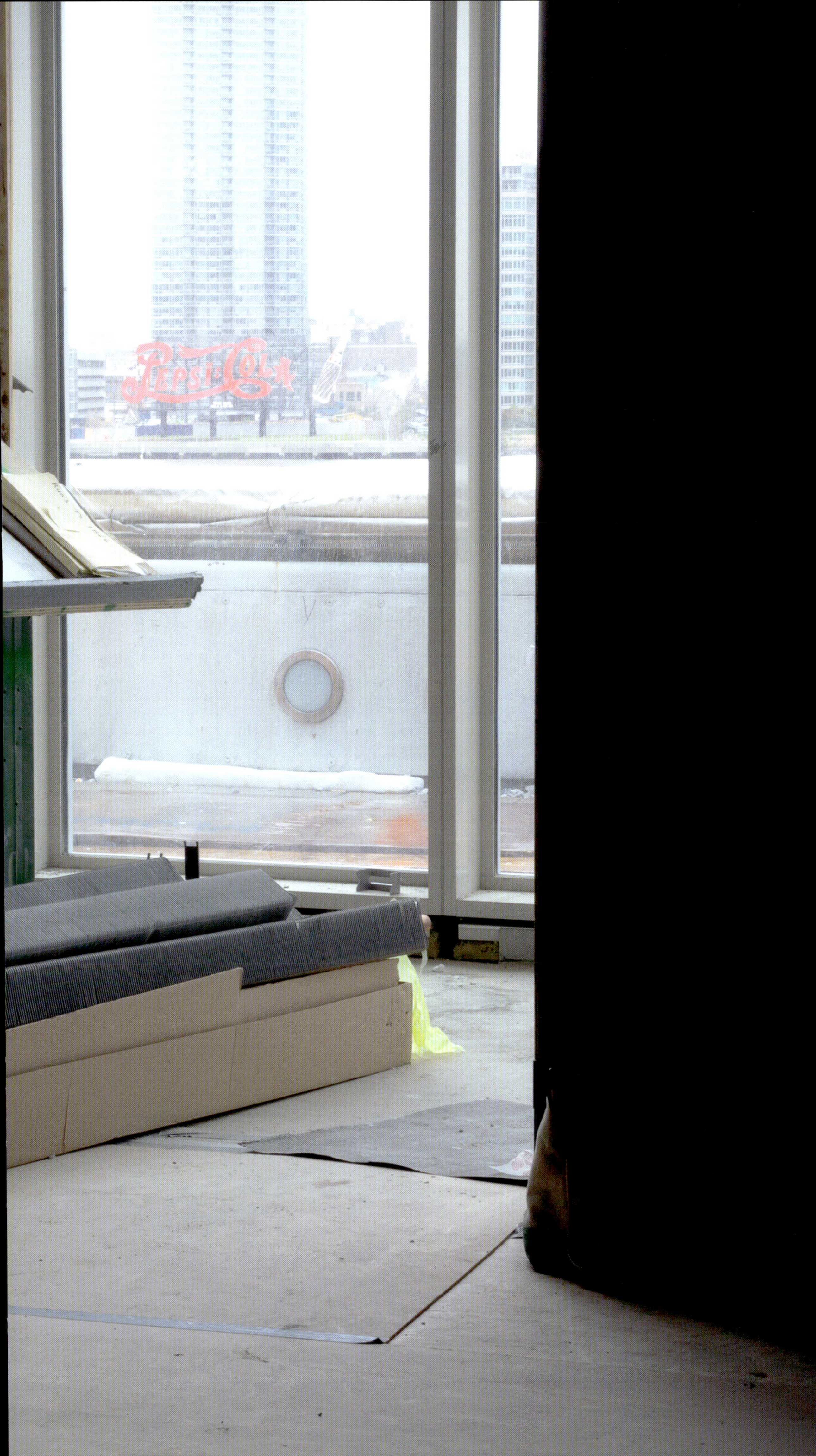

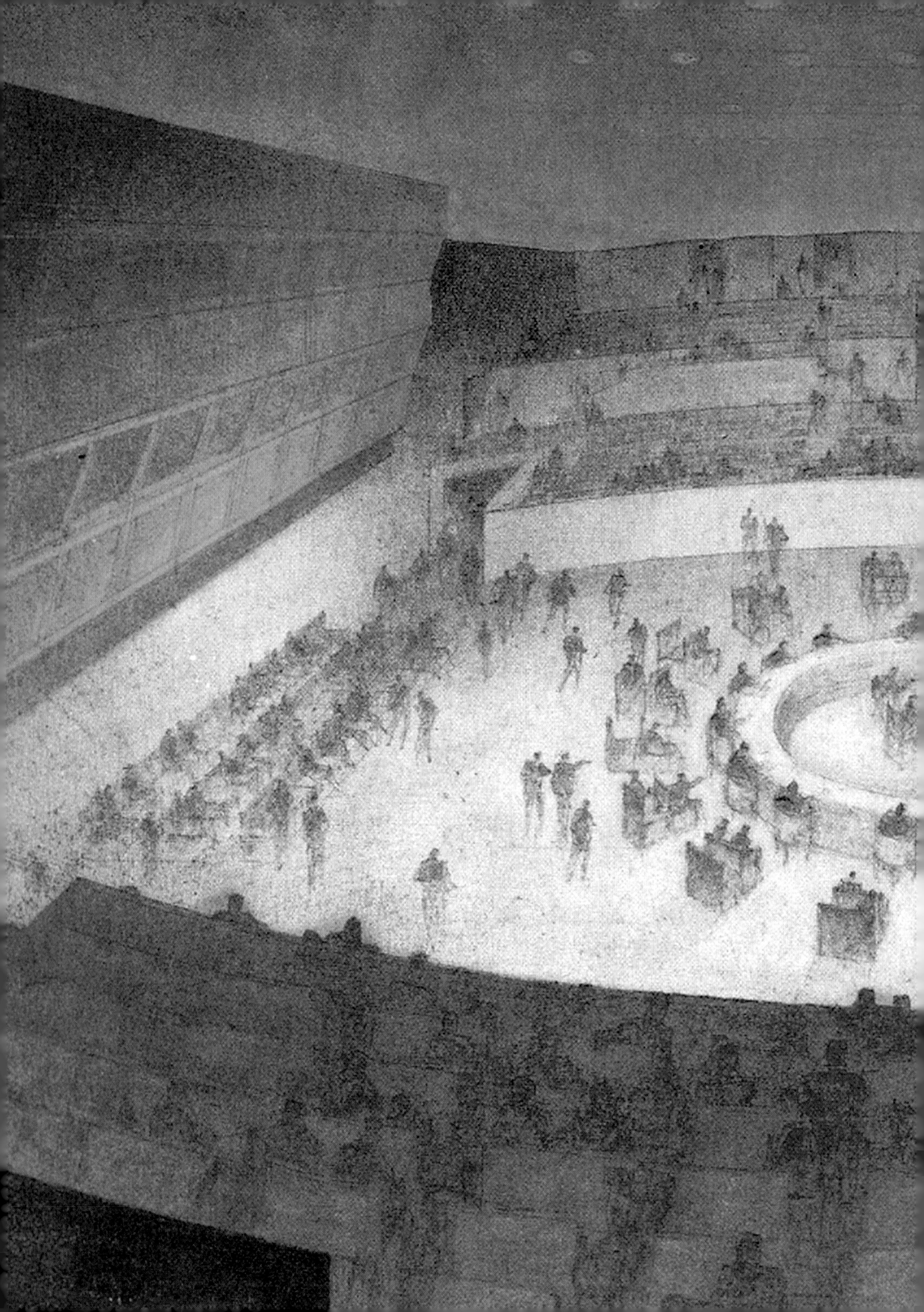

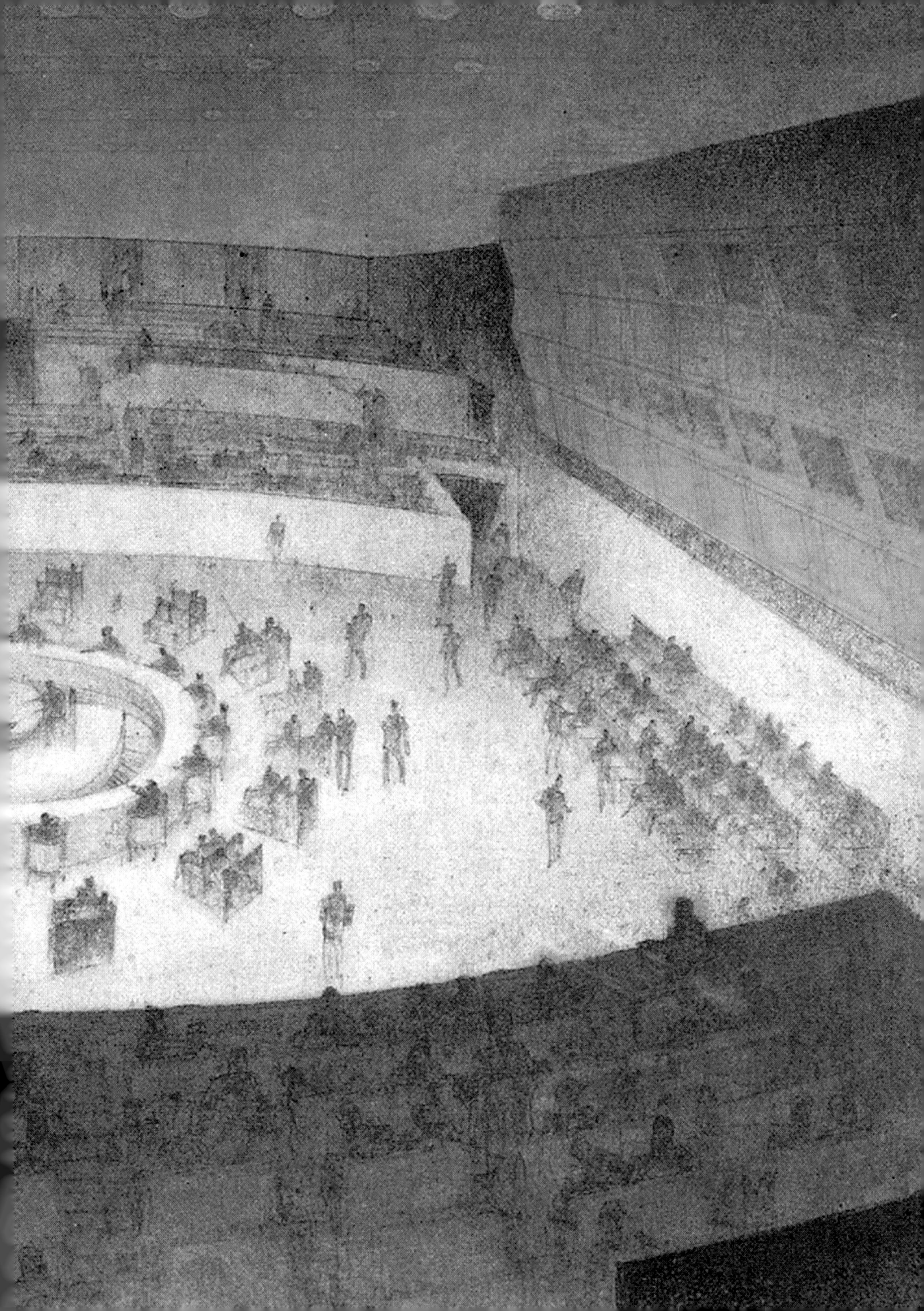

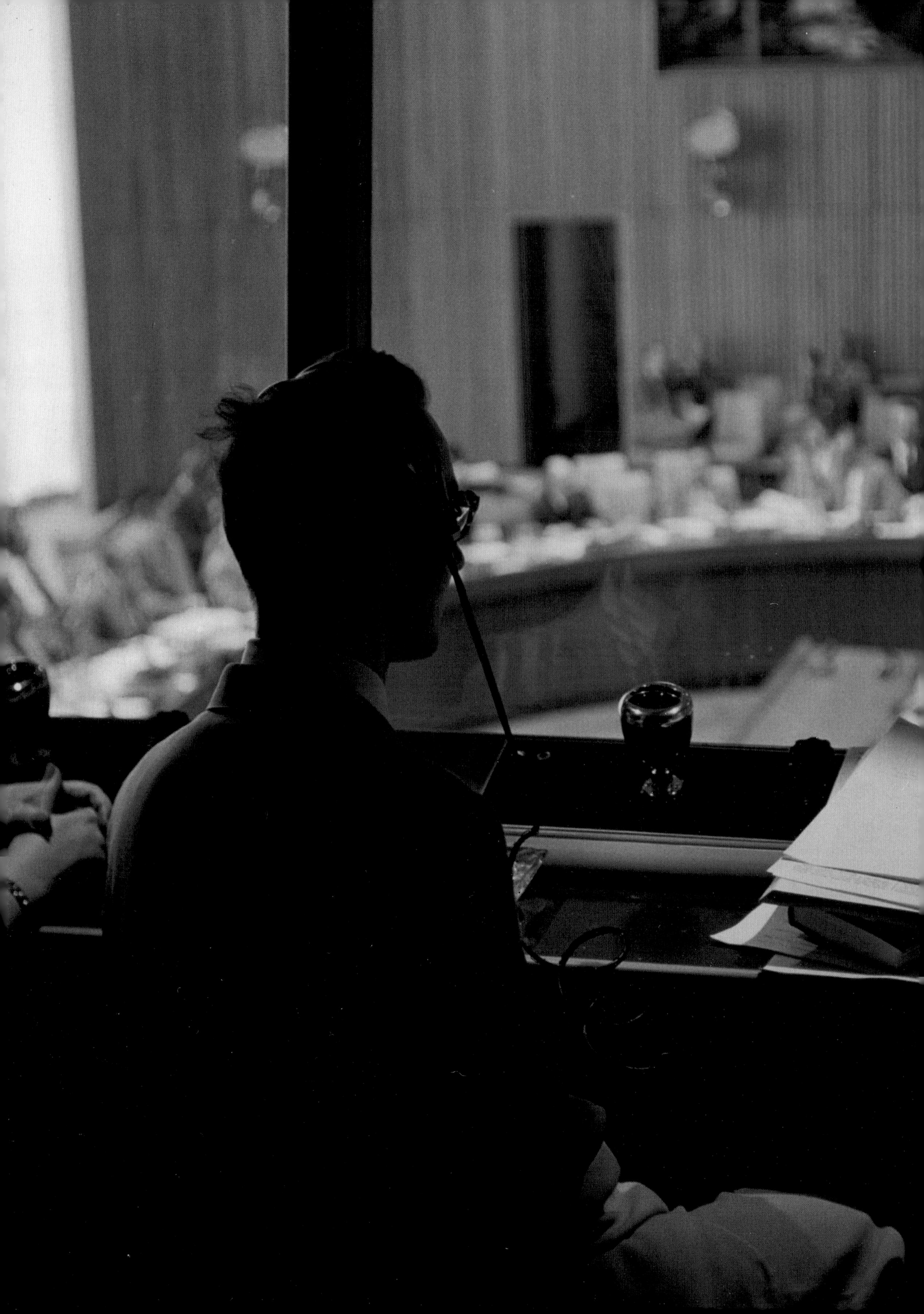

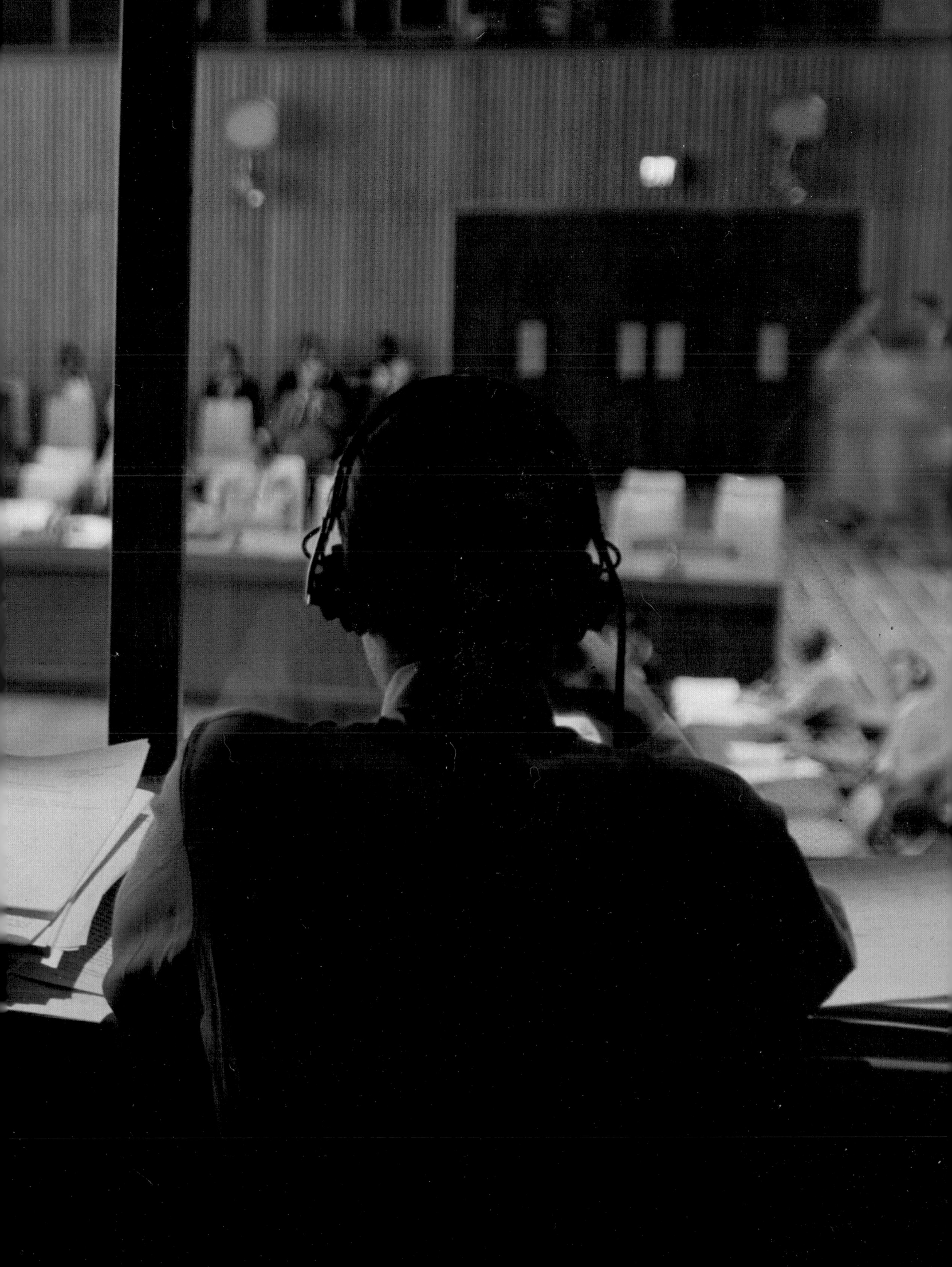

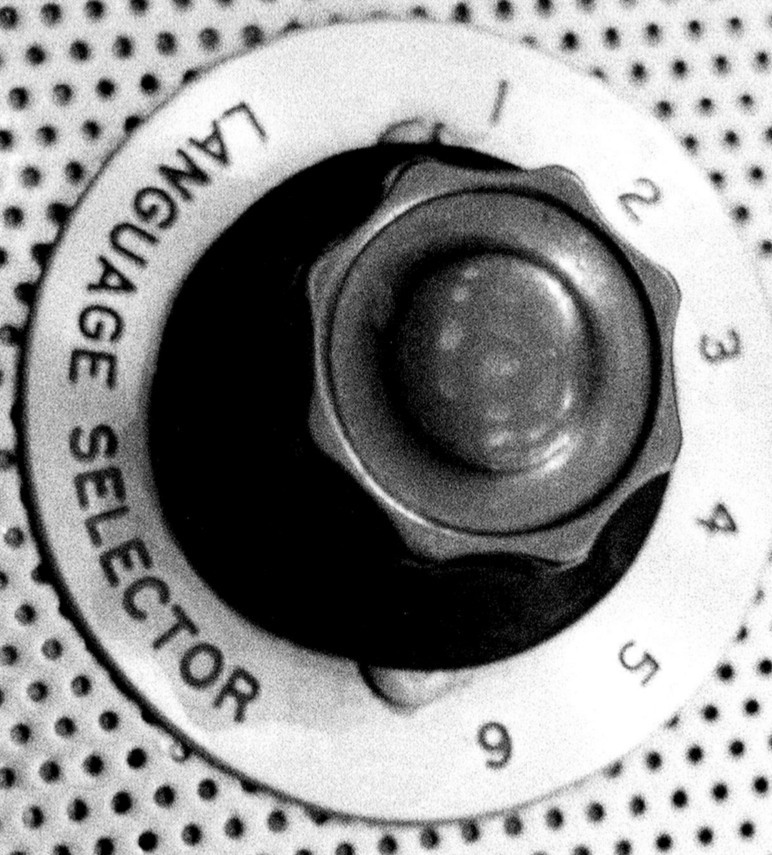

LANGUAGE SELECTOR
1 2 3 4 5 6

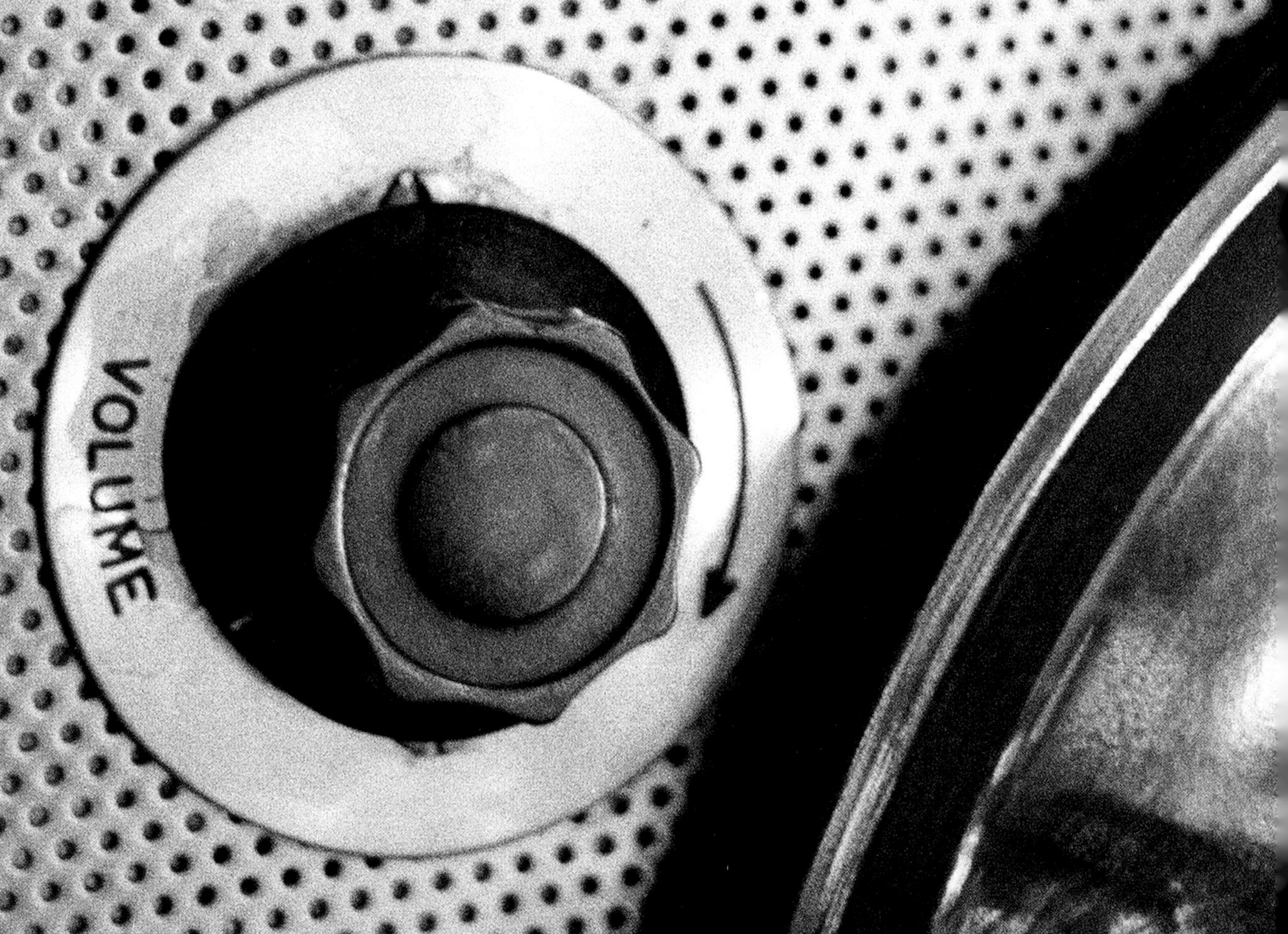

VOLUME

> DK
> (adjusting headphones)

Ok, we can talk now; we won't have to work again for a
while. I'm listening to you with one ear.

> ND

Are you interpreting just the French speakers? How does
this work?

> JM

Whatever is said in French, Spanish, or Russian, we
interpret into English. In our case, we both have French,
so we take turns with French. I work from Spanish and my
colleague works from Russian. And we also have something
called a "relay"... if someone is speaking Arabic from
the floor, the Arabic booth will interpret into English
or French. So, if it's English on the floor, obviously we
don't go into action; we just listen.

> DK

This is an unusual meeting; the panel are mostly speaking
English, and now they are making casual, sort of impromptu,
closing statements.

> (laughter from the floor)

> ND

How do you translate humor?

> JM

It depends. Sometimes you can say it directly and
sometimes the joke is more open. That is to say, you don't
necessarily interpret the words verbatim, but try to render
a similar sense. But if it's a pun or if it's an idiom,
that can be tricky. There is an old story about somebody in
the Security Council; an ambassador was telling a joke and
he was going on and on about this cat...

> DK

Oh no...

> JM

The interpreter thought he knew where it was going and
he chose to render it differently, something culturally
specific for these listeners. So, while the speaker was
going on and on about a cat, the interpreter had been going
on about a dog. Then the speaker said, "But what if the cat
decides to climb a tree?" It was a big mess.

> ND

How can you translate a joke if you don't know the punch
line?

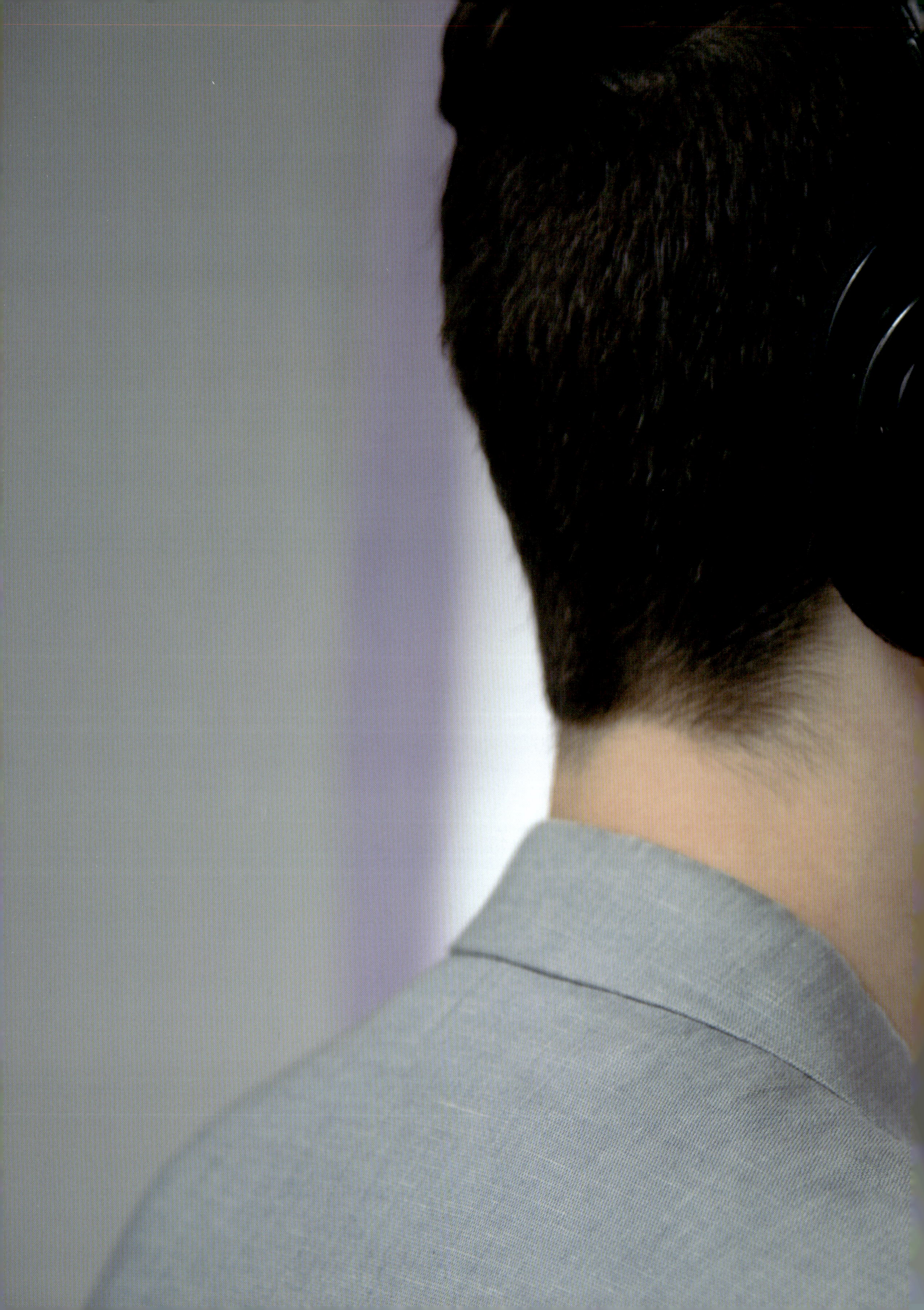

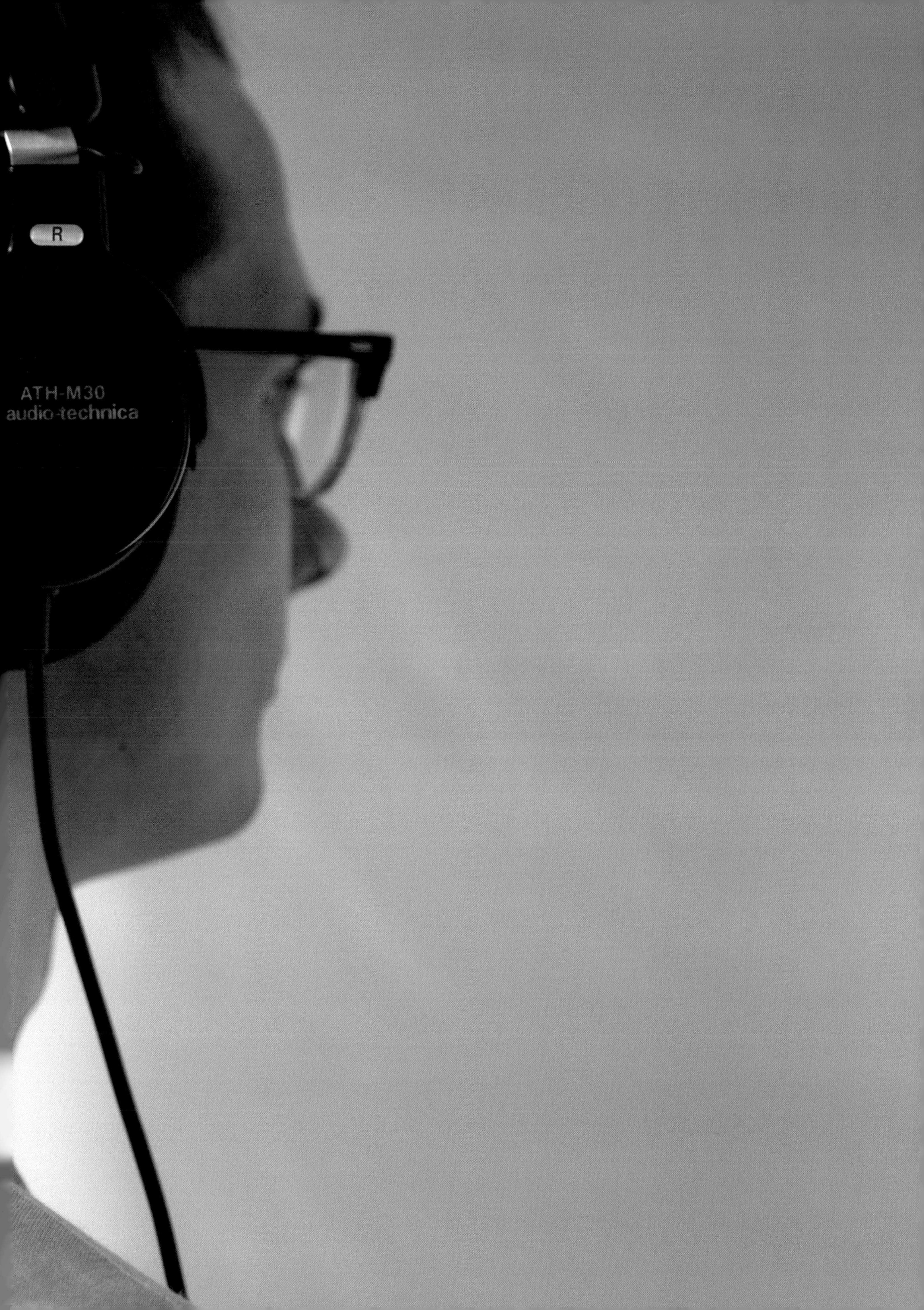
R
ATH-M30
audio-technica

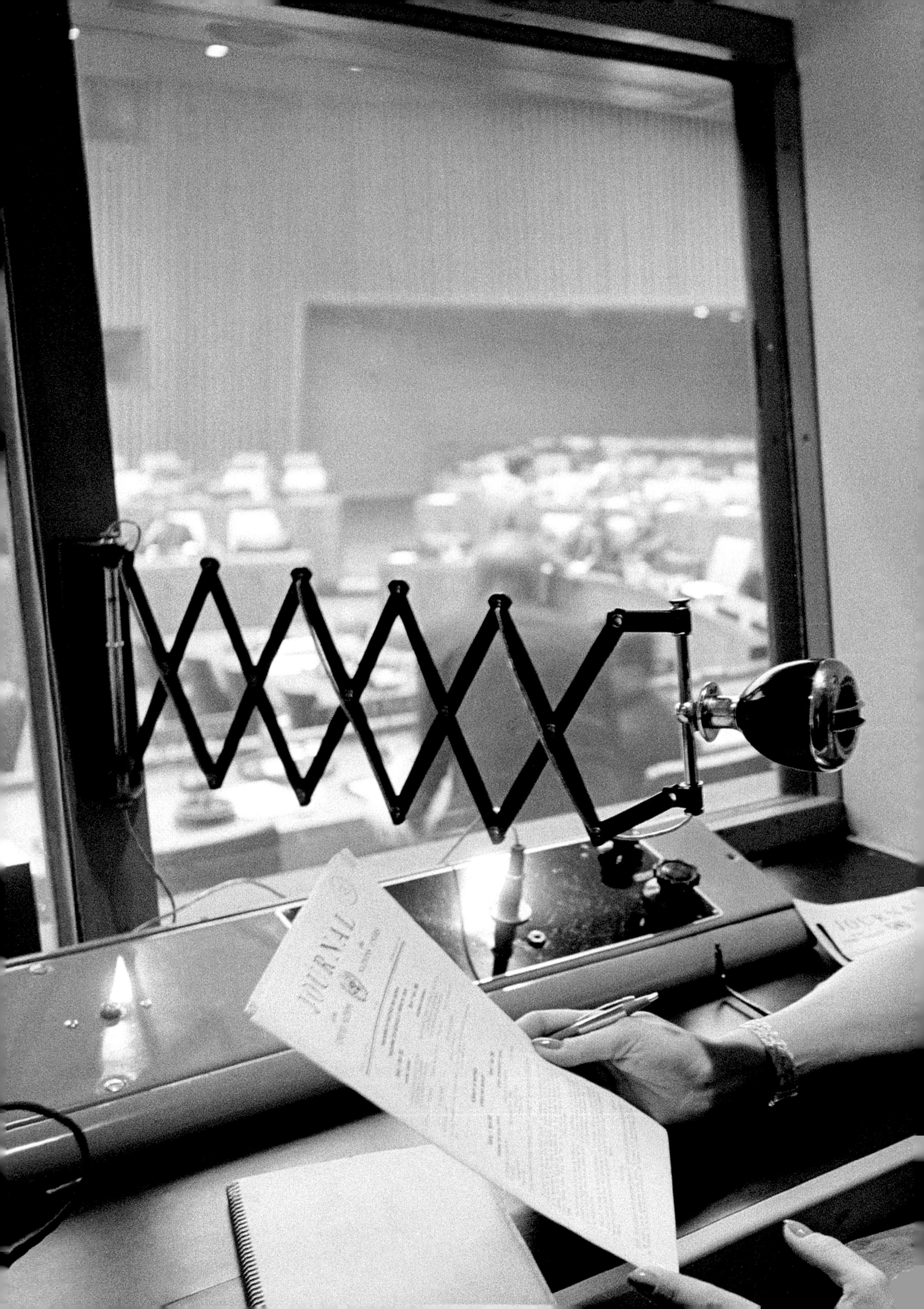

                              DK
          You can do it; you just do it.

                              JM
          You listen for meaning and more often than not, you can
          find the appropriate cultural metaphor or register to
          communicate the spirit of a joke. You know, adrenaline
          becomes more active when you're at the microphone.

                              DK
          Yes, it's very interesting, you get this adrenaline rush
          and you come out with words you didn't even know you knew.
          But you never, never laugh into the microphone.

                              JM
          Right, no matter what they say. I mean, at the European
          Parliament, the MPs will use more humor -- and swearwords,
          my God. It's difficult to translate swearwords.

                              DK
          But my point was about laughing. Sometimes it's not
          the intention of the speaker to be funny, but they say
          something in anger, an outrageous insult and you have
          to adapt your voice to the tone and emotions of the
          speaker... sometimes it's hard to suppress a laugh.

                              JM
          Right, the whole floor might be laughing but we can never
          laugh. Like the "straight man" -- the tsukkomi.

                              ND
          What does that mean?

                              JM
          In Japan, there is a tradition of two performers -- there
          is a funny man and a distinguished man who doesn't laugh.

                              ND
          Oh, the "straight man." Like in, "Who's on first?"...

                              JM
          I don't know...

                              DK
          No, the straight man sets up the jokes so the funny guy
          can give the punch line. Like Dean Martin and Jerry Lewis.

                              ND
          Like Zeppo Marx?

                              DK
          Well, anyway. The tone is very different at the UN.
          Here, there is more innuendo, things left unsaid.

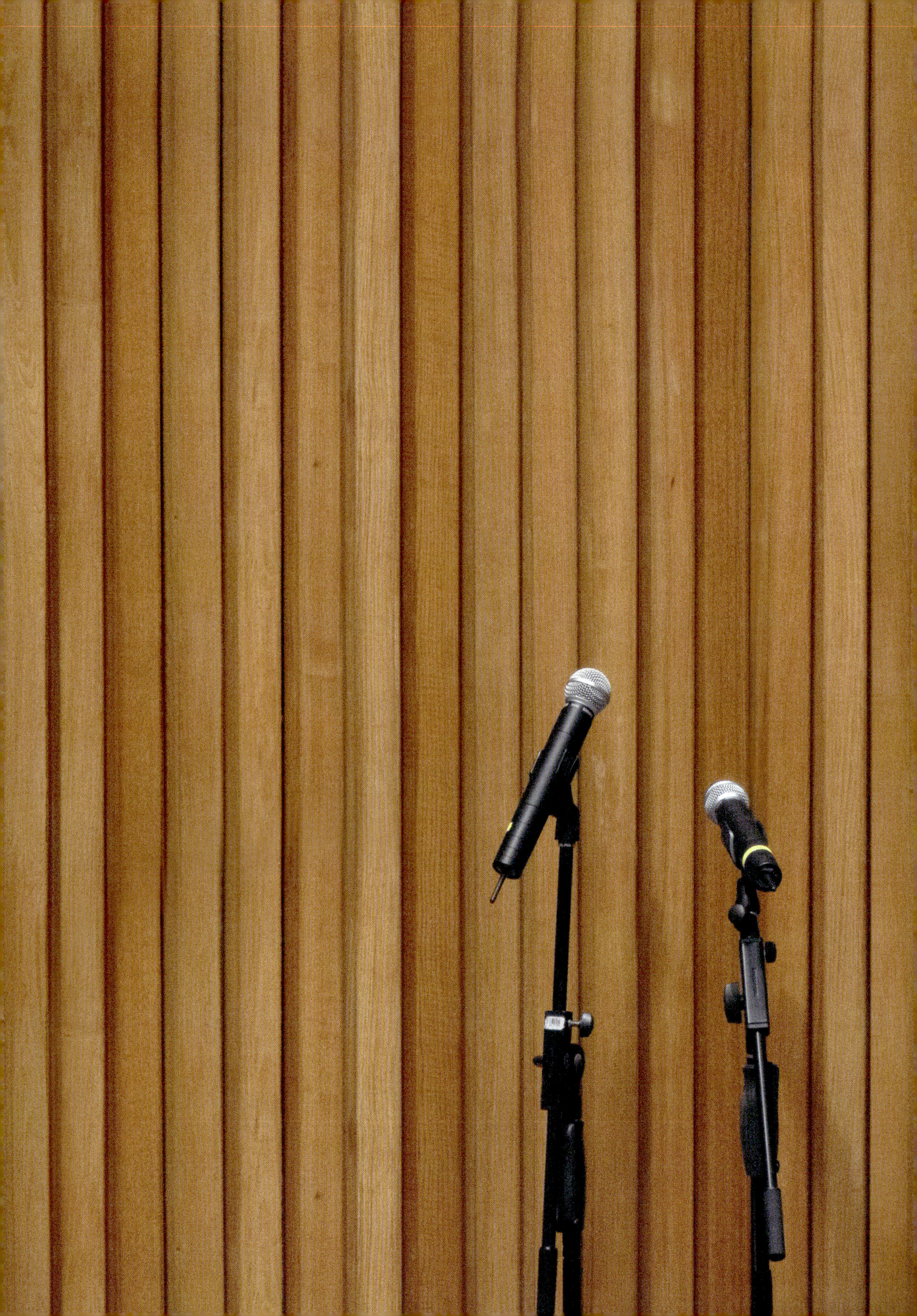

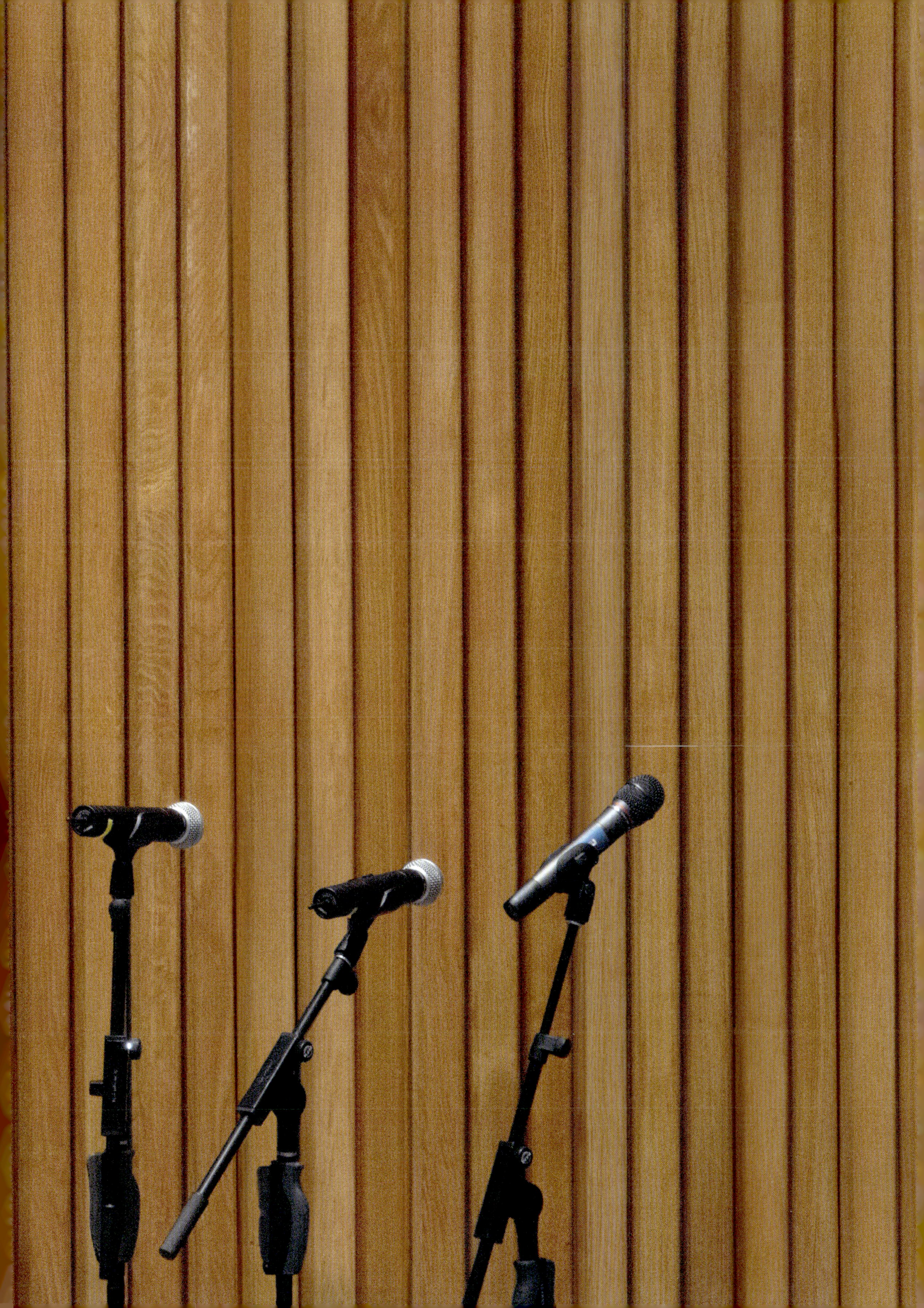

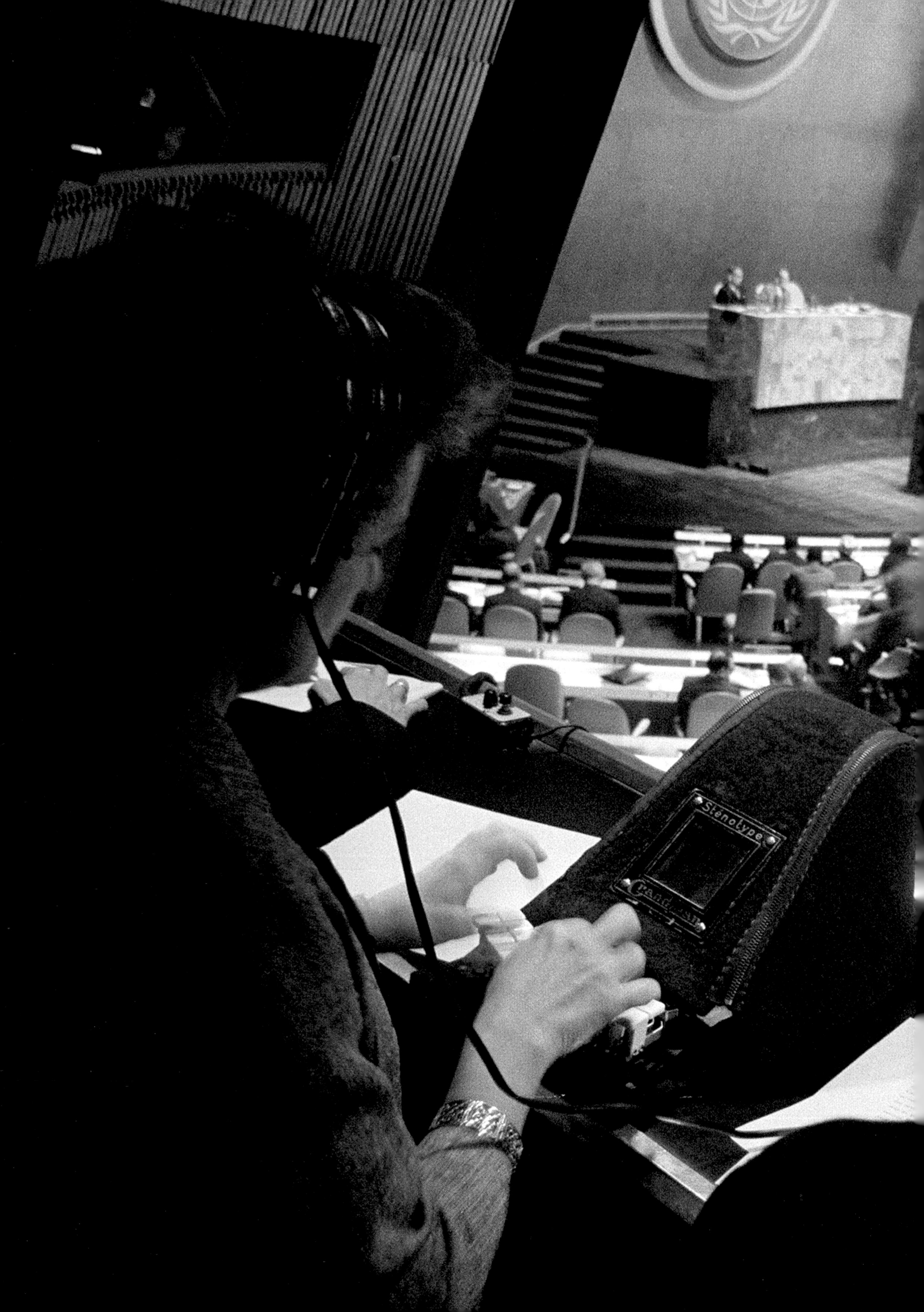

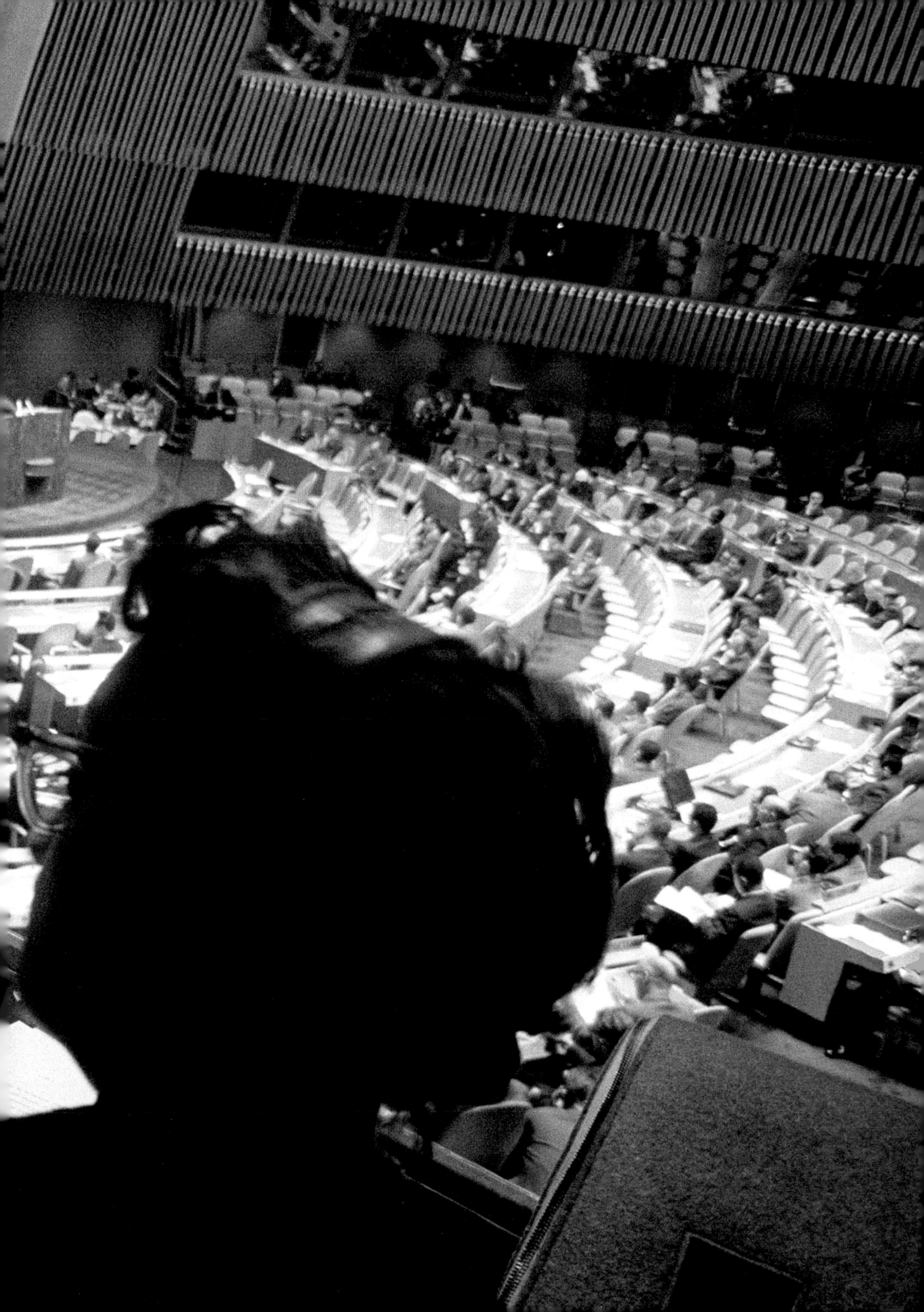

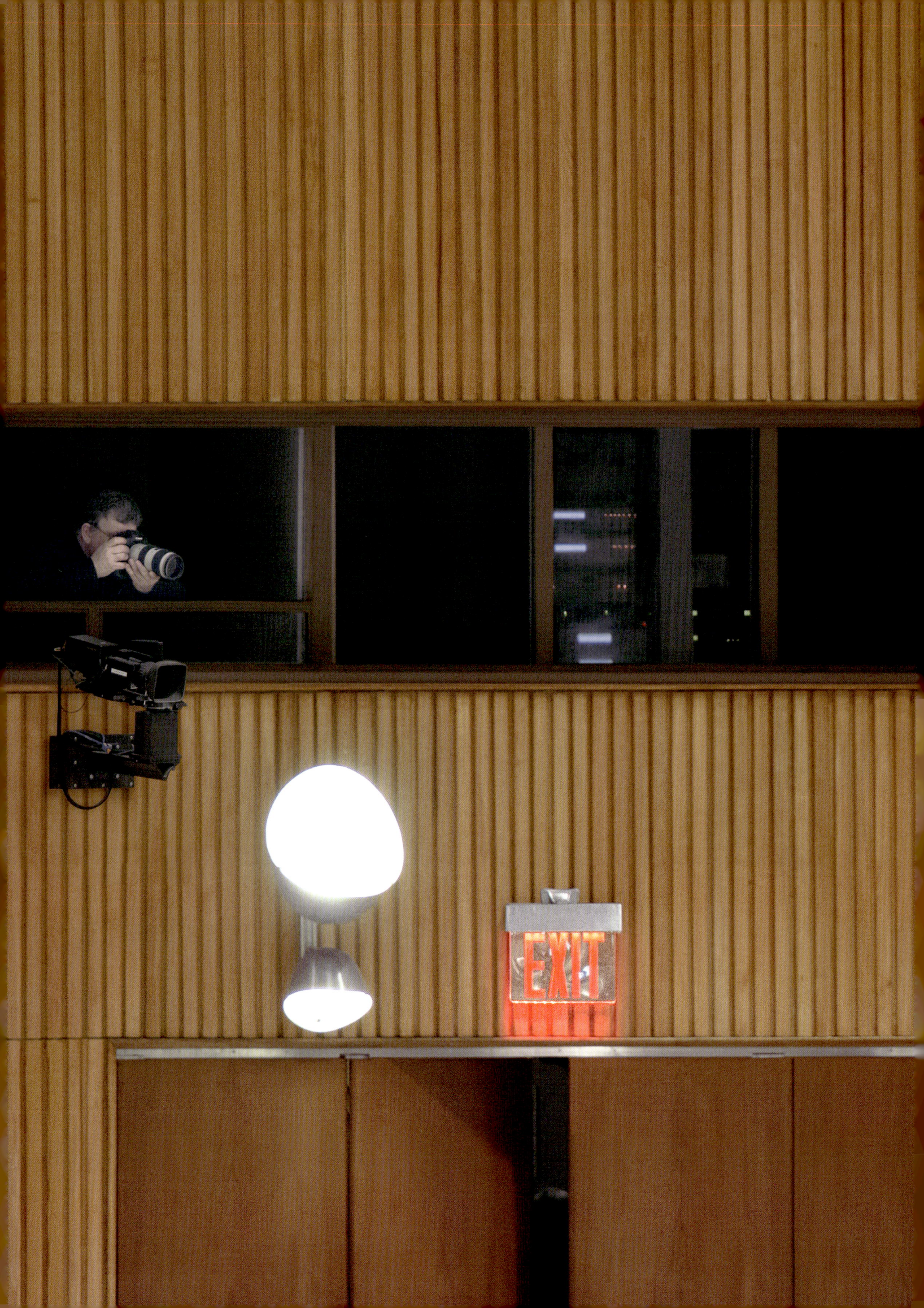

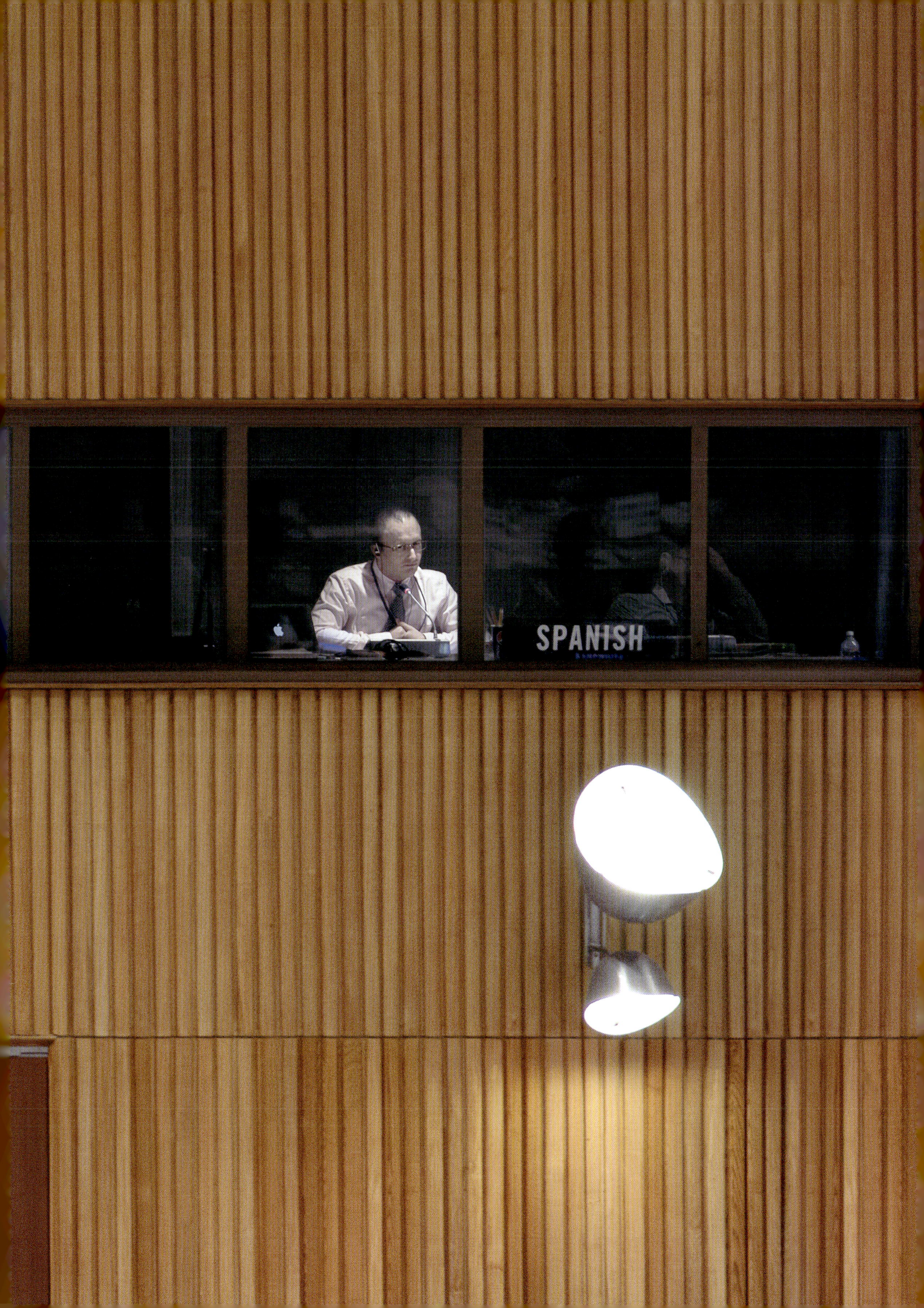
SPANISH

Translator collapsed during Khadafy's rambling diatribe

By Chuck Bennett

After struggling to turn Khadafy's insane ramblings at the UN into English for 75 minutes, the Libyan dictator's personal interpreter got lost in translation.

"I just can't take it any more," Khadafy's interpreter shouted into the live microphone - in Arabic. At that point, the U.N.'s Arabic section chief, Rasha Ajalyaqeen, took over and translated the final 20 minutes of the speech.

Breaking with protocol, Khadafy brought his own interpreters from Tripoli for Wednesday's speech rather than use one of the 25 Arabic interpreters supplied by the United Nations, staff interpreters said.

"This is the best team in the world - most heads of state prefer to use U.N. interpreters because then - no matter what happens - they can blame the interpreter," one staffer said.

Khadafy has a habit of repeating the same phrase over and over again, "which is good because if you don't understand what he says the first time you can get it right the second or third time," the interpreter said.

It's not just zany conspiracy theories about the Kennedy assassination and swine flu that are a challenge, but the loony Libyan's strange mannerisms.

Although a red warning light illuminates after the 15-minute time limit, after being introduced in the General Assembly Hall as the "leader of the revolution,

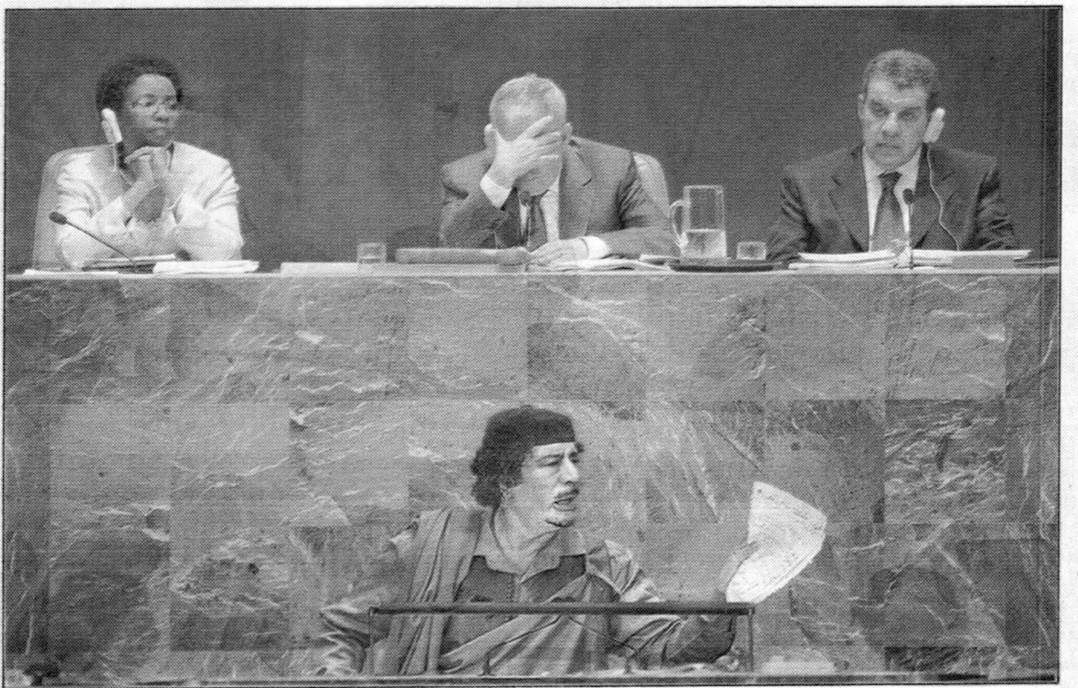

Libyan leader Colonel Moamer Kadhafy holds a copy of the UN Charter as he speaks during the United Nations General Assembly.

president of the African Union, the king of kings of Africa," Colonel Khadafy shattered protocol by giving a rambling speech that stretched for 90 minutes instead of the allotted 15.

He also suggested that those who caused "mass murder" in Iraq be tried; defended the right of the Taliban to establish an Islamic emirate; wondered whether swine flu was cooked up in a laboratory as a weapon; and demanded a thorough investigation of the assassinations of John F. Kennedy and Martin Luther King.

He offered to move the United Nations headquarters to Libya because leaders coming here had to endure jet lag and because the understandable security against another attack on New York. Khadafy blamed the United Nations for the world's most

                              ND

I read that Qaddafi brought his personal interpreters from
Tripoli because he was speaking a Libyan dialect, a local
dialect that is very difficult to understand. You were the
Arabic Section Chief at the UN at that time; is that what
the Libyan delegation told you?

                              RA

Yes. You know, the staff interpreters at the UN, we
don't second-guess delegations. But it was probably a
matter of trust. They don't know that we work under
oath -- literally, we work under oath. One of the basic
requirements is to put aside your biases.

                              ND

By "oath," do you mean specifically the AIIC's "Code of
Professional Ethics"? Or are you making reference to
ethical standards for UN interpreters? Or both?

                              RA

By "oath," I mean that interpreters see their job as
that of accurately and faithfully conveying the feelings
and ideas of the speaker. This is the main criterion in
evaluating the quality of interpretation. It is a UN
requirement, the fulfillment of which determines whether or
not someone is eligible to become an interpreter. I am not
an AIIC member but I am confident they also consider this
the cornerstone of their code.

So, that morning I was asked to find a place for the
interpreters provided by the delegation. I told them,
"You don't need to provide interpreters; there is an
Arabic booth. Arabic is an official language at the UN and
whatever the Colonel, His Excellency, would say would be
interpreted properly." And that was exactly the answer I
was given: "It's a local dialect and you're not going to
understand."

Yes, there are dialects that differ between one Arab
country and another, but when they speak classical Arabic,
we understand it.

                              ND
Qaddafi was speaking standard Arabic?

                              RA

Yes, he was speaking standard Arabic! You know, sometimes
there might be a variation that does not ring a bell
immediately, and in an interpretation context, you have to
respond immediately. This is more likely to happen when
the speaker is citing proverbs. For example, if they say
a culturally specific proverb, something like, "This will
only happen when flint stones produce leaves," in the
Libyan dialect, they would say "the year of the fenugreek."

It could throw you off for a minute, but you would be able
to figure something out. In the worst-case scenario, you
would use a neutral expression that wouldn't influence the
flow of the speech and hope that whatever he's going to
say next will give you an idea where to go.

                              ND
That's interesting because one British newspaper wrote
that "Qaddafi speaks almost exclusively in the Libyan
dialect, which is not always intelligible to Arabic
speakers farther afield." And I've also read that Qaddafi
wasn't able to speak standard Arabic very well.

                              RA
No, that's absolutely not true. Oh, maybe they were
talking about another speech? Do you remember, during the
Libyan uprising, there was a widely shown TV clip where
Qaddafi was saying, "We will cleanse Libya, inch by inch,
house by house...," something like that. In this case,
he was speaking a heavy Libyan dialect, but we still
understood it.

                              ND
Did you meet with Mr. Zlitni before the speech?

                              RA
I met him very briefly. I was the chief of booth at the
time and I was working in the meeting that directly
preceded Mr. Qaddafi, which was... I think it was Mr.
Obama's statement. So I met him briefly as I was exiting
my shift.

                              ND
I've listened to this speech a number of times and even
from the beginning, Zlitni sounds completely overwhelmed.
His voice was sort of staccato, shaky; it's really hard to
follow.

                              RA
I do believe it was definitely inferior to anything we can
provide at the UN. It was substandard, if I may say so.

But to be fair, no interpreter on God's earth can work
for an hour and forty minutes -- no one, no one. All of
your attention is committed in a very intense way and even
if it's a more casual meeting, it becomes too draining,
you lose focus. We're not suppose to be working in shifts
longer than thirty minutes.

                              ND
When you met him before the speech, did he ask for
assistance?

                              RA

No, the funny thing was that he asked for assistance on
the public address system.

                              ND

So, it's true that he said into the live mic...?

                              RA

I think he said something like, "I can't take it any
more," but I would have to go back to the record to be
sure.

                              ND

Were you listening to the whole speech?

                              RA

We were listening to the public address system in our
office. I was listening, but kind of zooming in and out.
And then I heard him say, "I can't take it anymore" rather
loudly. So, I had to (laughs), I literally had to run four
blocks; our office is near 42nd Street, it's all the way
over by the East River.

                              ND

Was he all alone in the booth?

                              RA

He had decided to sit in the English booth and so he was
with an English interpreter who didn't speak Arabic.
Usually, if someone is speaking Arabic from the floor, the
Arabic booth will take that into English or French and the
other five languages would interpret from us. But in this
case, Qaddafi didn't even trust someone else to go from
English to French. They wanted their own interpreters to
take Arabic into English and Arabic into French directly.

                              ND

All the papers mentioned that Mr. Zlitni "collapsed." Or
did he just stop?

                              RA

I think he just stopped, but really I don't know how it
happened because I didn't go into the English booth. I
went straight to my booth. I was thinking: "Now they're
asking the Arabic interpreters to take over..." I don't
want to sound as if I was second-guessing my colleagues.
I did ask the team; I asked my colleague who would have
normally been on-shift, "Would you like to work?" and she
said no, which was understandable. I mean, we were aware
that the world would be trying to listen to Qaddafi.
This was his first appearance at the UN. Libya had only
recently opened relations with much of the international
community after twenty years; there is a political burden
when you jump into that.

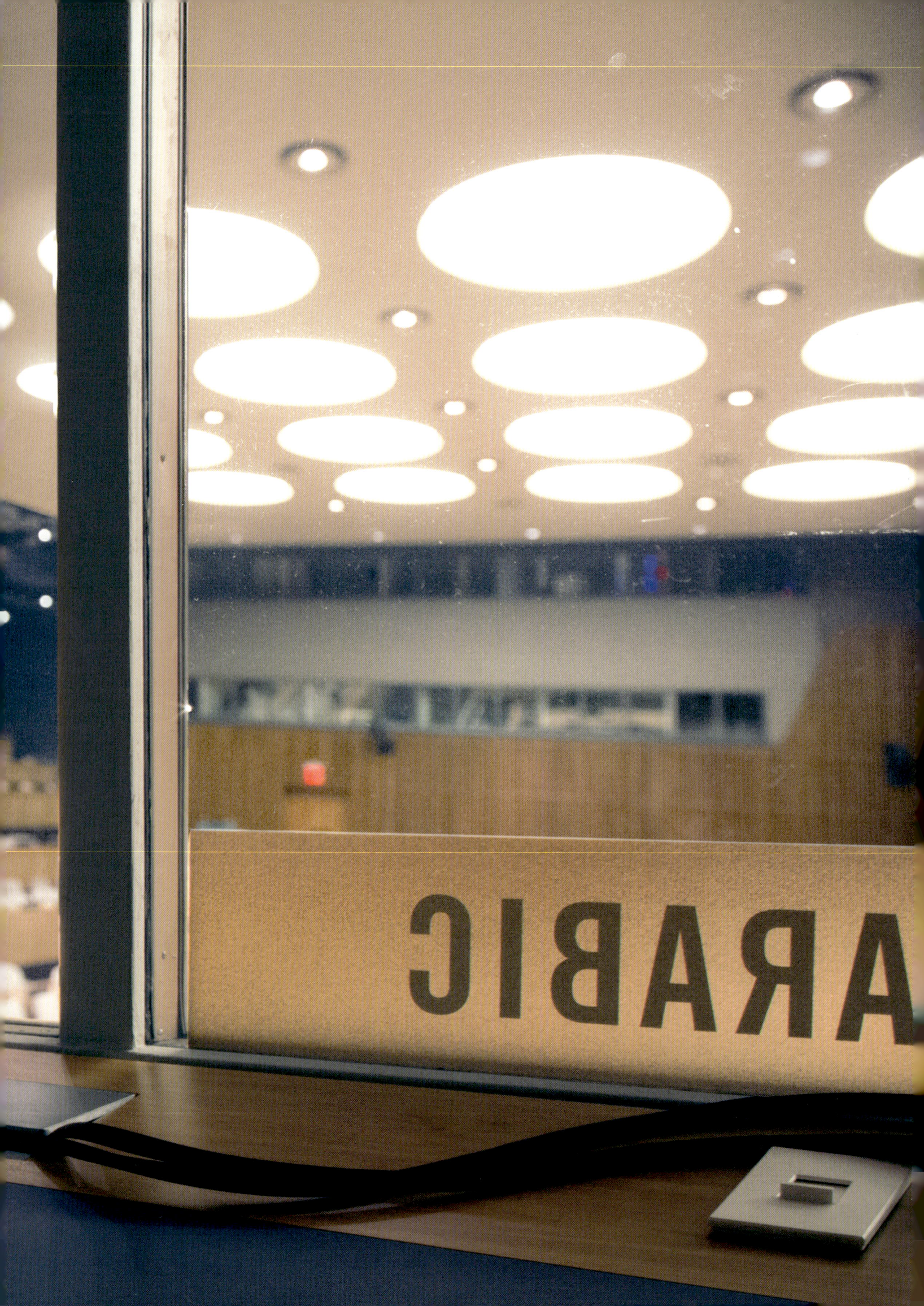

                              ND
Did you hear Mr. Zlitni's version of what happened?

                              RA
No.

                              ND
Among other things, he claims that he did not say, "I
just can't go on," or anything like that, into a live
microphone.

                              RA
No, I'm sorry. He said it, because I heard him. That's how
we knew! That's how we knew he needed help. Listen, you
can get to a point of mental exhaustion where you can't
make sense of words any more.

                              ND
Actually, he sounded completely lost from the beginning,
completely freaked out. You've worked at high-level
meetings for a number of years. How do you deal with the
stress?

                              RA
Let me tell you that I do have a propensity for
hypertension. I had to start taking medication after
September 11. There's no way to completely avoid the
stress, no matter how well you succeed in hiding your
emotions. My cardiologist told me to change professions
and I said, "Oh, would you like me to tell you, 'Go become
a plumber now?'"

You know what added to the stress with the Qaddafi speech?
There were a few times when he paused, to check on the
interpretation, to check whether I rendered it properly...

                              ND
Really? In the middle of the speech?

                              RA
Yes! There was a section where he said, "... and this
added insult to injury." In Arabic, they would say
something like, "It was already soil and he added water
to make mud, he made it more muddy." Qaddafi said, "Now,
let's see how they interpret this!" and put on his
earpiece... by which time, I had already spoken. I mean,
there was no way for him to check.

                          ND
He spoke for ninety-eight minutes, and there is a fifteen-
minute time limit in the General Assembly. Do speakers
often run over?

                          RA
Yes, unless there is a very tough president. But they
rarely interrupt delegations and definitely not heads of
state. From our booth, we were able to see Mr. Treki, who
was chairing the meeting during Qaddafi's speech.

                          ND
I was going to ask you about that!

                          RA
Did you see how he looked?

                          ND
He was shaking his head around, holding his head in his
hands, he was so upset!

                          RA
Yes, he was in bad shape. I wondered if he would survive
this meeting.

                          ND
So, what do you do when you notice that the audience is so
exasperated? As an interpreter, what can you do?

                          RA
You don't do anything. You carry the tone of the speaker.
Let me tell you, an interpreter cannot be a judge.
Accuracy, faithfulness to the emotions and the linguistic
expressions of the speaker, is very important. And in
this case, it was difficult because there was a point when
Qaddafi... did he throw the UN Charter at the podium?

                          ND
Yes, he tore it and threw it over his shoulder.

                          RA
He tore it up. And I think that whoever was sitting at the
podium had to duck down.

                          ND
I was listening very closely whether your voice would
change and I must say, you were very good.

                          RA
Oh, there was a hint of laughter, which let me tell
you, wasn't supposed to be audible. But some things are
reasonably acceptable under the pressure of circumstances.

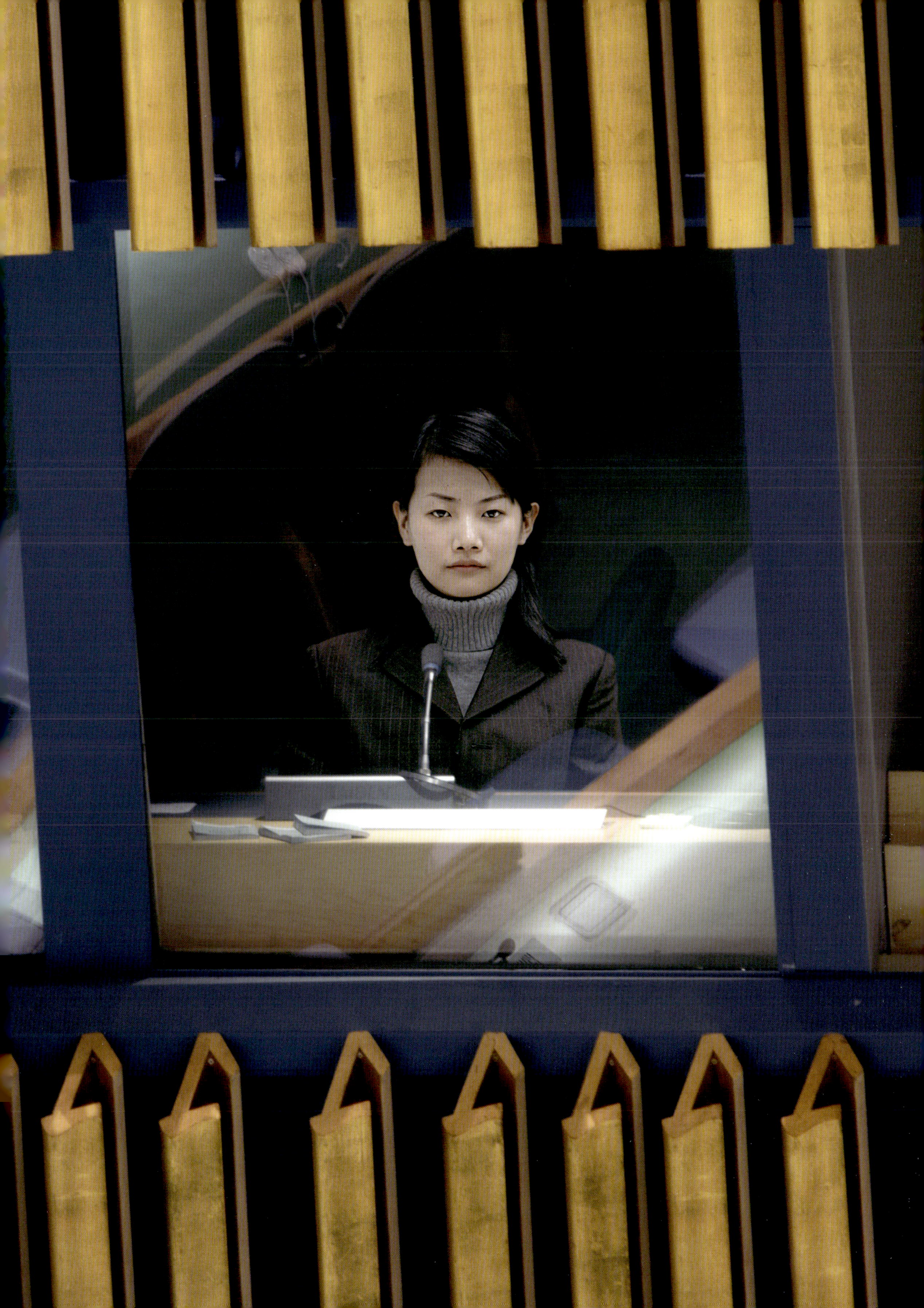

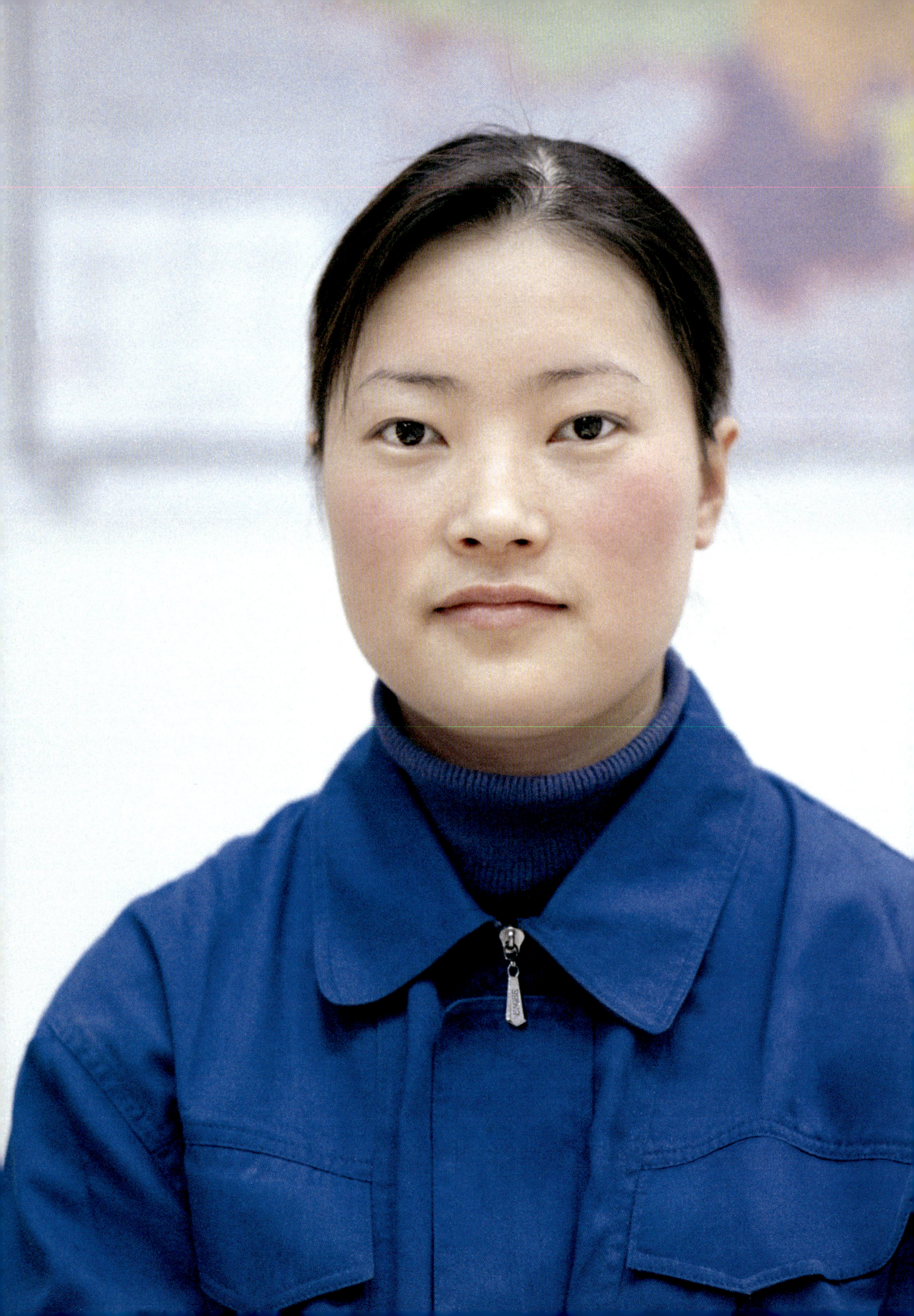

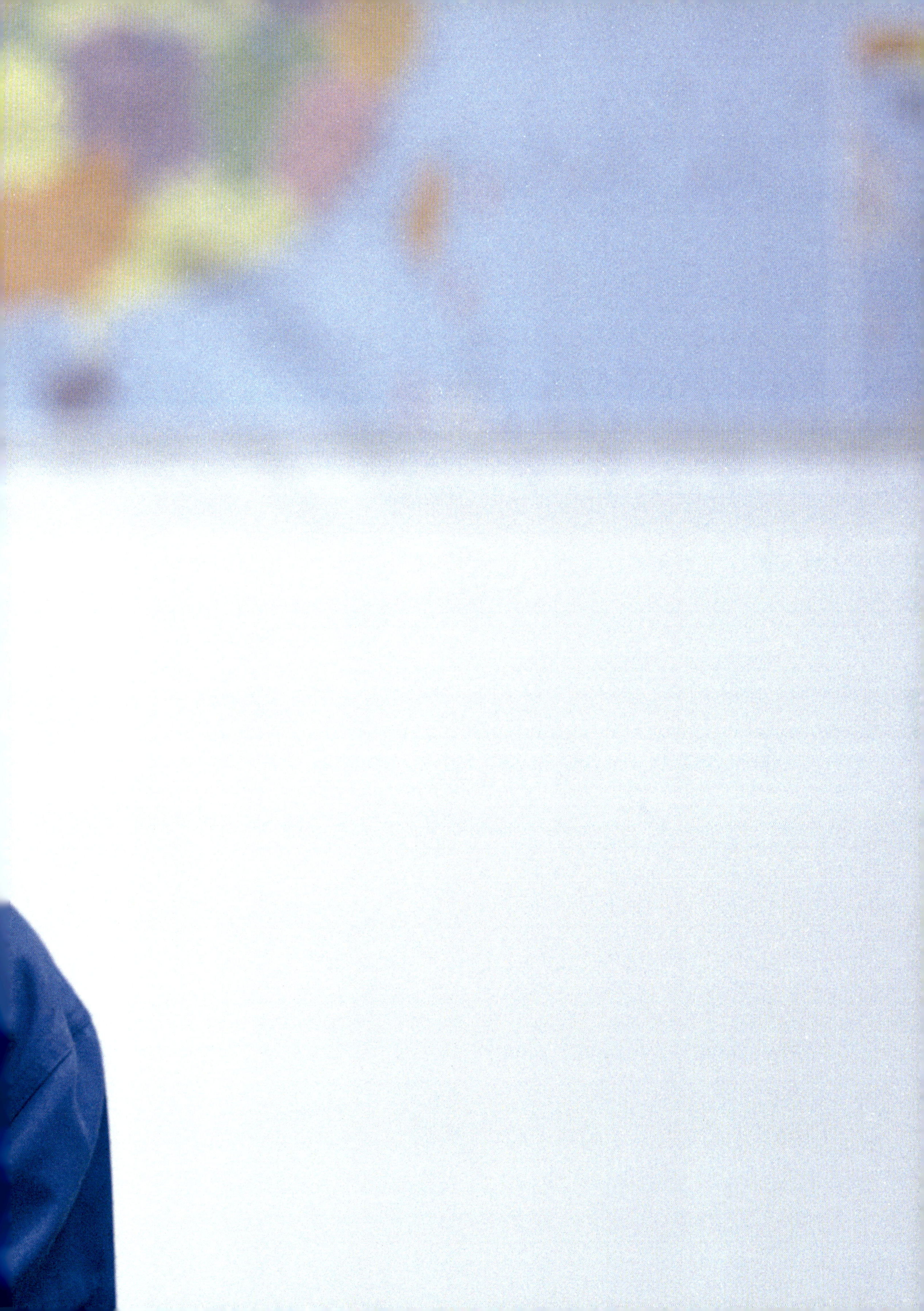

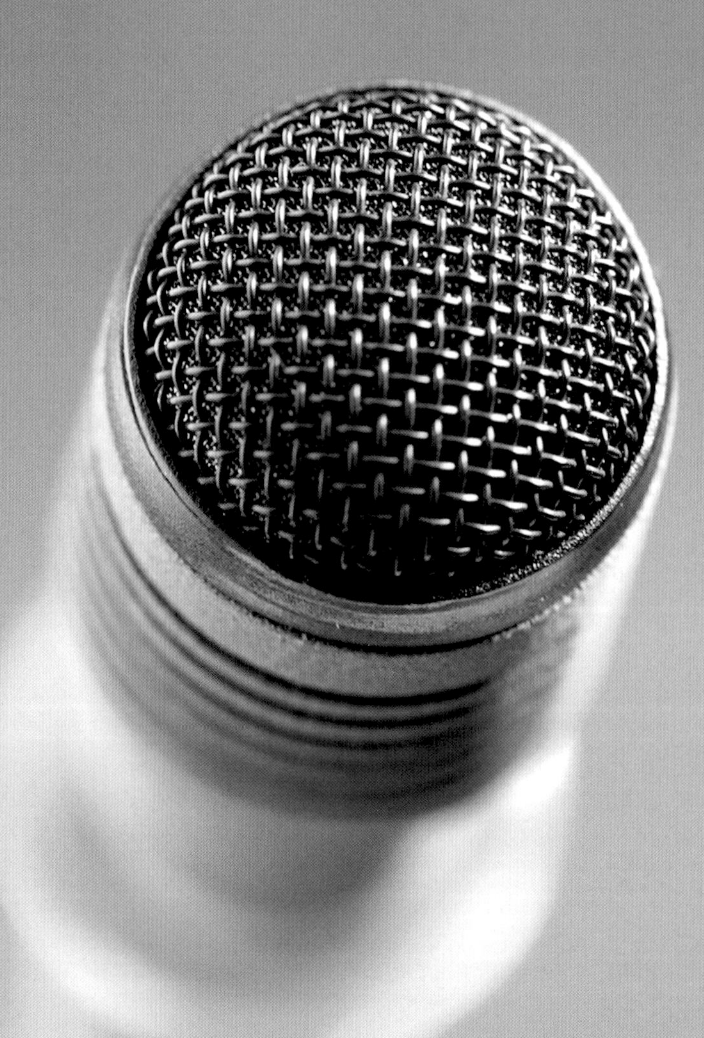

                            ND
You have often emphasized the importance of "invisibility"
as an interpreter. Could you explain what you mean?

                            RA
Again, the task you assign yourself and the task the world
expects of you is to be a mediator between two cultures.
And there is a responsibility for you to be faithful
to the emotions and the linguistic expressions of the
speaker. When I said "invisible," I meant that you have no
right to second-guess your speaker. It is what he says,
how he feels, what he's trying to say... this is what's
important.

I always give an example of one speech that I interpreted,
I think it was Yitzhak Rabin's last speech to the United
Nations before he was assassinated. And his speechwriter...
honestly, the writer did such a beautiful job. Ok, first
I'll tell you about my own cultural sensitivities, to
contextualize this. My mother is a Palestinian. My mother
was born in Nablus in 1926. She left what was Palestine at
the time, in 1938, because it was under mandate and the
British exiled both my grandparents from the West Bank.
Let me give you just that much. When I began to interpret
Rabin's speech, all I could think of was the language,
that it was such a beautiful speech. Next to me, there
was an interpreter who was never known for expressing her
emotions, and afterwards, she turned to me and said, "Oh
my God, Rasha, that was beautiful!"

I could not think of anything else, only what the
speechwriter wanted, what Rabin wanted -- rightly or...
hypocritically (laughs). I can say that as a political
judgment, after the fact. But when I was on duty, during
that speech, I did it to the best of my ability. I did
it as if I were an Israeli citizen proud of her prime
minister. This is what I mean by "invisible." As an
interpreter, I have no right to be anything in between.

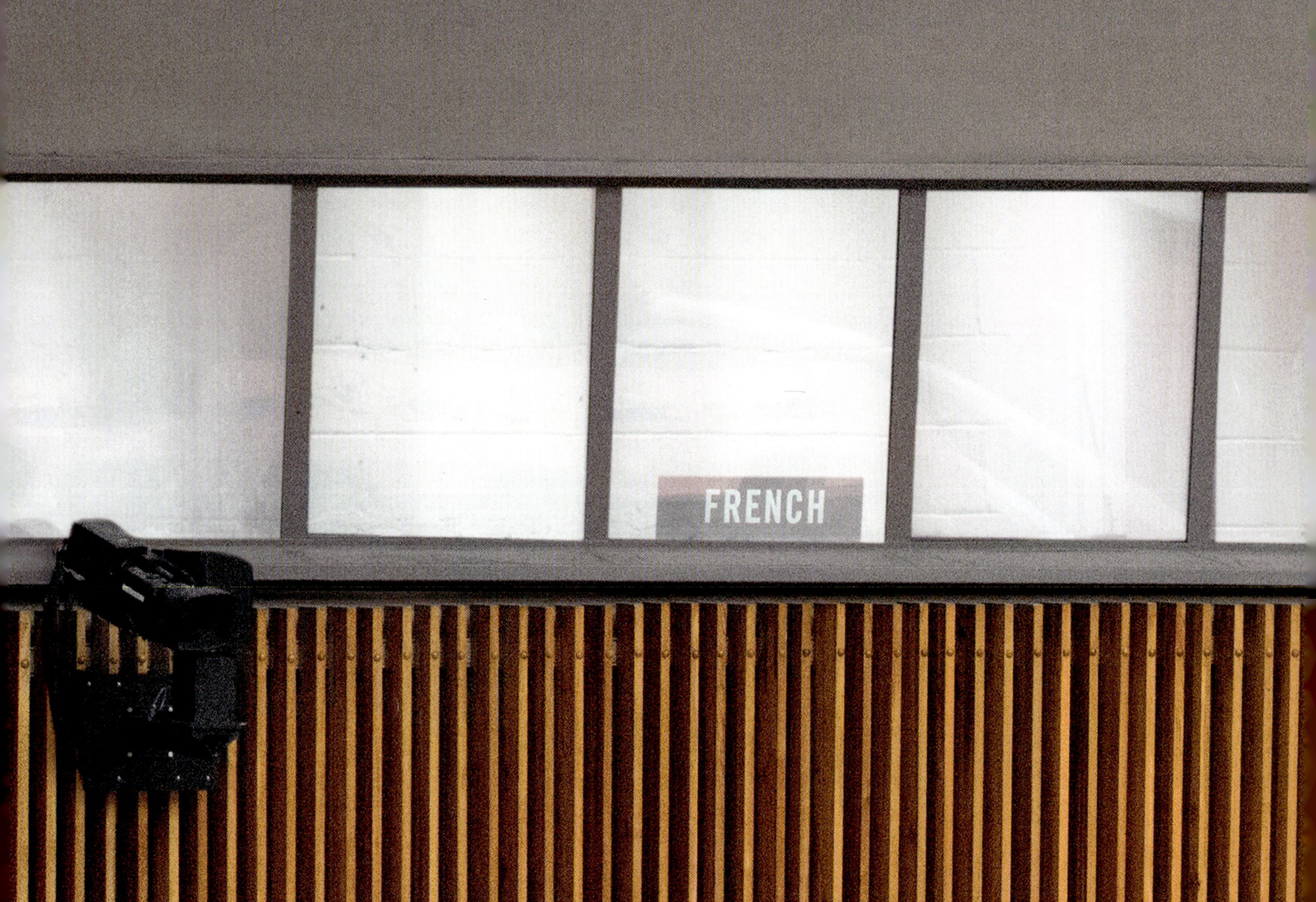
FRENCH

RUSSIAN

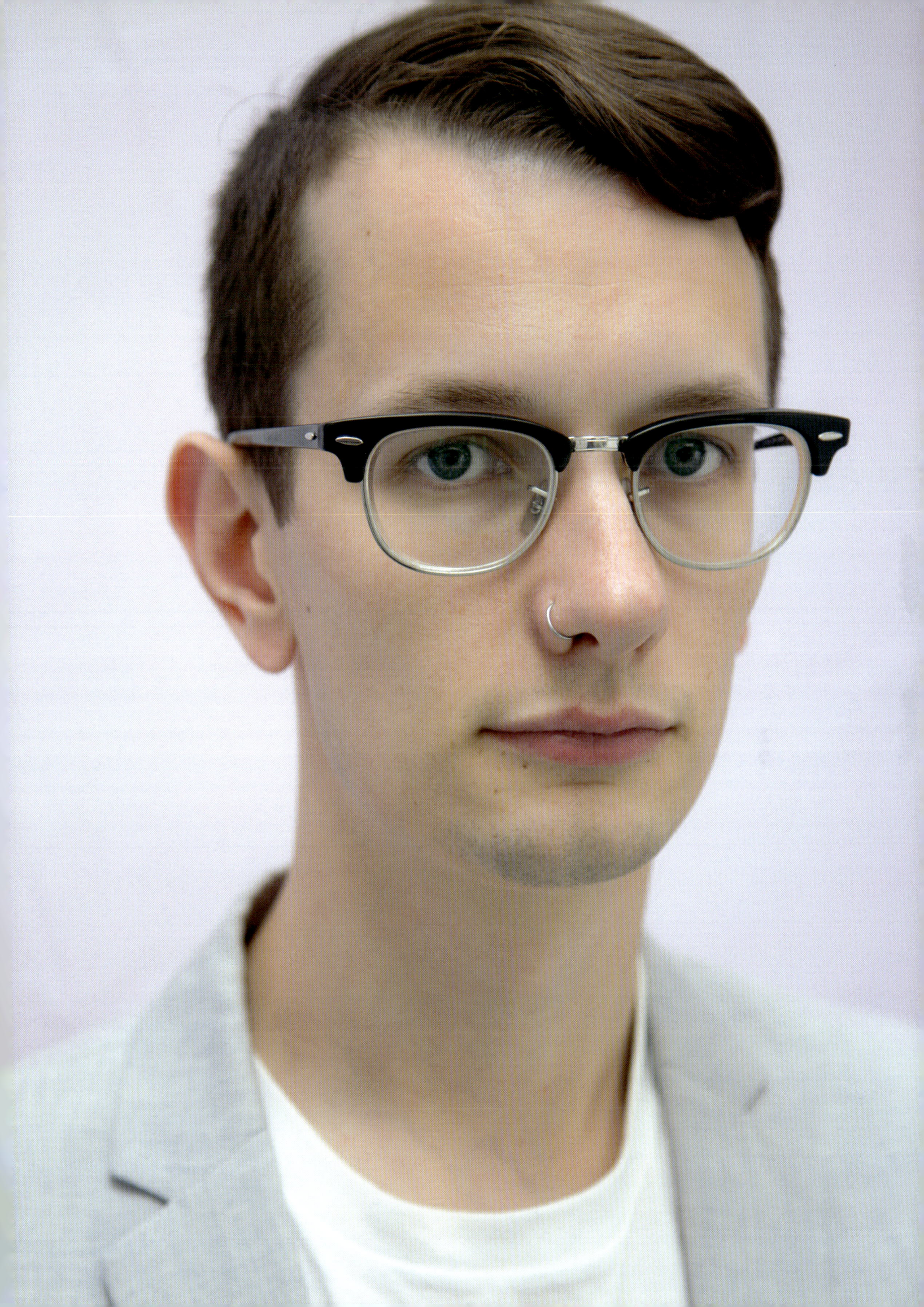

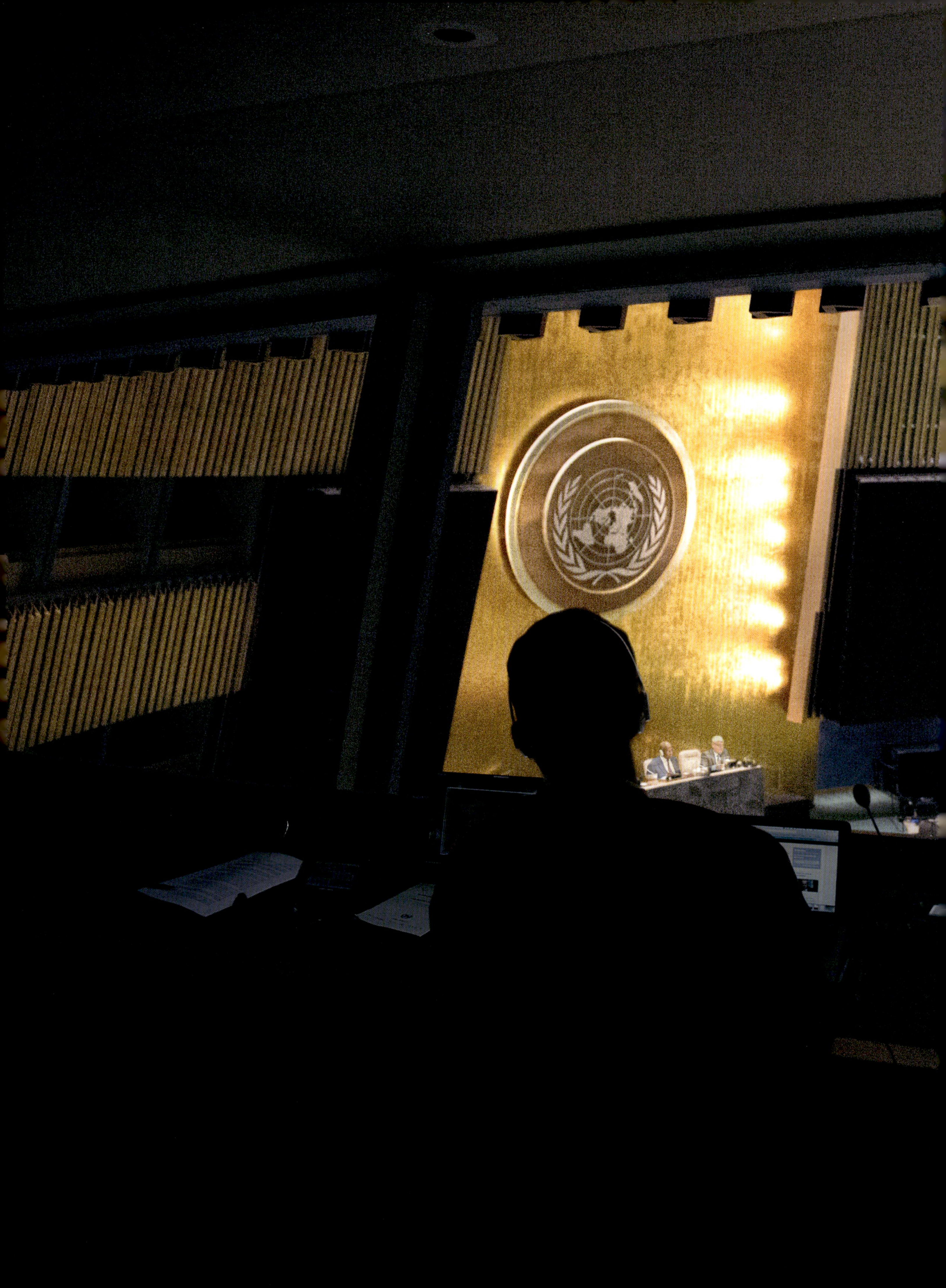

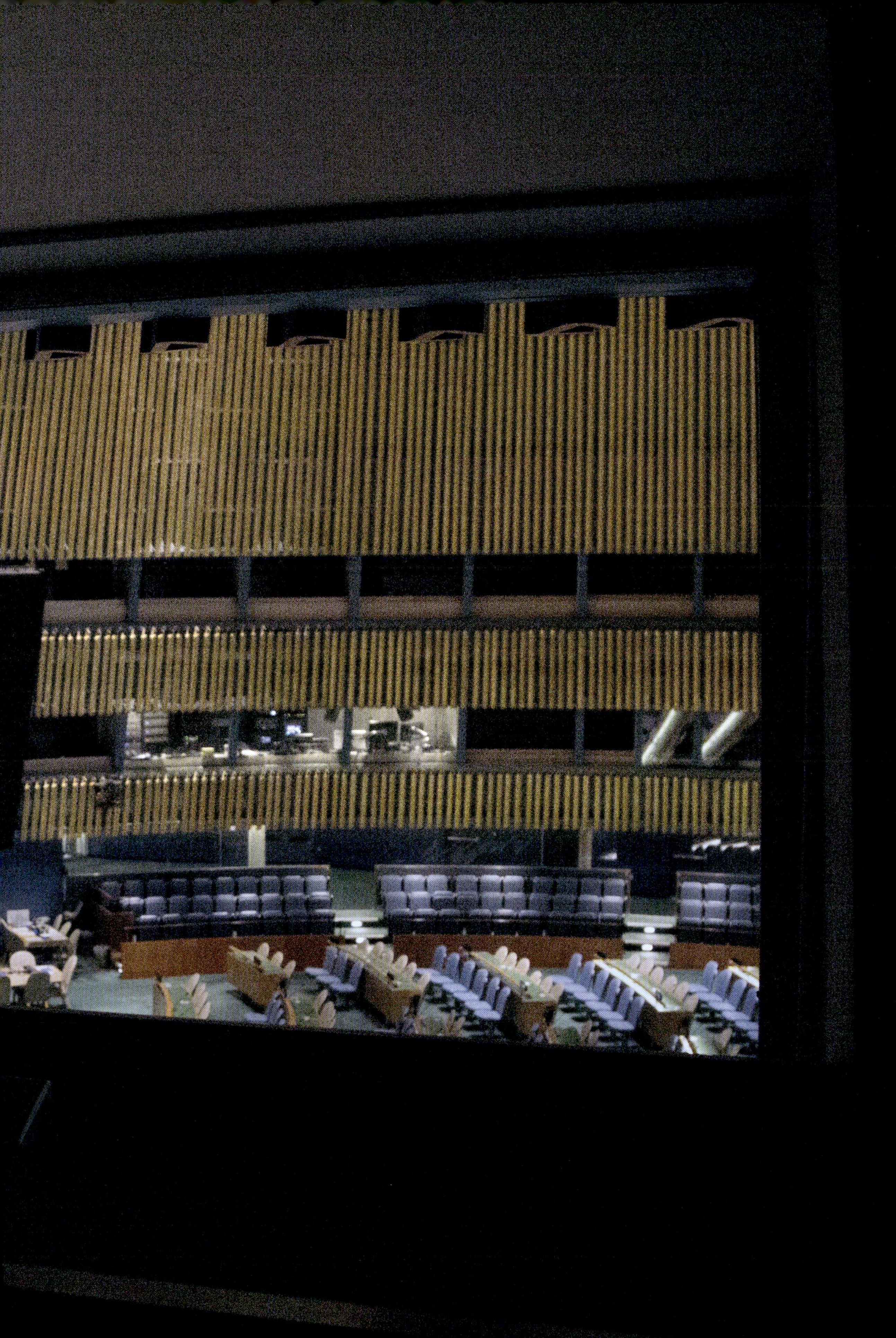

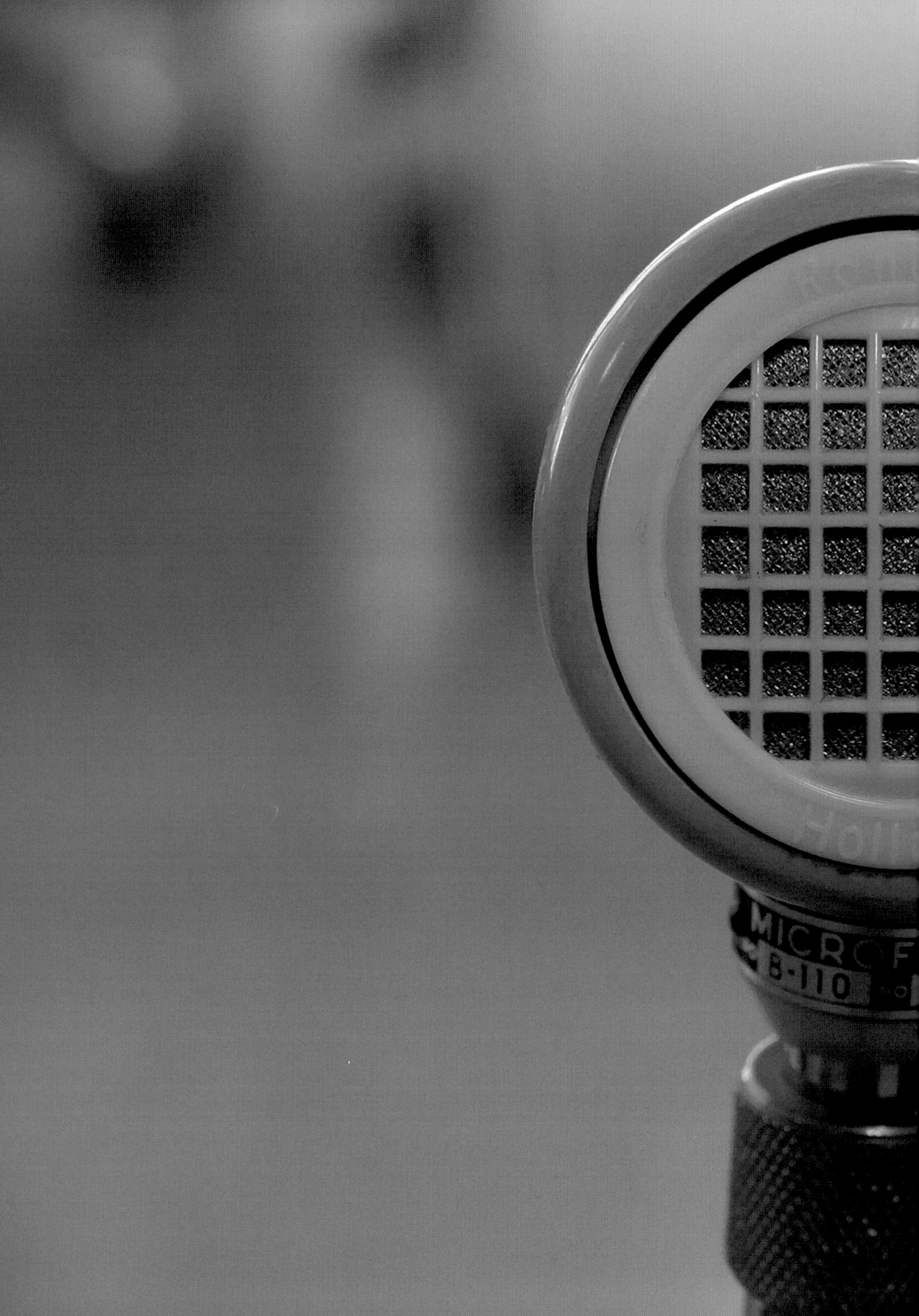
MICROF
CB-110

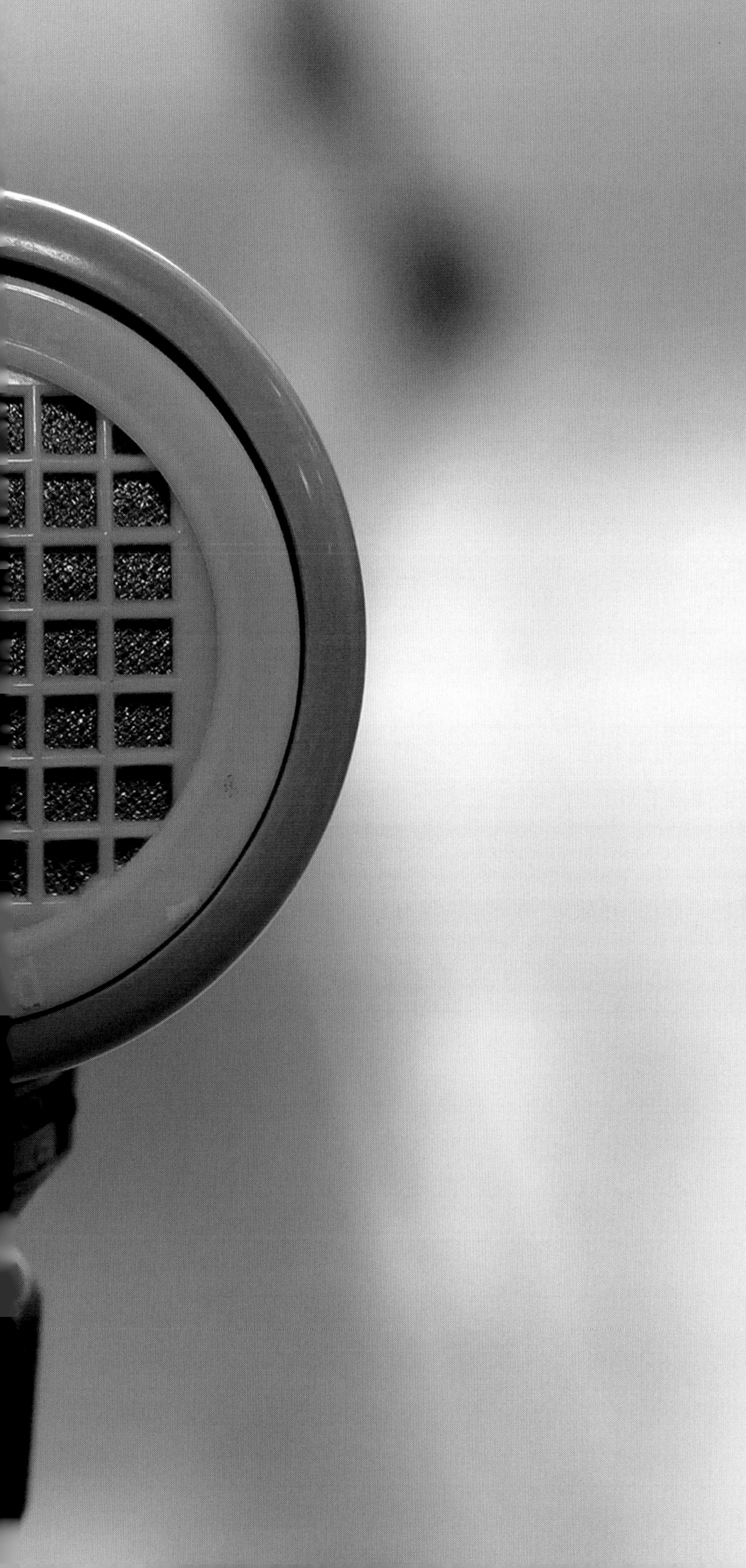

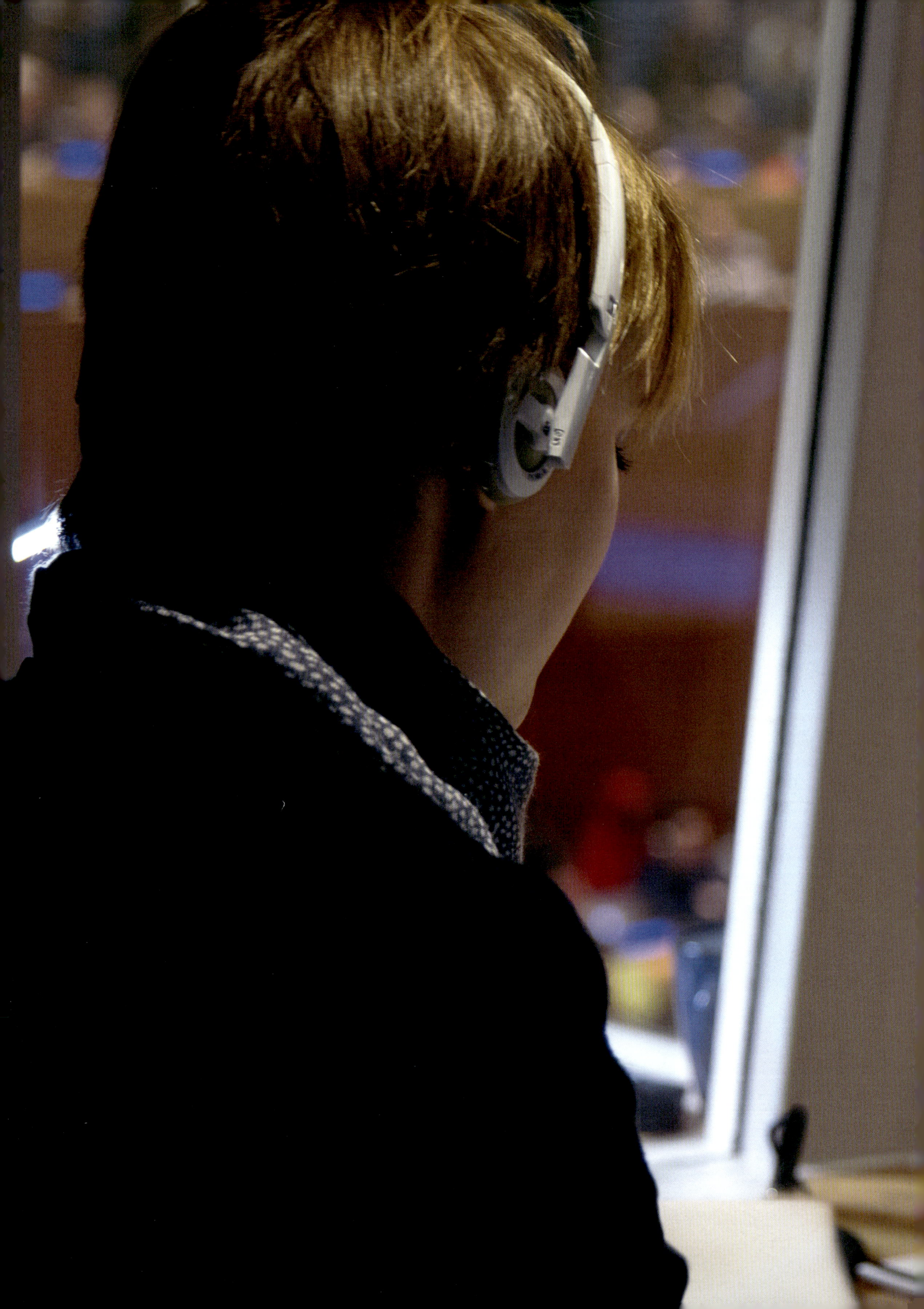

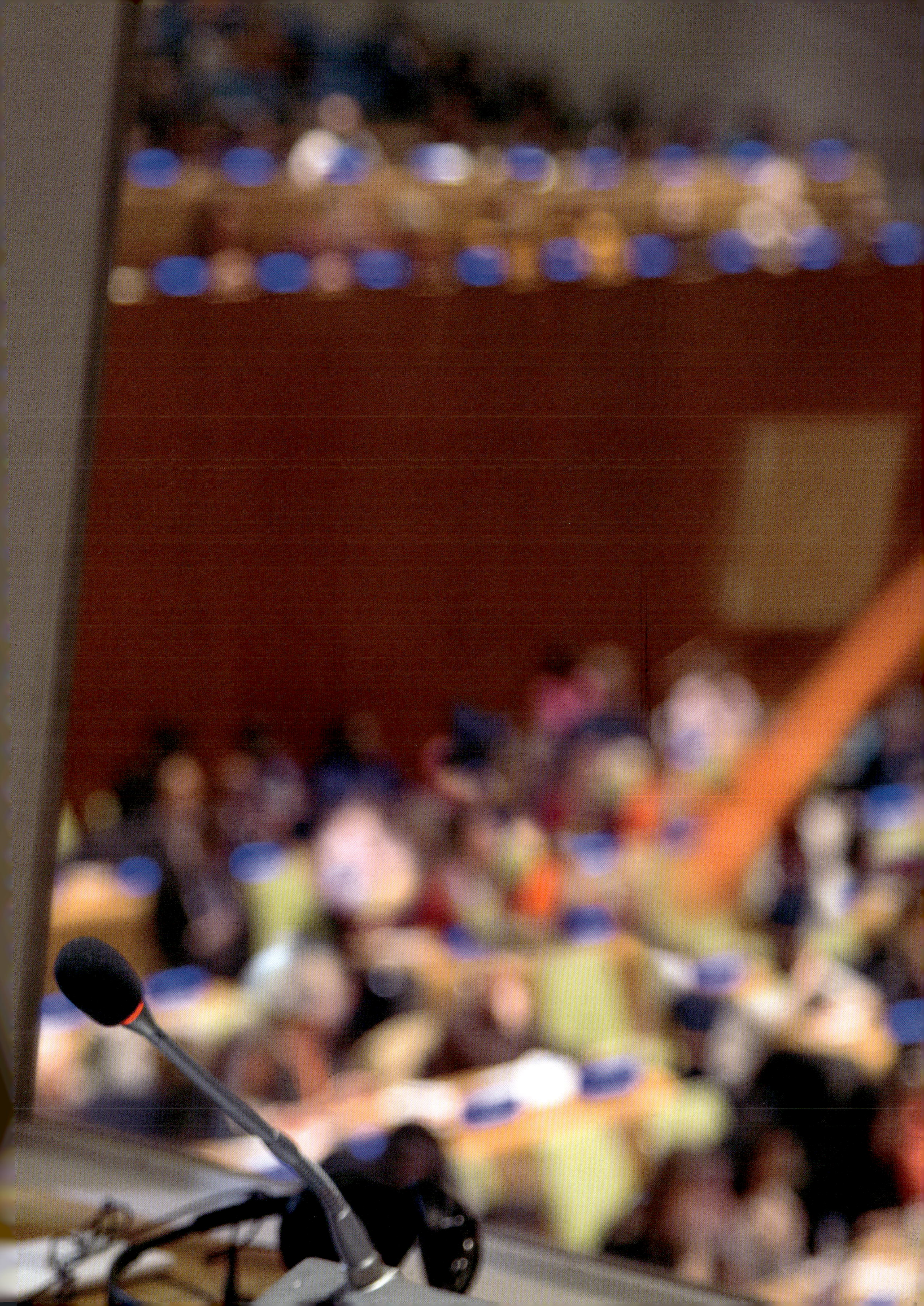

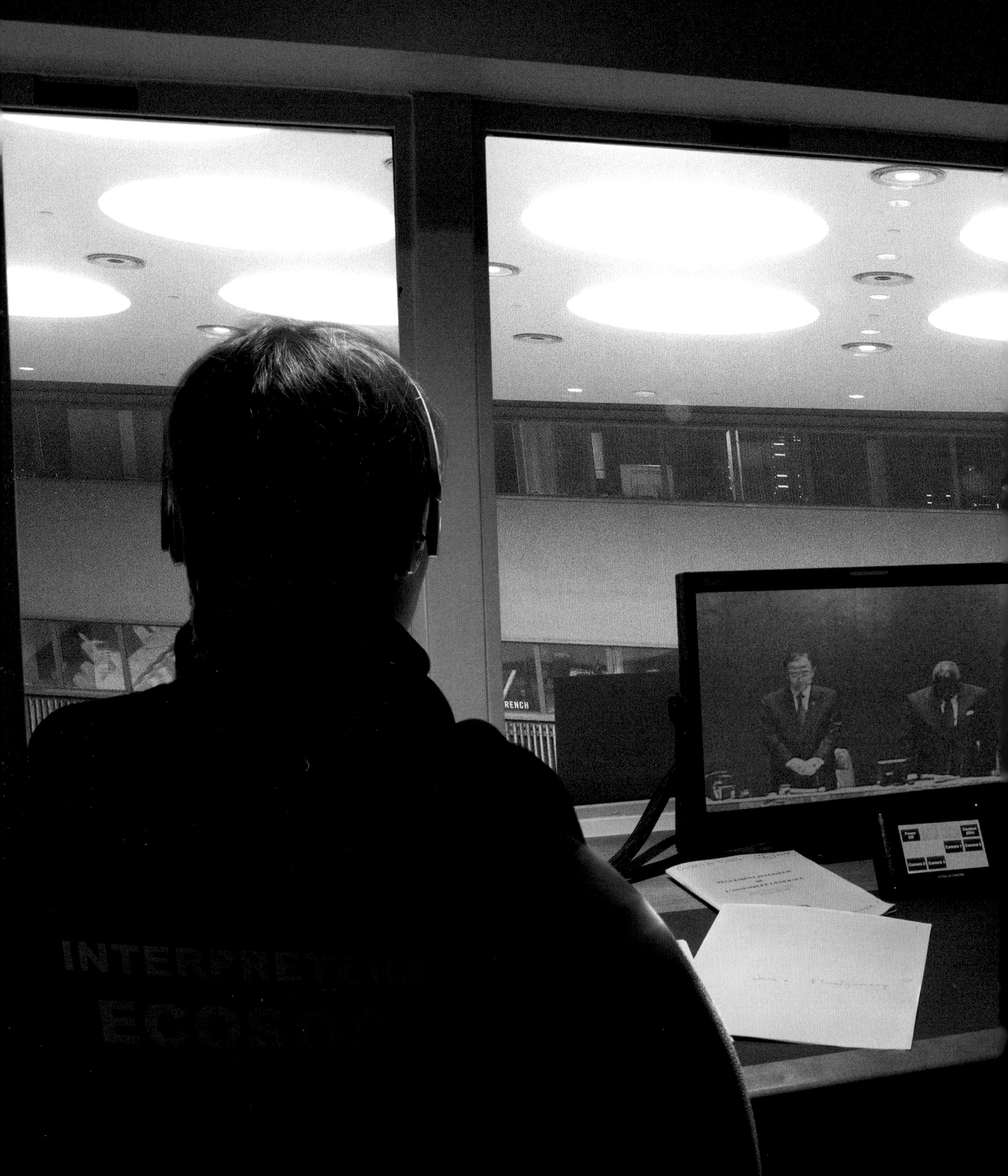

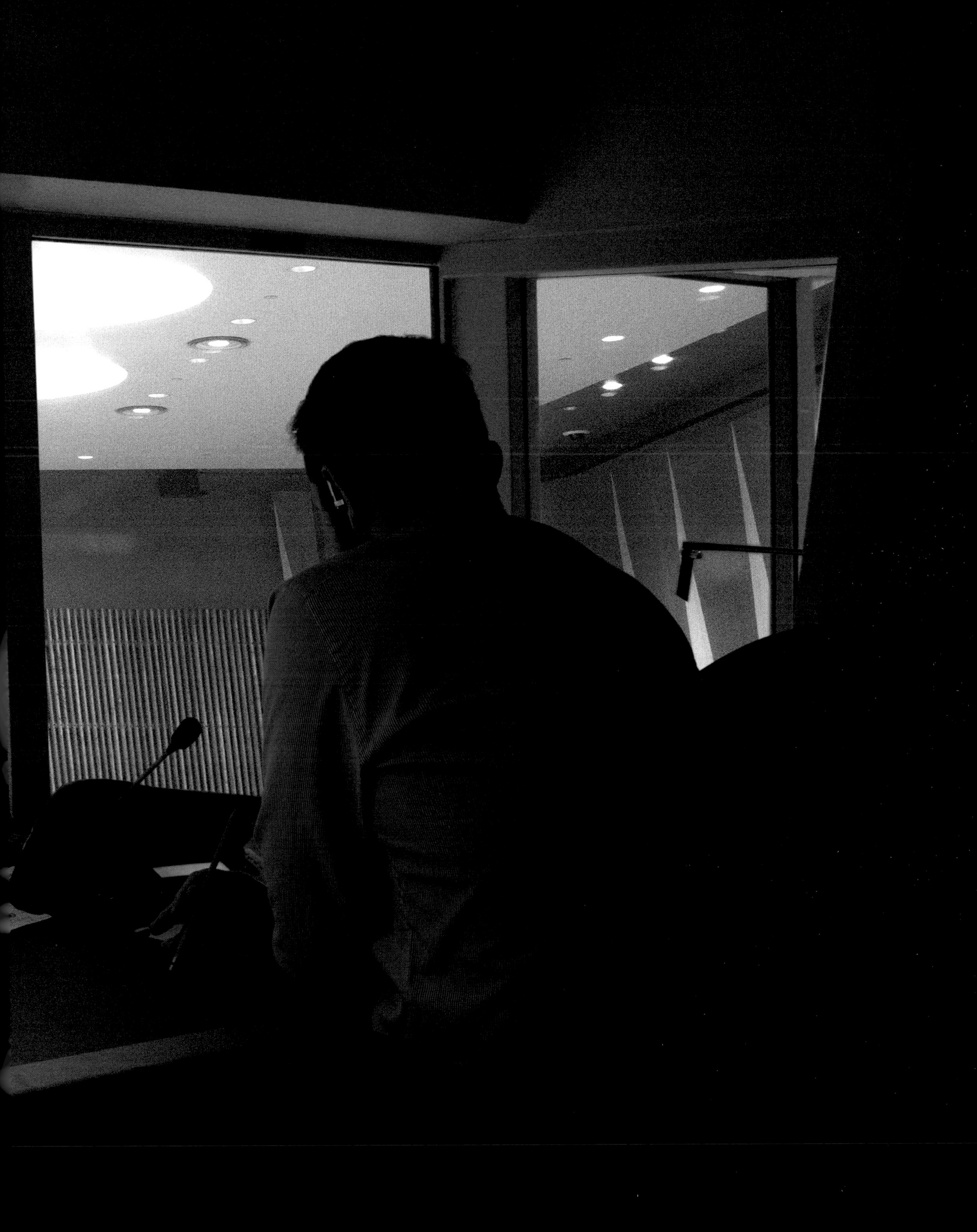

DEMAIN, LE CODE D

LE M

diplor

5,40 € - Mensuel - 28 pages

DOSSIER : FIN DE CYCLE POUR LA SOCI

Le temps des c

TRAVAIL HORS LA LOI ? – pa

ONDE
natique

DÉMOCRATIE

lères

BÂILLONNER LA

Israël à 1
de l'Inqu

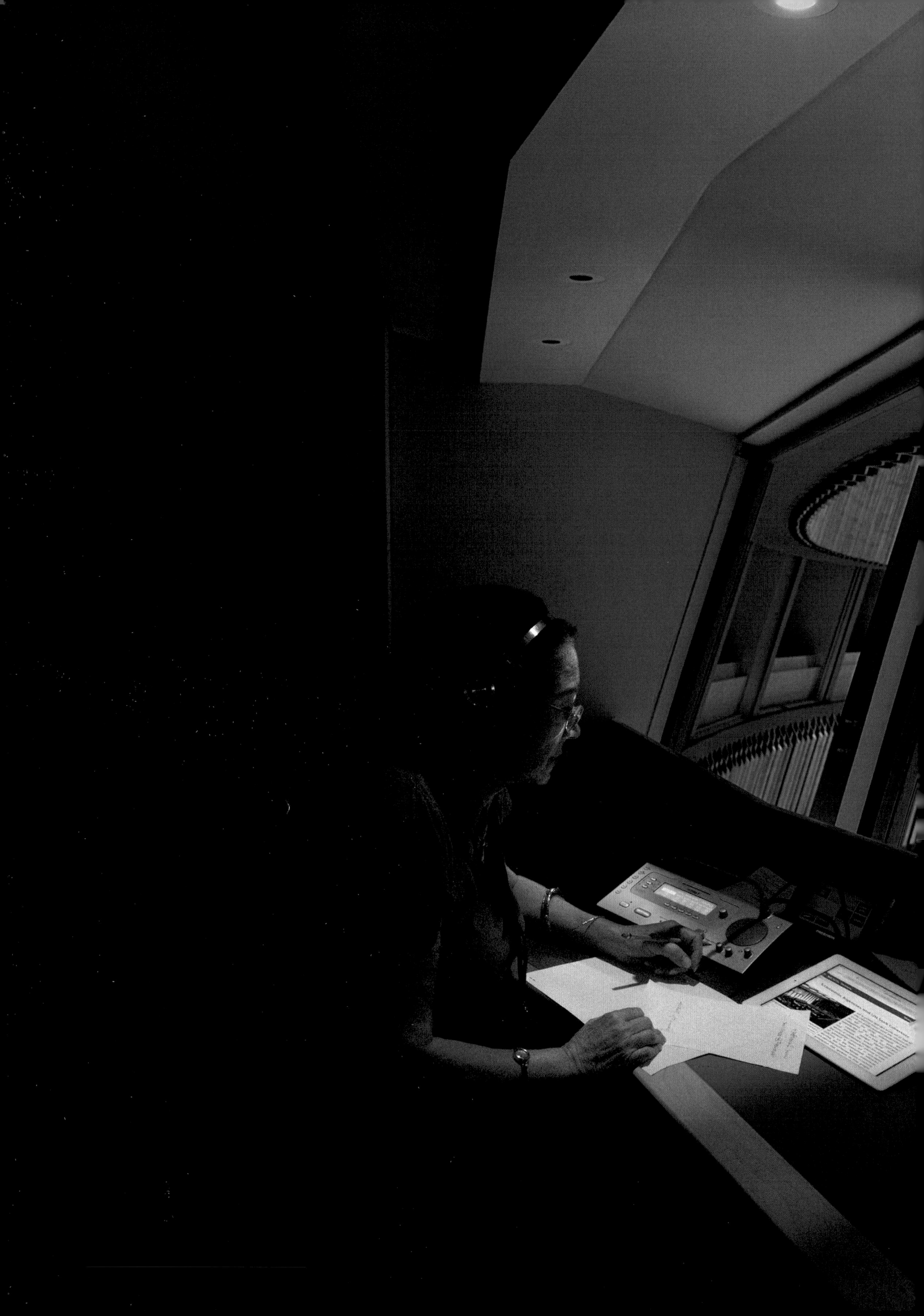

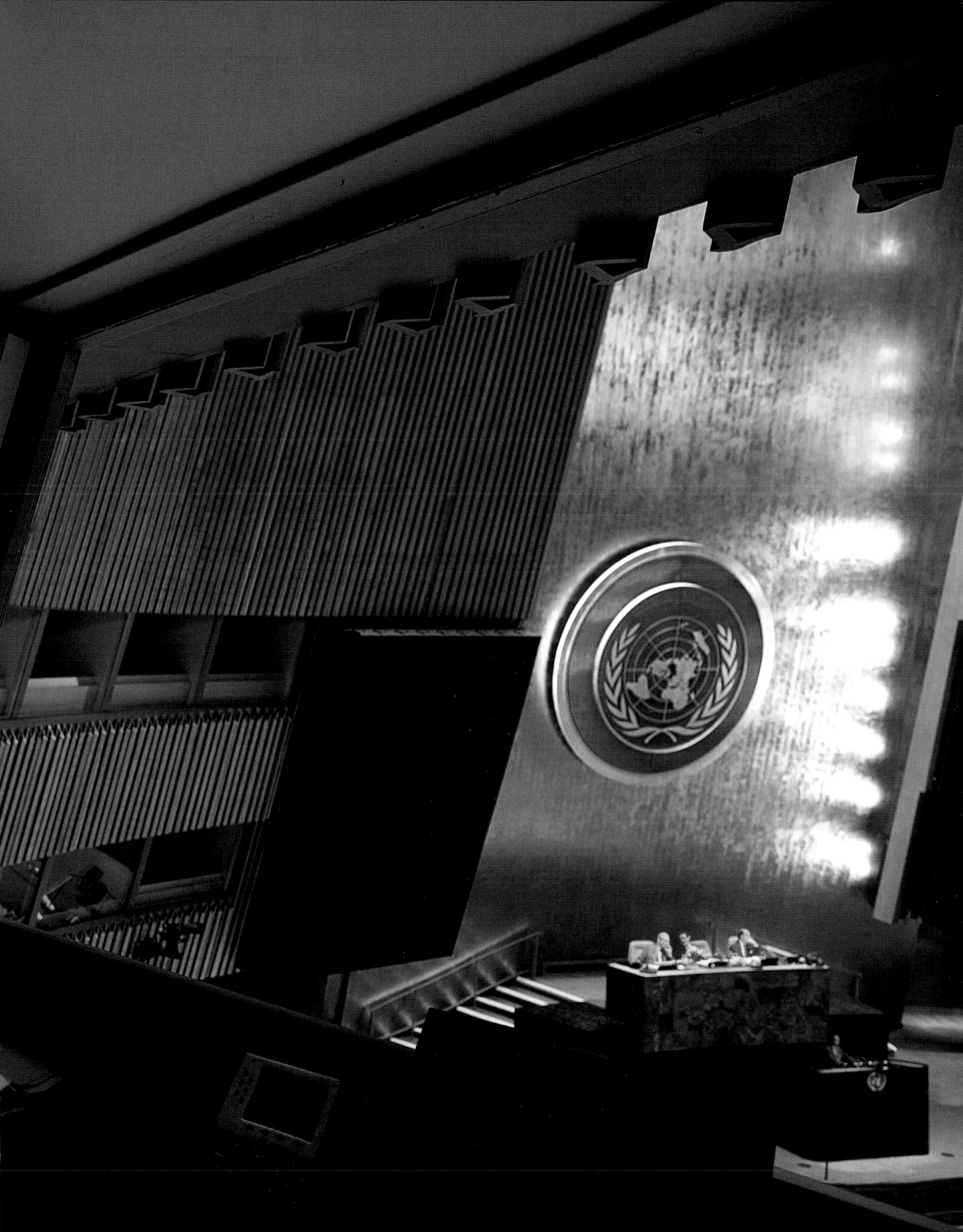

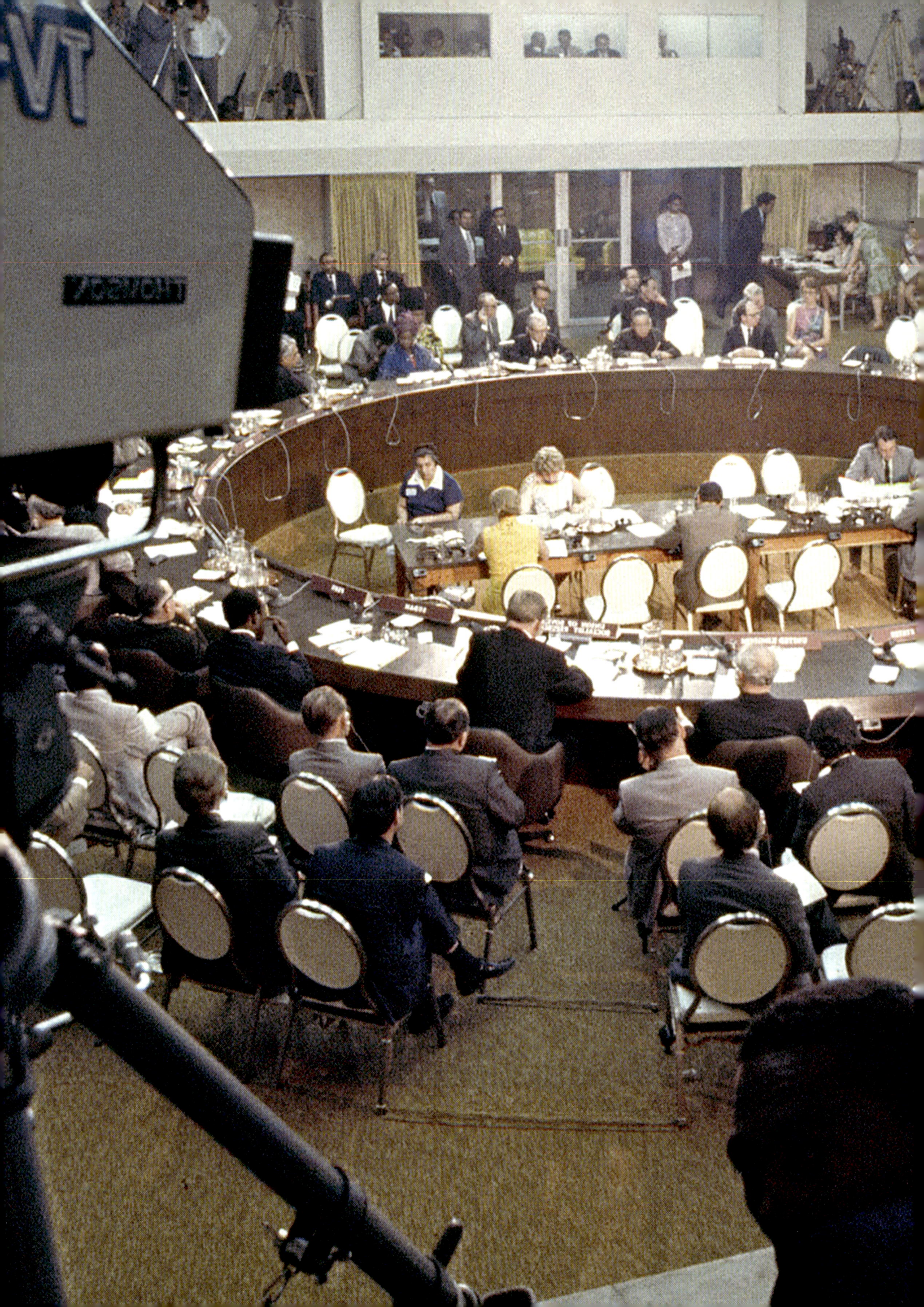

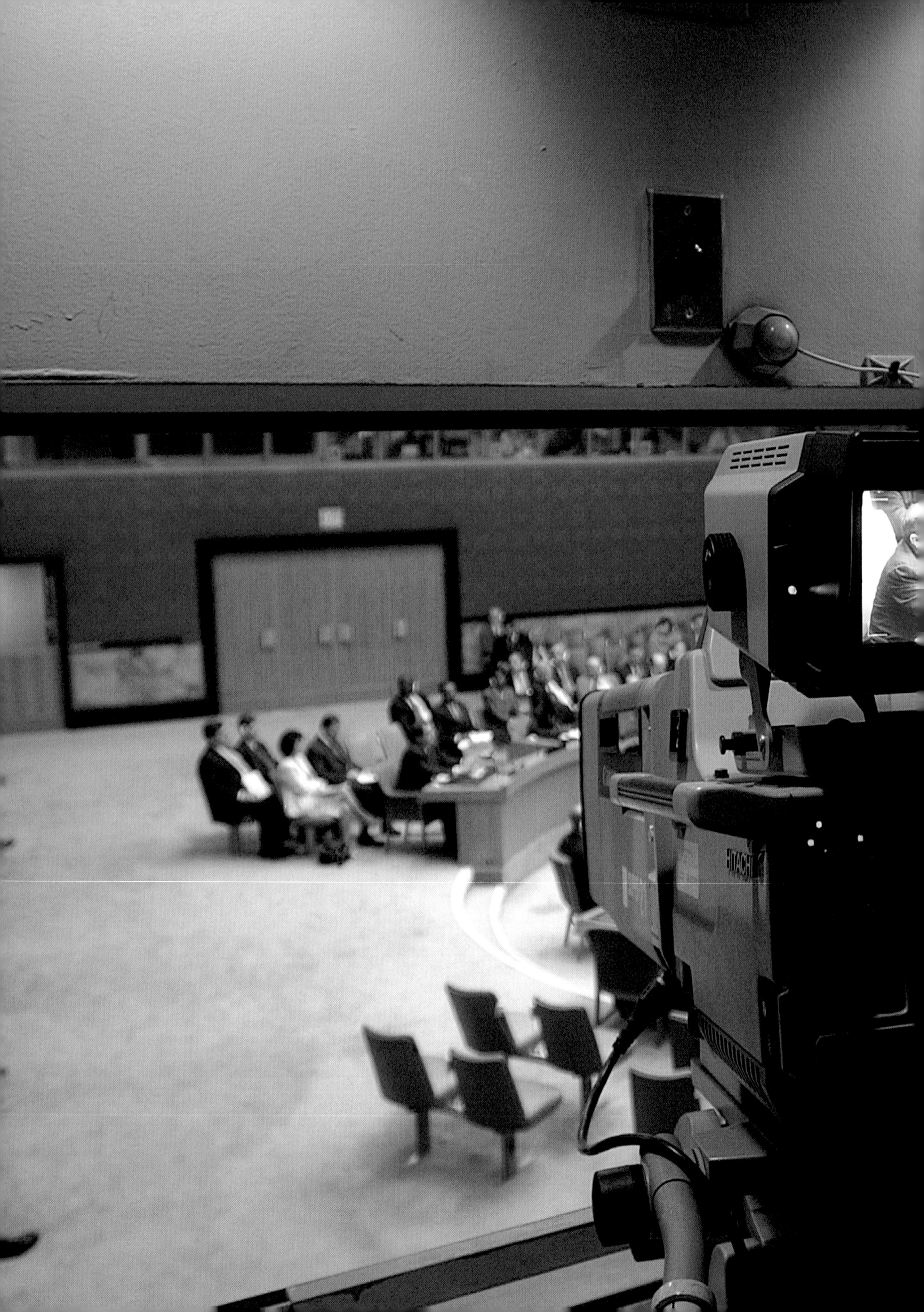

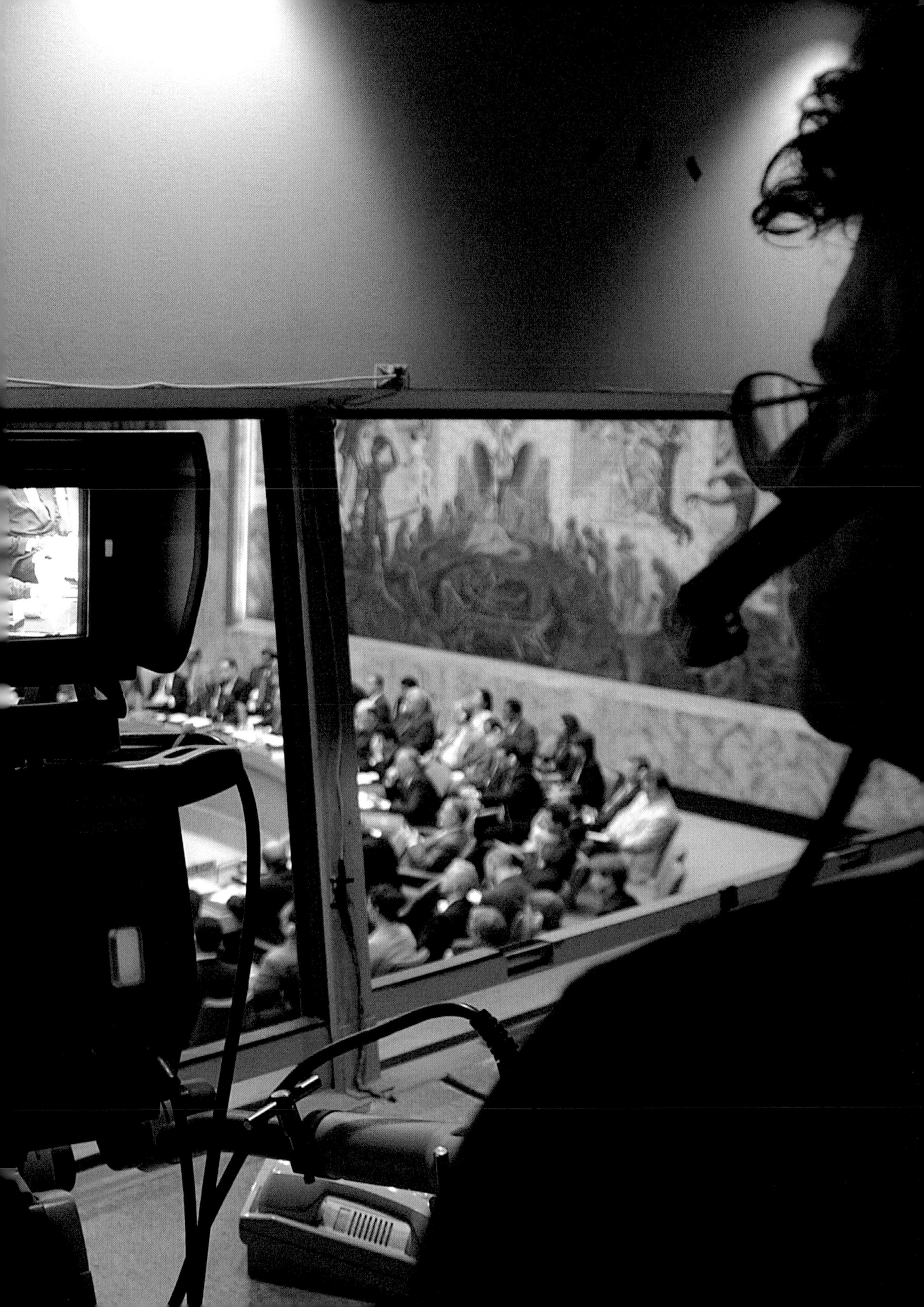

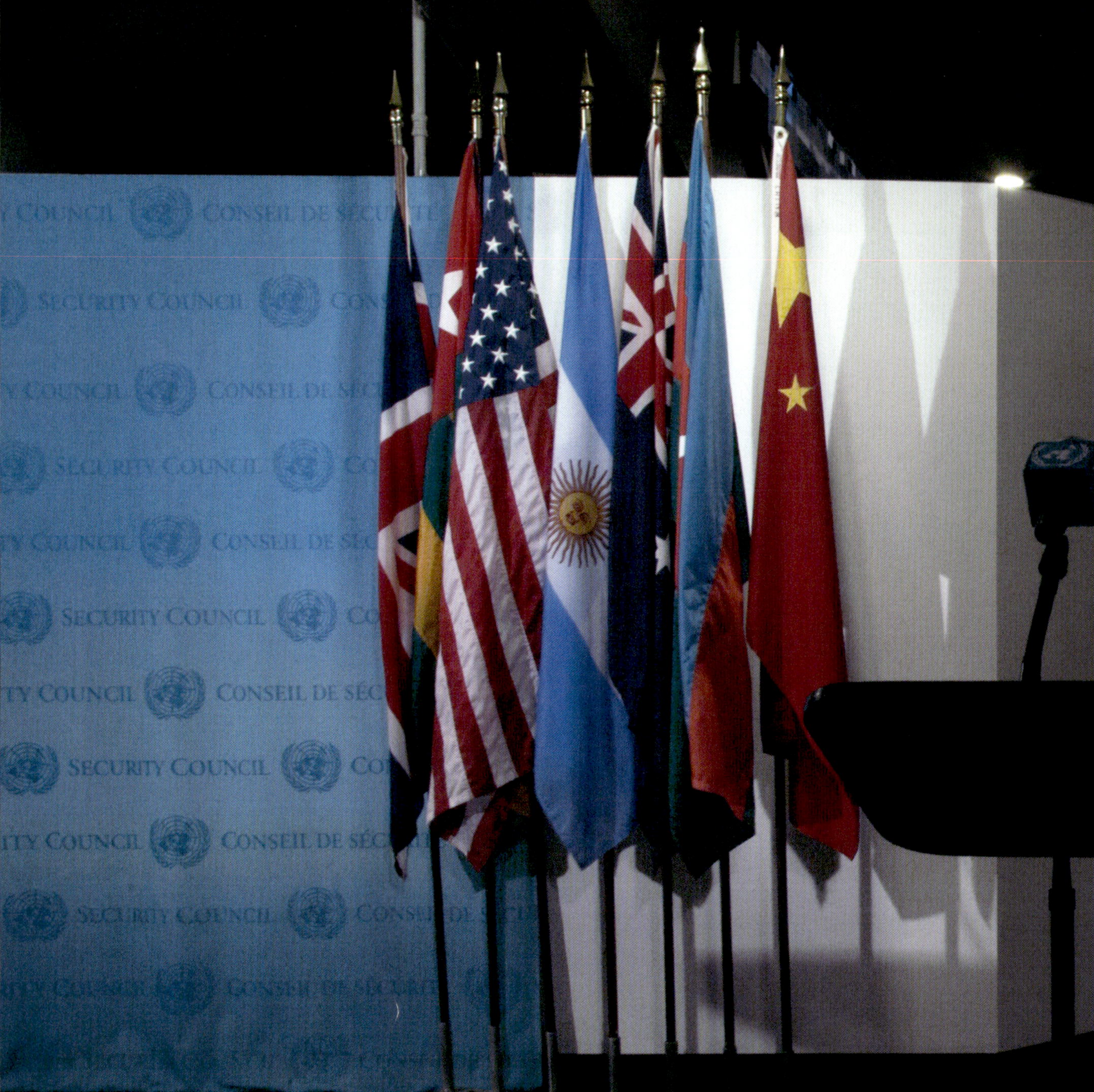

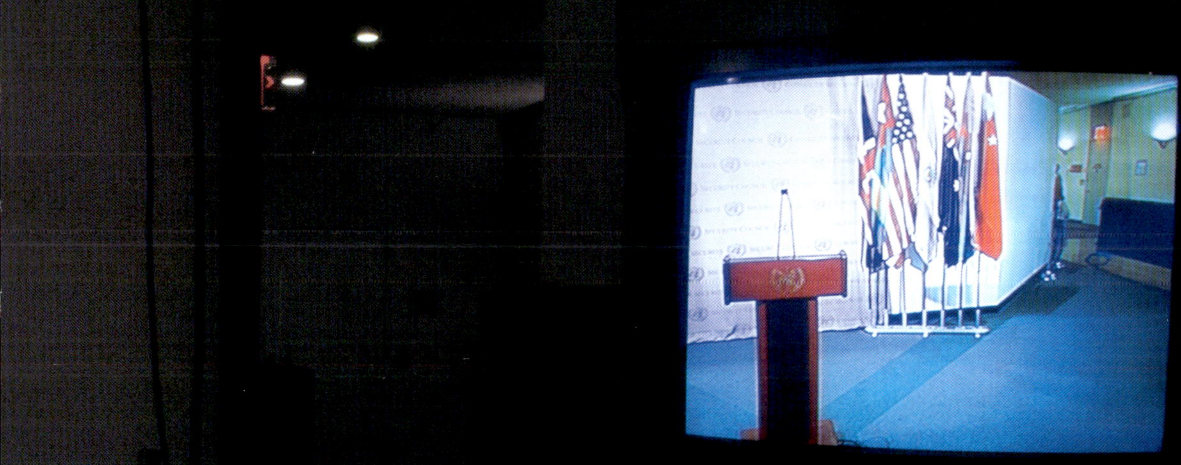

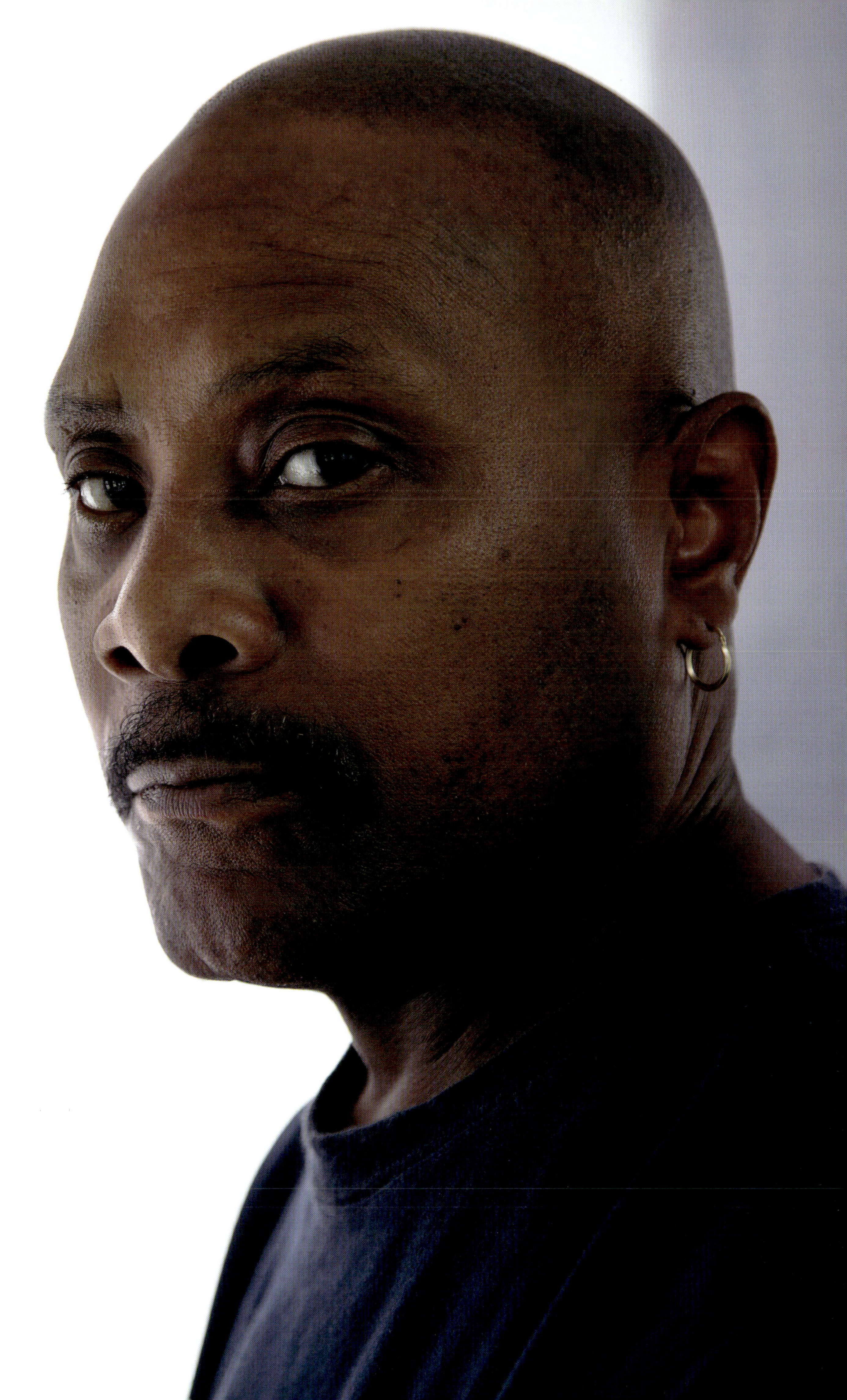

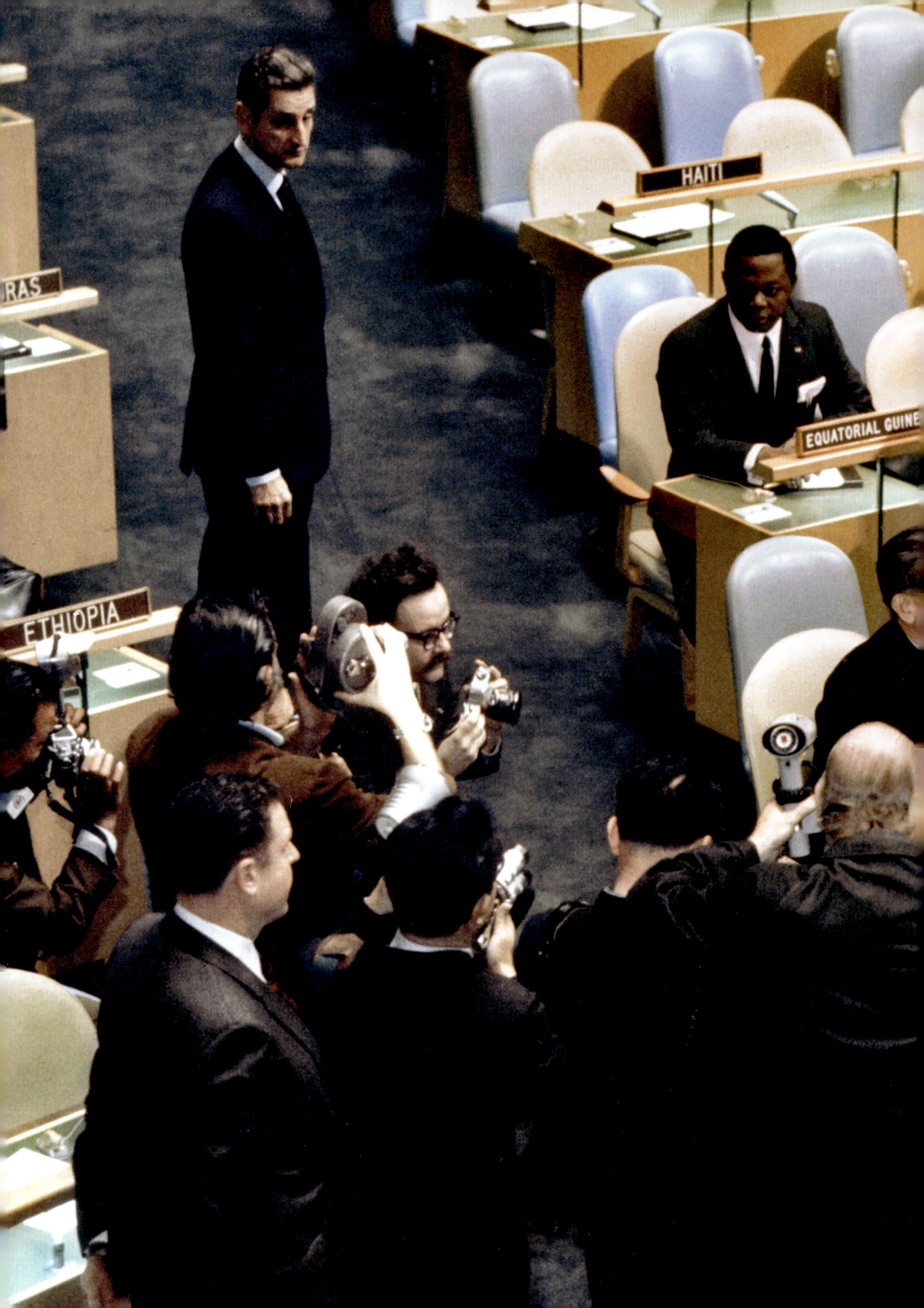

HAITI
EQUATORIAL GUINE
ETHIOPIA
RAS

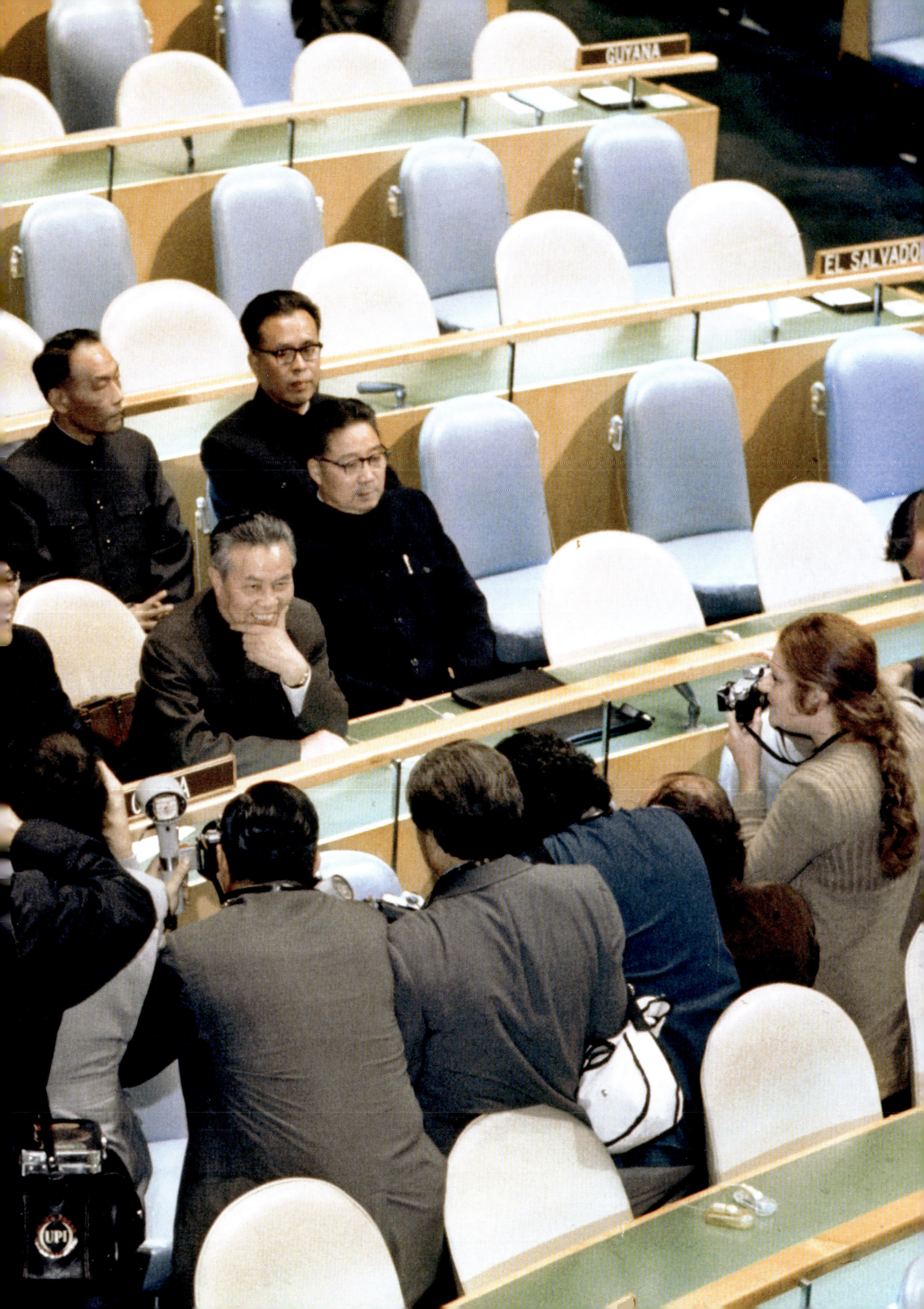

GUYANA
EL SALVADOR
UPI

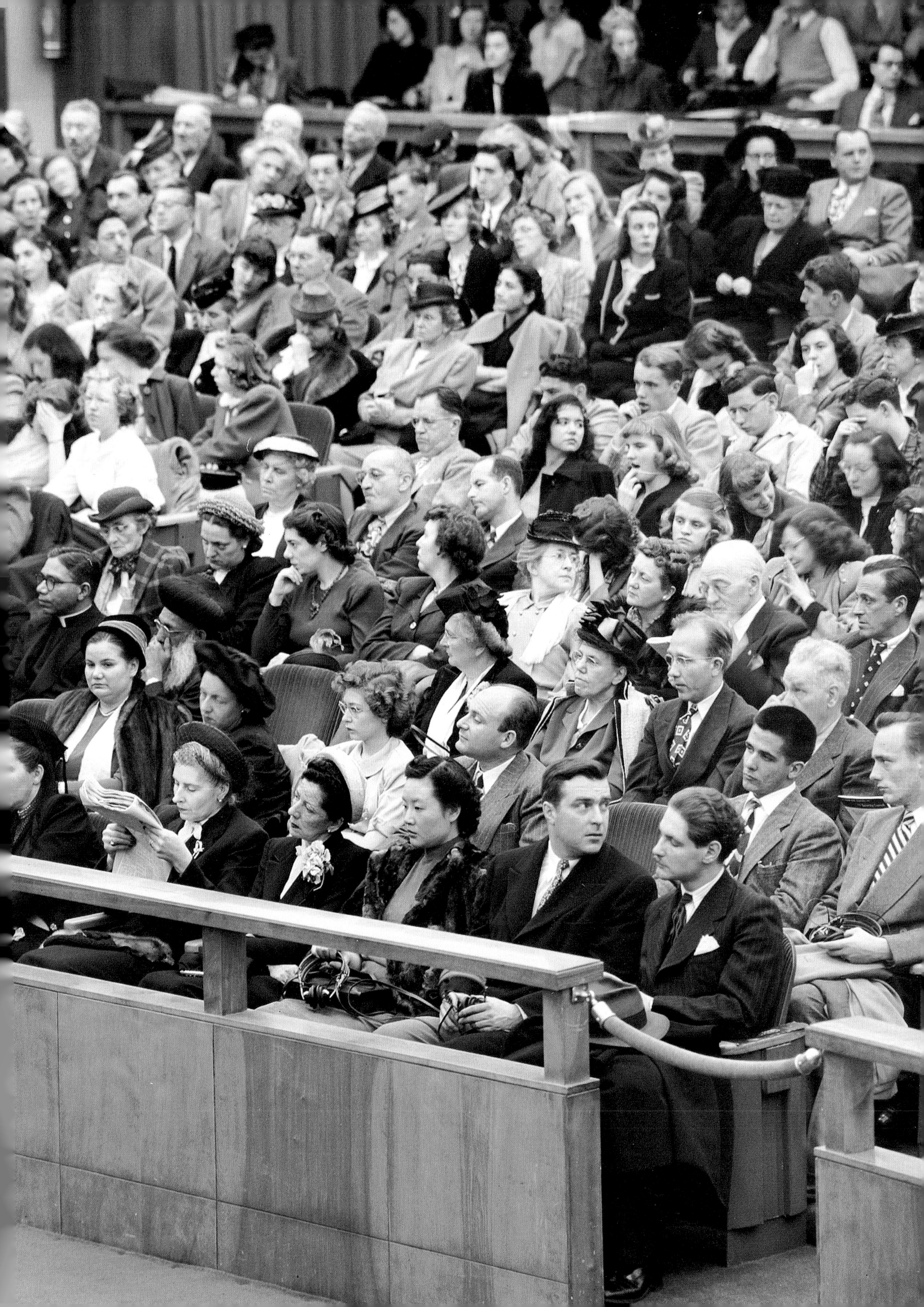

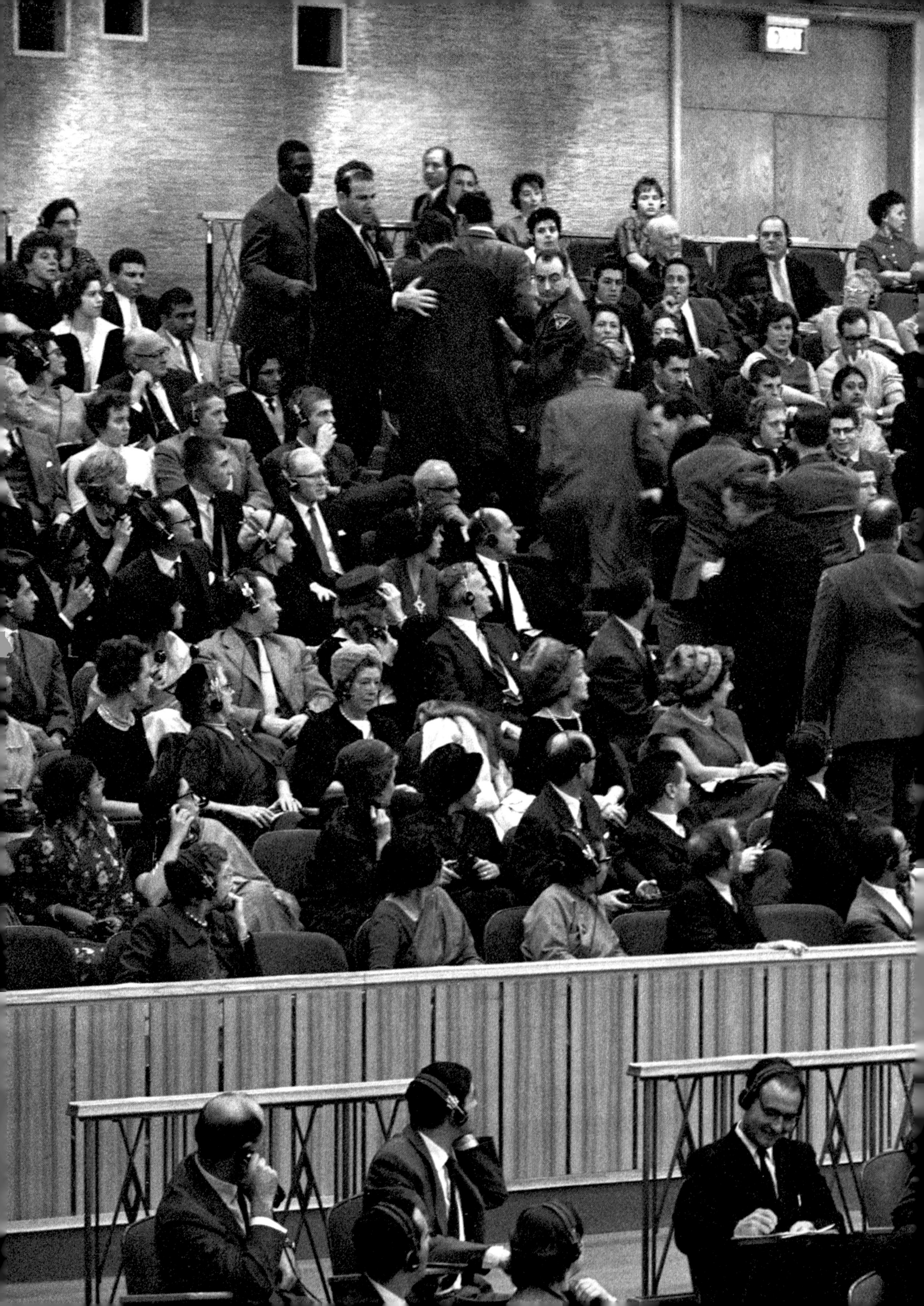

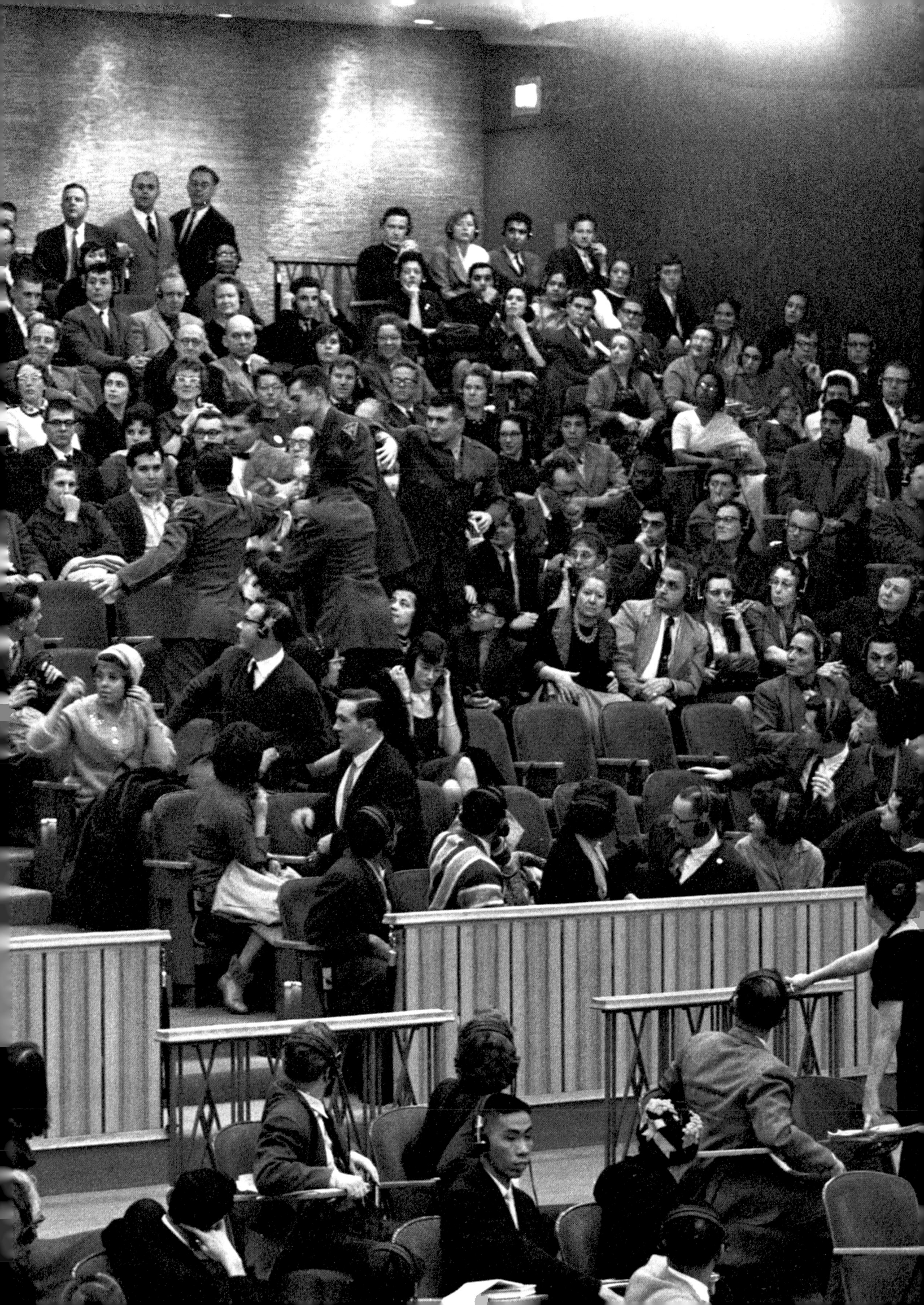

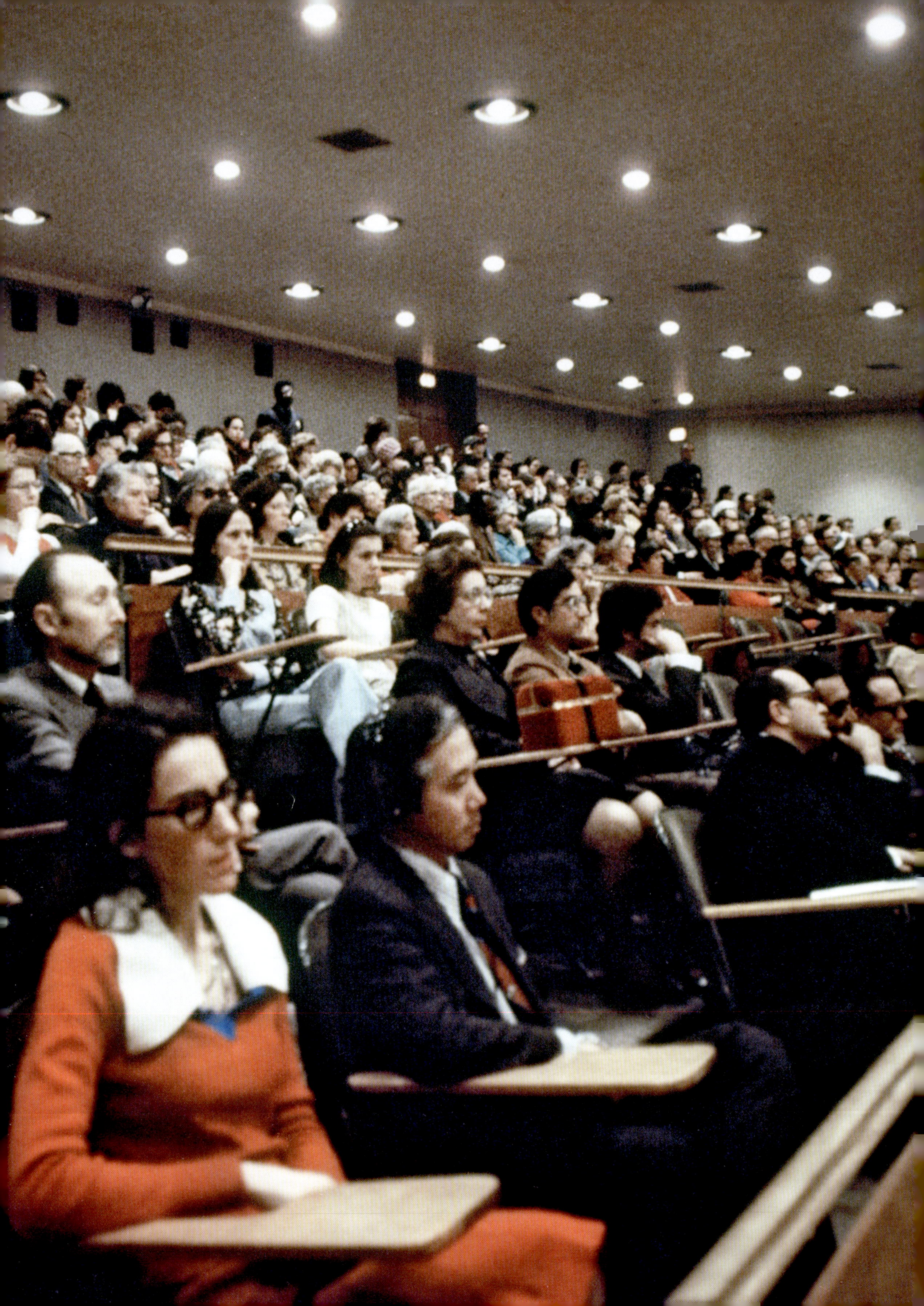

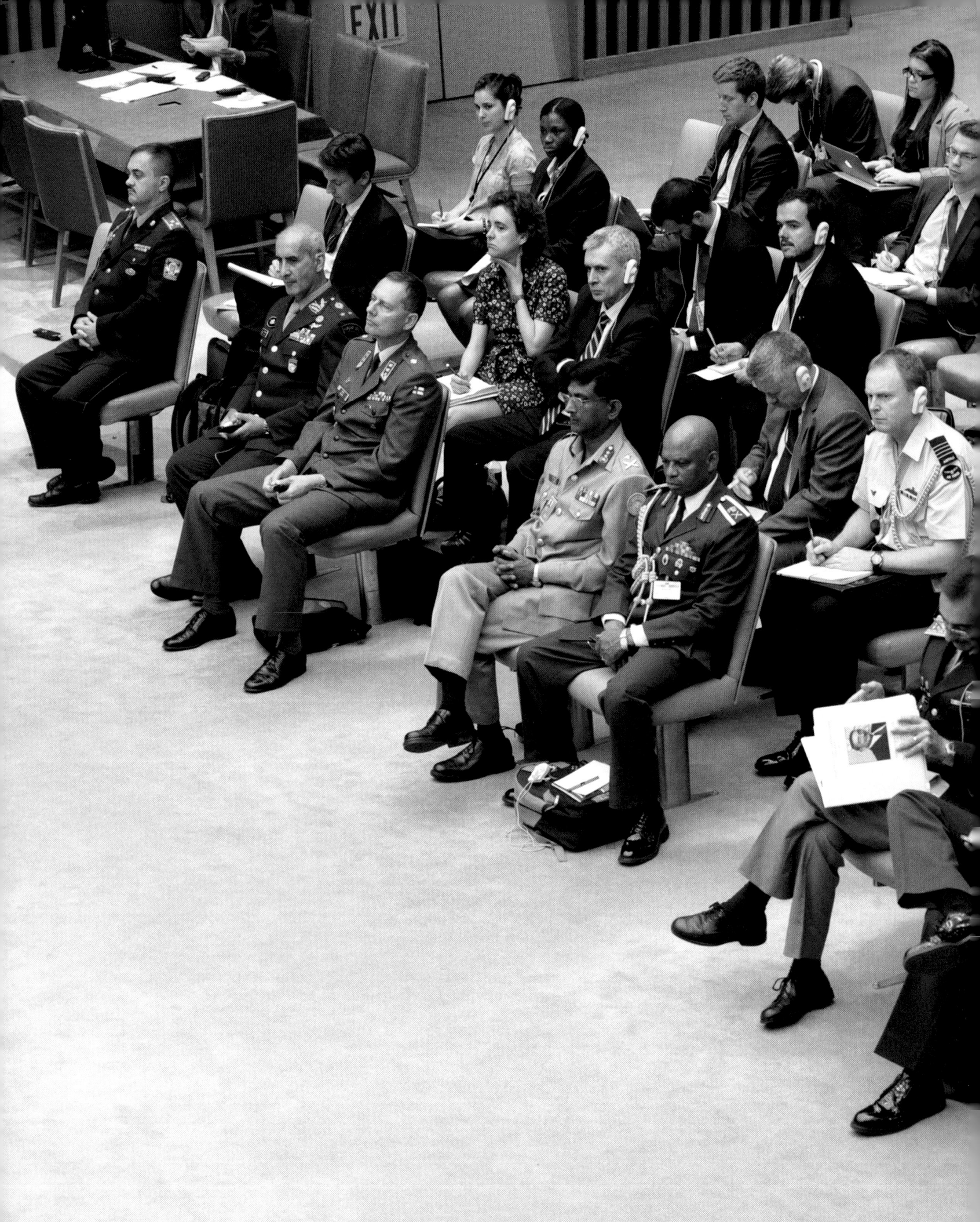

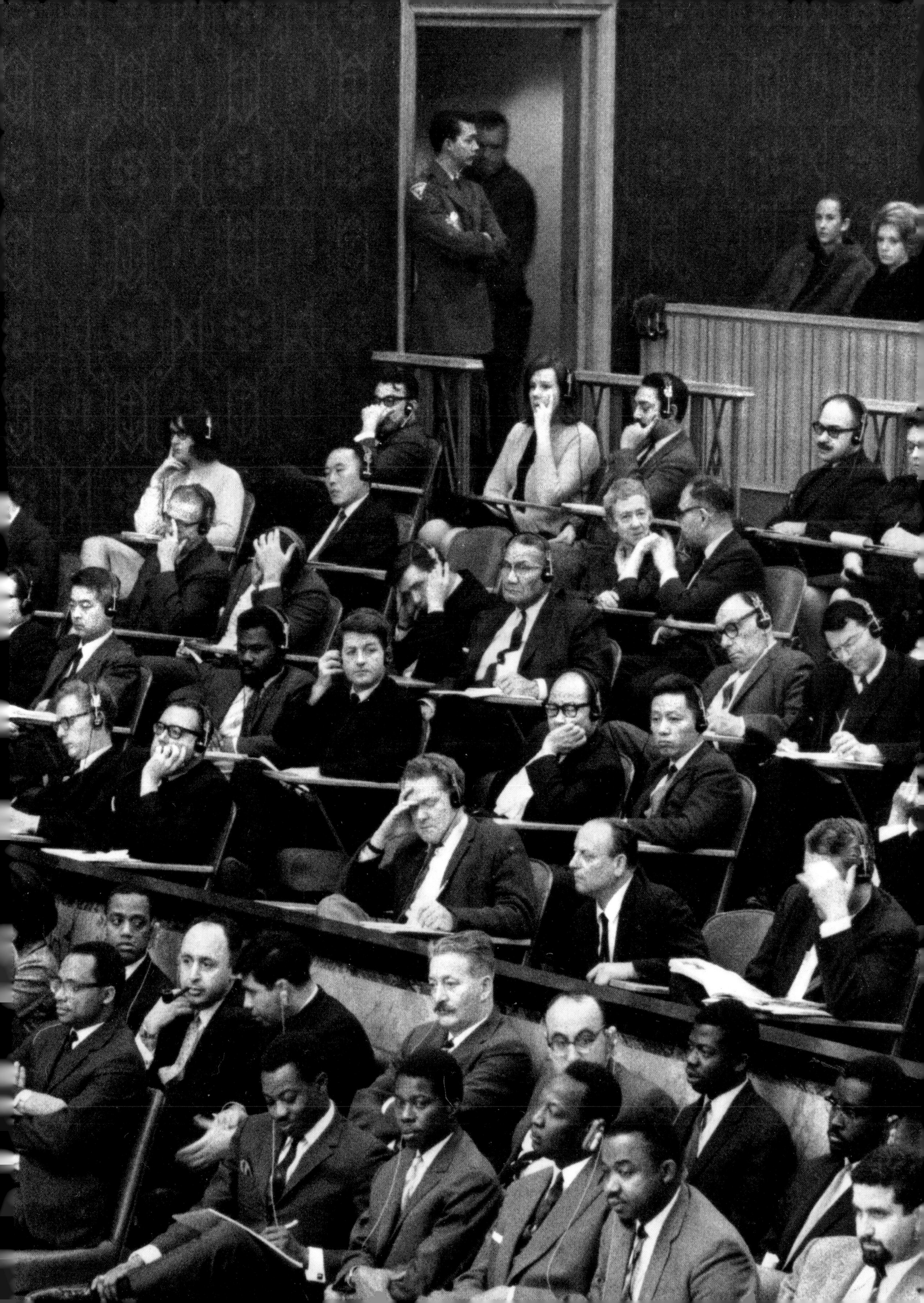

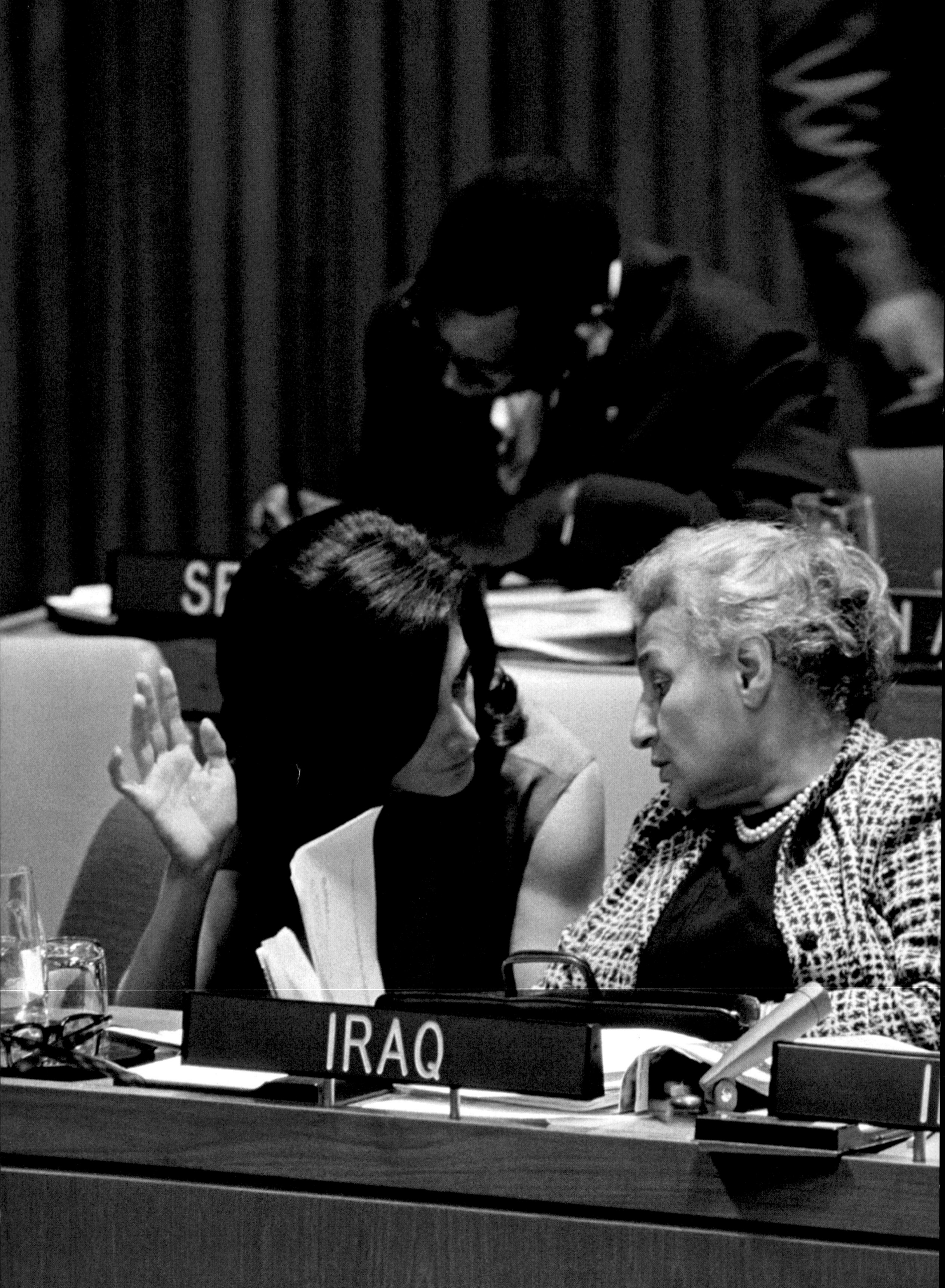
IRAQ

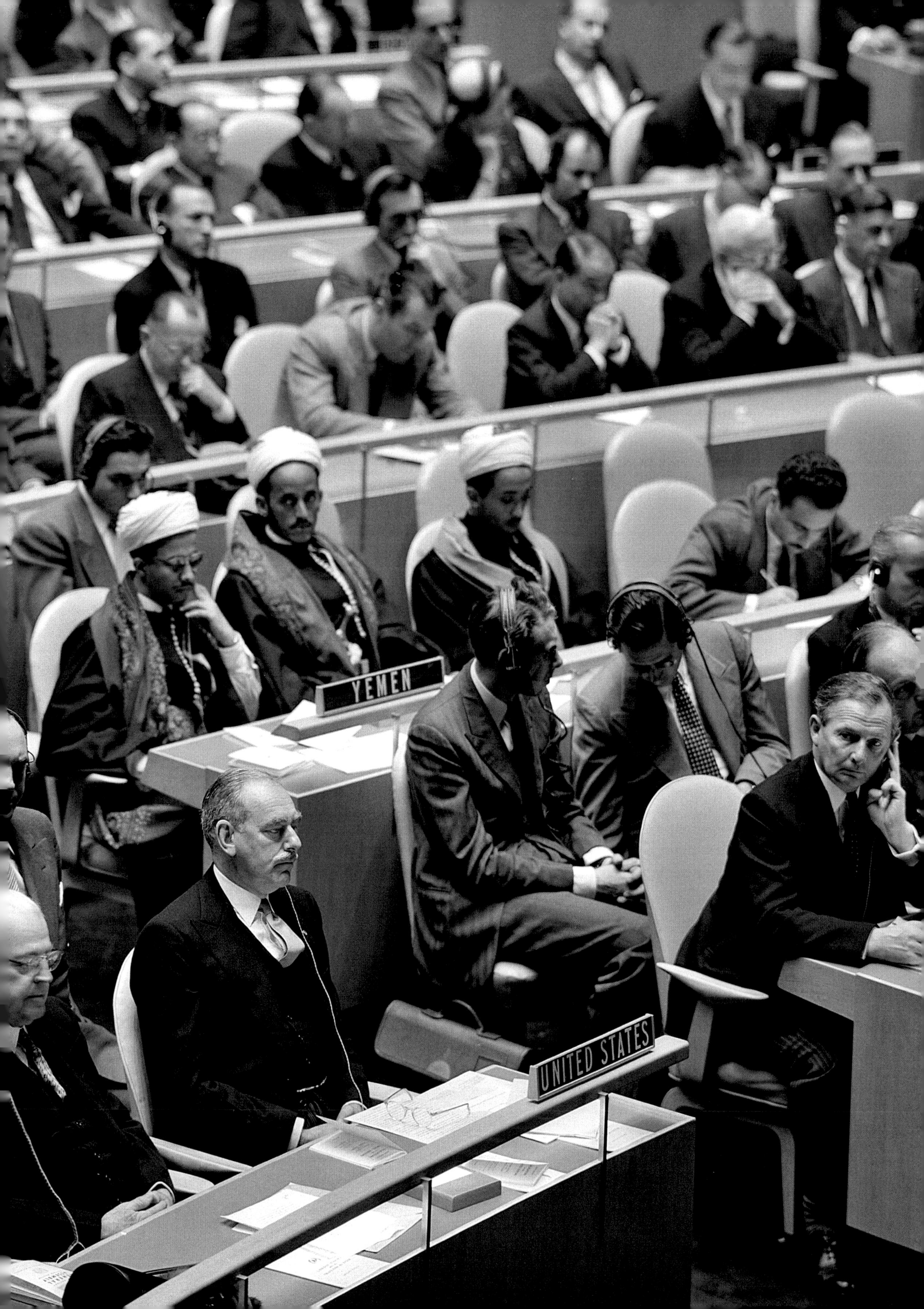
YEMEN
UNITED STATES

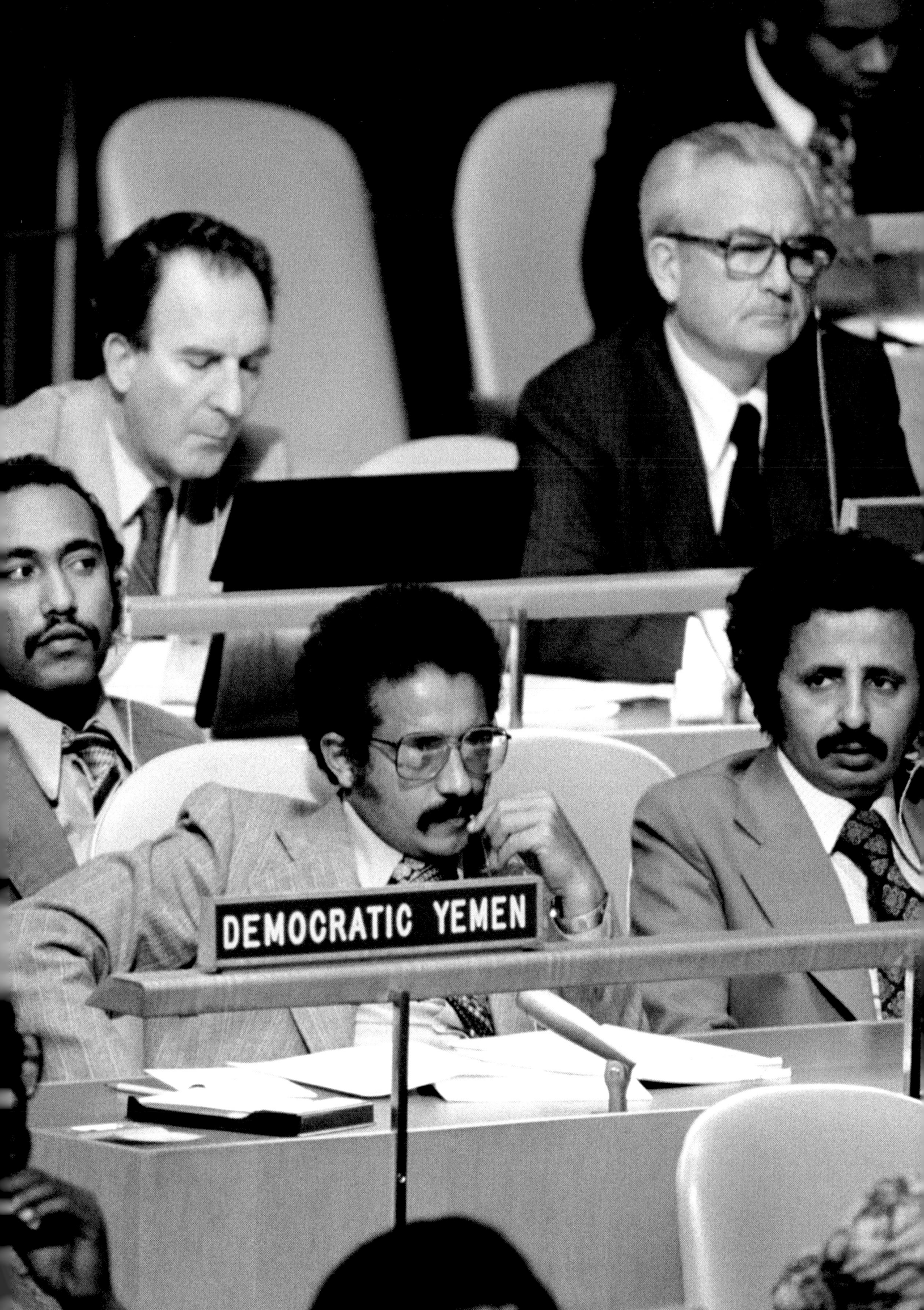

DEMOCRATIC YEMEN

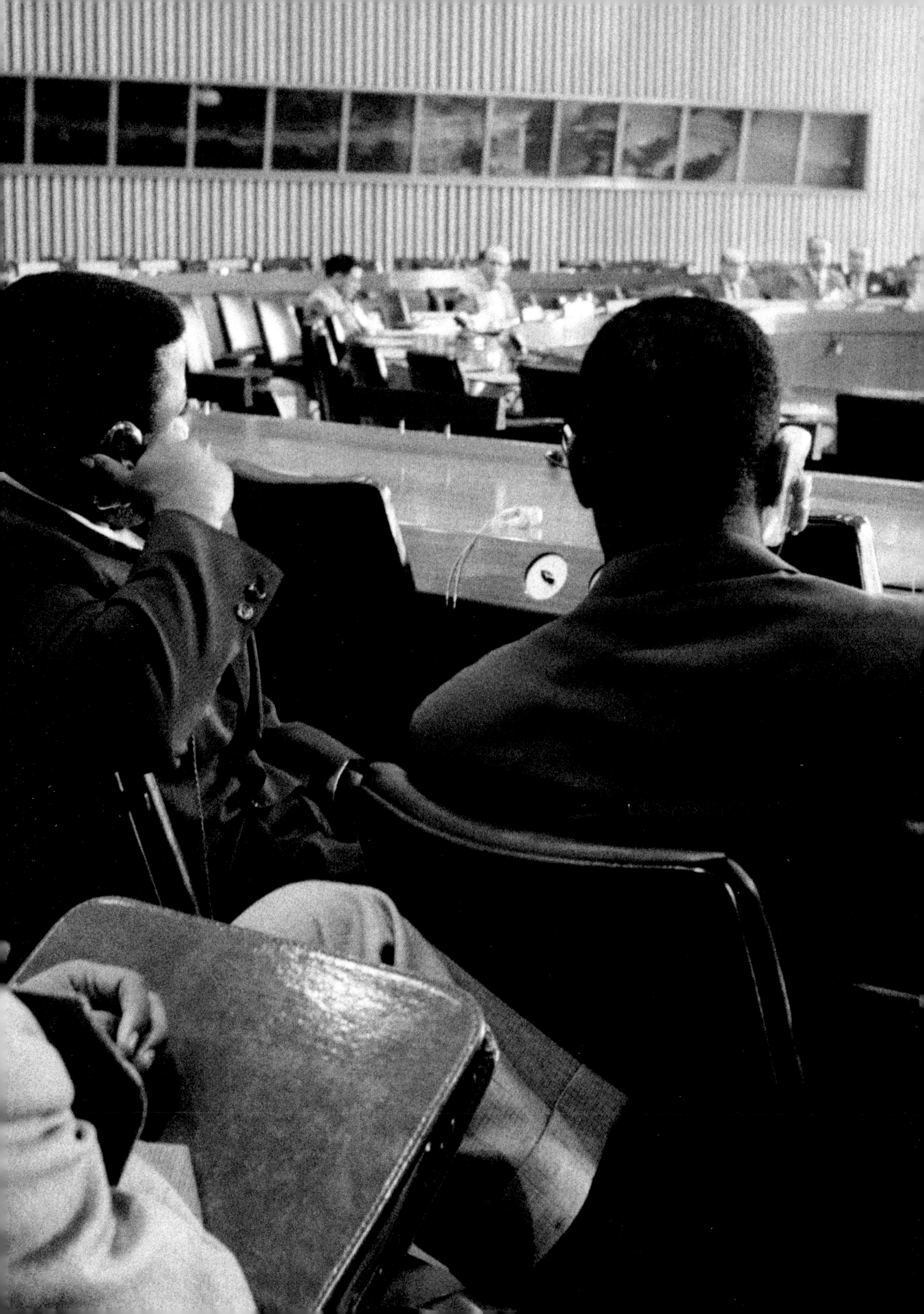

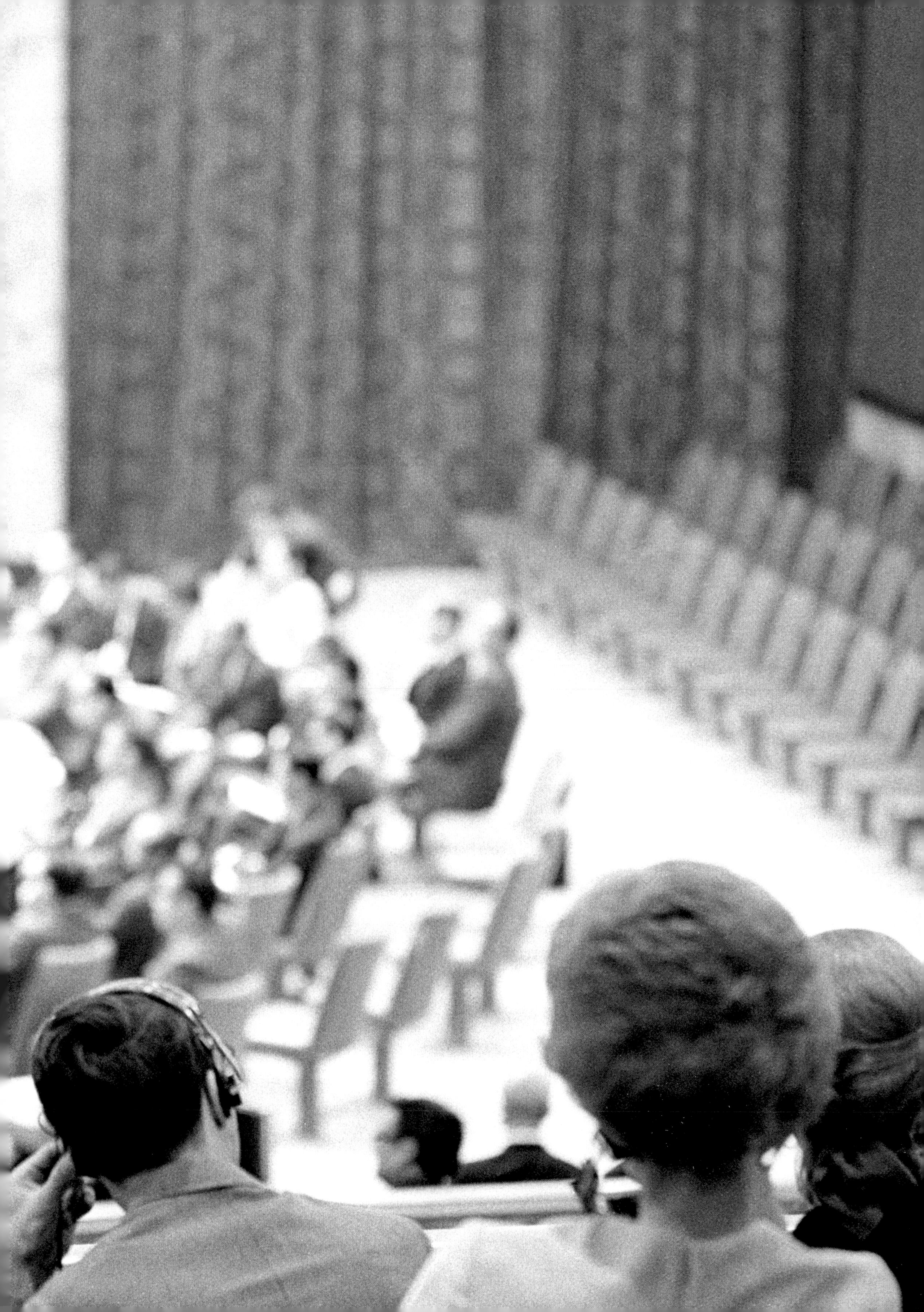

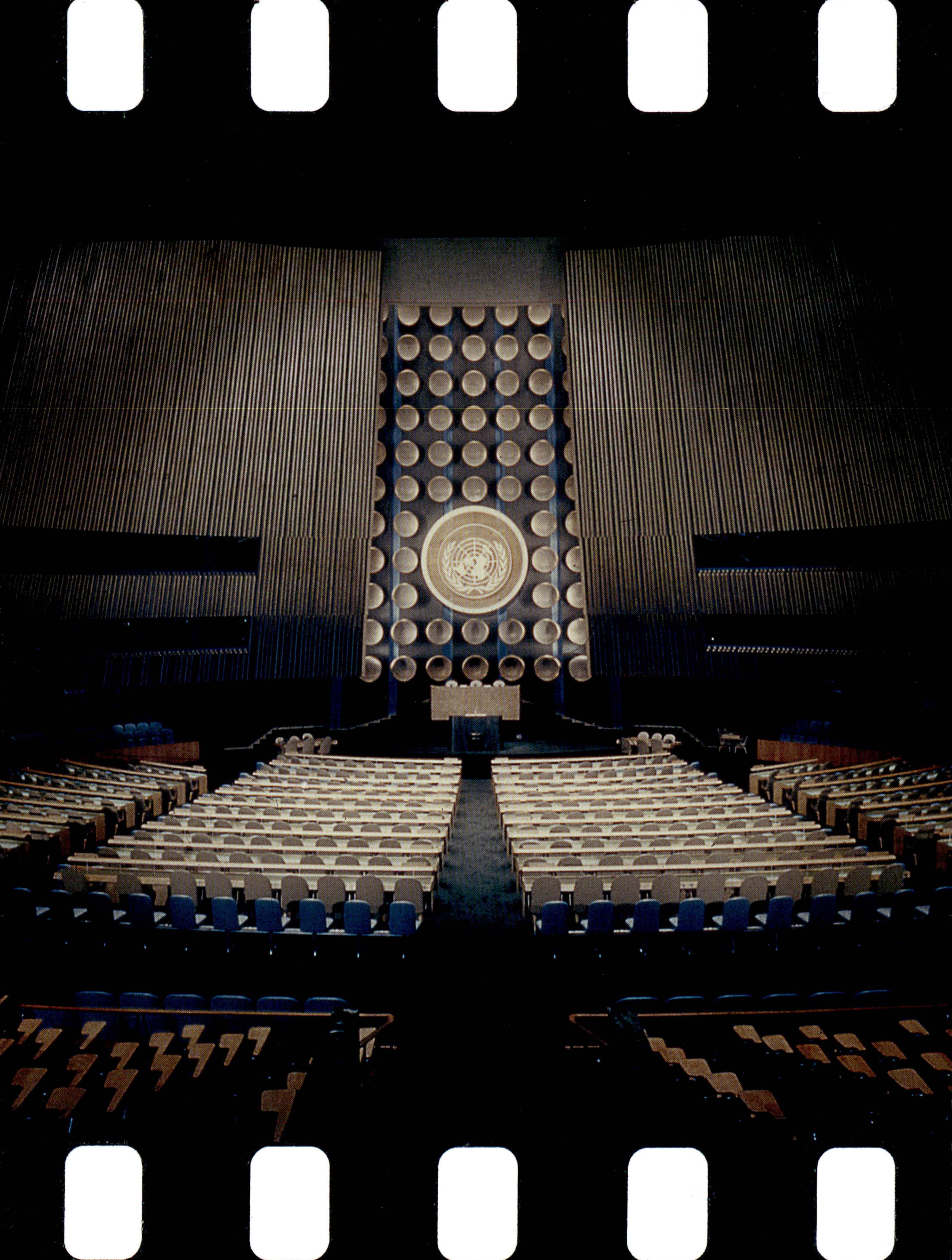

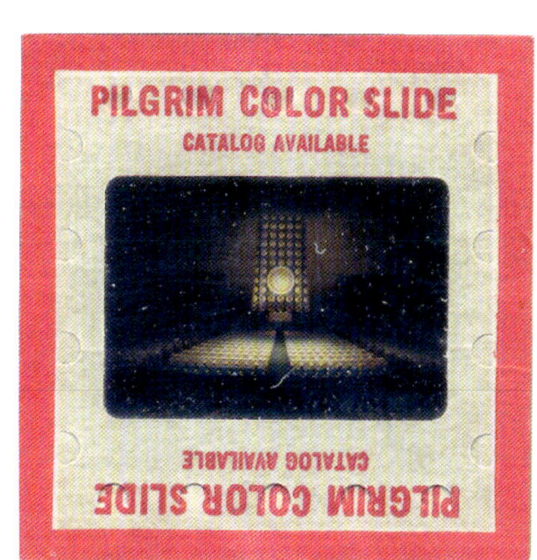
PILGRIM COLOR SLIDE
CATALOG AVAILABLE
PILGRIM COLOR SLIDE
CATALOG AVAILABLE

Nancy Davenport is a Canadian artist whose work has been exhibited at a variety of venues, including the Metropolitan Museum of Art, New York; the Liverpool Biennial; the Istanbul Biennial; the São Paulo Biennial; the National Gallery of Canada, Ottawa; the International Center of Photography, New York; and the MIT List Visual Arts Center, Cambridge, Massachusetts. She lives in New York and teaches at the University of Pennsylvania.

Reinaldo Laddaga is an Argentine writer and critic who lives in New York. His latest books are a collection of short stories and sound pieces titled *Things That a Mutant Needs to Know* (Amsterdam: Unsounds, 2013) and, with Jorge Carrion in Spanish, a collective rewriting of Robert Ripley's *Believe It or Not!* titled *Riplay* (Buenos Aires: Adriana Hidalgo, 2014).

Published by
Cabinet Books
Immaterial Incorporated
181 Wyckoff Street
Brooklyn, NY 11217 USA
<www.cabinetmagazine.org>

Cabinet Books is the book imprint of
Immaterial Incorporated, a non-profit 501(c)3
organization whose core activity is the
publication of *Cabinet* magazine.

This book has been made possible by support
from the Mellon Humanities, Urbanism, and
Design (H+U+D) Initiative at the University
of Pennsylvania and from the University of
Pennsylvania Faculty Research Fund.

Cabinet Books would additionally like to
thank the Lambent Foundation and the
Orphiflamme Foundation.

Nancy Davenport would like to thank Werner
Schmidt at the Office of the Under-Secretary-
General for Management, United Nations,
New York. Thanks also to Terry Adkins, Rasha
Ajalyaqeen, Shimon Attie, George Baker,
Nayland Blake, Michael Brenson, Martin
Brody, Klaus vom Bruch, Carol Bugger, Sarah
Charlesworth, Mei-Fang Chian, Wei-Ren Chiu,
Tommy Cos, Ann Burke Daly, Micah Danges,
Jason Degraff, J. DiGanji, Eshrat Erfanian,
Matt Freedman, Don Garland, Jessica Green,
Joshua Green, Tom Griffiths, Richard Hogan,
James Kanter, Homay King, Paul Kennedy,
Nicole Klagsbrun, Blaise Kropf, Vladmir
Laksin, Yves Le Bleiz, Tyrone Lester, Sophie
Louyot, Xing-Jun Lu, Ken Lum, Jeannette
Morrison, Joshua Mosley, Sina Najafi,
Thomas Pihl, Barbara Pollock, Karen Redrobe,
Christian Siekmeier, Kaja Silverman, Orkan
Telhan, Jackie Tileston, and John Zeppetelli.

Davenport would like to extend her deepest
thanks and gratitude to Margaret Sundell,
Reinaldo Laddaga, Tsipora Primor, Florence
Davenport, David Charles Davenport, and
Amit Primor.

Distributed worldwide by
D.A.P. / Distributed Art Publishers
155 Sixth Avenue, 2nd floor
New York, NY 10013
tel: + 1 212 627 1999
fax: + 1 212 627 9484
email: dap@dapinc.com

ISBN: 978-1-932698-75-6
Printed in Belgium by Die Keure
First printing, 2016

Design: Everything Studio